21世纪高等院校英语专业系列规划教材
安徽省高等学校"十三五"规划教材
安徽省一流本科教材建设项目成果

Selected Readings in English Literature

英国文学选读

（第2版）

主　编　林玉鹏
副主编　陈光明　谢劲秋
编　者　姜　敏　陈　静　林玉霞
　　　　陈　曦　罗　佳　林绪芹

北京师范大学出版集团
BEIJING NORMAL UNIVERSITY PUBLISHING GROUP

安徽大学出版社

图书在版编目(CIP)数据

英国文学选读:英文/林玉鹏主编. —2版. —合肥:安徽大学出版社,2018.6
(2024.7重印)
21世纪高等院校英语专业系列规划教材
ISBN 978-7-5664-1571-4

Ⅰ.①英… Ⅱ.①林… Ⅲ.英语－阅读教学－高等学校－教材②英国文学－文学欣赏 Ⅳ.①H319.4:I

中国版本图书馆 CIP 数据核字(2018)第 091530 号

英国文学选读(第 2 版)　　　　主编　林玉鹏

出版发行:	北京师范大学出版集团
	安 徽 大 学 出 版 社
	(安徽省合肥市肥西路 3 号 邮编 230039)
	www.bnupg.com
	www.ahupress.com.cn
印　　刷:	安徽省人民印刷有限公司
经　　销:	全国新华书店
开　　本:	710 mm×1010 mm　1/16
印　　张:	28
字　　数:	643 千字
版　　次:	2018 年 6 月第 2 版
印　　次:	2024 年 7 月第 4 次印刷
定　　价:	65.00 元

ISBN 978-7-5664-1571-4

策划编辑：李　梅　　　　　　　　　装帧设计：李　军
责任编辑：李　雪　　　　　　　　　美术编辑：李　军
责任印制：陈　如　孟献辉

版权所有　侵权必究

反盗版、侵权举报电话：0551－65106311
外埠邮购电话：0551－65107716
本书如有印装质量问题，请与印制管理部联系调换。
印制管理部电话：0551－65106311

1. 英国文学的发展概貌

英国文学的发展历史与英语语言的发展史紧密相连。要勾勒英国文学的发展概貌,有必要首先简要介绍英语语言发展的大致轨迹。英语属于日耳曼语族中的一支,是早先居住在欧洲大陆莱茵河流域的盎格鲁·撒克逊原居住地居民使用的语言。盎格鲁·撒克逊人来到英伦时也将他们的语言带到不列颠。英语语言的发展大致经历了三个时期:古英语时期(450~1150),这个时期以英语史诗《贝尔武甫》为代表;中古英语时期(1150~1500),这个时期的文学代表是乔叟(Geoffrey Chaucer,1343~1400)的《坎特伯雷故事集》(*The Canterbury Tales*);现代英语时期(1500~),这个时期的代表作家为莎士比亚。英国文学的发展主要经历了盎格鲁·撒克逊、文艺复兴、新古典主义(17~18世纪)、浪漫主义、现实主义、现代主义以及当代等时期。

(1) 中世纪文学

与世界上其他很多民族的文学一样,诗歌是英国文学史上最早发展繁荣的文学体裁。大约3000行的英语史诗《贝尔武甫》(*Beowulf*)是盎格鲁·撒克逊人的祖先日耳曼人从其莱茵河流域的居住地带到英伦的,最先是口头相传,约于公元8~11世纪之间由寺庙僧侣根据口头传说用古英语记录而成。该诗叙述了英国民族的祖先贝尔武甫带领人民与大自然的化身怪物格兰代尔及其母亲作斗争的故事,是英国文学中最早使用头韵手法的作品。浪漫传奇以亚瑟王和他的圆桌骑士传奇为代表,其中最为著名的是《高文爵士和绿衣骑士》(Sir Gawain and the Green Knight),它歌颂了勇敢、忠贞等美德。

朗格兰(William Langland,1330～1386)的《农夫皮尔斯》(Piers the Plowman)通过一系列梦幻场景,以诗体形式和讽喻的笔触描绘了当时社会各方面的图景,揭露了富人的腐败和统治者的腐朽。该诗使用头韵法。中世纪和新时代之交时期的乔叟的代表作《坎特伯雷故事集》由总序和24个故事构成,讲述了当时社会的方方面面和各色人等的故事,反映了人们希望冲破中世纪宗教戒律、追求人性解放的愿望。作者刻画了很多栩栩如生的人物,强调必须由女性作为家庭的主导,其中最为著名的是巴斯妇,她先后有多名丈夫和情人。该作品由英雄双行体写成,开创了英语文学中使用该诗体的先河。此外,乔叟的创作对推动伦敦方言成为英国全民语言起了积极作用,他被誉为"英国诗歌之父"。

从1200～1700年间,在英格兰北部和苏格兰地区存在着一种民间叙事文学:一种通常用抑扬格四行诗体构成、用于传唱的民间歌谣(ballad),最为著名的是关于绿林好汉罗宾汉劫富济贫的故事。

(2) 文艺复兴时期文学

文艺复兴时期英国文学出现了一次繁荣,代表作家西德尼(Sir Philip Sidney,1554～1586)的传奇故事《阿卡迪亚》(The Arcadia)、李利(John Lyly,1554～1606)的传奇故事《尤菲伊斯》(Euphues)、斯宾塞(Edmund Spenser,1552～1599)的诗歌代表作《仙后》(Faerie Queene)对英语诗歌的发展和英语语言规范产生了积极的影响。这些为莎士比亚(William Shakespeare,1564～1616)作品的出现奠定了基础。

英国戏剧的历史可追溯到中世纪。15～16世纪流行的奇迹剧(miracle plays)、道德剧(morality plays)和幕间剧(interludes)对英国戏剧发展有直接的影响。其中道德剧因其不像奇迹剧那样受制于宗教故事,赋予了作家更大的创作空间。在此期间,一些被称为"大学才子"(University Wits)、与大学有联系的作家,将以命运为主题的古罗马悲剧推上英国舞台,促进了英国戏剧的发展。其中重要的剧作家有罗伯特·格林(Robert Green,1558~1592)、基德(Thomas Kyd,1558~1594)和马洛(Christopher Marlowe,1564~1593)。这些剧作家都对莎士比亚影响很大,马洛的代表作《帖木尔大帝》(*Tamburlaine the Great*)中激情充沛的人物、开拓进取的人文主义精神和雄辩有力的素体诗(blank verse)尤其对莎士比亚戏剧产生了直接的影响。

莎士比亚被认为是英国文学中最伟大的作家,也是世界文学中伟大的作家之一。他的37(或38)部戏剧(包括悲剧、喜剧、历史剧和传奇剧)是英国文学乃至世界文学中的瑰宝。他对人性的洞悉,他创造的性格复杂和丰富多彩的人物、曲折的剧情、广阔的社会画面,以及他对英语语言创造性的使用等均达到了很高的艺术高度。他的四大悲剧《哈姆雷特》(*Hamlet*)、《李尔王》(*King Lear*)、《奥赛罗》(*Othello*)和《麦克白》(*Macbeth*)尤其具有高度的艺术感染力和永恒的艺术魅力。莎士比亚同时也是一位诗人,他的诗歌成就体现在154首十四行诗和2首长诗上。与莎士比亚同时代的戏剧家本·琼生(Ben Johnson,1573~1637)倡导古典主义戏剧的"三一律"原则,在其《个性各异》(*Everyman In His Humour*)和《人各有癖》(*Everyman Out of His Humour*)中首创英国性情喜剧。

培根(Francis Bacon,1561~1626)既是哲学家,又是重要的散文作家。其《论述文集》(*Essays*)包括58篇题材广泛、短小简练、富有哲理、文笔质朴的随笔(或称小品文),主要谈论处世之道和人生哲理,包含很多警句格言,在英国文学史上具有独特的地位。

(3) 17 世纪文学

17世纪产生了4位名叫约翰的作家,其中3位在文学史上很有影响。约翰·弥尔顿(John Milton,1608~1674)的人生经历与英国革命紧密相连,其代表作《失乐园》(*Paradise Lost*)以圣经故事为原型,描写了撒旦与上帝的斗争。撒旦失败后,为了报复上帝,引诱亚当和夏娃偷吃禁果，使得他们被上帝逐出伊甸园。由于有类似的情感经历，诗人将撒旦塑造成敢于反抗暴政和强权的英雄。该诗创造了以宏大的主题、磅礴的气势和强有力的素体诗为特征的"弥尔顿诗体"。约翰·邓恩(John Donne,1572~1631)是玄学诗派的主要代表，他的诗以充满理性思辨的"奇喻"而著称，对 20 世纪现代主义尤其是艾略特的诗歌产生了很大的影响。属于该诗派的其他诗人还有赫伯特(George Herbert,1593~1633)和马维尔(Andrew Marvell,1621~1678)。

约翰·班扬(John Bunyan, 1628~1688)的《天路历程》(*The Pilgrim's Progress*)描写了主人公基督徒和他的朋友忠诚从毁灭城到天国的途中所经历的种种艰难与诱惑，以寓言的形式描写了人的灵魂的救赎，其中最为著名的是有关名利场的描写。该书深受《圣经》的直接影响，叙事使用生动的日常语言。约翰·德莱顿(John Dryden, 1631~1700)的创作标志着诗歌中注重清晰精确表达、韵律严整、强调克制情感的新古典主义的开端，它将在 18 世纪得到进一步发展。这个时期还出现了一些保皇党诗人或称宫廷诗人(Cavalier Poets)，其抒情诗通常有关爱情，轻松高雅，语言机智，通常表达及时行乐(carpe diem)的主题。

17 世纪还出现了以韦伯斯特(John Webster,1580~1625)为代表的所谓流血悲剧(tragedy of blood or blood-and-thunder plays)，其代表作《白魔鬼》(*White Devil*)和《麦尔菲的女公爵》(*The Duchess of Malfi*)充满对恐怖、暴力和犯罪细节的描述，同时也刻画了一些令人难忘的人物。这些对 20 世纪作家如艾略特等产生了巨大的影响。此外，沿袭本·琼生家庭戏剧传统的米德尔顿(Thomas Middleton,1580~1627)的代表作《逮住老家伙的诀窍》(*A Trick to Catch the Old One*)和麦辛杰(Philip Massinger,1583~1639)的代表作《新法还旧债》(*A New Way to Pay Old Debts*)开启了现实主义家庭生活喜剧之风，为后来的风俗喜剧(comedy of manners)奠定了基础。风俗喜剧是 17 世纪末王政复辟时期出现的一种揭露宫廷奢靡腐化风气的戏剧，其喜剧场景的刻画、机智语言的表达对很多后世作家产生了影响。代表作家有埃塞瑞吉(Sir George Etherege,1635~1691)、维彻利

(William Wycherley，1640～1716)和康格利乌（William Congreve，1670～1729），其中以康格利乌最为重要。

(4) 18 世纪文学（启蒙时期文学）

新古典主义发端于 17 世纪的法国，17 世纪后期在英国出现，18 世纪早中期达到高潮。新古典主义尊崇古希腊罗马文学艺术，强调合乎经典规范，节制情感，讲求形式的和谐平衡和表达的清晰明了。蒲伯（Alexander Pope，1688～1744）是英国新古典主义的重要代表，他强调古典文学的条理性，强调品位、得体、理智、逻辑、均衡、克制情感等规则。其文体优雅、精练，混合讽刺和机智，使英雄双行体臻于完善。他用该诗体写成的《论批评》（*On Criticism*）是对新古典主义文学主张的阐释和总结，其中有很多著名引语。约翰逊（Samuel Johnson，1709～1784）被其同时代人当作文学的"立法者"而受到推崇。他赞同新古典主义的文学主张，在文学批评、散文写作和词典编纂等方面均取得出色成就。

18 世纪是英国小说发端、发展和成熟的时期，出现了多位重要的小说家。笛福（Daniel Defoe，1661～1731）的《鲁滨逊漂流记》（*Robinson Crusoe*）是英国文学中第一部真正意义上的现代小说。它采用现实主义手法，用第一人称的直接叙述方式，以平实的语言、生动的情节、逼真的细节描写了主人公在荒岛上的经历，颂扬了殖民主义时代对外扩张的冒险精神。理查森（Samuel Richardson，1689～1761）以《帕米拉》（*Pamela*）十分偶然地确立了自己在英国小说史中的地位。他原本打算写一本指导青年人写信的书，结果写成一部描写女仆帕米拉的德行得到回报的书信体小说。该小说以细腻的人物心理刻画和情感描绘见长。

同时代的作家菲尔丁（Henry Fielding，1707～1754）受塞万提斯的《堂吉诃德》影响，提出了小说新观念，认为小说应该是"用散文写成的喜剧史诗"，作品中多有滑稽讽刺成分。他具有小说形式意识，关注小说的结构，采用第三人称叙述，使小说趋于成熟。其主要作品有《汤姆·琼斯》（*Tom Jones*）和《约瑟夫·安德鲁斯》（*Joseph Andrews*）等。

斯沫莱特(Tobias George Smollett,1721~1771)按照流浪汉小说传统写成的《兰登传》(Roderick Random)开启了英国航海小说之先河。斯威夫特(Jonathan Swift,1667~1745)的《格列弗游记》(Gulliver's Travels)用丰富的想象描写了主人公在小人国、大人国、飞岛国和智马国的奇异经历,同时也以寓言的方式对英国社会的方方面面进行了讽刺和批判。

18世纪中期英国文学中出现了一种过分沉溺情感、怀念宗法社会的感伤主义(Sentimentalism)思潮。感伤主义也是社会不公正造成下层人民苦难在文学上的一种曲折反映,在小说、戏剧和诗歌中均有体现。斯泰恩(Laurence Stern,1713~1768)的《一次感伤的旅行》(A Sentimental Journey)是感伤主义名称的来源。小说中很多片段抒发了作者的感伤情绪。此外,他的《项狄传》(Tristram Shandy)是一部没有故事情节的奇书,被认为是现代主义小说的先驱。至此,英国小说臻于成熟。哥尔德斯密(Oliver Goldsmith,1728~1774)的感伤主义分别体现在他的表现工业化侵蚀下农民悲惨生活的诗歌《荒村》(The Deserted Village)和反映相似主题的小说《威克菲尔德牧师传》(The Vicar of Wakefield)中。此外,他还有一部风格近于风俗喜剧的著名戏剧《屈身求爱》(She Stoops to Conquer),曾在舞台上长演不衰。

与此同时,英国诗歌中还出现了表现自然和死亡的诗歌。墓园诗派代表作家格雷(Thomas Gray,1716~1771)的《墓畔哀歌》(Elegy Written in a Country Churchyard),沉溺生命和死亡的思考,表达对农民俭朴生活的同情。此外,汤姆逊(James Thomson,1700~1748)的《四季》(Seasons)、科林斯(William Collins,1721~1759)的《黑夜颂》(Ode to Evening)等都表现了类似的主题。还有一些诗人向往古代文学。麦克弗森(James Macpherson,1736~1796)伪托公元3世纪爱尔兰诗人创作了所谓"奥西诗篇"。珀西(Thomas Percy,1729~1811)在《古诗遗稿》(Reliques)中为恢复英国古代民谣做出了努力,对英国浪漫主义诗人产生了很大的影响。

18世纪末期出现了沃尔普尔(Horace Walpole,1717~1797)的

《奥特兰多城堡》(*The Castle of Otranto*),开英国哥特小说之先河。瑞德克利夫(Mrs. Ann Radcliffe,1764~1823)的《尤道尔弗的秘密》(*The Mysteries of Udolpho*)最为著名。该类小说通常描写性虐狂式的人物对无辜而敏感的年轻女性的摧残,其中有很多超自然的神秘因素和恐怖成分,因其故事多发生在中世纪的哥特式城堡而得名。瑞德克利夫对同时代的许多作家如拜伦、雪莱和勃朗特姐妹等都有很大的影响。

18世纪初期的戏剧代表作有盖伊(John Gay,1685~1732)的讽刺音乐剧《乞丐歌剧》(*The Beggar's Opera*)、李罗(George Lillo,1693~1739)的家庭悲剧和哥尔德斯密(Oliver Goldsmith,1728~1774)的妙趣横生的喜剧《屈身求爱》。谢立丹(Richard Brinsley Sheridan,1751~1816)的《造谣学校》(*The School for Scandal*)和《情敌》(*The Rivals*)等剧的喜剧场景和机智对话秉承了17世纪末和18世纪初的风俗喜剧的传统,对上层社会道德堕落进行了讽刺和批判。谢立丹的戏剧在英国戏剧史上具有承上启下的作用,对19世纪末20世纪初萧伯纳等人的戏剧具有深远的影响。

(5) 浪漫主义时期文学(1798~1830s)

彭斯(Robert Burns,1759~1796)和布莱克(William Blake,1757~1827)二人被称为浪漫主义诗歌黎明时期的诗人。带着泥土气息的苏格兰农民诗人彭斯以朴实的笔触、独具特色的苏格兰方言和真挚的情感讴歌美好的爱情,表达对故国家园的热爱以及对友谊的渴望。他的诗音乐性强,闪烁着纯真的美。布莱克的诗用质朴的语言、充满童真意趣的意象和象征手法,触及社会的阴暗面,表现了独到的思想深度。他的诗意象瑰丽,高度抒情,带有神秘色彩,有一种独特的艺术美。华兹华斯(William Wordsworth,1770~1850)和柯勒律治(S. T. Coleridge,1772~1834)在1798年共同出版的《抒情谣曲》(*Lyrical Ballads*)标志着英国浪漫主义文学运动的开端。他们和骚塞(Robert Southey,1774~1843)被称为英国第一代浪漫主义诗人。他们长期住在英国的湖区,因而又被称为湖畔派诗人。华兹华斯在《抒情谣曲》第二版序言中提出了自己的诗歌原则，认为诗歌应该用日常语言描写普通事件，诗歌是感情的自然流露，而平静中回忆的情感最为强烈。柯勒律治的诗歌充满瑰丽的意象和神秘色彩，显示了他独特的想象力。以长诗《古舟子咏》(The Rime of the Ancient Mariner)为代表的一些诗篇描绘了梦幻般的超自然世界，具有奇特之美。

年轻一代的诗人拜伦(George Gordon Byron, 1788～1824)将讽刺、哲学沉思和景色描绘等融为一体，写出了激情充沛的抒情诗。在长诗《唐璜》(Don Juan)和《查尔德·哈罗德的漫游》(Childe Harold's Pilgrimage)中，他创造了与暴政和社会弊端孤军奋战的"拜伦式英雄"。雪莱(Percy Bysshe Shelley, 1792～1822)的诗表现了浪漫主义和理想主义，他的一些长诗描绘了理想社会，描写自然的诗具有很高的抒情性和精致的美。济慈(John Keats, 1795～1821)崇尚"美就是真，真就是美"的观点，其短暂的一生致力于使自然界转瞬即逝的美在诗中永驻。他的以多首颂诗为代表的诗歌以诉诸感官的意象创造的美而著称。

在此期间，被称为英国历史小说之父的司格特(Sir Walter Scott, 1771～1832)在《艾凡赫》(Ivanhoe)和《罗伯·罗耶》(Rob Roy)等作品中，根据苏格兰、英格兰和欧洲历史，描绘了广阔的社会生活画面，首次使山川河流等环境背景成为小说情节的一部分。其小说人物众多，情节曲折生动，注重行动。生活在浪漫主义时期的简·奥斯丁(Jane Austen, 1775～1817)独树一帜，其描写同时代中产阶级日常生活的《傲慢与偏见》(Pride and Prejudice)等6部作品为英国现实主义小说做出了新贡献。她的小说结构严谨，细节刻画精致、逼真、生动，语言精练，对话幽默，妙趣横生，没有曲折的情节和波澜壮阔的事件，对家庭婚姻和乡村生活日常琐事娓娓道来，引人入胜。

(6) 现实主义时期文学(1830s～1918)

维多利亚时代是英国历史上的繁荣时期之一，洋溢着积极乐观的氛围。丁尼生(Alfred Tennyson, 1809～1892)和布朗宁(Robert Browning, 1812～1889)是这个时期最重要的诗人。生活在现实主义时期的这两位诗人深受浪漫主义诗人影响,故被称为第三代浪漫主义诗人。丁尼生在抒情诗和戏剧独白诗方面均取得了成就。他的《国王田园诗》(*The Idylls of the King*)表现了对工业化社会的厌恶以及对古代或中世纪的怀念。受济慈影响,他的诗中有对感官愉悦的追求,同时也流露出一种不易察觉却深沉的感伤。他用词考究,语言很有音乐性。布朗宁学习的是雪莱对音韵的追求,其主要成就和贡献在于让人物自我揭示的戏剧独白诗。阿诺德(Matthew Arnold,1822~1888)是一位批评家和诗人,他的诗常表现孤独的情绪和对难以企及的宁静的渴求。其名诗《多佛海滩》("Dover Beach")采用戏剧独白的形式,用鲜明的意象和富有节奏的音韵,渲染了月夜海滩的凄美意境,表达了主人公对世纪之交人们信仰丧失的忧郁,在英语诗歌中有独特的地位。

19世纪中至20世纪初是英国文学中现实主义小说的又一高潮时期,出现了一些重要的女性小说家。夏洛蒂·勃朗特(Charlotte Bronte,1816~1855)的《简·爱》(*Jane Erye*)以强烈的情感和具有表现力的语言在英国文学中第一次塑造了独立、自强、自尊的女性人物形象。夏洛蒂妹妹艾米丽·勃朗特(Emily Bronte,1818~1848)的《呼啸山庄》(*Wuthering Heights*)讲述了男女主人公刻骨铭心的爱情以及男主人公希斯克利夫的复仇故事,塑造了令人难忘的独特人物形象。两部作品的语言均富有表现力,充满情感张力。

19世纪出现了一些重要的批判现实主义小说家。狄更斯(Charles Dickens,1812~1870)在《匹克威克外传》(*Pickwick Papers*)、《奥列弗·退斯特》(*Oliver Twist*)、《大卫·科普菲尔德》(*David Copperfield*)和《双城记》(*A Tale of Two Cities*)等数量众多的小说中,以史诗般的笔触描述了英国和欧洲社会的广阔画面,揭露社会罪恶,对下层人民给予深切同情,同时也表现了生活和人性中的美。其笔触幽默生动,语言富有表现力,众多人物和场景令人难忘。

与狄更斯同时代的另一位批判现实主义作家萨克雷(William Makepiece Thackeray,1811~1863)在很多方面与狄更斯形成对照。在其代表作《名利场》(*Vanity Fair*)中,他用冷峻和讽刺的笔触,揭露了上层社会形形色色人物的可笑和丑恶行为，塑造了一个独特的、不择手段往上爬的女冒险家比基·夏泼的形象。另一位现实主义作家凯斯凯尔夫人(Mrs. Gaskell, 1810～1865)在其《玛丽·巴顿》(Mary Barton)和《北与南》(North and South)中揭露了工业社会的罪恶，表现了劳资双方的冲突。作为一名女性作家，乔治·艾略特(George Eliot, 原名 Mary Ann Evans, 1819～1880)在《弗洛斯河上的磨坊》(The Mill on the Floss)、《亚当·彼得》(Adam Bede)和《织工马南》(Silas Marner)等小说作品中以其细致的人物心理分析和对生活悲剧的道德探讨在英国小说中独树一帜。麦瑞迪斯(George Meredith, 1828～1909)在《个人主义者》(The Egoist)等小说中以细腻的笔触描写女性心理，探讨生活中的喜剧因素。

哈代(Thomas Hardy, 1840～1928)尽管是一位诗人，却同时也以小说闻名于世。在以《德伯家的苔丝》(Tess of the D'Urbervilles)为代表的数量众多的小说中，他以同情的笔触描绘了威塞克斯农民的悲剧生活，表现了19世纪末农民阶级在大工业的挤压下破产的命运。哈代把人物的悲剧归结为冥冥中的命运，小说中充满了神秘主义的宿命论，在对人物命运的描写上具有自然主义倾向。另一位维多利亚时代小说家巴特勒(Samuel Butler, 1835～1902)在《众生之路》(The Way of All Flesh)和《艾瑞横》(Erewhon)等作品中以机智和讽刺的语言描写了资本主义社会的弊病，探讨伦理问题。斯蒂文森(Robert Louis Stevenson, 1850～1894)在《金银岛》(Treasure Island)等为代表的作品中使小说回到浪漫传奇故事的传统。柯南·道尔(Conan Doyle, 1859～1930)的福尔摩斯(Sherlock Holmes)探案系列小说在英国探案小说发展上具有里程碑意义。吉卜林(Rudyard Kipling, 1856～1936)的《丛林之书》(The Jungle Book)和《吉姆》(Kim)等小说作品以丰富的想象和生动的笔触展现了以印度等异域为背景的故事，蕴含着对英国海外殖民历史的肯定。康拉德(Joseph Conrad, 1857～1924)在《黑暗的心》(Heart of Darkness)等代表作中描写殖民者在海外的冒险经历，展现了人性中的黑暗。小说情节曲折生动，善于渲染气氛和刻画人物心理。

高尔斯华绥(John Galsworthy,1867～1933)秉承了现实主义文学传统,在其三部曲《福赛特家史》(*The Forsyte Saga*)中以现实主义的手法描绘了资产阶级代表索米斯·福赛特家族几代人的发展和衰落的过程,对资本主义做了伦理上的批评。本涅特(Arnold Bennet,1867～1931)的代表作《老妇谭》(*The Old Wives's Tales*)以现实主义的笔触和充分的细节展现了人物的平庸生活。威尔斯(Herbert George Wells,1866～1946)的《时间机器》(*The Time Machine*)等小说用科幻的手法对资本主义社会和人性的弱点进行了批判。毛姆(Somerset Maugham,1874～1965)对人类命运持悲观观点,在《人性枷锁》(*Of Human Bondage*)等小说中表现了人性的弱点、社会对个人的压制以及独立自由精神的可贵。

剧作家王尔德(Oscar Wilde,1854～1900)的《温德米尔夫人的扇子》(*Lady Windermere's Fan*)、《无足轻重的女人》(*A Woman of No Importance*)、《理想丈夫》(*An Ideal Husband*)和《作为厄内斯特的重要性》(*The Importance of Being Earnest*)等剧作语言机智,戏剧场景富喜剧性,具有风俗喜剧的特征。沁孤(John Millington Synge,1871～1909)的《骑马下海的人》(*Riders to the Sea*)表现了命运中的黑暗力量,具有古希腊悲剧特征。

(7) 现代文学(1918～1945)

奥凯西(Sean O'Casey,1880～1964)的戏剧将现实主义、象征主义和浪漫传奇相结合。萧伯纳(George Bernard Shaw,1856～1950)深受易卜生的影响,将戏剧作为表达思想的工具。他的《华伦夫人的职业》(*Mrs. Warren's Profession*)、《鳏夫的房产》(*Widowers' Houses*)和《皮革马利翁》(*Pygmalion*)等多部剧作善于用悖论手法,探讨各种社会问题,其机智幽默的语言显示了风俗喜剧的特征。诗人艾略特也写了很多戏剧,最为著名的是《大教堂谋杀案》(*Murder in the Cathedral*)。他试图在现代社会恢复古希腊悲剧的形式。

福斯特(E. M. Forster,1879～1970)在代表作《印度之行》(*A Passage to India*)中关注人际关系,试图探究不同民族之间相互理解和信任的途径。其笔调冷峻克制,善用反讽和象征。他的《小说面面观》(Aspects of the Novel)是对小说理论的贡献。劳伦斯(D. H. Lawrence,1885~1930)认为现代工业文明扼杀了人类情感。他的小说呼唤情感,尤其是男女之情的复苏。他在《儿子与情人》(Sons and Lovers)、《查特莱夫人的情人》(Lady Chatterley's Lover)等一系列小说中探究人际的感情联系,尤其是男女之间的肉体之爱。他突破题材禁区,用一种象征性的语言描写男女肉体之爱,在英国文学史上具有独到之处。

20世纪初出现了形式创新的现代主义小说。乔伊斯(James Joyce,1882~1941)被认为是意识流小说及现代主义小说的创始人。他试图打破时空、意识和无意识等的界限,在代表作《尤利西斯》(Ulysses)中,以高度试验性、多样化的语言风格,表现了思绪、印象、回忆、梦境等在人物内心的"流动",全面展现了现代社会的尤利西斯等人物的日常生活,象征西方社会现代人性的复杂、生活的琐屑和无意义。《芬尼根守灵》(Finnegans Wake)则更进一步,完全探究人物的无意识。伍尔夫(Virginia Woolf,1882~1941)几乎与乔伊斯同时尝试用意识流手法写作。她的《达罗卫夫人》(Mrs. Dalloway)和《到灯塔去》(To the Lighthouse)等小说通过压缩时间,给人物的意识提供更多的细节描绘,逼真地表现人物的"意识的原子",具有很强的情感力度。赫胥黎(Aldous Huxley,1884~1963)创作了《美好的新世界》(Brave New World)等一系列社会讽刺小说。乔伊斯·凯瑞(Joyce Cary,1888~1957)在《约翰逊先生》(Mister Johnson)以及以《她本人大吃一惊》(Herself Surprised)和《恩宠的囚徒》(Prisoner of Grace)等为首的多部三部曲中,表达了现代生活的矛盾和对立、东西方文化之间的冲突和人生艰辛、幸福飘忽不定等主题,强调爱的重要性。其三部曲均以一个即将走到生命尽头的人物回顾一生、解释事件原因为叙事模式。小说情节通常涉及一个女人和两个情人之间的关系。

艾略特(Thomas Stearns Eliot,1888~1965)和叶芝(William Butler Yeats,1865~1939)是现代主义诗歌里程碑式的诗人。现代主义诗歌从反对维多利亚时代诗歌的滥情和词义不确定开始,强调理性,用反讽、口语、意象和象征表达思想,强调城市题材。艾略特的《普鲁弗洛克的情歌》("The Love Song of J. Alfred Prufrock")(1917)标志着现代主义诗歌的开端。诗中运用很多反讽、反传统的意象和来自文学经典的隐喻,表现了现代人空虚、颓废的情绪。他的《荒原》(*The Waste Land*)使用了大量的典故,将当代西方社会喻为精神荒原,强调其需要用信仰救赎。叶芝在浪漫主义的影响下开始诗歌创作,后来转向法国象征主义。他受东方神秘主义影响,构建了自己的象征体系"世界之灵"。他用象征的手法,探讨时间和变化、爱情和年龄、生命和艺术等主题。思想上他受历史循环论影响。他的诗歌中有很多象征循环的意象,如陀螺、旋转的楼梯等。

第一次世界大战是影响现代主义诗歌的因素之一。这个时期的代表诗人是布鲁克(Rupert Brooke,1887~1915)、萨松(Siegfried Sassoon,1886~1967)和欧文(Wilfred Owen,1893~1918)。除萨松之外,其余两位均战死沙场。布鲁克用浪漫主义的眼光看待战争,而欧文则以愤怒的态度揭示了战争残酷的现实。一战之后最为突出的诗人是被称为"奥登一代"的一批诗人,他们都受到艾略特和欧文的影响。其领袖人物奥登(Wystan Hugh Auden,1907~1973)诗艺娴熟,致力于试验创新。斯彭德(Stephen Spender,1909~1995)的诗更具个性和情感色彩。刘易斯(Day Lewis,1904~1972)是其中最具抒情性、最率真同时也是最传统的诗人。他们一起为英国诗歌带来了新手法和新观点。

叶芝领导的爱尔兰文学复兴也给苏格兰诗人指明了方向。麦克迪亚米德(Hugh MacDiarmid,1892~1978)领导了苏格兰文学复兴,重新将充满活力的苏格兰文学语言引入诗歌。麦克尼斯(Louis MacNeice,1907~1963)是叶芝之后最为杰出的诗人,他采用爱尔兰的写作方式描写现代社会问题。迪伦·托马斯(Dylan Thomas,1914~1953)是现代主义时期威尔士最有才华的诗人,其诗植根于威尔士传统,激情充沛,想象力丰富,音乐性强,描写自然和乡村、出生、性和死亡等的力量。其诗《羊齿山》("Fern Hill")以成人的视角和儿童的想象描写了在农庄度过的童年时光,其瑰丽的意象和其中暗含的对时间和生死的思考以及语言运用的高度灵活性和潜力令人赞叹。

一战后还出现了关注社会和政治的小说。伊夫琳·沃(Evelyn Waugh,1903~1966)的《罪恶的躯体》(Vile Bodies)和《一捧尘土》(A Handful of Dust)等作品揭示了社会生活方面的种种弊端。普里斯特利(J. B. Priestley,1894~1984)的笔触深入各阶层,展现世间百态。被称为"侦探小说女皇"的克里斯蒂(Agatha Christie,1890~1976)是英国的畅销作家,她在《东方快车谋杀案》(Murder on the Orient Express)、《尼罗河上的惨案》(Death on the Nile)和《捕鼠器》(The Mousetrap)等70多部作品中,讲述了跌宕起伏、扣人心弦的故事。

现代主义时期还有两位风格独特的作家。格雷厄姆·格林(Graham Greene,1904~1991)的作品包括《斯坦堡特快车》(Stamboul Train)等多部惊险小说和《这是个战场》(It's a Battlefield)等多部关注社会的小说。在皈依天主教之后,他创作了《权力和荣耀》(The Power and the Glory)等多部宗教主题的小说。他善于刻画人物内心,擅长讽刺手法的运用,作品情节生动。罗伯特·格雷夫斯(Robert Graves,1895~1985)是一位作品多达140多部的多产诗人、小说家和翻译家,其历史小说《我,克劳底乌斯》(I, Claudius)等善于从失败者的角度重构历史。

(8) 当代文学(1946~)

二战后出现了一批重要的作家。奥威尔(George Orwell,1903~1950)在《动物农场》(Animal Farm)和《1984》(Nineteen Eighty-four)等小说中,采用政治寓言的方式对社会和政治的弊端进行了讽刺。戈尔丁(William Golding,1911~1993)的《蝇王》(Lord of the Flies)通过描写飞机失事后迫降在荒岛上的一群男孩的生存状况,以寓言的方式探讨了人性的善恶,表达了对人性中邪恶的担忧。

20世纪50年代影响英国诗坛的"运动派"诗人,试图走理智、高雅和自我克制风格的中间道路,既反对浪漫主义,又反对贝克特式存在主义的现代主义。作为运动派的主要诗人,拉金(Philip Larkin,1922~1985)的诗风典雅、清晰、简洁,题材广泛,表现了生活中勇气的必要性。戴维(Donald Davie,1922～1995)是运动派的重要批评家,他要求诗人使用散文句法,使用可以表达真正生活感觉的词语,避免抽象。他的诗显示了语言运用的功力。20世纪60年代主导英国诗坛的是休斯(Ted Hughes,1930～1998),其诗以充沛的想象力、鲜明的意象、强烈的情感和粗犷的风格表现了自然的野性。其以《栖息的鹰》("Hawk Roosting")为代表的动物诗,令人觉得诗人进入了动物体内,感受到了它们原始的活力。休斯的诗也反映了现代主义与浪漫主义相结合的特征。冈恩(Thom Gunn,1929～2004)早期与休斯共同出版一本诗集,后来定居美国。其诗具有理性的力量,语言灵活简练。被称为爱尔兰的华兹华斯的希尼(Seamus Heaney,1939～2013)关注祖祖辈辈生活的乡村,其对乡村风景如沼泽地等的描绘中同时包含着对爱尔兰厚重历史的追寻。

战后还出现了一批"愤怒的青年"作家。金斯利·艾米斯(Kingsley Amis,1922～1995)的代表作《幸运的吉姆》(*Luky Jim*)描写了主人公在社会环境中由愤世嫉俗的知识分子变成一个玩世不恭之人的过程,因而他被视为"愤怒的青年"的代表。其小说以反讽见长,喜剧性强,题材广泛。除社会小说之外,他还创作了惊险、犯罪、侦探和科幻等类型的小说。另一位"愤怒的青年"的代表约翰·韦恩(John Wain,1925～1994)的小说《每况愈下》(*Hurry on Down*)表现了战后大学毕业生谋职的经历以及对社会不公的愤怒。约翰·福尔斯(John Fowles,1926～2005)的《法国中尉的女人》(*The French Lieutenant's Woman*)将事实和虚幻融为一体,将维多利亚时代和现代进行时空交替,提供了多种结尾让读者选择。该小说作为现代小说艺术佳作受到推崇。

诺贝尔奖获得者莱辛(Doris Lessing,1919～2013)是战后最重要的作家,创作了《小草在歌唱》(*The Grass Is Singing*)和《金色笔记》(*Golden Notebook*)等多部长篇小说。她关注社会和政治,关注人类尤其是女性的生存状况。其短篇小说尤其是描写非洲生活的短篇小说具有独特的艺术魅力。默多克(Iris Murdoch,1919～1999)关注社会和政治,她的《在网下》(*Under the Net*)、《沙堡》(*The Sandcastle*)等

20多部作品善用隐喻和象征，描写知识分子生活，具有很强的哲理性，故其被称为观念小说家。

20世纪50年代中叶之后出现了一批实验性剧作家。贝克特（Samuel Beckett, 1906~1989）出生于爱尔兰，长期定居法国，用英语和法语创作。其代表作《等待戈多》(Waiting for Godot) 描写了两个流浪汉在荒野等待一个叫戈多的人，但戈多是谁及为什么要等他，剧中人和观众皆一无所知。该剧生动地表现了人生的无意义以及人在荒诞世界中孤立无援的境地，是荒诞派戏剧的典型代表，开启了存在主义戏剧之先河。奥斯本（John Osborne, 1929~1994）被认为是"愤怒的青年"在戏剧界的代表，其代表作《愤怒的回顾》(Look Back in Anger) 表现了社会的腐败和人的生存困境以及战后青年对现实的愤怒和不满。其作品擅长心理刻画，语言运用娴熟。品特（Harold Pinter, 1930~2008）的代表作三幕剧《看房者》(The Caretaker) 描写了主人公千方百计想保住自己待在房子里面的权利，但最终被赶走。这部作品反映了动荡社会人们不安的心理和生活中不可知的威胁。品特将他自己的这一类剧作称为"威胁喜剧"。韦思克（Arnold Wesker, 1932~2016）的代表作三部曲之一《大麦鸡汤》(Chicken Soup with Barley) 描写了犹太工人一家两代人长达20年的生活，表现了不同思想观点的对立。

60年代末期又掀起新的戏剧浪潮。斯托帕托（Tom Stoppard, 1937~）也是荒诞派戏剧代表之一，其成名作《罗森格兰茨和吉尔登斯特恩都已死去》(Rosencrantz and Guildenstern Are Dead) 等作品运用荒诞的表现手法，揭示了发人深思的主题。剧作家彼得·沙弗（Peter Shaffer, 1926~2016）以描写人物的嫉妒、憎恶和仇恨等激情的剧作见长，此外他还担任多部成功影视作品、音乐剧等的编剧。其孪生兄弟安东尼·沙弗（Anthony Shaffer, 1926~2001）主要写作侦探和恐怖情节剧，剧情曲折生动，常采用巴洛克式的背景。兄弟二人还一起发表过小说。

著名作家金斯利·艾米斯之子马丁·艾米斯（Martin Amis, 1949~）在《金钱》(Money) 和《伦敦场地》(London Fields) 等小说中表现了人的欲望、人与人之间的隔阂以及生存的困境,他善用讽刺和黑色幽默对社会弊端进行揭露和批评。艾克罗伊德(Peter Ackroyd,1949~)在《王尔德的最后证词》(*The Last Testament of Oscar Wild*)等作品中,用虚拟自传的方式,将历史和虚幻融合,利用历史上作家、艺术家的生平,表现伦敦既不断变迁又保持固有特征的主题。新一代女性作家的重要代表拜厄特(A. S. Byatt,1936~)在《太阳的影子》(*The Shadow of the Sun*)、《游戏》(*The Game*)和《花园处女》(*The Virgin in the Garden*)等多部小说中表现了家庭主题。其作品尤其关注女性在社会中的困境,弥漫着悲观情绪。拜厄特的妹妹德拉布尔(Margaret Drabble,1939~)在其《夏日鸟笼》(*A Summer Bird Cage*)、《磨盘》(*The Millstone*)等小说中关注个体,尤其是女性与社会的关系,人物悲剧性的缺陷反映了政治经济环境的弊端,揭示所谓富裕国家的阴暗面。

奈保尔(V. S. Napaul,1932~)与拉什迪(Salman Rushdie,1947~)、石黑一雄(Kazuo Ishguro,1954~)一起被称为"英国移民文学三雄"。他的《比斯瓦斯先生有其屋》(*A House for Mr. Biswas*)表现了人的普遍而抽象的孤独、"失根"的生存境遇和殖民地外裔劳工的艰辛。其《抵达之谜》(*The Enigma of Arrival*)记叙了殖民地作家的心路历程。奈保尔的作品以真切的细节和简洁、明快、幽默的语言,表现了失去文化之根的困境和"外来者"的疏离感,以及异质文化间的冲突和融合,表达了作者对人性的怀疑、对社会的批判和对人生的思考。拉什迪的代表作《午夜的孩子》(*Midnight's Children*)从后殖民主义的视角,表现了东西方世界之间的联系、断裂和迁移,以及漂浮无根、身份认同危机和文化冲突。该书融历史、神话、传奇、纪实、新闻和广告于一体,内容浩瀚,场面恢宏,情节曲折,叙事在历史、现实和虚幻之间随意地转换,形成了其独特的魔幻现实主义。其《撒旦诗篇》(*The Satanic Verses*)被认为影射《古兰经》而引起了巨大争议,遭到穆斯林世界的抗议。日裔作家石黑一雄的小说《长日留痕》(*The Remains of the Day*)和《别让我走》(*Never Let Me Go*)等以历史为背景,采用第一人称叙事和含蓄的笔法,描写了欧亚文明和多元文化碰撞之中的帝国、阶级及童真的失去等，表现了人性的弱点、人生的孤独和情感的压抑。书中往往有一种悲观的宿命情绪，结尾常常是开放式的。

2. 本书特点

（1）本书每单元包括作家简介、作品简介、作品选读、注释、帮助理解作品的问题、作品欣赏精要、深入学习讨论思考题、建议拓展阅读和文学知识等内容，与选文讲解阐释紧密相扣，有助于自主学习，加深理解。作家和作品简介力求简洁精练，提供有关作家作品的最重要信息。有关理解作品的问题设计得较为直接，有助于读者对作品要点的把握。作品欣赏要点则更进一步从作品内涵和艺术手法上对读者进行引导和启发。为了帮助读者更全面地了解作家，我们列出了拓展或深入阅读的作品简要目录。深入学习的讨论题是为了拓展和加深对特定作家的理解，具有一定的深度，可以作为讨论题，也可以作为写作题目。此外，根据需要有些单元安排了文学知识内容。文学知识从具体话题出发，结合所选作品特征，对相关文学现象或艺术特征从一定的高度进行发挥阐释，使之更具普遍性，读者从中可以获得文学基本知识。这种安排可以引导学生由入门而逐渐登堂入室，激发兴趣，进而对作品作出探幽发微的探讨研究。

（2）本书所选作品均为文学史上具有代表性和典型性的作品。尽管有些作品频频出现在各种选本中，作为教材本书再选似有新意不足之嫌，但我们认为，那些各选本必选的名篇佳作是在文学史的长河中经历了时间考验的人类文化瑰宝。如果为求新而不用，既是对作者不公，也是对刚刚步入英美文学门廊的学生的不公，初学者有必要阅读这些人类文化精华。

（3）由于具有以上提到的释阐、欣赏和思考诸方面的特点，本书可用作英国文学课堂教学用书，也可用作自学教材，还可以作为文学欣赏的读本。

（4）按照英美文学选读教材的惯常做法，本书的重点是小说、诗歌和戏剧。散文作品仅选培根一人的作为样例。

（5）本书编写人员均是多年从事英国文学教学的教师。本书编者根据各自研究专长分别具体负责小说、诗歌或戏剧中的一种，而不是按照通常的做法以文学史时期分配任务。这样更有利于发挥编写人员的专长，提高教材质量。

3. 具体分工

全书由上海外国语大学虞建华教授担任总主编，主编为合肥工业大学林玉鹏教授，副主编为安庆师范大学陈光明教授和安徽师范大学谢劲秋教授。主编负责确定本书内容、制定编写体例和编写细则、提供编写样例、负责统稿和审阅全书书稿并提出修改意见。同时，主编还负责诗歌编写的总体安排和相关具体作品编写。副主编陈光明教授除了协助主编工作之外，还负责全部小说部分的编写；副主编谢劲秋教授负责全部戏剧部分，包括莎士比亚戏剧和诗歌部分的编写，安徽师范大学林绪芹老师参加了该部分的编写。

诗歌部分的具体分工如下。林玉鹏负责邓恩、布莱克、济慈、丁尼生、布朗宁、叶芝、迪伦·托马斯、特德·休斯部分的编写；合肥工业大学姜敏副教授负责乔叟、弥尔顿和雪莱部分的编写；陈静副教授负责彭斯和格雷部分的编写；安徽农业大学林玉霞副教授负责华兹华斯和科勒律治部分的编写；合肥工业大学陈曦副教授负责拉金和希尼部分的编写；合肥学院罗佳老师负责拜伦和阿诺德部分的编写。除诗歌之外，林玉鹏还负责散文家培根部分的编写。

本书疏漏之处，敬请同行专家和广大读者指正。

本书为安徽省教育厅人文社会科学重点专项基金项目(SK2012A100)成果。

林玉鹏
2013年6月于合肥斛兵塘畔
修订于2018年4月

Table of Contents

I. Middle Ages 1

Geoffrey Chaucer 1
   The Canterbury Tales 2

II. The English Renaissance 9

William Shakespeare 9
   Hamlet 9
   The Merchant of Venice 14
   Sonnet 18 35
Francis Bacon 38
   Of Studies 38

III. The Seventeenth Century 43

John Donne 43
   The Flea 43
John Milton 47
   Paradise Lost 48

John Bunyan ·· 54
   The Pilgrim's Progress ·· 54

IV. The Restoration and the Eighteenth Century ······ 62

Daniel Defoe ·· 62
   Robinson Crusoe ··· 63
Jonathan Swift ··· 70
   Gulliver's Travels ·· 71
Thomas Gray ·· 79
   Elegy Written in a Country Churchyard ····················· 80
Richard Brinsley Sheridan ·· 87
   The School for Scandal ··· 88

V. The Age of Romanticism ······ 95

Robert Burns ·· 95
   A Red, Red Rose ··· 96
   John Anderson, My Jo ·· 97
   My Heart's in the Highlands ··· 99
William Blake ··· 102
   The Tyger ·· 102
   The Sick Rose ··· 105
William Wordsworth ·· 108
   She Dwelt among the Untrodden Ways ························ 109
   My Heart Leaps Up When I Behold ······························ 111
   I Wandered Lonely as a Cloud ······································· 112
Samuel Taylor Coleridge ·· 116
   Kubla Khan ·· 117
George Gordon Byron ··· 122
   She Walks in Beauty ·· 122

Percy Bysshe Shelley ···· 124
   Ode to the West Wind ···· 125
John Keats ···· 133
   Ode on a Grecian Urn ···· 134
Jane Austen ···· 139
   Pride and Prejudice ···· 139

Ⅵ. Age of Realism (The Victorian Age) ···· 148

Charlotte Brontë ···· 148
   Jane Eyre ···· 149
Charles Dickens ···· 162
   Great Expectations ···· 163
William Makepeace Thackeray ···· 177
   Vanity Fair ···· 178
Alfred Lord Tennyson ···· 189
   The Eagle ···· 190
   Break, Break, Break ···· 191
   Crossing the Bar ···· 193
Robert Browning ···· 196
   My Last Duchess ···· 196
Matthew Arnold ···· 202
   Dover Beach ···· 202
Thomas Hardy ···· 205
   Tess of the D'Urbervilles ···· 206

Ⅶ. Modern Age ···· 222

W. B. Yeats ···· 222
   The Second Coming ···· 223

Bernard Shaw ········· 226
  Major Barbara ········· 226
E. M. Forster ········· 250
  A Passage to India ········· 252
D. H. Lawrence ········· 267
  Sons and Lovers ········· 268
James Joyce ········· 281
  Araby ········· 282
Virginia Woolf ········· 290
  The Mark on the Wall ········· 291

Ⅷ. Contemporary Period ········· 302

William Golding ········· 302
  Lord of the Flies ········· 303
Doris Lessing ········· 315
  A Road to the Big City ········· 315
John Fowles ········· 325
  The French Lieutenant's Woman ········· 325
Antonia Susan Byatt ········· 333
  Possession: A Romance ········· 334
Dylan Thomas ········· 348
  Fern Hill ········· 348
Philip Larkin ········· 353
  Toads ········· 354
  Cut Grass ········· 357
Ted Hughes ········· 360
  Hawk Roosting ········· 360
Seamus Heaney ········· 364
  Digging ········· 364
  The Forge ········· 367
John Osborne ········· 369

Table of Contents

Look Back in Anger 370
Harold Pinter 387
The Dumb Waiter 387

References **418**

Middle Ages

Geoffrey Chaucer
(1343~1400)

About the Author

Geoffrey Chaucer(1343~1400), noted as the father of English poetry, was the most influential poet of the English Middle Ages. His work played a significant role in the establishment of English as the prime vehicle for literature written in England and made the dialect of London the foundation for the modern English language. His varied career acquainted him with all walks of life of his time, making his writing a great source for studying the English medieval society. His travels to the European Continent enabled him to learn and introduce various forms of rhymed stanzas to English poetry. Most of Chaucer's works are long narrative poems and are conventionally divided into three periods: the French, the Italian and the English, reflecting the degree to which he was influenced by the foreign established writers such as Dante, Petrarch and Boccaccio. Among his many works are *The Book of the Duchess*, *The House of Fame*, *The Legend of Good Women* and the long philosophical romance *Troilus and Criseyde*, and he is best loved today for *The Canterbury Tales*. He was buried in Westminster Abbey and unconsciously started the famous Poet Corner there. Many notable critics believe that he stands as one of the great shapers of literary narrative and character today.

★ The Canterbury Tales

About the Poem

The Canterbury Tales, written in Middle English chiefly in the years 1387~1400, is the most famous and well acclaimed masterpiece of Geoffrey Chaucer. The frame of the story is that the narrator joins a company of twenty-nine pilgrims from all walks of life, such as a knight, a squire, a prioress, a tradesman, a drunken cook and a plowman. There are also monks, nuns and priests, a doctor, a lawyer, a sailor, a miller, a carpenter, an Oxford scholar etc., and the wife of Bath, at an inn in Southwark near London, and travels to a saint's shrine in Canterbury. The inn-keeper suggests that each pilgrim tell two tales on the way to Canterbury and two on the way back in order to entertain one another. The finished work is a collection of about twenty-four tales linked up by introductions with a prologue and an epilogue. Chaucer never finished his tales. Among them, the Knight's tale, the Nun's tale and the Wife of Bath's tale are the most popular ones. In the General Prologue, Chaucer presents a panorama of his contemporary society through vivid descriptions of the clothing, professions and social ranks of the pilgrims, each by his/her simplest and most striking characteristics.

The General Prologue
(Excerpt)

WHEN in April the sweet showers[1] fall
And pierce the drought of March to the root[2], and all
The veins are bathed[3] in liquor of such power[4]
As brings about the engendering of the flower[5],
When also Zephyrus[6] with his sweet breath
Exhales[7] an air in every grove and heath[8]
Upon the tender shoots, and the young sun
His half-course in the sign of the Ram[9] has run,
And the small fowl[10] are making melody
That sleep away the night with open eye
(So nature pricks them and their heart engages)
Then people long to go on pilgrimages[11]

And palmers[12] long to seek the stranger strands[13]
Of far-off saints, hallowed in sundry[14] lands,
And specially, from every shire's[15] end
In England, down to Canterbury[16] they wend[17]
To seek the holy blissful martyr[18], quick
To give his help to them when they were sick.
It happened in that season that one day
In Southwark[19], at The Tabard[20], as I lay
Ready to go on pilgrimage[21] and start
For Canterbury, most devout at heart,
At night there came into that hostelry[22]
Some nine and twenty in a company
Of sundry folk happening then to fall
In fellowship, and they were pilgrims all
That towards Canterbury meant to ride.
The rooms and stables of the inn were wide;
They made us easy, all was of the best.
And shortly, when the sun had gone to rest,
By speaking to them all upon the trip
I soon was one of them in fellowship
And promised to rise early and take the way
To Canterbury, as you heard me say.
But none the less, while I have time and space,
Before my story takes a further pace,
It seems a reasonable thing to say
What their condition was, the full array[23]
Of each of them, as it appeared to me
According to profession and degree,
And what apparel they were riding in;
And at a Knight I therefore will begin.
...

There was also a nun, a prioress,
Who, in her smiling, modest was and coy;
Her greatest oath was but "By Saint Eloy!"[24]
And she was known as Madam Eglantine[25].
Full well she sang the services divine
Intoning through her nose, becomingly;
And fair she spoke her French[26], and fluently.

At table she had been well taught withal[27],
And never from her lips let morsels fall,
Nor dipped her fingers deep in sauce, but ate
With so much care the food upon her plate
That never driblet fell upon her breast.[28]
In courtesy she had delight and zest.
Her upper lip was always wiped so clean
That in her cup was no iota[29] seen
Of grease, when she had drunk her draught of wine.
And certainly she was of great disport[30]
And full pleasant, and amiable of port[31]
And went to many pains to put on cheer
Of court, and very dignified appear
And to be thought worthy of reverence.
But, to say something of her moral sense,
She was so charitable and piteous
That she would weep if she but saw a mouse
Caught in a trap, though it were dead or bled.
She had some little dogs, too, that she fed
On roasted flesh, or milk and fine white bread[32].
But sore she'd weep if one of them were dead,
Or if men smote it with a rod to smart:
For pity ruled her, and her tender heart.
Full properly her wimple[33] pleated was.
Her nose was straight, her eyes as grey as glass,
Her mouth full small, and also soft and red;
But certainly she had a fair forehead;
It was almost a full span broad[34], I own[35],
For, truth to tell, she was not undergrown.
Full stylish was her cloak, I was aware.
Of coral small about her arm she'd bear
A string of beads[36], gauded[37] all round with green;
And from there hung a brooch of golden sheen
On which there was first written a crowned "A,"
And under, Amor Vincit Omnis[38].
...

I. Middle Ages

Notes

1. shower: brief fall of rain.
2. pierce… to the root: penetrate into the root.
3. The veins are bathed: the roots are hydrated.
4. in liquor of such power: such powerful liquid(rain).
5. the engendering of the flower: the flower being caused to bud and bloom.
6. Zephyrus: the name of the god of the west wind in Greco-Roman mythology; referring here to the west wind.
7. exhales: breathes out.
8. grove and heath: small wood and ever-green bush.
9. Ram: the constellation Aries.
10. small fowl: little birds.
11. pilgrimage: a journey to a sacred place. In Chaucer's time, good Christians were supposed to make a yearly pilgrimage to a significant religious site. Some of these locations, like Canterbury Cathedral, were places where martyrs for the Christian faith had died.
12. palmers: pilgrims.
13. strands: shores.
14. sundry: various.
15. shire's: countryside's.
16. Canterbury: cathedral in the southeast of England, an important destination for Christian pilgrims because it was the location of the murder of the Saint Thomas à Becket.
17. wend: go.
18. Martyr: Thomas à Becket, who was martyred at Canterbury. He was Archbishop of Canterbury from 1162 until his assassination by followers of King Henry II of England for their conflict over the rights and privileges of the church. He is venerated as a saint and martyr by both the Roman church and the Anglican Communion.
19. Southwark: an area south of London bridge; in Chaucer's time, it had many inns and taverns.
20. Tabard: the inn where the pilgrims are staying.
21. go on pilgrimage: it is said that the poem probably is based on Chaucer's own pilgrimage seeking the saint's blessing for his sick wife.
22. hostelry: inn.
23. array: dress.

24. Saint Eloy: or St. Eligius; patron saint of goldsmiths.
25. Madam Eglantine: her name means "honeysuckle".
26. French: usually spoken by the upper classes.
27. withal: (archaic) in addition.
28. This part describes the nun's dainty manners.
29. iota: the ninth Greek letter; (fig) smallest amount.
30. of great disport: well-bred ladies were supposed to be cheerful at social events.
31. port: behavior.
32. fine white bread: this kind of bread is very expensive.
33. wimple: nun's head covering.
34. a full span broad: broad foreheads were highly fashionable then.
35. own: agree, recognize.
36. beads: prayer beads.
37. gauded: interspersed(点缀).
38. Amor Vincit Omnia: love conquers all.

Questions for Understanding

1. Why do people long for pilgrimage in April in England? What is the pilgrimage for?
2. How much do you know about the Christianity in the Middle Ages?
3. From what order will the narrator introduce each of his companions?
4. How does the narrator like the nun? Do you think his tone is ironic?
5. Can you get some idea about the women's fashion in Chaucer's society from the detailed description of the refined prioress?

Aspects of Appreciation

1. Frame story

A frame story (also frame tale, frame narrative, etc.) is usually about a gathering of people in one place for the exchange of stories with each character telling his/her tale. It employs a narrative technique in which an introductory main story organizes a set of shorter stories. An early example of the frame story is *Arabian Nights* (《一千零一夜》) and the historically famous frame stories include Boccaccio's *Decameron* (《十日谈》) and Chaucer's *The Canterbury Tales* (《坎特伯雷故事》). It is known that Chaucer was influenced by Boccaccio to some degree, but Chaucer, instead of addressing an over-refined society as Boccaccio did, took his characters from all walks of life, and with these varied figures and their respective tales, he presents to his people a mosaic-like panorama of his contemporary society of England.

2. The opening of the General Prologue

The narrator presents an imagery of spring's return and rebirth. The hydrating sweet showers, the engendering of the roots and flowers, the constellation of Ram in the sky, the gentle west wind and the chirping birds, are all familiar landscape of England in April. According to Patrick Gardner and Miriam Jacobson, the verbs used to describe Nature's actions—piercing, engendering, inspiring and pricking—conjure up images of conception. After a long sleep in the winter, people, as well as nature, begin to stir, and feel the need to travel to some saints' shrine to have a spiritual cleansing and renewal. This famous opening was once imitated and parodied by T. S. Eliot in the very beginning of his renowned poem *The Waste Land*.

3. Poetic devices: the heroic couplet(英雄双韵体)

Geoffrey Chaucer pioneered the use of the heroic couplet, which is among his many contributions to the reform of English poetry. A heroic couplet is a rhymed iambic pentameter(五步抑扬格), which is always in masculine(阳韵的) end rhyme(尾韵), replacing the older traditional alliteration(头韵). A heroic couplet is commonly used for epic and narrative poetry. The original version of *The Canterbury Tales* is mostly written in heroic couplet and sounds beautiful. This selection of the modern version translated by Nevill Coghill also mainly employs this rhyme scheme nicely.

4. Lady-like manners

As manners and language became increasingly important in defining the "gentle" classes in the later Middle Ages, some people, besides the noble class, devoted a great deal of attention to the manners proper to a would-be lady. Books of manners became popular and influenced even more people. Part of this fashion is echoed in Chaucer's portrait of Madame Eglentyne, the Prioress. She speaks French "fair" and "fluently"; she never lets bits of food fall from her lips nor stain her breast. When she reaches for food on the table she does not dip her fingers deep in sauce; she wipes her lips very clean of grease before drinking from her wine cup. Her personality is pleasant and amiable, and she is cheerful at social events. In a word, she appears to be very dignified and worth respect. Besides, she is obviously compassionate towards animals, which shows her high moral sense. However, more than one point of these details seems to carry a hint of irony in the description of this member of the clergy who imitates the manners of the royal court.

Suggested Further Reading

The rest part of General Prologue, the Knight's tale, the Nun's tale and the Wife of Bath's tale in *The Canterbury Tales*.

Topics for Further Study

1. Do you think the return of spring has also inspired the poet to compose his lines as the classical poet (like Homer) relied on a muse to start his writing?
2. Some critics said that the narrator (Chaucer) probably had a crush on the prioress. Can you find out how differently her image as a female is described from the other women in the poem?
3. What does the narrator look like? Can you characterize him after reading the whole poem?

Knowledge of Literature

Estates Satire

Medieval social theory divides society into three broad classes, called "estates": the clergy, the military (including the nobility), and the laity (including the peasantry). Estates Satire is a medieval genre which satirizes the corruption that occurs within the three medieval social estates. The General Prologue constitutes an example of Medieval Estates Satire through characterizing the group members of the pilgrims, who represent a diverse cross-section of 14th-century English society. For example, the prioress' life style, and her bejeweled rosary with a motto of "love conquers all" which seems more like a love token than a sign of her devotion to Jesus Christ, satirizes the corruption of the estate of the clergy to some degree. However, as is noted by many critics, the General Prologue also provides an ideal member of each estate as a model with which the others can be compared and contrasted—the Parson, the Knight, and the Plowman, for instance.

II

The English Renaissance

William Shakespeare
(1564~1616)

About the Author

William Shakespeare, English playwright and poet, belongs to those rare geniuses of mankind who have become landmarks in the history of world culture. His plays communicate a profound knowledge of the wellsprings of human behaviour, reveal through portrayals of a wide variety of characters. His use of poetic and dramatic means to create a unified aesthetic effect out of a multiplicity of vocal expressions and actions is recognized as a singular achievement, and his use of poetry within his plays to express the deepest levels of human motivation in individual, social, and universal situations is considered one of the greatest accomplishments in literary history.

No wonder that Shakespeare's works are so fondly cherished by the greatest minds of mankind, and among them Karl Marx, who regards Aeschylus and Shakespeare as "the two greatest dramatic geniuses the world has ever known". It is well known in what high esteem Shakespeare is held by such giants of world literature as Milton, Goethe, Stendhal and Pushkin.

★ Hamlet

About the Play

Hamlet is considered to be the summit of Shakespeare's art. It was written in 1601~1602 and first published in 1603. Shakespeare took a certain story of Prince Amleth from old sources which could be traced to the 12th century. He, however, was not the first to dramatize Hamlet's history. In the eighties, a play that bore the same name gained popularity among the English public. Thomas Kyd was supposed to have been the author of this play.

Under Shakespeare's pen, the medieval story assumed new meaning and significance. Danish names could not hide from the spectators and readers the fact that it was England which the great writer described in his play. The whole tragedy is permeated with the spirit of Shakespeare's own time. *Hamlet* is the profoundest expression of Shakespeare's humanism and his criticism of the contemporary life.

Act Ⅲ, Scene Ⅰ

(A room in the castle.)
HAMLET.
To be, or not to be: that is the question[1]:
Whether 'tis nobler in the mind to suffer
The slings[2] and arrows of outrageous fortune,
Or to take arms against a sea of troubles[3],
And by opposing end them. To die: to sleep;
No more[4]; and by a sleep to say we end
The heart-ache and the thousand natural shocks
That flesh is heir to, 'tis a consummation[5]
Devoutly to be wish'd. To die, to sleep;
To sleep! perchance to dream: aye, there's the rub[6];
For in that sleep of death what dreams[7] may come,
When we have shuffled off this mortal coil[8],
Must give us pause: there's the respect[9]
That makes calamity of so long life[10];
For who would bear the whips and scorns of time[11],
The oppressor's wrong, the proud man's contumely,
The pangs of despised love, the law's delay,
The insolence of office and the spurns
That patient merit of the unworthy takes,
When he himself might his quietus make[12]
With a bare bodkin[13]? who would fardels bear,

To grunt and sweat under a weary life,
But that the dread of something after death,
The undiscover'd country, from whose bourn[14]
No traveler returns, puzzles the will,
And makes us rather bear those ills we have
Than fly to others that we know not of?
Thus conscience does make cowards of us all,
And thus the native hue of resolution
Is sicklied o'er with the pale cast of thought[15],
And enterprises of great pitch and moment[16]
With this regard their currents turn awry,
And lose the name of action[17].

Notes

1. To be or not to be: to be—to exist or to live. The question—Hamlet expands in the next four lines, debating with himself which is the more honourable course—patiently to endure earthly misfortunes, or boldly to oppose them.
2. slings: i. e. missiles thrown by slings.
3. take arms against a sea of troubles: put an end to one's troubles by fighting against them.
4. No more: that is all.
5. consummation: a completion of one's life.
6. "Rub" is the technical term in bowls for any obstacle which hinders the bowl from keeping on its proper course—e. g. an uneven bit of ground, a stone, etc. Hence the sense "obstacle, hindrance", as in this now proverbial phrase "there's the rub".
7. what dreams: i. e. the thought of what dreams may come.
8. mortal coil: turmoil of mortality, confused trouble of mortal life.
9. respect: consideration = "regard".
10. of so long life: so long-lived.
11. time: the times, the world, one's contemporaries.
12. might his quietus make: might give himself his release from life's troubles.
13. bare bodkin: dagger without the cover.

14. bourn: boundary, limit.
15. thought: anxiety.
16. pitch and moment: magnitude and importance.
17. And lose the name of action: even as a river may lose itself in a sandy waste and so after its long course never reach the sea, a wonderful symbol, indeed, of frustration and failure.

Questions for Understanding

1. What is the question asked by Hamlet? What is the real implication of "to be" and "not to be"?
2. Why is sleep so frightening since it can "end" the heartache and the thousand natural shocks?
3. Why would people rather bear the sufferings of the world than die to avoid them, according to Hamlet?
4. What makes people lose their determination to take action?
5. Many critics take a deterministic view of the plot of *Hamlet*, arguing that the prince's inability to act and tendency toward melancholy reflection is a "tragic flaw" that leads inevitably to his demise. Is this an accurate way of understanding the play?

Aspects of Appreciation

The character of Hamlet

From the play and Hamlet's soliloquy, we know that Hamlet is Prince of Denmark. In the play from Ophelia's comment on him and his friendly conversations with Horatio, we know he is a man of Renaissance with humanist's ideal—a soldier, scholar, courtier, the glass of fashion and the mold of form.

When he first appears in the play, he is in the state of depression, because, first he finds the evil and corruption in his country: the world to him is "an unweeded garden, the time is out of joint. O cursed spite, that ever I was born to set it right". Secondly, he, from the ghost, knows the real cause of his father's death. Therefore, the most important problem he is facing now is to avenge his father's death. But the situation he is in is very dangerous, because he has to fight against that stronghold of feudalism with his uncle on the top. So he pretends to be mad. Here we can say he is a little resourceful himself. In addition, he is a melancholy, hesitant, reasonable and philosophical man as well as a great moralizer, and a slow avenger of his father's death. At other times, he does have chance to act but he remains puzzled, undecided, and skeptical, dallies with his purposes, till the occasion is lost, and finds out some pretense to relapse into indolence and thoughtfulness again. For this reason, he refuses to kill the king when the latter is at his prayers.

He is also disgusted at evil things, such as his loathing of his mother's sensuality, his astonishment and horror at her shallowness, his contempt for everything pretentious or false. He is far from a perfect humanist and he is a man himself.

Suggested Further Reading

Shakespeare's tragedies *King Lear*, *Macbeth*, and *Othello*.

Topics for Further Study

1. Humanism in Shakespeare's *Hamlet*.
2. Throughout the play, Hamlet feigns madness, but his portrayal of a madman is so intense and so convincing that many readers believe that Hamlet actually slips into insanity at certain moments in the play. Comment on Hamlet's insanity.
3. Hamlet's relationship with Ophelia.

Knowledge of Literature

1. Tragedy

Tragedy, as a literary term, refers to a serious drama in which a heroic protagonist meets an unhappy or calamitous end, brought about by some fatal flaw of character, by circumstances outside his or her control, or simply by destiny. According to Aristotle, "a tragedy … is the imitation of an action that is serious and also, as having magnitude, complete in itself; in language with pleasurable accessories, each kind brought in separately in the parts of the work; in a dramatic, not in a narrative form; with incidents arousing pity and fear, wherewith to accomplish its catharsis of such emotions."

2. Soliloquy

It is a speech, often of some length, in which a character, alone on the stage, expresses his thoughts and feelings. In classical drama the soliloquy is rare, but the playwrights of Elizabethan and Jacobean period used it extensively and with great skill. The soliloquy enables a dramatist to convey directly to audience important information about a particular character: his state of mind and heart, his most intimate thoughts and feelings, his motives and intentions.

★ The Merchant of Venice

About the Play

The Merchant of Venice is a comedy by William Shakespeare, believed to have been written between 1596 and 1598. Though classified as a tragic comedy in the First Folio and sharing certain aspects with Shakespeare's other romantic comedies, the play is perhaps most remembered for its dramatic scenes, and is best known for Shylock and the famous "pound of flesh" speech. The plot involves Shylock, a greedy Jewish money-lender. Shylock has lost his beloved daughter when she elopes with a man who belongs to a virulently anti-Semitic society. Shylock seeks a literal "pound of flesh" from the Merchant of Venice— Antonio when he fails to pay the debt. Portia defends Antonio from Shylock's legal suit. He ends by renouncing his faith and his fortune.

Act IV Scene I

(Venice. A court of justice.

Enter the DUKE, the MAGNIFICOES, ANTONIO, BASSANIO, GRATIANO, SOLANIO, SALARINO, and others.)

DUKE OF VENICE.

What, is Antonio here?

ANTONIO.

Ready[1], so please your Grace.

DUKE OF VENICE.

I am sorry for thee: thou art come to answer

A stony adversary, an inhuman wretch

Uncapable of pity; void and empty

From[2] any dram[3] of mercy.

ANTONIO.

I have heard

Your Grace hath ta'en great pains to qualify[4]

His rigorous course, but since he stands obdurate,

II. The English Renaissance

And that no lawful means can carry me
Out of his envy's reach, I do oppose
My patience to his fury; and am arm'd
To suffer, with a quietness of spirit,
The very tyranny and rage of his.
DUKE OF VENICE.
Go one, and call the Jew into the court.
SOLANIO.
He's ready at the door: he comes, my lord.
(Enter SHYLOCK.)
DUKE OF VENICE.
Make room, and let him stand before our face. —
Shylock, the world thinks and I think so too,
That thou but lead'st this fashion of thy malice[5]
To the last hour of act; arid then 'tis thought
Thou'lt show thy mercy and remorse[6] more strange
Than is thy strange apparent cruelty;
And where thou now exact'st the penalty,—
Which is a pound of this poor merchant's flesh,—
Thou wilt not only loose[7] the forfeiture,
But, toucht with human gentleness and love,
Forgive a moiety[8] of the principal;
Glancing an eye of pity on his losses,
That have of late so huddled on his back,
Enow[9] to press a royal merchant[10] down,
And pluck commiseration of his state
From brassy bosoms and rough hearts of flint,
From stubborn Turks aud Tartars, never train'd
To offices of tender courtesy.
We all expect a gentle answer, Jew.
SHYLOCK.
I have possest[11] your Grace of what I purpose;
And by our holy Sabbath have I sworn
To have the due and forfeit[12] of my bond
If you deny it, let the danger light
Upon your charter and your city's freedom.
You'll ask me, why I rather choose to have

A weight of carrion-flesh than to receive
Three thousand ducats: I'll not answer that;
But say it is my humour: is it answer'd?
What if my house be troubled with a rat,
And I be pleased to give ten thousand ducats
To have it baned[13]! What, are you answer'd yet?
Some men there are love not a gaping pig[14];
Some, that are mad if they behold a cat[15];
And others, when the bag-pipe sings i'th' nose,
Cannot contain their urine: for affection[16]
Mistress of passion, sways it to the mood
Of what it likes or loathes. Now, for your answer:
As there is no firm reason to be render'd,
Why he cannot abide a gaping pig;
Why he, a harmless necessary cat;
Why he, a woollen bag-pipe,—but of force
Must yield to such inevitable shame
As to offend himself, being offended
So can I give no reason, nor I will not,
More than a lodged[17] hate and a certain[18] loathing
I bear Antonio, that I follow thus
A losing suit against him. Are you answer'd?
BASSANIO.
This is no answer, thou unfeeling man,
To excuse the current[19] of the cruelty.
SHYLOCK.
I am not bound to please thee with my answer.
BASSANIO.
Do all men kill the things they do not love?
SHYLOCK.
Hates any man the thing he would not kill?
BASSANIO.
Every offence is not a hate at first.
SHYLOCK.
What, would'st thou have a serpent sting thee twice?
ANTONIO.
I pray you, think you question with the Jew:

II. The English Renaissance

You may as well go stand upon the beach,
And bid the main flood[20] bate[21] his usual height;
You may as well use question with the wolf,
Why he hath made the ewe bleat for the lamb;
You may as well forbid the mountain pines
To wag their high tops, and to make no noises
When they are fretten with the gusts of heaven[22];
You may as well do any thing most hard,
As seek to soften that,—than which what's harder?—
His Jewish heart:—therefore, I do beseech you,
Make no more offers, use no further means,
But, with all brief and plain conveniency[23],
Let me have judgement, and the Jew his will.
BASSANIO.
For thy three thousand ducats here is six.
SHYLOCK.
If every ducat in six thousand ducats
Were in six parts, and every part a ducat,
I would not draw[24] them,—I would have my bond.
DUKE OF VENICE.
How shalt thou hope for mercy, rendering none?
SHYLOCK.
What judgement shall I dread, doing no wrong?
You have among you many a purchased slave,
Which, like your asses and your dogs and mules,
You use in abject and in slavish parts[25]
Because you bought them:—shall I say to you,
Let them be free, marry them to your heirs?
Why sweat they under burdens? let their beds
Be made as soft as yours, and let their palates
Be season'd with such viands? You will answer,
The slaves are ours:—so do I answer you:
The pound of flesh, which I demand of him,
Is dearly bought, 'tis mine, and I will have it.
If you deny me, fie upon your law!
There is no force in the decrees of Venice.
I stand for judgement: answer,—shall I have it?

DUKE OF VENICE.
Upon my power I may dismiss this court,
Unless Bellario, a learned doctor,
Whom I have sent for to determine this,
Come here to-day.
SOLANIO.
My lord, here stays without
A messenger with letters from the doctor,
New come from Padua.
DUKE OF VENICE.
Bring us the letters; call the messenger.
BASSANIO.
Good cheer, Antonio! What, man, courage yet
The Jew shall have my flesh, blood, bones, and all,
Ere thou shalt lose for me one drop of blood.
ANTONIO.
I am a tainted wether[26] of the flock,
Meetest[27] for death: the weakest kind of fruit
Drops earliest to the ground; and so let me:
You cannot better be employ'd, Bassanio,
Than to live still, and write mine epitaph.
(Enter NERISSA, dressed like a lawyer's clerk)
DUKE OF VENICE.
Came you from Padua, from Bellario?
NERISSA.
From both, my lord. Bellario greets your Grace.
(Presents a letter)
BASSANIO.
Why dost thou whet thy knife so earnestly?
SHYLOCK.
To cut the forfeiture from that bankrout[28] there.
GRATIANO.
Not on thy sole, but on thy soul, harsh Jew,
Thou makest thy knife keen; but no metal can,
No, not the hangman's axe, bear half the keenness
Of thy sharp envy. Can no prayers pierce thee?
SHYLOCK.

II. The English Renaissance

No, none that thou hast wit enough to make.
GRATIANO.
O, be thou damn'd, inexecrable[29] dog!
And for thy life let justice be accused.
Thou almost makest me waver in my faith,
To hold opinion with[30] Pythagoras,
That souls of animals infuse themselves
Into the trunks of men; thy currish spirit
Govern'd a wolf, who, hang'd for human slaughter,
Even from the gallows did his fell[31] soul fleet,
And, whilst thou lay'st in thy unhallow'd dam,
Infused itself in thee; for thy desires
Are wolvish, bloody, starved, and ravenous.
SHYLOCK.
Till thou canst rail the seal from off my bond,
Thou but offend'st thy lungs to speak so loud;
Repair thy wit, good youth, or it will fall
To cureless ruin[32]—I stand here for law.
DUKE OF VENICE.
This letter from Bellario doth commend
A young and learned doctor to our court. —
Where is he?
NERISSA.
He attendeth here hard by[33],
To know your answer, whether you'll admit him.
DUKE OF VENICE.
With all my heart. —Some three or four of you
Go give him courteous conduct to this place. —
Meantime the court shall hear Bellario's letter.
CLERK (reads)

Your Grace shall understand, that at the receipt of your letter I am very sick; but in the instant that your messenger came, in loving visitation[34] was with me a young doctor of Rome; his name is Balthazar. I acquainted him with the cause in controversy between the Jew and Antonio the merchant; we turn'd o'er many books together; he is furnisht with my opinion, which, better'd with his own learning,—the greatness whereof I cannot enough commend,—comes with him, at my importunity, to fill up[35] your Grace's request in my stead. I beseech you, let his lack of years be no impediment to let him lack a reverend estimation[36]; for I never knew so young a body with so old a head. I leave him to your gracious acceptance, whose trial shall better publish his commendation[37].

DUKE OF VENICE.
You hear the learn'd Bellario, what he writes:
And here, I take it, is the doctor come.
(Enter PORTIA for BALTHAZAR.)
Give me your hand. Come you from old Bellario?
PORTIA.
I did, my lord.
DUKE OF VENICE.
You are welcome; take your place.
Are you acquainted with the difference
That holds this present question in the court?
PORTIA.
I am informed throughly[38] of the cause. —
Which is the merchant here, and which the Jew?
DUKE OF VENICE.
Antonio and old Shylock, both stand forth.
PORTIA.
Is your name Shylock?
SHYLOCK.
Shylock is my name.
PORTIA.
Of a strange nature is the suit you follow;
Yet in such rule[39], that the Venetian law
Cannot impugn you as you do proceed. —
You stand within his danger[40], do you not?
ANTONIO.
Ay, so he says.
PORTIA.
Do you confess the bond?
ANTONIO.
I do.
PORTIA.
Then must the Jew be merciful.

SHYLOCK.
On what compulsion must I? tell me that.
PORTIA.
The quality of mercy is not strain'd[41], —
It droppeth as the gentle rain from heaven
Upon the place beneath; it is twice blest. —
It blesseth him that gives, and him that takes:
'Tis mightiest in the mightiest: it becomes
The throned monarch better than his crown;
His sceptre shows the force of temporal power,
The attribute to awe and majesty,
Wherein doth sit the dread and fear of kings
But mercy is above this sceptred sway, —
It is enthroned in the hearts of kings,
It is an attribute to God himself;
And earthly power doth then show likest God's
When mercy seasons justice. Therefore, Jew,
Though justice[42] be thy plea, consider this, —
That, in the course of justice, none of us
Should see salvation: we do pray for mercy
And that same prayer[43] doth teach us all to render
The deeds of mercy. I have spoke thus much
To mitigate the justice of thy plea[44];
Which if thou follow, this strict court of Venice
Must needs give sentence gainst the merchant there.
SHYLOCK.
My deeds upon my head! I crave the law,
The penalty and forfeit of my bond.
PORTIA.
Is he not able to discharge the money?
BASSANIO.
Yes, here I tender it for him in the court;
Yea, thrice the sums if that will not suffice,
I will be bound to pay it ten times o'er,
On forfeit of my hands, my head, my heart;
If this will not suffice, it must appear
That malice bears down truth. And I beseech you,

Wrest[45] once the law to your authority;
To do great right, do a little wrong;
And curb this cruel devil of his will.
PORTIA.
It must not be; there is no power in Venice
Can alter a decree established:
'T will be recorded for a precedent;
And many an error, by the same example,
Will rush into the state: it cannot be.
SHYLOCK.
A Daniel[46] come to judgement! yea, a Daniel! —
O wise young judge, how I do honour thee!
PORTIA.
I pray you, let me look upon the bond.
SHYLOCK.
Here 'tis, most reverend doctor, here it is.
PORTIA.
Shylock, there's thrice thy money offer'd thee.
SHYLOCK.
An oath, an oath, I have an oath in heaven:
Shall I lay perjury upon my soul?
No, not for Venice.
PORTIA.
Why, this bond is forfeit;
And lawfully by this the Jew may claim
A pound of flesh, to be by him cut off
Nearest the merchant's heart. —Be merciful:
Take thrice thy money; bid me tear the bond.
SHYLOCK.
When it is paid according to the tenour. —
It doth appear you are a worthy judge;
You know the law, your exposition
Hath been most sound: I charge you by the law,
Whereof you are a well-deserving pillar,
Proceed to judgement; by my soul I swear
There is no power in the tongue of man
To alter me: I stay here on my bond.

II. The English Renaissance

ANTONIO.
Most heartily I do beseech the court
To give the judgement.
PORTIA.
Why then, thus it is:—
You must prepare your bosom for his knife.
SHYLOCK.
O noble judge! O excellent young man!
PORTIA.
For the intent and purpose of the law
Hath full relation to the penalty[47],
Which here appeareth due upon the bond.
SHYLOCK.
'Tis very true: O wise and upright judge!
How much more elder[48] art thou than thy looks!
PORTIA.
Therefore lay bare your bosom.
SHYLOCK.
Ay, his breast:
So says the bond:—doth it not, noble judge? —
Nearest his heart: those are the very words.
PORTIA.
It is so. Are there balance here to weigh
The flesh?
SHYLOCK.
I have them ready.
PORTIA.
Have by some surgeon, Shylock, on your charge[49],
To stop his wounds, lest he do bleed to death.
SHYLOCK.
Is it so nominated in the bond?
PORTIA.
It is not so exprest: but what of that?
'T were good you do so much for charity.
SHYLOCK.
I cannot find it; 'tis not in the bond.
PORTIA.

You, merchant, have you any thing to say?
ANTONIO.
But little: I am arm'd and well prepared. —
Give me your hand, Bassanio: fare you well!
Grieve not that I am fall'n to this for you;
For herein Fortune shows herself more kind
Than is her custom: it is still her use
To let the wretched man outlive his wealth,
To view with follow eye and wrinkled brow
An age of poverty; from which lingering penance
Of such a misery doth she cut me off.
Commend me to your honourable wife:
Tell her the process of Antonio's end;
Say how I loved you, speak me fair in death;
And, when the tale is told, bid her be judge
Whether Bassanio had not once a love[50].
Repent but you that you shall lose your friend,
And he repents not that he pays your debt;
For, if the Jew do cut but deep enough,
I'll pay it presently with all my heart[51].
BASSANIO.
Antonio, I am married to a wife
Which is as dear to me as life itself;
But life itself, my wife, and all the world,
Are not with me esteem'd above thy life:
I would lose all, ay, sacrifice them all
Here to this devil, to deliver you.
PORTIA.
Your wife would give you little thanks for that,
If she were by, to hear you make the offer.
GRATIANO.
I have a wife, whom, I protest, I love:
I would she were in heaven, so she could
Entreat some power to change this currish Jew.
NERISSA.
'Tis well you offer it behind her back:
The wish would make else an unquiet house.

II. The English Renaissance

SHYLOCK (aside).
These be the Christian husbands! I have a daughter;
Would any of the stock of Barabbas[52]
Had been her husband rather than a Christian! —
We triffle time[53]: I pray thee, pursue sentence.
PORTIA.
A pound of that same merchant's flesh is thine:
The court awards it, and the law doth give it.
SHYLOCK.
Most rightful judge!
PORTIA.
And you must cut this flesh from off his breast:
The law allows it, and the court awards it.
SHYLOCK.
Most learned judge! —A sentence! come, prepare!
PORTIA.
Tarry a little, there is something else.
This bond doth give thee here no jots[54] of blood,—
The words expressly are, "a pound of flesh":
Take then thy bond, take thou thy pound of flesh;
But, in the cutting it, if thou dost shed
One drop of Christian blood, thy lands and goods
Are, by the laws of Venice, confiscate
Unto the state of Venice.
GRATIANO.
O upright judge! —Mark, Jew:—O learned judge!
SHYLOCK.
Is that the law?
PORTIA.
Thyself shalt see the act.
For, as thou urgest justice, be assured
Thou shalt have justice, more than thou desirest.
GRATIANO.
O learned judge! —Mark, Jew:—a learned judge!
SHYLOCK.
I take his offer, then:—pay the bond thrice,
And let the Christian go.

BASSANIO.

Here is the money.

PORTIA.

Soft!

The Jew shall have all justice;—soft[55]! no haste:—

He shall have nothing but the penalty.

GRATIANO.

O Jew! an upright judge, a learned judge!

PORTIA.

Therefore prepare thee to cut off the flesh.

Shed thou no blood; nor cut thou less nor more

But just a pound[56] of flesh: if thou cutt'st more

Or less than a just pound,—be it but so much

As makes it light or heavy in the substance,

Or the division of the twentieth part

Of one poor scruple[57], nay, if the scale do turn

But in the estimation of a hair,—

Thou diest, and all thy goods are confiscate.

GRATIANO.

A second Daniel, a Daniel, Jew!

Now, infidel, I have you on the hip[58].

PORTIA.

Why doth the Jew pause? take thy forfeiture.

SHYLOCK.

Give me my principal and let me go.

BASSANIO.

I have it ready for thee; here it is.

PORTIA.

He hath refused it in the open court:

He shall have merely justice and his bond.

GRATIANO.

A Daniel, still say I, a second Daniel! —

I thank thee, Jew, for teaching me that word.

SHYLOCK.

Shall I not have barely my principal?

PORTIA.

Thou shalt have nothing but the forfeiture,

To be so taken at thy peril, Jew.

SHYLOCK.
Why, then the devil give him good of it!
I'll stay no longer question[59].
PORTIA.
Tarry, Jew:
The law hath yet another hold on you.
It is enacted in the laws of Venice,—
If it be proved against an alien[60]
That by direct or indirect attempts
He seek the life of any citizen,
The party, 'gainst the which he doth contrive
Shall seize one half his goods; the other half
Comes to the privy coffer of the state;
And the offender's life lies in the mercy
Of the duke only, 'gainst all other voice[61]
In which predicament, I say, thou stand'st;
For it appears, by manifest[62] proceeding,
That indirectly, and directly too,
Thou hast contrived against the very life
Of the defendants; and thou hast incurr'd
The danger formerly by me rehearsed[63].
Down, therefore, and beg mercy of the duke.
GRATIANO.
Beg that thou mayst have leave to hang thyself:
And yet, thy wealth being forfeit to the state,
Thou hast not left the value of a cord[64]
Therefore thou must be hang'd at the state's charge[65].
DUKE OF VENICE.
That thou shalt see the difference of our spirits,
I pardon thee thy life before thou ask it:
I or half thy wealth, it is Antonio's;
The other half comes to the general state,
Which humbleness may drive unto a fine[66].
PORTIA.
Ay, for the state,—not for Antonio.

SHYLOCK.
Nay, take my life and all; pardon not that:
You take my house, when you do take the prop[67]
That doth sustain my house; you take my life,
When you do take the means where by I live.
PORTIA.
What mercy can you render him, Antonio?
GRATIANO.
A halter gratis[68]; nothing else, for God's sake.
ANTONIO.
So please my lord the duke and all the court
To quit[69] the fine for one half of his goods,
I am content; so he will let me have
The other half in use, to render it,
Upon his death, unto the gentleman
That lately stole his daughter:
Two things provided more,—that, for this favour,
He presently become a Christian;
The other, that he do record a gift,
Here in the court, of all he dies possest,
Unto his son Lorenzo and his daughter.
DUKE OF VENICE.
He shall do this; or else I do recant
The pardon that I late pronounced here.
PORTIA.
Art thou contented, Jew? what dost thou say?
SHYLOCK.
I am content.
PORTIA.
Clerk, draw a deed of gift.
SHYLOCK.
I pray you, give me leave to go from hence,
I am not well: send the deed after me,
And I will sign it.
DUKE OF VENICE.
Get thee gone, but do it.
GRATIANO.

In christening shalt thou have two godfathers:
Had I been judge, thou shouldst have had ten more[70],
To bring thee to the gallows, not the font.
(Exit SHYLOCK.)
DUKE OF VENICE.
Sir, I entreat you home with me to dinner.
PORTIA.
I humbly do desire your Grace of pardon:
I must away this night toward Padua,
And it is meet I presently set forth.
DUKE OF VENICE.
I am sorry that your leisure serves you not[71].
Antonio, gratify[72] this gentleman;
For, in my mind, you are much bound to him.
(Exeunt DUKE and his TRAIN.)
BASSANIO.
Most worthy gentleman, I and my friend
Have by your wisdom been this day acquitted
Of grievous penalties; in lieu whereof
Three thousand ducats, due unto the Jew,
We freely cope your courteous pains[73] withal.
ANTONIO.
And stand indebted, over and above,
In love and service to you evermore.
PORTIA.
He is well paid that is well satisfied;
And I, delivering[74] you, and satisfied,
And therein do account myself well paid:
My mind was never yet more mercenary.
I pray you, know me when we meet again:
I wish you well, and so I take my leave.
BASSANIO
Dear sir, of force I must attempt you further[75]:
Take some remembrance of us, as a tribute,
Not as a fee: grant me two things, I pray you,—
Not to deny me, and to pardon me.
PORTIA.

You press me far, and therefore I will yield.
(to ANTONIO) Give me your gloves, I'll wear them for your sake;
(to BASSANIO) And, for your love, I'll take this ring from you;—
Do not draw back your hand; I'll take no more;
And you in love shall not deny me this.
BASSANIO.
This ring, good sir,—alas, it is a trifle!
I will not shame myself to give[76] you this.
PORTIA.
I will have nothing else but only this;
And now methinks I have a mind to it.
BASSANIO.
There's more depends on this than on the value,
The dearest ring in Venice will I give you,
And find it out by proclamation:
Only for this, I pray you, pardon me.
PORTIA.
I see, sir, you are liberal in offers:
You taught me first to beg and now methinks
You teach me how a beggar should be answer'd.
BASSANIO.
Good sir, this ring was given me by my wife;
And, when she put in on, she made me vow
That I should neither sell nor give nor lose it.
PORTIA.
That's scuse[77] serves many men to save their gifts.
And if your wife be not a mad woman,
And know how well I have deserved this ring,
She would not hold out enemy for ever
For giving it to me. Well, peace be with you!
(Exeunt PORTIA and NERISSA.)
ANTONIO.
My Lord Bassanio, let him have the ring:
Let his deservings, and my love withal[78],
Be valued 'gainst your wife's commandment.
BASSANIO.
Go, Gratiano, run and overtake

II. The English Renaissance

Give him this ring; and bring him, if thou canst,
Unto Antonio's house:—away! Make haste.
(Exit GRATIANO.)
Come, you and I will thither presently[79];
And in the morning early will we both
Fly toward Belmont: come, Antonio. (Exeunt.)

※ ※

Notes

1. ready: the standard answer in court.
2. from: of.
3. dram: minute quantity; drop.
4. qualify: moderate; soften.
5. lend'st this fashion of thy malice: pretend to carry through this spiteful action.
6. remorse: pity; compassion.
7. loose: release.
8. moiety: part; portion.
9. enow: enough.
10. royal merchant: a merchant with the resources of the kingdom behind him.
11. possest: informed.
12. due and forfeit: the forfeit which is due.
13. baned: poisoned.
14. a gaping pig: a suckling pig served at the table with a lemon or some other fruit in its mouth.
15. behold a cat: some people have a natural antipathy to cats.
16. affection: sympathetic feeling; one's likes and dislikes.
17. lodged: deep-seated.
18. certain: sure; fixed.
19. current: course.
20. main flood: ocean.
21. bate: abate.
22. fretten with the gusts of heaven: ruffled or tossed by high winds.
23. plain conveniency: simple procedure.
24. draw: take.

25. parts: services, tasks.
26. wether: gelded sheep.
27. meetest: most fit.
28. bankrout: bankrupt.
29. inexecrable: so execrable, or evil, that you are beyond enough cursing.
30. to hold opinion with: to agree with.
31. fell: cruel; deadly.
32. cureless ruin: insanity.
33. hard by: near by.
34. in loving visitation: on a friendly visit.
35. to fill up: to comply with.
36. reverend estimation: thoughtful consideration.
37. Whose trial shall better publish his commendation: His performance will prove his ability better than I can describe it.
38. throughly: thoroughly.
39. in such rule: so much within the rules.
40. danger: reach or control.
41. strain'd: restricted to a few persons.
42. justice: Shylock's plea was judgment, not justice.
43. that same prayer: the Lord's Prayer.
44. mitigate the justice of thy plea: temper your insistence on strict justice.
45. wrest: bend.
46. Daniel: a Biblical reference to Daniel convicting the elders for spying on Susannah.
47. Hath full relation to the penalty: fully recognizes the validity of the penalty.
48. more elder: wiser in years.
49. on your charge: at your expense.
50. love: friend.
51. with all my heart: a jest that enhances the pathos of the scene.
52. Barabbas: a thief.
53. We trifle time: We waste time with trivialities.
54. jot: smallest particle.
55. soft: slowly.
56. just a pound: an exact pound.
57. scruple: a small unit of weight in ancient Rome.
58. I have you on the hip: I have you at my mercy.

59. I'll stay no longer question: I'll remain here no longer to be questioned.
60. alien: non-Christian.
61. voice: jurisdiction.
62. manifest: evident.
63. rehearsed: enumerated.
64. cord: rope for hanging.
65. charge: expense.
66. humbleness may drive unto a fine: if you repent and bear yourself humbly, this may be reduced to a mere fine.
67. prop: wealth.
68. halter gratis: a free rope.
69. quit: satisfy.
70. thou shouldst have had ten mores: you would have had ten more men; that is, a jury of twelve men.
71. your leisure serves you not: you do not have the time at your disposal.
72. gratify: reward.
73. We freely cope your courteous pains: We freely offer repayment for your courteous services.
74. delivering: saving.
75. of force I must attempt you further: I am forced to try to prevail on you again.
76. to give: by giving.
77. scuse: excuse.
78. withal: at the same time.
79. presently: at once.

Questions for Understanding

1. Why does Shylock prefer to take his pound of flesh instead of accepting the money from Bassanio?
2. What is the result of this play?
3. Discuss Shylock's dramatic function in *The Merchant of Venice*.
4. Pay special attention to Shylock's rhetoric—his use of metaphor and repetition, for instance. How do his speeches reflect his character as a whole?
5. Discuss Portia's character. How does she compare to the men around her? Is Bassanio a worthy husband for her?

Aspects of Appreciation

1. The theme of *The Merchant of Venice*

Through the successful characterization of a group of characters, like Portia, Bossanio, Antonio, even Shylock, Shakespeare highlights the theme of this comedy: on eulogy of the triumph of justice and love over insatiable greed and brutality.

2. Shakespeare's language

Shakespeare is the least educated of all the Elizabethan dramatists, yet his command of vocabulary is the largest. He uses more than 16,000 different words and enriches the English language with his own coinage. Under his pen, each word glows with life, which vitalizes the printed pages with beauty, melody, humor, pathos, tenderness, force, or whatever effect he chooses to produce. He uses the English language with the greatest freedom and ease, so that all the speeches fit all the characters who use them.

Suggested Further Reading

William Shakespeare's comedies *A Midsummer Night's Dream*, *As You Like it*, *Twelfth Night*.

Topics for Further Study

1. Features of Shakespeare's comedies.
2. Characterization of Shylock, Portia, Bassanio and Antonio.
3. Symbols in *The Merchant of Venice*, such as the pound of flesh, the three caskets, and the ring.

Knowledge of Literature

Comedy

All literary forms contains comic elements, but the term comedy is here used primarily to describe a genre of humorous plays that deal with ordinary or domestic events and end happily. Humor(or wit) is the essential element of any comedy. Comic effect may be subtle or coarse; it is typically achieved through some incongruity, whether physical, verbal, or conceptual. Although comedies aim to evoke laughter, they may also have a serious purpose.

★ Sonnet 18

About the Poem

One of the best-known of Shakespeare's sonnets, "Sonnet 18" is memorable for the skillful and varied presentation of subject matter, in which the poet's feelings reach a level of rapture unseen in the previous sonnets. The speaker opens the poem with a question addressed to the beloved: "Shall I compare thee to a summer's day?" In Line 2, the speaker stipulates what mainly differentiates the lady or the man from the summer's day: he or she is "more lovely and more temperate". Summer's days tend toward extremes: they are shaken by "rough winds"; in them, the sun("the eye of heaven") often shines "too hot", or too dim. And summer is fleeting: its date is too short, and it leads to the withering of autumn, as "every fair from fair sometime declines". The final quatrain of the sonnet tells how the beloved differs from the summer in that respect: his or her beauty will last forever("Thy eternal summer shall not fade…") and never die. In the couplet, the speaker explains how the beloved's beauty will accomplish this feat, and not perish because it is preserved in the poem, which will last forever; it will live "as long as men can breathe or eyes can see".

>   Shall I compare thee to a summer's day[1]?
>   Thou art more lovely and more temperate:
>   Rough winds do shake the darling buds of May,
>   And summer's lease hath all too short a date[2];
>   Sometime too hot the eye of heaven shines
>   And often is his gold complexion dimmed;
>   And every fair from fair sometime declines,
>   By chance or nature's changing course untrimmed[3];
>   But thy eternal summer shall not fade,
>   Nor lose possession of that fair thou ow'st[4];
>   Nor shall death brag thou wander'st in his shade,
>   When in eternal lines[5] to time thou grow'st[6];
>   So long as men can breathe, or eyes can see,
>   So long lives this, and this gives life to thee[7].

Notes

1. a summer's day: Here it may refer to a period or the season of summer.
2. a date: the period of a lease.
3. untrimmed: stripped of gay apparel.
4. ow'st: ownest, own.
5. lines: such as the lines of this poem and other sonnets.
6. When in eternal lines to time thou grow'st: When in (this) immortal poem, you become even with time.
7. So long lives this, and this gives life to thee: The boast of immortality for one's verse is a Renaissance convention and it goes back to the classics. It implies, not egotism on the part of the poet, but a faith in the permanence of poetry.

Questions for Understanding

1. Why does the poet compare "thee" to a summer's day?
2. What does the poet mean when he says "But thy eternal summer shall not fade"?
3. The poet also promises, "Nor shall death brag thou wander'st in his shade." Does this seem possible or plausible as a promise?
4. How does the speaker use natural imagery to create a picture of the person's beauty?

Aspects of Appreciation

1. Poetic devices

The poet applies personification, images and metaphors in the poem, giving human characteristics to abstract ideas.

2. "Thee" in the poem

"Thee" in "Sonnet 18" has always been controversial in the academic circle. "Thee" can be a lady beloved by the poet, or a male friend with eternal friendship, or even "love" or "beauty" in the abstract sense.

3. The theme of "Sonnet 18"

In admiring the eternal beauty of his friend, Shakespeare is actually singing of the eternal beauty of human beings. Moreover, the poet in the poem tries to say that literature can contend with time; literature is created by man and at the same time, it declares man's greatness and immortality. This reflects Shakespeare's ideal of humanism.

Suggested Further Reading

Shakespeare's "Sonnet 29" "Sonnet 106" "Sonnet 116", and "Sonnet 139".

Topics for Further Study

1. Features of imagery in Shakespeare's sonnets.
2. Themes of Shakespeare's sonnets.

Knowledge of Literature

Sonnet

Sonnet derives from the Italian "sonetto" meaning a "little sound" or "song" consisting of fourteen lines, usually in iambic pentameter with considerable variations in rhyme scheme.

The Italian form is the commonest. The sonnet came to England via Sir Thomas Wyatt and Earl of Surry early in the 16th century and it was Petrarchan form which they imported. However, it was not until the last decade of the 16th century that the sonnet was finally established in England. In England, actually there are several types of it, among which Petrarchan and Shakespearean sonnet are the most important ones.

All the sonnets are in iambic pentameter. The rhyme scheme of Petrarchan sonnet is *abbaabba cdecde* or some variants such as *cdcdcd* or *cdc cdc*. This type of sonnet is divided into two sections: the octave and sestet. The octave usually proposes a question, develops a narrative or delineates an idea; the accompanying sestet will answer the question, comment on the story, or countermand the idea. This thought-division is often signaled by an enjambment (run-on-line) in Line 9.

The rhyme scheme of Shakespearean sonnet is *abab cdcd efef gg*. The Shakespearean sonnet's thought-division is a 4-4-4-2 plan. There are four sections: three quatrains and a final couplet. In Shakespearean sonnet, each quatrain deals with a different aspect of the subject and the couplet either summarizes the theme or makes a final, sometimes contradicting comment.

Two other variations of the sonnet are the Miltonic and Spencerian sonnets. Milton follows the Petrarchan rhyme scheme, but makes his sestet merely a continuation of his original octave, not an answer to or comment on it. Spencer's original sonnet's rhyme scheme has been passed down to us also. Spencer follows the English thought-division of three quatrains and a couplet. The rhyme scheme of it is *abab bcbc cdcd ee*.

Francis Bacon
(1561~1626)

About the Author

Francis Bacon was an English philosopher, statesman, scientist, lawyer, jurist, author and pioneer of the scientific method. Although his political career ended in disgrace, he remained extremely influential through his works. Bacon has been called the father of empiricism and he died of pneumonia contracted while studying the effects of freezing on the preservation of meat. As a literary figure, Bacon's fame lies in his *Essays*, the 1625 version of which contains 58 essays and for which he is considered as the first practitioner of the genre in the English language. His essays cover a variety of subjects, including love, truth, friendship, parents and children, beauty, riches, youth and age, death, studies and high place. His style is marked by use of plain words, clarity of expression, eloquence of argument, use of erudite quotations and examples from daily life.

★ Of Studies

About the Work

One of the most famous, most frequently anthologized essays, "Of Studies" can serve as an example of Bacon's essays both in ideas and style. The essay is about the usefulness of studies for improving one's mind, character and abilities and there is a lot of practical wisdom in it. This has contributed to the popularity of the essay and it has become the source of many memorable quotations. The use of parellel structures, especially of trinomials, may be one of the factors which make the essay one of the logical strength and rhetorical eloquence.

Studies serve for delight, for ornament, and for ability. Their chief use for delight is in privateness and retiring[1]; for ornament, is in discourse[2]; and for ability, is in the judgment and disposition of business. For expert men[3] can execute, and perhaps judge of particulars, one by one; but the general counsels, and the plots[4] and marshalling of affairs, come best from those that are learned. To spend too much time in studies is sloth[5]; to use them too much for ornament, is affectation; to make judgment wholly by their rules, is the humor[6] of a scholar. They perfect nature, and are perfected by experience: for natural abilities are like natural plants, that need pruning[7], by study; and studies themselves do give forth directions too much at large[8], except they be bounded in by experience. Crafty men[9] condemn studies, simple men[10] admire them, and wise men use them; for they teach not their own use; but that is a wisdom without[11] them, and above them, won by observation. Read not to contradict and confute; nor to believe and take for granted; nor to find talk and discourse[12]; but to weigh and consider. Some books are to be tasted, others to be swallowed, and some few to be chewed and digested; that is, some books are to be read only in parts; others to be read, but not curiously[13]; and some few to be read wholly, and with diligence and attention. Some books also may be read by deputy, and extracts made of them by others; but that would be[14] only in the less important arguments[15], and the meaner sort of books, else distilled books are like common distilled waters, flashy[16] things. Reading maketh a full man; conference[17] a ready[18] man; and writing an exact man. And therefore, if a man write little, he had need[19] have a great memory; if he confer little, he had need have a present wit[20]: and if he read little, he had need have much cunning, to seem to know that he doth not. Histories make men wise; poets witty[21]; the mathematics subtile[22]; natural philosophy[23] deep; moral[24] grave; logic and rhetoric able to contend[25]. *Abeunt studia in mores*[26]. Nay, there is no stond[27] or impediment in the wit[28] but may be wrought out[29] by fit studies; like as[30] diseases of the body may have appropriate exercises. Bowling is good for the stone and reins[31]; shooting[32] for the lungs and breast; gentle walking for the stomach; riding for the head; and the like. So if a man's wit be wandering[33], let him study the mathematics; for in demonstrations[34], if his wit be called away never so little[35], he must begin again. If his wit be not apt to distinguish or find differences, let him study the schoolmen[36]; for they are *cymini sectores*[37]. If he be not apt to beat over[38] matters, and to call up one thing to prove and illustrate another, let him study the lawyers' cases. So every defect of the mind may have a special receipt[39].

Notes

1. in privateness and retiring: in solitude and retreat.
2. discourse: conversation.
3. expert men: men who are skillful in doing things.
4. plots: arrangements or plans.
5. sloth: lazy.
6. humor: whimsical disposition.
7. pruning: cut off branches of a tree to make it grow better.
8. too much at large: too general.
9. crafty men: men of craft.
10. simple men: simple-minded men.
11. without: outside.
12. find talk and discourse: find material for talk and discourse.
13. curiously: carefully.
14. would be: ought to be.
15. arguments: subjects.
16. flashy: bright-looking but worthless.
17. conference: conversation or discussion.
18. ready: quick to act or quick-minded.
19. had need: ought to.
20. present wit: quick wit.
21. witty: (archaic) ingenious.
22. subtile: (archaic) subtle.
23. natural philosophy: the science of physics.
24. moral: moral philosophy.
25. contend: argue.
26. *Abeunt studia in mores*: Studies pass into and influence manners or character.
27. stond: obstacle.
28. wit: mind.
29. wrought out: removed.
30. like as: as.
31. stone and reins: testicles and kidneys.
32. shooting: archery.
33. wit be wandering: mind be distracted.
34. demonstrations: solve a mathematics problem.

35. never so little: ever so little, no matter how little.
36. schoolmen: philosophers or divines of the Middle Ages.
37. *cymini sectores*: splitters of hairs.
38. beat over: investigate.
39. receipt: a list of drugs written by a physician.

Questions for Understanding

1. What can studies serve for and in what respective aspects?
2. Besides studies what else does one need?
3. What are the attitudes people have toward studies?
4. What is the right attitude toward studies?
5. What are the different ways of reading different books?
6. What are the functions of different disciplines?
7. What can reading contribute to the making of a person's character?
8. What are some of the functions of exercises to improve our physical health mentioned by the author?
9. Do you agree with the author in his ideas of studies?

Aspects of Appreciation

1. One of the most striking features of Bacon's style is that he expresses an abstract idea through the commonest objects and everyday life experience. Thus, "Men in great place are thrice *servants*" "Virtue is like a 'rich stone, best plain set'" "He that hath wife and children 'hath given hostages to fortune'". Selfish statesmen are compared to ants in an orchard. Some of the other famous quotations from Bacon are: "We take cunning for a sinister or crooked wisdom"; "I cannot call riches better than the baggage of virtue"; "Men fear death, as children fear to go in the dark".
2. Western culture seems to favour the figure "three" and the parellel of three elements or trinomials in the structure. From Shelley's line "Lift me as a wave, a leaf, a cloud", to Lincoln's famous "Government of the people, by the people, for the people", trinomials are widely used to achieve the effect of climax. Trinomials abound in this essay, "for delight, for ornament, and for ability" and "Crafty men … simple men … and wise men … ", adding much to the effect of the writing.

Suggested Further Reading

Francis Bacon's essays "Of Marriage and Single Life" "Of Great Place" and "Of Beauty".

Topics for Further Study

1. Discuss the overall structure of this essay and the features of Bacon's style.
2. Compare the style of Bacon with that of Shakespeare.
3. How can this essay help you in your own studies?

Knowledge of Literature

Essay

The word "essay" came from the French "essai", literally meaning "attempt". As a genre of brief nonfiction reflections in prose, essay (also known as familiar essay and personal essay) was developed by the French writer Montaigne (1533~1592) and Francis Bacon, and popularized by Joseph Addison (1672~1719) and Richard Steele (1672~1729). In the course of its development, many other writers have made their contributions. As distinguished from the article or feature story, both of which, however informal, are devoted mostly to informing, the essay is devoted to entertaining, or reflecting, or inspiring. It tends to be relaxed and philosophic, or witty, or poetic, or all of these at once. And it is comparatively brief—approximately five hundred words but rarely longer than a thousand. The style of an essay is both informal and urbane—the voice of a civilized speaker in conversation with a civilized audience, and audience well-read enough to recognize and appreciate allusions. In writing an essay, no matter how commonplace the topic is, the writer should strive for unusual treatment.

III The Seventeenth Century

John Donne
(1572~1631)

About the Author

John Donne(1572~1631) was a major representative of the metaphysical poets of the period. In 1601 Donne secretly married Anne Moore with whom he had 12 children. In 1615 he became an Anglican priest and he was appointed the Dean of St Paul's Cathedral in London in 1621.

His works include sonnets, love poetry, religious poems, Latin translations, epigrams, elegies, songs, satires and sermons and they are notable for their realistic and sensual style. His early works were shaped by satire, irony, and eroticism and his later poems, with great power and grace, expressed his desire for a close relationship with God. His poetry is noted for its vitality of language, ingenious use of intellectual and theological concepts in surprising conceits(奇喻): strange metaphors, paradoxes, far-fetched imagery and complicated reasoning. In his poems he described women in love with suggestions of sensual and physical love.

★ The Flea

About the Poem

The speaker of the poem may be a man trying to persuade a lady to enjoy love with him by the argument based upon a flea, which has obviously bitten them both. Since the 17th century idea of sex was a "mingling of the blood", he argues that by mixing their bloods together in the flea's body, they are practically married and of "one flesh"! Therefore if she kills the flea, she will kill three lives in one and commit three sins.

Mark[1] but[2] this flea, and mark in this,
How little that which thou deny'st me is[3];
Me it suck'd first[4], and now sucks thee,
And in this flea our two bloods mingled be;
Thou know'st that this cannot be said[5]
A sin, or shame, or loss of maidenhead[6],
Yet this enjoys before it woo[7],
And pamper'd swells[8] with one blood made of two,
And this, alas, is more than we would do.

Oh stay[9], three lives in one flea spare,
When we almost, nay[10] more than married are.
This flea is you and I, and this
Our marriage bed, and marriage temple is;
Though parents grudge[11], and you, we are met,
And cloisterd[12] in these living walls of jet[13].
Though use[14] make thee apt to kill me,
Let not to this, self murder added be[15],
And sacrilege[16], three sins in killing three.

Cruel and sudden, hast thou since
Purpled thy nail, in blood of innocence?
In what could this flea guilty be,
Except in that drop which it sucked from thee?
Yet thou triumph'st, and say'st that thou
Find'st not thyself, nor me the weaker now;
'Tis true, then learn how false, fears be[17];
Just so much[18] honor, when thou yield'st to me,
Will waste, as this flea's death took life from thee[19].

Notes

1. mark: look at, observe, note.
2. but: only.
3. How little that which thou deny'st me is: What you have refused me is very little (compared with what the flea has done to you).
4. me it suck'd first: it sucked me first.
5. said: called.
6. maidenhead: maidenhood.
7. woo: try to persuade someone to love you. Here the poet is deliberately being ambiguous. The whole line means that yet it enjoys this before it woos.
8. pamper'd swells: swells pampered, that is, becomes large because of gratification or satisfaction.
9. stay: stop or wait.
10. nay: not only that, but also.
11. grudge: give with reluctance.
12. cloisterd: confined or secluded. Note the religious implication of this word.
13. jet: a deep, glossy black stone. This is a reference to the colour of a flea.
14. use: custom.
15. Let not to this, self murder added be: Let self murder not be added to this (murder, killing).
16. sacrilege: treat something holy without respect.
17. These two lines mean that since you do not find yourself and me any weaker, then your fears are ungrounded or unreasonable.
18. Just so much: only so much, only so little.
19. The last two lines mean that if you give in to my wishes you will not lose much of your honor the same way that the flea's death will not take much of your life.

Questions for Understanding

1. What is the situation of this poem and what characters are involved?
2. What is the speaker's argument?
3. What may be the conceit(s) in the poem?
4. What is implied by the word "cloisterd" in terms of love between man and

woman?
5. What is suggested of the flea by "pamper'd swells"?
6. What is the character of the speaker and what may be the character of the lady in the poem?

Aspects of Appreciation

1. Use of conceits

   The poetry of John Donne is noted for its use of conceits. A conceit is a fanciful notion, something conceived, or created, out of imagination; or a very new and striking image; or a comparison. Metaphysical conceits, according to Samuel Johnson (1709~1784), "sometimes struck out unexpected truth" although they are "far-fetched". The most striking conceit or image in this poem is the flea, which is compared to the unity of man and woman, the marriage bed, and the marriage temple. Therefore, the killing of the flea is thought of as committing three sins: murder, self-murder and sacrilege.

2. Poetic devices

   Besides conceits or unusual images and metaphors, such devices as apostrophe, repetition and hyperbole are also used in this poem.

3. Sexual implications

   Donne's poems are noted for their implications of physical love and this poem is no exception. For instance, "one blood made of two" implies sex and/or pregnancy.

4. Dramatic elements

   This poem is like a short play in which a man tries to persuade a woman to yield to his desires or marriage proposal by an argument centred on a flea. Though the woman does not have speech, the reader or the audience can feel her presence, her reaction to the man-speaker's invitation and her action. There is action, development, climax and resolution of a play in this poem.

Suggested Further Reading

   John Donne's poems: "Holy Sonnet 10: Death, Be not Proud" "A Valediction: Forbidding Mourning" "The Sun Rising" "Song(go and catch a falling star)" "The Canonization" and his sermon "Meditation XVII".

Topics for Further Study

1. Features of conceits in John Donne's poetry.
2. Similarities and differences in John Donne's poems of worldly love and his

religious poems.
3. Differences in John Donne's poems and those of Elizabethan poets in their lyrical expression and use of imagery.

Knowledge of Literature

Love and religion

    In English literature, or for that matter, in western literature, there has been tradition of treating man's relationship with God allegorically by describing love between man and woman. Or the relationship between man and woman is interpreted as the relationship between man and God, as is the case of the Bible. John Donne's poetry is also noted for its treatment of religious themes in terms of love, or the other way round. That is, the poet deals with religious theme as if it were theme of love, or uses terms or ideas from religion to describe love, as is the case of this poem. In his poems love and religion are closely related. For instance, there are words with religious implications such as "cloister" "sacrilege" and "temple"; and also religious concepts such as "three lives in one flea" which implies holy trinity. Besides, there are also biblical allusions in the poem.

John Milton
(1608~1674)

About the Author

    John Milton (1608 ~ 1674), as a poet, an English revolutionary and social critic writing in English and Latin, ranks among the most important writers in the English language and remains a thinker of world importance. Milton was born in a Puritan family and was educated at Cambridge. When he toured Europe, he met the astronomer Galileo and was exposed to republicanism. His early masterpieces are *L'Allegro*, *Il Penseroso* (1632) and *Lycidas* (1637). From 1641 to 1654 he wrote essays and pamphlets, including *The Reason of Church Governments* (1642), *The Doctrine and Discipline of Divorce* (1643), *Of Education* (1644), *Areopagitica* (1644), *The Defense of the English People* (1651) and *The Second Defense of the English People* (1654). He used his pen in defense of the republican principles represented by the Commonwealth and once worked as a secretary for Oliver Cromwell. Even after becoming blind in 1654, he continued his massive output. He wrote (through dictating) *Paradise Lost* (1665), *Paradise Regained* (1667) and *Samson Agonistes* (1671). With his revolutionary humanist ideas and his unique artistic achievements, he had an international reputation during his lifetime and has influenced the later writers widely. William Blake even saw himself as Milton's poetical son.

★ Paradise Lost[1]

About the Poem

Paradise Lost (written between 1658 and 1663) is generally considered as one of the greatest works in the English language. It fulfilled John Milton's dream of producing a national epic. This Protestant epic contains twelve books in blank verse and is famous for its grand style and sublime theme. It is based on the Christian story of the Fall of Man and begins with the defeated Satan trying to organize other rebel angels in hell to revenge against God. God has sent Archangel Raphael to warn Adam and Eve, but Satan, in disguise of a serpent, successfully tempts them to disobey God and eat the forbidden fruit from the Tree of Knowledge. Then they are exiled as sinners from the Garden of Eden, thus they lose their paradise. Satan and his followers are finally turned into serpents. Milton's ambiguous way of presenting Satan as a hero-like protagonist has aroused critics' interest since its publication in 1667.

> Nine times the Space that measures Day and Night
> To mortal men, he[2] with his horrid crew
> Lay vanquished, rolling in the fiery Gulf[3]
> Confounded though immortal: But his doom
> Reserv'd him to more wrath; for now the thought
> Both of lost happiness and lasting pain
> Torments him; round he throws his baleful[4] eyes
> That witness'd[5] huge affliction and dismay
> Mixt with obdurate pride and steadfast hate:
> At once as far as Angels kenn[6] he views
> The dismal Situation waste and wild,
> A Dungeon horrible, on all sides round

As one great Furnace flam'd, yet from those flames
No light, but rather darkness visible
Serv'd only to discover sights of woe,
Regions of sorrow, doleful shades, where peace
And rest can never dwell, hope never comes[7]
That comes to all; but torture without end
Still urges[8], and a fiery Deluge, fed
With ever-burning Sulphur unconsum'd:
Such place Eternal Justice had prepar'd
For those rebellious, here thir[9] Prison ordain'd
In utter[10] darkness, and thir portion set
As far remov'd from God and light of Heav'n
As from the Center[11] thrice to th' utmost Pole[12].
O how unlike the place from whence they fell!
There the companions of his fall, o'erwhelm'd
With Floods and Whirlwinds of tempestuous fire,
He soon discerns, and weltring[13] by his side
One next himself in power, and next in crime,
Long after known in *Palestine*, and nam'd
Beëlzebub[14]. To whom th' Arch-Enemy,
And thence in Heav'n call'd Satan[15], with bold words
Breaking the horrid silence thus began.
...
"... All is not lost; the unconquerable Will,
And study[16] of revenge, immortal hate,
And courage never to submit or yield:
And what is else not to be overcome[17]?
That Glory never shall his wrath or might
Extort from me. To bow and sue for grace[18]
With suppliant knee[19], and deify[20] his power,
Who from the terror of this Arm so late
Doubted his Empire[21], that were low indeed,
That were an ignominy[22] and shame beneath
This downfall; since by Fate the strength of Gods[23]
And this Empyreal substance cannot fail[24],
Since through experience of this great event[25]
In Arms not worse, in foresight much advanc't[26],

We may with more successful hope resolve
To wage by force or guile eternal War[27]
Irreconcilable, to our grand Foe,
Who now triumphs, and in th' excess of joy
Sole reigning holds the Tyranny[28] of Heav'n."

✲ ✲

Notes

1. original text: John Milton, *Paradise Lost*. 2nd edn. 1674. Edited by Hugh MacCallum, A. S. P. Woodhouse.
2. he: Satan.
3. fiery Gulf: the burning lake.
4. baleful: full of woe.
5. witness'd: bore witness to.
6. kenn: range, which in the case of angels must be presumed to be nearly limitless.
7. hope never comes: an allusion of Dante's *Inferno* 3.9: "All hope abandon ye who enter here."
8. urges: afflicts (Latin).
9. thir.: their. Milton's preferred spelling was "thir".
10. utter: outer.
11. centre: the centre of the earth.
12. th'utmost Pole: the pole of the outermost sphere according to the Ptolemaic system with the earth at the center of nine concentric spheres.
13. weltring: weltering, rolling about (翻滚).
14. Beëlzebub: "God of the flies" or "Chief of the devils", a manifestation of Baal, worshipped by the Philistines at Ekron.
15. call'd Satan: originally called Lucifer, "bringer of light"; his name in heaven is changed to Satan. Satan signifies "The Adversary" or "enemy".
16. study: zealous pursuit.
17. what is else not to be overcome: what other things that cannot be conquered.
18. sue for grace: beg for mercy.
19. suppliant knee: falling down on one's knees submissively.

20. deify: worship.
21. doubted his Empire: lost confidence in his authority or power.
22. ignominy: shame, disgrace.
23. Gods: empyreal angels, virtually gods.
24. this Empyreal substance cannot fail: Satan refuses to admit that he owes his being to God, but boasts that the angels have their being from their empyreal, celestial (literally, of pure fire) essence, which is indestructible.
25. this great event: the battle between God and Satan.
26. advanc't: advanced.
27. eternal War: it indicates he is quite doubtful about the prospects for victory.
28. Tyranny: Satan contends that God rules as a tyrant.

Questions for Understanding

1. What is the situation in hell?
2. What is the tone of Satan's speech?
3. What is the character of Satan? Do you think he is a hero?
4. If one does not know the story of the Fall of Man, will he enjoy this poem?
5. What is implied by "To wage by force or guile eternal War / Irreconcilable, to our grand Foe"?
6. Do you think Milton's poetry is difficult? Why or why not?

Aspects of Appreciation

1. Character analysis of Satan

It is hard to say which side John Milton was on in *Paradise Lost*: God's or Satan's, because the figure of Satan is one of the most complicated and subtle characters in all literature.

Satan's impassioned speeches succeed in portraying God as a tyrant. His wish to democratize Heaven, his opposition to injustice, his heroic perseverance, his desire for glory, and his brave sort of self-sacrificing leadership make him the most interesting and likable character in the poem. The reader has found it difficult to avoid sympathizing with him to some degree, if not completely. So, Satan is claimed to be one of the earliest examples of an anti-hero by critics and his resemblance to Milton is noticeable.

However, a devoted Christian would feel hard to accept that Milton is on Satan's side, for Satan is really an evil and dangerous devil. His pride, his unhealthy desire for revenge, his refusal to repent, his violence toward Adam and Eve all prove that he is still the Satan in the Holy Bible in which he represents pure evil and is plotting against God. Milton claims in Book I the purpose of writing this poem is "justifying the ways of God to man". He begins the poem by describing Satan as a just-fallen angel whereas ends it by reducing him back to Hell as an ugly serpent. The sequence of different shapes assumed by Satan indicates the gradual derogation of his soul.

Critics have explained the possible reason why Milton portrayed Satan in such a way is that he wants us to be lured by Satan's infectious speech "only so he could show us the error of our ways". In other words, he is testing his readers. The reader should never neglect the fact that John Milton is a very serious Christian.

It is possible that readers with democratic principles and revolutionary spirit are likely to behold the figure of Satan differently from the ones with strong religious beliefs, and it happens Milton represents both of them: a Christian revolutionary writing on "Christian liberty".

2. Epithets of God in the poem

The ways Satan refers to God are neither positive, nor insulting as to offend the devoted Christians. In the excerpts, he calls God "Arch-Enemy" "our grand Foe" "Who … holds the Tyranny of Heav'n". Those epithets reflect Milton's and his Satan's attitude towards God. Milton, as a serious Christian, has never failed to respect and believe in the Almighty God. Satan, though a proud rebel, is not so arrogant as to believe in his superiority to God. The epithets can be seen as marks of a piece of Protestant writing.

3. Miltonic style

Milton is the first one to use blank verse in the epic genre. He improved it to be "the noblest medium for verse" and created his own elevated, Latinate style, namely, Miltonic style. It is a grand style and "majesty" can be said to be its unique and essential quality.

Milton's grand style originates from the formalities of classical prose. He emulates Virgil's Latinate style (In Latin, word order does not matter). Milton deliberately distorts the normal syntax and sound-patterns of a line and he likes using difficult, unusual words and allusions, which T. S. Eliot points out, are "not based upon common speech or common prose, or direct communication of meaning". Besides keeping the normal metrical characteristics of the ordinary blank verse, such as the absence of rhyme and stanza, he writes large extended verse paragraphs (large numbers of run-on lines centering on a common mood or thought) with a cunning variety in the rhythm and skillful variation of the pauses. In this way he makes the epic sonorously move forward with sustained rhythmic nobility.

The nobility of Miltonic style conforms to the epic's great theme and the lofty personality of its author. Readers often find Milton difficult to read because of the artificiality of the Latinized diction, idiom, syntactical structure and the unnatural speech rhythms of Milton's style. This does not affect his position as an artist of the highest rank in the great style. Of all English writers, Milton's style is said to be best entitled to the name of classic in all English. His blank verse was widely imitated in the 18th century though with much more artificiality.

Suggested Further Reading

John Milton's *Paradise Lost* and some short lyrics.

Topics for Further Study

1. Is it reasonable to identify John Milton himself with Satan in *Paradise Lost*?
2. The relationship between religious myth and secular politics.
3. Imagery and symbolism of Fall in *Paradise Lost*.

Knowledge of Literature

1. Epic

An epic is a long narrative poem, usually concerning a serious subject containing details of heroic deeds and events significant to a culture or nation. Virgil's *Aeneid*, Homer's *Iliad*, and John Milton's *Paradise Lost* are all epics.

2. Blank verse

Blank verse is the poetry written in unrhymed iambic pentameter. It has been described as "probably the most common and influential form that English poetry has taken since the sixteenth century". Paul Fussel has claimed that "about three-quarters of all English poetry is in blank verse". Christopher Marlowe is said to be the first English author to make full use of the potential of blank verse, and established it as the dominant verse form for English drama. The major achievements in English blank verse are made by William Shakespeare and John Milton.

John Bunyan
(1628~1688)

About the Author

Bunyan was born into a poor tinker's family in a small village near Bedford. He had little education. Honest, sincere, and endowed with a sensitive imagination, he was fired with an irresistible earnestness to teach people to be good and virtuous. He read the Bible, reformed himself, and wrote and preached among the common people. He became a man of the people, and the kindest man of all. As his popularity and dissenting voice seemed a threat to the monarchy and the Anglican Church, he was arrested and stayed in prison for 12 years (1660~1672), and was again imprisoned for six months in 1675. But he never succumbed to the authorities' request to stop preaching as a condition for his release, and continued to write and also make laces to support his family when in prison. He wrote over 60 books and pamphlets, all in the service of God and his fellow men. Bunyan became a public figure in his last 10 years, preaching at a London meeting house, his down-to-earth, humorous, and impassioned style drawing hundreds of people. He died working for his parish in 1688.

★ The Pilgrim's Progress

About the Book

The full title of the book is *The Pilgrim's Progress from This World to That Which Is to Come*. It is probably the most widely-read book in the English language, and one which has been translated into more languages than any other book except *The Bible*.

The story is told in the form of a dream by the author. He sees Christian, with a burden on his back and reading a book, from which he learns that the city in which he and his family dwell will be burned with fire. Part I describes his pilgrimage through the Slough of Despond, the Interpreter's House, the House Beautiful, the Valley of Humiliation, the Valley of the Shadow of Death, Vanity Fair, Doubting Castle, the Delectable Mountains, the Country of Beulah, to the Celestial City. On

III. The Seventeenth Century

the way he encounters various allegorical personages, such as Mr. Worldly Wiseman, Faithful (Who accompanies Christian on his way but is put to death in Vanity Fair), Hopeful (who next joins Christian), Giant Despair, the foul fiend Apollyon, and many others. Part II relates how Christian's wife Christiana, moved by a vision, sets out with her children on the same pilgrimage.

The work is a moral and religious allegory as well as a reflection of the reality of a specific historical period.

Chapter 6, Book I

Then I[1] saw in my dream, that when they[2] were got[3] out of the wilderness, they presently saw a town before them, and the name of that town is Vanity; and at the town there is a fair kept, called Vanity Fair. It is kept all the year long; it beareth[4] the name of Vanity Fair, because the town where it is kept is lighter than vanity; and also because all that is there sold or that cometh thither is vanity. As is the saying of the wise, all that cometh is vanity.

This fair is no new-erected business, but a thing of ancient standing; I will show you the original[5] of it.

Almost five thousand years agone[6], there were pilgrims walking to the Celestial City[7], as these two honest persons[8] are; and Beelzebub, Apollyon, and Legion[9], with their companions, perceiving by the path that the pilgrims made, that their way to the city lay through this town of Vanity, they[10] contrived here to set up a fair; a fair wherein should be sold all sorts of vanity, and that it should last all the year long: therefore at this fair are all such merchandise sold, as houses, lands, trades, places, honours, preferments[11], titles, countries, kingdoms, lusts, pleasures, and delights of all sorts, as whores, bawds[12], wives, husbands, children, masters, servants, lives, blood, bodies, souls, silver, gold, pearls, precious stones, and what not[13].

And, moreover, at this fair there is at all times to be seen juggling, cheats, games, plays, fools, apes[14], knaves, and rogues, and that of every kind.

Here are to be seen, too, and that for nothing[15], thefts, murders, adulteries, false swearers, and that of a blood-red colour[16].

And as in other fairs of less moment[17], there are the several[18] rows[19] and streets, under their proper[20] names, where such wares are vended[21]; so here likewise you have the proper places, rows, streets (viz.[22] countries and kingdoms), where the wares of this fair are soonest[23] to be found. Here is the Britain Row, the French Row, the Italian Row, the Spanish Row, the German Row, where several sorts of vanities are to be sold. But, as in other fairs, some one commodity is as the chief of all the fair, so the ware of Rome and her merchandise[24] is greatly promoted[25] in this fair; only our English nation, with some others, have taken a dislike thereat[26].

Now, as I said, the way to the Celestial City lies just through this town where this lusty[27] fair is kept; and he that will go to the City, and yet not go through this town, must needs[28] go out of the world. The Prince of Princes[29] himself, when here[30], went through this town to his own country, and that upon a fair day too; yea[31], and as I think, it was Beelzebub, the chief lord of this fair, that invited him to buy of[32] his vanities; yea, would have made[33] him lord of the fair, would he but[34] have done him reverence as he went through the town. Yea, because he was such a person of honour, Beelzebub had him from street to street, and showed him all the kingdoms of the world in a little time, that he might, if possible, allure the Blessed One[35] to cheapen[36] and buy some of his vanities; hut he had no mind to the merchandise, and therefore left the town without laying out[37] so much as one farthing[38] upon these vanities. This fair, therefore, is an ancient thing, of long standing, and a very great fair.

Now these pilgrims, as I said, must needs go through this fair. Well, so they did: but, behold, even[39] as they entered into the fair, all the people in the fair were moved[40], and the town itself as it were in a bubbub[41] about them; and that for several reasons: for—

First, the pilgrims were clothed with such kind of raiment[42] as was diverse from[43] the raiment of any that traded in that fair. The people therefore of the fair, made a great gazing upon them: some said they were fools, some they were bedlams[44], and some, they are outlandish men[45].

Secondly, and as they[46] wondered at their apparel, so they did likewise at their speech; for few could understand what they said. They naturally spoke the language of Canaan[47], but they that kept the fair were the men of this world; so that, from one end of the fair to the other, they. seemed barbarians[48] each to the other[49].

Thirdly, but[50] that which did not a little amuse[51] the merchandisers, was that these pilgrims set very light by[52] all their wares; they care not so much as to look upon them; and if they[53] called upon them to buy, they[54] would put their fingers in their eats, and cry, Turn away mine[55] eyes from beholding vanity, and look upwards, signifying that their trade and traffic[56] was in heaven.

One chanced mockingly, beholding the carriages[57] of the men[58], to say unto them: What will ye buy? But they, looking gravely upon him, answered: We buy the truth. At that there was an occasion taken to despise the men the more; some mocking, some taunting, some speaking reproachfully, and some calling upon others to smite them. At last things came to a hubbub and great stir in the fair, insomuch that all order was confounded. Now was word presently brought to the great one[59] of the fair, who quickly came down, and deputed some of his most trusty friends to take these men into examination[60], about whom the fair was almost overturned…

(A trial is held, in which Faithful is accused by three witnesses, Envy, Superstition, and Pickthank.)

Then went the jury out, whose name were Mr. Blind-man, Mr. Nogood, Mr. Malice, Mr. Love-lust, Mr. Live-loose, Mr. Heady, Mr. High-mind, Mr. Enmity, Mr. Liar, Mr. Cruelty, Mr. Hate-light, and Mr. Implacable; who every one[61] gave in his private verdict against him among themselves, and afterwards unanimously concluded to bring him in guilty before the Judge. And first, among themselves, Mr. Blind-man, the foreman[62], said, I see clearly that this man is a heretic. Then said Mr. Nogood: Away with such a fellow from the earth. Ay, said Mr. Malice, for I hate the very looks of him. Then said Mr. Love-lust, I could never endure him. Nor I, said Mr. Live-loose, for he would always be condemning my way. Hang him, hang him, said Mr. Heady. A sorry scrub[63], said Mr. High-mind. My heart riseth against him, said Mr. Enmity. He is a rogue, said Mr. Liar. Hanging is too good for him, said Mr. Cruelty. Let's dispatch[64] him out of the way, said Mr. Hate-light. Then said Mr. Implacable, might I have all the world given me, I could not be reconciled to him; therefore, let us forthwith bring him in guilty of death. And so they did; therefore he was presently condemned to be had from the place where he was, to the place from whence[65] he came, and there to be put to the most cruel death that could be invented.

They therefore brought him out to do with him according to their law; and, first, they scourged him, then they buffeted him, then they lanced his flesh with knives; after that, they stoned him with stones, then pricked him with their swords; and, last of all, they burned him to ashes at the stake.

Thus came Faithful to his end.

Now I saw that there stood behind the multitude a chariot and a couple of horses, waiting for Faithful, who (so soon as his adversaries had despatched him) was taken up into it, and straightway was carried up through the clouds, with sound of trumpet, the nearest way to the celestial gate.

But as for Christian, he had some respite, and was remanded back to prison. So he there remained for a space; but He that overrules all things, having the power of their rage in his own hand, so wrought it about, that Christian for that time escaped them, and went his way…

Notes

1. I: the author himself.
2. they: Christian and his friend Faithful.
3. were got: had got.
4. beareth: bears.
5. original: origin.
6. agone: (archaic) ago.
7. the Celestial City: Paradise.
8. these two honest persons: Christian and Faithful.
9. Beelzebub, Apollyon, and Legion: All are fellows of Satan. Legion: basic army unit of Roman.
10. they: Beelzebub, Apollyon, and Legion.
11. preferments: promotions.
12. bawds: procuresses.
13. and what not: and other things of similar kind.
14. apes: mimics, imitators.
15. for nothing: free of charge.
16. a blood-red colour: something very striking.
17. moment: importance.
18. several: different.
19. rows: short streets.
20. proper: own.
21. vended: sold.
22. viz: the shortened form for "videlicet" in Latin, meaning "namely".

III. The Seventeenth Century

23. soonest: easiest.
24. the ware of Rome and her merchandise: the goods of Roman Catholic Church and her trade, implying that within the Roman Catholic Church there was much corruption and that many things were bought and sold there.
25. promoted: publicized in order to sell.
26. only our English nation, with some others, have taken a dislike thereat: our English nation, with some others, have disapproved of the ware of Rome (referring to the separation of the Anglican Church from the Roman Catholic Church). Thereat: at "the ware of Rome and her merchandise".
27. lusty: full of vitality; merry, cheerful.
28. needs: necessarily.
29. the Prince of Princes: Jesus Christ.
30. when here: when he was alive.
31. yea: (archaic) yes, moreover.
32. of: some of.
33. would have made: The subject of this is the previous "that".
34. would he but: if only he would.
35. the Blessed One: Jesus Christ.
36. cheapen: (archaic) buy.
37. laying out: spending, expending.
38. farthing: former British coin, equal to 1/4 penny.
39. even: just.
40. moved: excited.
41. in a hubbub: in a disturbance.
42. raiment: clothes.
43. diverse from: different from.
44. bedlams: madmen.
45. outlandish men: foreigners.
46. they: Christian and Faithful.
47. Canaan: the Promised Land, ultimately conquered by the children of Israel and settled by them, hence the pilgrims speak the language of the Bible and of the true religion.
48. barbarians: foreigners. The Greeks and Romans designated all those who spoke a foreign tongue.
49. each to the other: the two pilgrims and the other people in the fair.

50. Thirdly, but: But, thirdly.
51. amuse: bewilder.
52. set very light by: regard as valueless.
53. they: the tradesmen.
54. they: Christian and Faithful.
55. mine: my.
56. trade and traffic: dealings, business.
57. carriages: bearing, posture.
58. the men: Christian and Faithful.
59. the great one: "the chief lord of this fair".
60. examination: investigation.
61. who every one: every one of whom.
62. the foreman: the head of the jury.
63. A sorry scrub: a wretched, dwarfish person, here referring to Faithful.
64. despatch: dispatch, send away.
65. whence: where.

Questions for Understanding

1. Why is the market called Vanity Fair?
2. Why did Christian and his friend cause noise in the fair?
3. What did people in the fair do to Christian and his friend when they wanted to buy truth?
4. What can you learn about the jury from their names? What happened to Christian at the end of this selection?

Aspects of Appreciation

1. *The Pilgrim's Progress* as an allegory

Allegory is a narrative, in which the characters and actions, and sometimes the setting as well, are contrived to make coherent sense on the literal level of signification, and at the same time to signify a second, correlated order of signification. The allegory of ideas is that the literal characters represent concepts and the plot allegorizes an abstract doctrine or thesis. The central device of allegory is the personification of abstract entities such as virtues, vices, states of mind, modes of life, and types of character. In some explicit allegories, such reference is specified by the names given to characters and places.

The Pilgrim's Progress indicates the nature of an explicit allegorical narrative, allegorizing the Christian doctrine of salvation by telling how the character named Christian, flees the City of Destruction and makes his way laboriously to the Celestial City.

The novel, owing to its plain style and rich meanings, circulated at first mainly in uneducated circles, and became an allegorical classic, regarded by generations of readers as a manual moral instruction and an aid to literacy, as well as a delightful tale.

2. The realistic and satirical aspects of the novel

The book gives a real picture of how life was like during the 17th century in England. Many allegorical figures and places Christian meets on the way are what might have been seen in Bunyan's day on any English market road. The landscapes and houses in the story seem to be no other than those of Restoration England. It is a faithful panoramic reflection of the age.

The most well known is the description of the Vanity Fair, by which the author gives a symbolic picture of London. In the Fair, all things are bought and sold, including honour, title and even kingdom, and lust, cheating, roguery, murder, and adultery prevail. He satirizes the society he lives in, where vices violate the teachings of the Christian religion.

By the combination of the realistic description with allegorical symbolism and satire, Bunyan develops the tradition of name symbolism, making the book a seminal text in the development of the English realistic novel and producing a great influence upon later novelists as Charles Dickens and William Makepeace Thackeray.

Suggested Further Reading

1. John Bunyan. *The Life and Death of Mr. Badman* (1680).
2. Tamsin Spargo. *The Writings of John Bunyan*. VT, USA: Ashgate, 1997.

Topics for Further Study

1. How does Bunyan combine the personalities with the abstract human virtues in his allegoric characterization?
2. Discuss Bunyan's prose style. Compare the style of *The Pilgrim's Progress* with that of the Bible.
3. In what aspects is *The Pilgrim's Progress* still inspiring readers in the modern time?

IV

The Restoration and the Eighteenth Century

Daniel Defoe
(1660～1731)

About the Author

Daniel Defoe was born into a Protestant background and detested the repressive rule of Anglican Church and the Roman Catholic Church. In his seventy years of life, Defoe passed through all kinds of ups and downs, from poverty to wealth, from prosperity to obscurity, from prison to immense popularity and royal favors. All these are obscure enough in detail, but several facts stand out clearly and are worth mentioning. First, Defoe was a jack-of-all-trades, as well as a writer. In English literature, he was often given the credit for the pioneering of the modern novel. But Defoe, the novelist, came out of Defoe, the journalist; he once conducted several papers, of which the most popular one was *The Review*. As a journalist, he had a reporter's eye for the picturesque and a newspaperman's instinct for making a good story with simple, smooth, colloquial English. This partially accounts for the great popularity of his works. Another fact about Defoe is that he knew about prison life. His prison experience and his knowledge of criminals helped the creation of his numerous stories of thieves and pirates, such as *Captain Singleton*.

When he was nearly 60 years old, Defoe wrote the great work *Robinson Crusoe*, for which he was remembered. It was an instant success. Other stories followed rapidly: *Captain Singleton* (1720), *Colonel Jacque* (1722) and *Moll Flanders* (1722). The list grew with astonishing rapidity, ending

IV. The Restoration and the Eighteenth Century

with *the History of the Devil* in 1726.

As the first major novelist in English literary history, Defoe was a highly conscious writer. He knew what he was doing and tried to do it well with his heightened awareness of the novel as an art form. His views on the novel, mostly explained in the prefaces to his novels, focus on two things of significance to the emerging genre: its realism and its moral aesthetic, which are the salient features of his novels.

★ Robinson Crusoe

About the Novel

The Life and Strange Surprising Adventures of Robinson Crusoe is based on the adventures of one real sailor, Alexander Selkirk, who ran away from home and was left on an uninhabited island for five years (1704~1709). The novel's hero, Robinson Crusoe, goes out to sea, experiences a shipwreck, and is left alone on a wild island(the first part). Then he goes back to colonize it and engages in trade with distant countries(the second part), and has some further adventures and musings and moralizations on his experiences(the third part). The popular *Robinson Crusoe* story as people normally know is in fact the narrative focus of the first part(1719); the second part(1719) was never popular and is no longer read, and the third part has never gone beyond its first printing in 1720.

As the story goes, Robinson Crusoe, a strong individual, does not feel happy with the easy comforts that his father has provided him with. He heads out to sea and becomes a planter in South America, but he is insatiable. He ventures further out, experiences a shipwreck, and is left all by himself on an island without any trace of civilized life. He soon overcomes his despair, and sets out building a life for himself. With the things he salvages from the ship, he builds a shelter, and then a house, finds food, raises goats, plants crops, makes clothing, makes boats, beats back savages from other islands, saves someone, Friday as he names him, and makes him his servant. Later on he saves Friday's father and a Spaniard and becomes the master on the island. He begins to enjoy some comfort and stays there for some 28 years. When an English ship goes by later, he saves its captain from mutiny, and returns to England on it. This is about the end of the first part of the book.

From the part subtitled "I Am Very Seldom Idled"(Excerpt)

I, that was reduced to a meer state of nature, found this to my daily discouragement, and was made more and more sensible of it every hour, even after I had got the first handful of seed-corn, which, as I have said, came up unexpectedly, and indeed to a surprise.

First, I had no plow to turn up the earth, no spade or shovel to dig it. Well, this I conquered, by making a wooden spade, as I observed before; but this did my work in but a wooden manner[1], and tho' it cost me a great many days to make it, yet for want of iron it not only wore out the sooner, but made my work the harder, and made it be performed much worse.

However, this I bore with, and was content to work it out with patience, and bear with the badness of the performance. When the corn was sowed, I had no harrow, but was forced to go over it myself and drag a great heavy bough of a tree over it, to scratch it, as it may be called, rather than rake or harrow it.

When it was growing and grown, I have observed already how many things I wanted, to fence it, secure it, mow or reap it, cure and carry it home, thrash, part it from the chaff, and save it. Then I wanted a mill to grind it, sieves to dress it, yeast and salt to make it into bread, and an oven to bake it, yet all these things I did without, as shall be observed; and yet the corn was an inestimable comfort and advantage to me too. All this, as I said, made every thing laborious and tedious to me, but that there was no help for; neither was my time so much loss to me, because, as I had divided it, a certain part of it was every day appointed to these works; and as I resolved to use none of the corn for bread till I had a greater quantity by me; I had the next six months to apply myself wholly by labour and invention to furnish myself with utensils proper for the performing all the operations necessary for the making the corn(when I had it) fit for my use.

But first, I was to prepare more land, for I had now seed enough to sow above an acre of ground. Before I did this, I had a weeks-work at least to make a spade, when it was done was but a sorry one indeed, and very heavy, and required double labour to work with it; however, I went thro' that, and sowed my seed in two large flat pieces of ground, as near my house as I could find them to my mind[2], and fenced them in with a good hedge, the stakes of which were all cut of that wood which I had set before,

IV. The Restoration and the Eighteenth Century

and knew it would grow, so that in one year's time I knew I should have a quick or living-hedge, that would want but little repair. This work was not so little as to take me up less than three months, because great part of that time was of the wet season, when I could not go abroad.

Within doors, that is, when it rained, and I could not go out. I found employment on the following occasions; always observing, that all the while I was at work I diverted myself with talking to my parrot, and teaching him to speak, and I quickly learned him to know his own name, and at last to speak it out pretty loud, Poll, which was the first word I ever heard spoken in the island by any mouth but my own. This, therefore, was not my work, but an assistant to my work, for now, as I said, I had a great employment upon my hands, as follows, viz. I had long study'd, by some means or other, to make myself some earthen vessels, which indeed I wanted sorely, but knew not where to come at them. However, considering the heat of the climate, I did not doubt but if I could find out any such clay, I might botch up some such pot as might, being dry'd in the sun, be hard enough and strong enough to bear handling, and to hold any thing that was dry and required to be kept so; and as this was necessary in the preparing corn, meal, etc. , which was the thing I was upon, I resolved to make some as large as I could, and fit only to stand like jars to hold what should be put into them.

It would make the reader pity me, or rather laugh at me, to tell how many awkward ways I took to raise this paste, what odd, mishapen, ugly things I made; how many of them fell in, and how many fell out, the clay not being stiff enough to bear its own weight; how many cracked by the over violent heat of the sun, being set out too hastily; and how many fell in pieces with only removing, as well before as after they were dry'd; and in a word, how after having laboured hard to find the clay, to dig it, to temper it, to bring it home and work it, I could not make above two large earthen ugly things, I cannot call them jars, in about two months labor.

However, as the sun baked these two very dry and hard, I lifted them very gently up, and set them down again in two great wicker-baskets which I had made on purpose for them, that they might not break, and as between the pot and the basket there was a little room to spare, I stuffed it full of the rice and barley straw, and as these two pots being to stand always dry. I thought would hold my dry corn, and perhaps the meal, when the corn was bruised.

Tho' I miscarried so much in my design for large pots, yet I made several smaller things with better success, such as little round pots, flat dishes, pitchers and pipkins, and any things my hand turned to, and the heat of the sun baked them strangely hard.

But all this would not answer my end, which was to get an earthen pot to hold what was liquid, and bear the fire, which none of these could do. It happened after some time, making a pretty, large fire for cooking my meat, when I went to put it out after I had done with it, I found a broken piece of one of my earthen-ware vessels in the fire, burnt as hard as a stone, and red as a tile. I was agreeably surprised to see it, and said to myself, that certainly they might be made to burn whole if they would burn broken.

This set me to studying how to order my fire, so as to make it burn me some pots. I had no notion of a kiln, such as the potters burn in, or of glazing them with lead, tho' I had some lead to do it with; but I placed three large pipkins and two or three pots in a pile one upon another, and placed my fire-wood all round it with a great heap of embers under them; I ply'd the fire with fresh fuel round the out-side, and upon the top, till I saw the pots in the inside red hot quite thro', and observed that they did not crack at all; when I saw them clear[3] red, I let them stand in that heat about five or six hours, till I found one of them, tho' it did not crack, did melt or run, for the sand which was mixed with the clay melted by the violence of the heat, and would have run into glass if I had gone on; so I slacked my fire gradually till the pots began to abate of the red colour, and watching them all night, that I might not let the fire abate too fast, in the morning I had three very good, I will not say handsome, pipkins, and two other earthen pots, as hard burnt as cou'd be desired; and one of them perfectly glazed with the running of the sand.

After this experiment, I need not say that I wanted no sort of earthen ware for my use; but I must needs say, as to the shapes of them, they were very indifferent[4], as any one may suppose, when I had no way of making them but as the children make dirt-pies, or as a woman would make pies that never learned to raise paste.

No joy at a thing of so mean a nature was ever equal to mine, when I found I had made an earthen pot that would bear the fire; and I had hardly patience to stay till they were cold, before I set one upon the fire again, with some water in it, to boil me some meat, which it did admirably well; and with a piece of a kid I made some very good broth, though I wanted oatmeal,

IV. The Restoration and the Eighteenth Century

and several other ingredients requisite to make it so good as I would have had it been.

My next concern was to get me a stone mortar, to stamp or beat some corn in; for as to the mill, there was no thought at arriving to that perfection of art, with one pair of hands. To supply this want I was at a great loss; for, of all trades in the world, I was as perfectly unqualify'd for a stone-cutter as for any whatever; neither had I any tools to go about it with. I spent many a day to find out a great stone big enough to cut hollow and make fit for a mortar, and could find none at all; except what was in the solid rock, and which I had no way to dig or cut out; nor indeed were the rocks in the island of hardness sufficient, but were all of a sandy crumbling stone, which neither would bear the weight of a heavy pestle, nor would break the corn without filling it with sand; so after a great deal of time lost in searching for a stone, I gave it over, and resolved to look out for a great block of hard wood, which I found indeed much easier; and getting one as big as I had strength to stir, I rounded it, and formed it in the out-side with my axe and hatchet, and then with the help of fire, and infinite labour, made a hollow place in it, as the Indians in Brazil made their canoes. After this, I made a great heavy pestle or beater, of the wood called the ironwood, and this I prepared and laid by against I had my next crop of corn, when I proposed to my self to grind, or rather pound, my corn into meal to make my bread.

My next difficulty was to make a sieve, or search, to dress my meal, and to part it from the bran and the husk, without which I did not see it possible I could have any bread. This was a most difficult thing, so much as but to think on; for to be sure I had nothing like the necessary thing to make it; I mean fine thin canvas, or stuff, to search the meal through. And here I was at a full stop for many months; nor did I really know what to do; linnen I had none left, but what was meer rags; I had goats hair, but neither knew I how to weave it or spin it; and had I known how, here was no tools to work it with; all the remedy that I found for this was, that at last I did remember I had among the seamen's clothes which were saved out of the ship, some neckcloths of callicoe or muslin; and with some pieces of these I made three small sieves, but proper enough for the work; and thus I made shift for some years; how I did afterwards, I shall shew in its place.

The baking part was the next thing to be considered, and how I should make bread when I came to have corn; for first I had no yeast; as to that part, as there was no supplying the want, so I did not concern my self much about it; but for an oven, I was indeed in great pain. At length I found out an experiment for that also, which was this: I made some earthen vessels, very broad, but not deep; that is to say, about two foot in diameter, and not above nine inches deep; these I burnt in the fire, as I had done the other, and laid them by; when I wanted to bake, I made a great fire upon my hearth, which I had paved with some square tiles of my own making and burning also; but I should not call them square.

When the fire-wood was burnt pretty much into embers, or live coals, I drew them forward upon this hearth so as to cover it all over, and there I let them lye till the hearth was very hot; then sweeping away all the embers, I set down my loaf or loaves, and whelming down the earthen pot upon them, drew the embers all round the out-side of the pot, to keep in, and add to the heat; and thus, as well as in the best oven in the world, I baked my barley loaves, and became in little time a meer pastry-cook into the bargain; for I made my self several cakes of the rice, and puddings; indeed I made no pies, neither had I any thing to put into them, supposing I had, except the flesh either of fowl or goats.

It need not be wondered at, if all these things took me up most part of the third year of my abode here; for it is to be observed that in the intervals of these things, I had my new harvest and husbandry to manage; for I reaped my corn in its season, and carry'd it home as well as I could, and laid it up in the ear in my large baskets, till I had time to rub it out; for I had no floor to thrash it on, or instrument to thrash it with.

And now indeed, my stock of corn increasing, I really wanted to build my barns bigger. I wanted a place to lay it up in; for the increase of the corn now yielded me so much, that I had of the barley about twenty bushels, and of the rice as much, or more; insomuch that now I resolved to begin to use it freely; for my bread had been quite gone a great while; also I resolved to see what quantity would be sufficient for me a whole year, and to sow but once a year.

Upon the whole, I found that the forty bushels of barley and rice was much more than I could consume in a year; so I resolved to sow just the same quantity every year that I sowed the last, in hopes that such a quantity would fully provide me with bread, etc.

IV. The Restoration and the Eighteenth Century

Notes

1. in but a wooden manner: in but a clumsy manner.
2. to my mind: to my liking.
3. clear: completely.
4. they were very indifferent: they were not very good.

Questions for Understanding

1. What is the selection about?
2. What do you find admirable in *Robinson Crusoe* from this selection?
3. What is your comment on the writing style of this selection?

Aspects of Appreciation

1. Realistic depiction

The charm of *Robinson Crusoe* lies in its intense reality, in the succession of thoughts, feelings, incidents, which every reader recognizes to be absolutely true to life. The detailed descriptions of the steps taken by the hero to provide for himself a shelter, food, clothing and the other simple comforts of life, are managed with great skill by the author in a simple, straightforward style. This adds to the realistic effects of the story.

2. A success story

A self-made success such as Benjamin Franklin's can always touch the human heart and engrave itself upon the human mind. Robinson Crusoe is a self-made man. He succeeds in creating a life all through his own efforts.

3. Reading from political perspective

To read it politically, the reader may interpret the story as an artistic projection of colonial expansion. Crusoe, backed by advanced technology, the gun, conquers a less civilized people represented by Friday. Friday has remained a servant, if not a slave, to his master Crusoe since the first day they met.

4. Reading from social perspective

To read it socially, the reader can find that Crusoe's adventures imply different Western cultural values. The novel sings highly of the dignity of labour, a slogan which the bourgeoisie used to justify their accumulation of wealth through diligent work and colonial expansion.

5. Reading from religious perspective

There is also the theme of religious devotion. *Robinson Crusoe* is filled with religious aspects. Defoe was himself a Puritan moralist, and wrote many books on how to be a good Puritan Christian. *Robinson Crusoe* shares many of the same themes.

Suggested Further Reading

1. Daniel Defoe. The *Fortunes and Misfortunes of the Famous Moll Flanders*, 1722.
2. W. R. Owens & Philip Nicholas Furbank. *A Critical Bibliography of Daniel Defoe*, 1998.

Topics for Further Study

1. Realistic description of everyday routine pervades the novel, but the story does not lack in descriptions of the psychology of the hero. Find examples of the hero's feelings and emotions to show this feature.
2. What is the major appeal of the novel *Robinson Crusoe*? What of the novel appeals to you most?
3. Cite examples from the novel to illustrate the survival ability of the hero, and analyse his character.

Jonathan Swift
(1667～1745)

About the Author

Jonathan Swift was born in Dublin, Ireland. His father died before he was born, and he was compelled to accept aid from relatives. He once studied at Dublin University, where he detested the curriculum, reading only what appealed to his own nature. After graduation, he was sent to England and admitted to the household of a distant relative, Sir William Temple, a diplomat and a writer of some fame. During the next 10 years between 1689 and 1699, he acted as secretary to Temple and read and studied widely. After his relation with Temple grew unbearable, he left and worked in a little church in Ireland. There, Swift wrote a number of articles and pamphlets which brought him into notice as a satirist of the age and one of the most important figures in London. From 1704 to 1710 he wrote political pamphlets for the Whigs. Disgusted at its indifference to the welfare of the Anglican Church in Ireland, he abandoned the Whigs and

IV. The Restoration and the Eighteenth Century

went over to the Tories. In 1713 Swift was appointed the Dean of St. Patrick's Cathedral in Dublin. His life in Ireland gave him an intimate knowledge of the miserable condition of the people. There he wrote his best known literary work, *Gulliver's Travels* (1726), which is a satire on the whole English society of the early 18th century, and exposes the dark and evil sides in various parts of the society.

Besides satire, Swift is also known for his pamphlets which reveal the miseries of the Irish people and the social injustice in Ireland, particularly the cruel oppression and exploitation by the English government. During the last years of his life Swift suffered from a brain disease. He died in 1745.

Swift is one of the greatest English novelists, poets and prose writers. It is a great education in English to read Swift's prose. His language is simple, clear and vigorous. He is a master satirist. His satire is masked by an outward gravity and apparent earnestness. This makes his satire all the more powerful.

★ Gulliver's Travels

About the Novel

Gulliver's Travels records the four voyages of Lemuel Gulliver and his adventures in four astounding countries.

The first part tells of his voyage and shipwreck in Lilliput, where the inhabitants are about six inches high, everything on the island being in the proportion of an inch to a foot as compared with things that we know. The statesmen who obtain place and favour by cutting monkey capers on the tight rope before their sovereign, and the two great parties, the little-endians and big-endians, who plunge the country into civil war over the momentous question of whether an egg should be broken on its big or on its little end, are satires on the politics of Swift's own day and generation.

In the second part, Gulliver is accidentally left ashore on Brobdingnag, where the inhabitants are giants, and everything is done upon an enormous scale. When Gulliver tells about his own people, their ambitions and wars and conquests, the giants can only wonder that such great venom could exist in such little insects.

The third part is occupied with a visit to the flying island of Laputa, and its neighboring continent and capital Lagado. Here the satire is directed against philosophers, men of science, historians, and projectors.

In the fourth part, Swift describes the country of the Houyhnhnms, who are horses endowed with reason. Their rational, clean and simple society is contrasted with the filthiness and brutality of the Yahoos, beasts in human shape.

Part 1 A Voyage to Lilliput

Chapter 4

The first request I made after I had obtained my liberty, was, that I might have license to see Mildendo[1], the metropolis, which the Emperor easily granted me, but with a special charge to do no hurt either to the inhabitants or their houses. The people had notice by proclamation of my design to visit the town. The wall which encompassed it is two feet and a half high and at least eleven inches broad, so that a coach and horses may be driven very safely round it; and it is flanked with strong towers at ten feet distance. I stepped over the great Western Gate, and passed very gently, and sideling[2] through the two principal streets, only in my short waistcoat, for fear of damaging the roofs and eaves of the houses with the skirts of my coat. I walked with the utmost circumspection, to avoid treading on any stragglers, that might remain in the streets, although the orders were very strict, that all people should keep in their houses at their own peril. The garret windows and tops of houses were so crowded with spectators, that I thought in all my travels I had not seen a more populous place. The city is an exact square, each side of the wall being five hundred feet long. The two great streets, which run cross and divide it into four quarters, are five feet wide. The lanes and alleys, which I could not enter, but only viewed them as I passed, are from twelve to eighteen inches. The town is holding five hundred thousand souls[3]. The houses are from three to five stories. The shops and markets well provided.

The Emperor's palace is in the centre of the city, where the two great streets meet. It is enclosed by a wall of two feet high, and twenty feet distant from the buildings. I had his Majesty's permission to step over this wall; and the space being so wide between that and the palace, I could easily view it on every side. The outward court is a square of forty feet, and includes two other courts: in the inmost are the royal apartments, which I

IV. The Restoration and the Eighteenth Century

was very desirous to see, but found it extremely difficult; for the great gates, from one square into another, were but eighteen inches high and seven inches wide. Now the buildings of the outer court were at least five feet high, and it was impossible for me to stride over them without infinite damage to the pile, though the walls were strongly built of hewn stone, and four inches thick. At the same time the Emperor had a great desire that I should see the magnificence of his palace; but this I was not able to do till three days after, which I spent in cutting down with my knife some of the largest trees in the royal park, about a hundred yards distant from the city. Of these trees I made two stools, each about three feet high, and strong enough to bear my weight. The people having received notice a second time, I went again through the city to the palace, with my two stools in my hands. When I came to the side of the outer court, I stood upon one stool, and took the other in my hand: this I lifted over the roof, and gently set it down on the space between the first and second court, which was eight feet wide. I then stepped over the buildings very conveniently from one stool to the other, and drew up the first after me with a hooked stick. By this contrivance I got into the inmost court; and lying down upon my side, I applied my face to the windows of the middle stories, which were left open on purpose, and discovered the most splendid apartments that can be imagined. There I saw the Empress and the young Princes, in their several lodgings, with their chief attendants about them. Her Imperial Majesty was pleased to smile very graciously[4] upon me, and gave me out of the window her hand to kiss.

But I shall not anticipate the reader[5] with farther descriptions of this kind, because I reserve them for a greater work, which is now almost ready for the press, containing a general description of this empire, from its first erection, through a long series of princes, with a particular account of their wars and politics, laws, learning, and religion; their plants and animals, their peculiar manners and customs, with other matters very curious and useful; my chief design at present being only to relate such events and transactions as happened to the public, or to myself, during a residence of about nine months in that empire.

One morning, about a fortnight after I had obtained my liberty, Reldresal, principal Secretary(as they style him) of Private Affairs, came to my house attended only by one servant. He ordered his coach to wait at a distance, and desired I would give him an hour's audience; which I readily consented to, on account of his quality[6] and personal merits, as well as the many good offices[7] he had done me during my solicitations at court[8]. I offered to lie down, that he might the more conveniently reach my ear; but he chose rather to let me hold him in my hand during our conversation. He began with compliments on my liberty; said he might pretend to some merit in it[9]; but, however, added, that if it had not been for the present situation of things at court, perhaps I might not have obtained it so soon. For, said he, as flourishing a condition as we may appear to be in to foreigners, we labor under two mighty evils; a violent faction at home, and the danger of an invasion by a most potent enemy from abroad. As to the first, you are to understand, that for above seventy moons[10] past there have been two struggling parties in this empire, under the names of Tramecksan and Slamecksan[11], from the high and low heels on their shoes, by which they distinguish themselves.

It is alleged indeed, that the high heels are most agreeable to our ancient constitution: but however this be, his Majesty has determined to make use of only low heels[12] in the administration of the government, and all offices in the gift of the Crown[13] as you cannot but observe; and particularly, that his Majesty's Imperial heels are lower at least by a *drurr* than any of his court[14] (*drurr* is a measure about the fourteenth part of an inch). The animosities between these two parties run so high, that they will neither eat nor drink, nor talk with each other. We compute the Tramecksan, or High-Heels, to exceed us in number; but the power is wholly on our side. We apprehend his Imperial Highness, the Heir to the Crown[15], to have some tendency towards the High-Heels[16]; at least we can plainly discover one of his heels higher than the other, which gives him a hobble in his gait. Now, in the midst of these intestine disquiets, we are threatened with an invasion from the Island of Blefuscu[17], which is the other great empire of the universe, almost as large and powerful as this of his Majesty[18]. For as to what we have heard you affirm, that there are other kingdoms and states in the world inhabited by human creatures as large as yourself, our philosophers are in much doubt, and would rather conjecture that you dropped from the moon, or one of the stars; because it is certain, that a hundred mortals of your bulk would, in a short time, destroy all the fruits and cattle of his Majesty's dominions. Besides, our histories of six thousand moons[19] make no mention of any other regions, than the two great empires of Lilliput and Blefuscu. Which two mighty powers have, as I was going to tell you, been engaged in a most obstinate war for six and thirty moons past[20]. It began upon the following occasion. It is allowed on all hands[21], that the primitive way of breaking eggs, before we eat them, was upon the larger end: but his present Majesty's grandfather[22], while he was a boy, going to eat an egg, and breaking it according to the ancient practice, happened to cut one of his fingers. Whereupon the Emperor his father published an edict, commanding all his subjects, upon great penalties, to break the smaller end of their eggs. The people so highly resented this law, that our histories tell us there have been six rebellions raised on that account; wherein one Emperor[23] lost his life, and another[24] his crown. These civil commotions were constantly fomented by the monarchs of Blefuscu[25]; and when they were quelled, the exiles always fled for refuge to that empire. It is computed, that eleven thousand persons have, at several times, suffered death, rather than submit to break their eggs at the smaller end. Many hundred large volumes have been published upon this controversy: but the books of the Big-Endians have been long forbidden[26], and the whole party, rendered incapable by law of holding employments[27], During the course of these troubles, the Emperors of Blefuscu did frequently expostulate by their ambassadors, accusing us of making a schism in religion, by offending against a fundamental doctrine of our great prophet Lustrog, in the fifty-fourth chapter of the Blundecral (which is their *Alcoran*)[28]. This, however, is thought to be a mere strain upon the text[29]; for the words are these: *That all true believers shall break their eggs at the convenient end*; and which is the convenient end, seems, in my humble opinion, to be left to every man's conscience, or at least in the power of the chief magistrate to determine. Now the Big-Endian exiles have found so much credit in the Emperor of Blefuscu's court, and so much private assistance and encouragement from their party here at home, that a bloody war[30] has been carried on between the two empires for six and thirty moons with various success[31], during which time we have lost forty capital ships. and a much greater number of smaller vessels, together with thirty thousand of our best seamen and soldiers; and the damage received by the enemy is reckoned to be somewhat greater than ours. However, they have now equipped a numerous fleet, and are just preparing to make a descent upon us; and his Imperial Majesty, placing great confidence in your valor and strength, has commanded me to lay this account of his affairs before you.

I desired the Secretary to present my humble duty[32] to the Emperor, and to let him know, that I thought it would not become me, who was a foreigner, to interfere with parties; but I was ready, with the hazard of my life[33], to defend his person and state against all invaders.

❈❈❈❈❈❈❈❈❈❈❈❈❈❈❈❈❈❈❈❈❈❈❈❈❈❈❈❈❈

Notes

1. Mildendo: an anagram of London.
2. sideling: sideways.
3. five hundred thousand souls: The population of London in 1700 has been estimated at 550,000.
4. smile very graciously: perhaps an allusion to Queen Anne's inclination towards the Tories.
5. anticipate the reader: tell the reader beforehand what he can read later.
6. quality: high social position.
7. offices: help, favour done to others.
8. solicitations at court: various requirements made to court.
9. pretend to some merit in it: claim some credit for it.
10. above seventy moons: If Lilliputian "moons" can indicate years, this implies that party strife originated in the Civil War, which ended 74 years before 1725 (when Swift was writing his first version of *Gulliver's Travels*).
11. Tramecksan and Slamecksan: the High Church party (Tories), and Low Church party (Whigs).
12. his Majesty has determined to make use of only low heels: George Ⅰ favoured the Whigs.
13. all offices in the gift of the Crown: all the official posts (positions) the king could give to his ministers.
14. by a drurr than any of his court: George Ⅱ was more sympathetic to the Whigs than to the Tories; the Prince of Wales, later George Ⅱ, hobnobbed with the discontented of both parties. Drurr has been read as dirt or turd.
15. his Imperial Highness, the Heir to the Crown: Here the author satirizes the prince of England, who later became the king of England (i.e. George Ⅱ). He had friends in both Whigs and Tories. So the author in the following text satirizing his sitting on the fences, "one of his heels higher than the other".

IV. The Restoration and the Eighteenth Century

16. tendency towards the High-Heels: George II, then Prince of Wales, favoured the Tories.
17. the Island of Blefuscu: Here the author alludes to France at that time.
18. France and England were the main contenders in the War of the Spanish Succession(1701~1713).
19. six thousand moons: perhaps 6,000 years, the traditional history of the earth.
20. six and thirty moons past: England was at war with France from 1689 (35 years before 1725) until 1697(War of the League of Augsburg), and again 1701~1713(War of the Spanish Succession).
21. It is allowed on all hands: It is agreed unanimously.
22. grandfather: presumably Henry VIII, who cut his finger(felt injured at not being allowed to marry Anne Boleyn), because he approached his egg(symbol of Easter, and so of Christianity) from the larger end(the Catholic Church). To soothe his childish irritation, his father(i. e. Henry himself in his adult capacity of King) commanded his subjects to approach their eggs from the smaller end (the Church of England). Thus big-endians are Catholics, little-endians Anglicans.
23. one Emperor: Charles I.
24. another: James II. The big-endians and the little-endians represent the Catholics and Protestants; they also suggest England and Rome in the reign of King Henry VIII; the controversy between the two also suggests the Civil Wars in England in 1640s when Charles I was beheaded and James II exiled.
25. Blefuscu: France gave asylum and support to the Royalists during the Commonwealth, and to the Jacobites after 1688. Louis XIV declared the Pretender to be James III, King of England.
26. ... the books of the Big-Endians ... forbidden: i. e. by an Act of 1550, under which all Catholic literature was "abolished, extinguished, and forbidden for ever to be used".
27. rendred incapable by law of holding employments: Here the author alludes to and satirizes Test Act, which was passed in 1673 and which prohibited the Catholic believers to hold public offices.
28. *Alcoran*: the Koran.
29. a meer strain upon the text: an absolute distortion of the text of the Alcoran.
30. a bloody war: In *The Conduct of the Allies* (1711) Swift had argued

against prolonging the war.
31. various success: victories shared by both sides.
32. duty: respect.
33. with the hazard of my life: at the risk of losing my life.

Questions for Understanding

1. In this chapter, Swift describes the smallness of the Lilliputians. What does this "smallness" imply in the author's satire of the aristocratic-bourgeois society of the time?
2. What does Swift mean to satirize in his description of the differences between the two struggling parties in Lilliput?
3. What is the cause of the civil strife and war between Lilliput and the neighbouring empire of Blefuscu? What is the target of the author's satire?

Aspects of Appreciation

1. Themes

Gulliver's Travels is full of allusions to historical events. It gives an unparalleled satirical depiction of the vices of the age, expresses a satirical view of the state of European government, and of petty conflicts between religions, and also serves an inquiry into whether men are inherently corrupt or whether they become corrupted.

2. Artistic features

Artistically, *Gulliver's Travels* is both a fantasy and a realistic work of fiction. Though the four voyages are obviously invented and unreal, they are told in a vivid and convincing way and include many direct descriptions of men and things in the 18th century, besides the numerous indirect references to the situations of the writer's own day.

3. Cultural influences

Widely read and appreciated throughout the world by grown-ups and children alike, *Gulliver's Travels* is as valid today as it was originally produced. The popularity of the book even made the term "Lilliputian" enter the English language as an adjective meaning "small and delicate". The term "yahoo" is often encountered as a synonym for ruffian or thug. "Brobdingnagian" appears as synonym for "very large" or "gigantic". In the discipline of computer science, the terms big-endian and little-endian are used to describe two possible ways of laying out bytes in memory.

Suggested Further Reading

1. Jonathan Swift. "A Modest Proposal", 1729.
2. D. Nokes. *Jonathan Swift: A Critical Biography*, Oxford University Press, 1985.

Topics for Further Study

1. Some would argue that Swift was a misanthrope and that *Gulliver's Travels* proves his hatred of mankind. What is your opinion? Support your opinion with examples from the text.
2. Explain how Swift makes use of the character of Gulliver. Does Gulliver have a distinct and recognizable character or is he simply Swift's mouthpiece?
3. In his satire, Swift makes a correlation between "size" and "sense of morality". Cite examples from the description of Gulliver in Lilliput to explain how this works.

Thomas Gray
(1716~1771)

About the Author

Thomas Gray (1716~1771) was born in London into a lower middle class family. He was educated at Eton, where he befriended Richard West and Horace Walpole. He then studied and later settled at Cambridge. In his life he made a grand tour of France and Italy between 1739 and 1741 and several tours of the Lake District and Scotland in search of beauty and the sublime in nature. These things were not generally valued in the early 18th century, when the popular taste ran to classical styles in architecture and literature. Although Gray's output was small, his masterpiece, "Elegy Written in a Country Churchyard" (1751) once and for all established his fame as the leader of the sentimental poetry of the day, especially English graveyard school. Gray wrote with sincerity, honesty and integrity. His style is sophisticated and allusive, often marked with the trait of a highly artificial diction and a distorted word order. Although he still worked within the 18th century forms, he introduced new subject matter for poetry. His value for the picturesque, the sublime and the Gothic may be regarded as the first foreshadowing of the Romantic movement that dominated the early 19th century.

★ Elegy Written in a Country Churchyard
(Excerpt)

About the Poem

It is believed that Gray wrote his masterpiece in the graveyard of the church in Stoke Poges, Buckinghamshire. Written with classical precision and polish, "Elegy Written in a Country Churchyard" shows a keen interest in the English countryside and the life of the common people. The poet claims that life is short and transitory, as Line 36 makes clear "The paths of glory lead but to the grave" and meditates on the humble fate of those lying under the tombstones who might have been great in accomplishment, should they have just had the opportunities they deserve. This thought leads him to praise the dead for the honest, simple lives that they lived. It knits structure, rhyme scheme, imagery and message into a brilliant work that confers on Gray everlasting fame.

> The curfew[1] tolls the knell[2] of parting day,
> The lowing herd wind slowly o'er the lea[3]
> The plowman homeward plods[4] his weary way,
> And leaves the world to darkness and to me.
>
> Now fades the glimm'ring landscape on the sight,
> And all the air a solemn stillness holds,
> Save[5] where the beetle wheels his droning[6] flight,
> And drowsy tinklings lull the distant folds[7];
>
> Save that from yonder[8] ivy-mantled[9] tow'r
> The moping owl does to the moon complain
> Of such, as wand'ring near her secret bow'r[10],
> Molest her ancient solitary reign[11].
>
> Beneath those rugged elms, that yew-tree's shade,
> Where heaves the turf in many a mould'ring[12] heap,

IV. The Restoration and the Eighteenth Century

Each in his narrow cell for ever laid,
The rude[13] forefathers of the hamlet sleep.

The breezy call of incense-breathing Morn[14],
The swallow twitt'ring[15] from the straw-built shed,
The cock's shrill clarion, or the echoing horn,
No more shall rouse them from their lowly bed.

For them no more the blazing hearth shall burn,
Or busy housewife ply[16] her evening care:
No children run to lisp their sire[17]'s return,
Or climb his knees the envied kiss to share.

Oft did the harvest to their sickle yield,
Their furrow oft the stubborn glebe[18] has broke;
How jocund did they drive their team afield!
How bow'd the woods beneath their sturdy stroke!

Let not Ambition[19] mock their useful toil,
Their homely joys, and destiny obscure;
Nor Grandeur[20] hear with a disdainful smile
The short and simple annals[21] of the poor.

The boast of heraldry[22], the pomp[23] of pow'r,
And all that beauty, all that wealth e'er gave,
Awaits alike th' inevitable hour.
The paths of glory lead but to the grave.

Nor you, ye proud, impute to these the fault,
If Mem'ry[24] o'er their tomb no trophies[25] raise,
Where thro' the long drawn aisle and fretted vault[26]
The pealing anthem swells the note of praise.

Can storied urn[27] or animated bust
Back to its mansion call the fleeting breath[28]?
Can Honour's voice provoke the silent dust,
Or Flatt'ry soothe the dull cold ear of Death[29]?

Perhaps in this neglected spot is laid
Some heart once pregnant with celestial fire[30];
Hands, that the rod of empire might have sway'd,
Or wak'd to ecstasy the living lyre[31].

But Knowledge to their eyes her ample page
Rich with the spoils of time did ne'er unroll[32];
Chill Penury repress'd their noble rage,
And froze the genial current of the soul[33].

Full many a gem of purest ray serene,
The dark unfathom'd caves of ocean bear:
Full many a flow'r is born to blush unseen,
And waste its sweetness on the desert air.

Some Village-Hampden[34], that with dauntless breast
The little tyrant of his fields withstood;
Some mute inglorious Milton here may rest,
Some Cromwell guiltless of his country's blood.

...

For thee, who mindful of th'unhonour'd Dead
Dost in these lines their artless tale relate[35];
If chance, by lonely contemplation led,
Some kindred spirit shall inquire thy fate[36],

Haply[37] some hoary-headed swain[38] may say,
"Oft have we seen him at the peep[39] of dawn
Brushing with hasty steps the dews away
To meet the sun upon the upland lawn."

"There at the foot of yonder nodding beech
That wreathes its old fantastic roots so high,
His listless length[40] at noontide would he stretch,
And pore upon[41] the brook that babbles by."

"Hard by yon[42] wood, now smiling as in scorn,
Mutt'ring his wayward fancies[43] he would rove[44],

Now drooping, woeful wan, like one forlorn,
Or craz'd with care, or cross'd in hopeless love."

"One morn I miss'd him on the custom'd hill,
Along the heath and near his fav'rite tree;
Another came; nor yet beside the rill,
Nor up the lawn, nor at the wood was he;"

"The next with dirges[45] due in sad array
Slow thro' the church-way path we saw him borne.
Approach and read(for thou canst read) the lay[46],
Grav'd on the stone beneath yon aged thorn."

THE EPITAPH

Here rests his head upon the lap of Earth
A youth to Fortune and to Fame unknown.
Fair Science frown'd not on his humble birth,
And Melancholy mark'd him for her own.

Large was his bounty, and his soul sincere,
Heav'n did a recompense as largely send:
He gave to Mis'ry all he had, a tear,
He gain'd from Heav'n('twas all he wish'd) a friend.

No farther seek his merits to disclose,
Or draw his frailties from their dread abode,
(There they alike in trembling hope repose)
The bosom of his Father and his God[47].

Notes

1. curfew: in medieval Europe, the ringing of a bell to prompt people to extinguish fires and lights.
2. knell: the sound of a bell rung to announce a death or a funeral.
3. lea: meadow, field of grass.

4. plod: to make one's way or walk along (a path, road, etc.) with heavy, usually slow steps.
5. save: except.
6. droning: buzzing, humming, monotonous sound.
7. folds: small valley; level land between rolling hills; flocks of sheep.
8. yonder: distant, remote.
9. ivy-mantled: completely cloaked, dressed or adorned by ivy.
10. bow'r: bower, an enclosure surrounded by plant growth, in this case, ivy.
11. Molest her ancient solitary reign: bother the owl while it keeps watch over the churchyard and countryside.
12. mould'ring: mouldering, decaying, crumbling.
13. rude: unlearned; robust, sturdy.
14. breezy call of incense-breathing Morn: wind carrying the pleasant smells of morning, including dewy grass and flowers. Notice that Morn is a personification (It calls and breathes).
15. twitt'ring: chirping, making a short, shrill sound.
16. ply: be busy with.
17. sire: daddy.
18. glebe: [poetic] land, esp. when regarded as the source of growing things.
19. Ambition: a personification referring to the desire to succeed or to ambitious people seeking lofty goals.
20. Grandeur: a personification referring to people with wealth, social standing, and power.
21. annals: historical records; story.
22. heraldry: noble birth.
23. pomp: ceremonies, rituals, and splendid surroundings of nobles and royals.
24. Mem'ry: Memory, a personification referring to memorials, commemorations, and tributes—including statues, headstones, and epitaphs—used to preserve the memory of important or privileged people.
25. trophies: an ornamental or symbolic group of figures depicting the achievements of the dead man.
26. fretted vault: a carved or ornamented arched roof or ceiling.
27. storied urn: a funeral urn with an epitaph inscribed on it.
28. Can storied urn … breath: Can the soul (fleeting breath) be called back

IV. The Restoration and the Eighteenth Century 85

  to the body (mansion) by the urn or bust back?
29. Can Honour's ··· Death: Can honor (Honour's voice) attributed to the dead person cause that person (silent dust) to come back to life? Can flattering words (Flatt'ry) about the dead person make death more "bearable"?
30. pregnant with celestial fire: Full of great ideas, abilities, or goals (celestial fire).
31. wak'd ··· lyre: Played beautiful music on a lyre, a stringed instrument. In other words, one of the people in the cemetery could have become a great musician if given the opportunity, "waking up" the notes of the lyre.
32. Knowledge ··· unroll: Knowledge did not reveal itself to them (their eyes) in books (ample page) rich with treasures of information (spoils of time).
33. Chill ··· soul: Poverty (penury) repressed their enthusiasm (rage) and froze the flow (current) of ideas (soul).
34. Village-Hampden: allusion to John Hampden (1594～1643), who refused to pay an unfair tax imposed by the king and later died in battle in the English Civil Wars (1642～1651).
35. For thee ··· relate: Gray appears to be referring to himself. Mindful that the villagers deserve some sort of memorial, he is telling their story (their artless tale) in this elegy (these lines).
36. Gray is wondering what people would say about him if he died.
37. Haply: Perhaps; by chance; by accident.
38. hoary-headed swain: Gray-haired country fellow; old man who lives in the region.
39. peep: the first appearance.
40. listless length: his tired body.
41. pore upon: look at; watch.
42. yon: archaic dialect for that.
43. wayward fancies: unpredictable, unexpected, or unwanted thoughts; capricious or flighty thoughts.
44. rove: wander.
45. dirges: funeral songs.
46. lay: short poem, in this case, the epitaph below.
47. general meaning of the Epitaph: Here lies a man of humble birth, who did not know fortune or fame but who did become a scholar. Although he was depressed at times, he had a good life, was sensitive to the needs

of others, and followed God's laws. Don't try to find out more about his good points or bad points, which are now with him in heaven.

Questions for Understanding

1. What details from the landscape does the speaker notice and comment on?
2. What is the tone of the poem?
3. How does the speaker defend the dead in the remote churchyard cemetery from the contempt of abstractions like Ambition and Grandeur?
4. How does the poem display a sense of symmetry?
5. What effect does the Epitaph at the end have on the poem in terms of theme?

Aspects of Appreciation

1. Elegy stanza

This elegy adopts dignified iambic pentameter with traditional ABAB quatrain. After Gray's poem became famous, this stanza form is referred to as elegiac stanza.

2. Poetic devices

The poem uses personification to make Ambition, Grandeur, Memory, Honour, Flattery and Death, Knowledge, Penury, Luxury and Pride, Forgetfulness and Nature all allegorical figures who represent general traits of 18th century humanity. It also effectively employs metaphors such as "the gem" and "the flower" in Stanza 14 to represent a person of great and noble qualities yet undiscovered or may stand for anything in life that goes unappreciated. It also uses alliteration, assonance, consonance and parallel syntactic construction to make itself an organic whole.

3. Romantic features

First is the prevalence of nature and its importance as being a place where meditation and deeply spiritual epiphanies occur. Second is the use of visionary, fantastic, or drug-induced imagery such as "drowsy tinklings lull the distant folds" and the "breezy call of incense-breathing morn". Third is the emphasis on the inner world of the individual and tendency for meditation. The speaker stands in the sublimity of nature and has an intimate meditation on man's mortality. He displays his individual outlook of the world.

4. A collage of adopted lines

The Elegy contains many outstanding phrases which have entered the

IV. The Restoration and the Eighteenth Century

common English lexicon, either on their own or as references in other works. A few of these include: "Far from the madding crowd" "The paths of glory" "Celestial fire" "The unlettered muse" "Kindred spirit" "Some mute inglorious Milton", etc.

Suggested Further Reading

Thomas Gray's poems: "Ode to the Death of a Favorite Cat" and "Ode on a Distant Prospect of Eton College".

Topics for Further Study

1. The gothic elements displayed in Gray's poetry.
2. Read Percy Bysshe Shelley's "Ozymandias" and decide whether he agrees with Gray on the subject of glory.

Knowledge of Literature

Elegy

The word "elegy" comes from the Greek word meaning "lament". Originaly, in classical Greek and Roman poetry, elegies are poems written in distiches or couplets. They can be of any subject from love, lamentation, to war and politics. Since the 16th century, elegies have come to be associated mainly with lamentation and death, and composed on set metrical form.

Richard Brinsley Sheridan
(1751～1816)

About the Author

Richard Brinsley Sheridan (1751～1816) was an Irish-born playwright and poet and long-term owner of the London Theatre Royal, Drury Lane. For thirty-two years, he was also a Whig Member of the British House of Commons for Stafford (1780～1806), Westminster (1806～1807) and Ilchester (1807～1812). Such high esteem he was held in by his contemporaries when he died that he was buried in Westminster Abbey. His most famous play *The School for Scandal* is considered one of the greatest comedies of manners in English.

His masterpieces are *The Rivals* (1775) and *The School for Scandal* (1777), comedies of manners that blend the brilliant wit of the Restoration with 18th-century sensibility. Both plays affectionately satirize fashionable society with its materialism, gossip, and hypocrisy. Although each ridicules sentimentalism, neither is itself entirely free of that attribute. *The Rivals* and *The School for Scandal* are generally regarded as important links between the masterpieces of Shakespeare and Bernard Shaw. In his plays, morality is a constant theme.

★ The School for Scandal

About the Play

An Irish-born English dramatist, Richard Brinsley Sheridan is a master of the satirical comedy of manners. *The School for Scandal*, one of the most popular comedies in the English language, has the permanent hold on the public and its attraction to the audience is surpassed only by the plays of William Shakespeare. It reveals not only Sheridan's mastery of the mechanics of stage comedy, but also his flair for witty dialogue and obvious delight in skewering the affectation and pretentiousness of aristocratic Londoners of the 1770s. It is a sharp satire on the moral degeneracy of the aristocratic-bourgeois society in the 18th-century England, on the vicious scandal-mongering among the idle rich, on the reckless life of extravagance and love intrigues in the high society and, above all, on the immorality and hypocrisy behind the mask of honorable living and high-sounding moral principles. Its lasting appeal makes it one of the best produced of all theater classics today, and one of the most delightful to read.

Act IV, Scene I

[A picture room in Charles Surface's house. Enter Charles Surface, Sir Oliver Surface, Moses, and Careless]

Char: Walk in, gentlemen, pray walk in;—here they are, the family of the Surfaces, up to the Conquest[1].

Oliv: And, in my opinion, a goodly collection.

Char: Ay, ay, these are done in the true spirit of portrait-painting; no *volontiere grace* or expression. Not like the works of your modern Raphaels[2], who give you the strongest resemblance, yet contrive to make your portrait independent of you; so that you may sink the original and not

IV. The Restoration and the Eighteenth Century

hurt the pioture. No, no; the merit of these is the inveterate likeness—all stiff and awkward as the originals, and like nothing in human nature besides.

Oliv: Ah! we shall never see such figures of men again.

Char: I hope not. Well, you see, Master Premium[3], what a domestic character I am; here I sit of an evening surrounded by my family. But come, get to your pulpit, Mr. Auctioneer; here's an old gouty chair of my grandfather's will answer the purpose.

Care: Ay, ay, this will do. But, Charles, I haven't a hammer; and what's an auctioneer without his hammer?

Char: Egad, that's true. What parchment have we here? Oh, our genealogy in full. [Taking pedigree down] Here, Careless, you shall have no common bit of mahogany, here's the family tree for you, you rogue! This shall be your hammer, and now you may knock down my ancestors with their own pedigree.

Oliv: What an unnatural rogue! —an *ex post facto* parricide! [Aside]

Care: Yes, yes, here's a list of your generation indeed;—faith, Charles, this is the most convenient thing you could have found for the business, for 'twill not only serve as a hammer, but a catalogue into the bargain. Come, begin—A-going, a-going, a-going!

Char: Bravo, Careless! Well, here's my great uncle, Sir Richard Ravelin, a marvellous good general in his day, I assure you. He served in all the Duke of Marlborough's wars, and got that cut over his eye at the battle of Malplaquet. What say you, Mr. Premium? look at him—there's a hero! not cut out of his feathers, as your modern clipped captains are, but enveloped in wig and regimentals, as a general should be. What do you bid?

Oliv: [Aside to Moses] Bid him speak.

Mos: Mr. Premium would have you speak.

Char: Why, then, he shall have him for ten pounds, and I'm sure that's not dear for a staff-officer.

Oliv: [Aside] Heaven deliver me! his famous uncle Richard for ten pounds! —[Aloud] Very well, sir, I take him at that.

Char: Careless, knock down my uncle Richard. —Here, now, is a maiden sister of his, my great-aunt Deborah, done by Kneller, in his best manner, and esteemed a very formidable likeness. There she is, you see, a shepherdess feeding her flock. You shall have her for five pounds ten—the sheep are worth the money.

Oliv: [Aside] Ah! poor Deborah! a woman who set such a value on herself—[Aloud] Five pounds ten—she's mine.

Char: Knock down my aunt Deborah! Here, now, are two that were a sort of cousins of theirs.—You see, Moses, these pictures were done some time ago, when beaux wore wigs, and the ladies their own hair.

Oliv: Yes, truly, head-dresses appear to have been a little lower in those days.

Char: Well, take that couple for the same.

Mos: 'tis a good bargain.

Char: Careless!—This, now, is a grandfather of my mother's, a learned judge, well known on the western circuit.—What do you rate him at, Moses?

Mos: Four guineas.

Char: Four guineas! Gad's life, you don't bid me the price of his wig.—Mr. Premium, you have more respect for the woolsack; do let us knock his lordship down at fifteen.

Oliv: By all means.

Care: Gone.

Char: And there are two brothers of his, William and Walter Blunt, Esquires, both members of Parliament, and noted speakers; and, what's very extraordinary, I believe, this is the first time they were ever bought or sold.

Oliv: That is very extraordinary, indeed! I'll take them at your own price, for the honour of Parliament.

Care: Well said, little Premium! I'll knock them down at forty.

Char: Here's a jolly fellow—I don't know what relation, but he was mayor of Norwich: take him at eight pounds.

Oliv: No, no; six will do for the mayor.

Char: Come, make it guineas, and I'll throw you the two aldermen there into the bargain.

Oliv: They're mine.

Char: Careless, knock down the mayor and aldermen. But, plague on't! we shall be all day retailing in this manner; do let us deal wholesale: what say you, little Premium? Give me three hundred pounds for the rest of the family in the lump.

Care: Ay ay, that will be the best way.

IV. The Restoration and the Eighteenth Century

Oliv: Well, well, anything to accommodate you; they are mine. But there is one portrait which you have always passed over.

Care: What, that ill-looking little fellow over the settee?

Oliv: Yes, sir, I mean that; though I don't think him so ill-looking a little fellow, by any means.

Char: What, that? Oh; that's my uncle Oliver! 'Twas done before he went to India.

Care: Your uncle Oliver! Gad, then you'll never be friends, Charles. That, now, to me, is as stern a looking rogue as ever I saw; an unforgiving eye, and a damned disinheriting countenance! an inveterate knave, depend on't. Don't you think so, little Premium?

Oliv: Upon my soul, sir, I do not; I think it is as honest a looking face as any in the room, dead or alive. But I suppose uncle Oliver goes with the rest of the lumber?

Char: No, hang it! I'll not part with poor Noll. The old fellow has been very good to me, and, egad, I'll keep his picture while I've a room to put it in.

Oliv: [Aside] The rogue's my nephew after all! —[Aloud] But, sir, I have somehow taken a fancy to that picture.

Char: I'm sorry for't, for you certainly will not have it. Oons, haven't you got enough of them?

Oliv: [Aside] I forgive him everything! —[Aloud] But, sir, when I take a whim in my head, I don't value money. I'll give you as much for that as for all the rest.

Char: Don't tease me, master broker; I tell you I'll not part with it, and there's an end of it.

Oliv: [Aside] How like his father the dog is. —[Aloud] Well, well, I have done. —[Aside] I did not perceive it before, but I think I never saw such a striking resemblance. —[Aloud] Here is a draught for your sum.

Char: Why, 'tis for eight hundred pounds!

Oliv: You will not let Sir Oliver go?

Char: Zounds! no! I tell you, once more.

Oliv: Then never mind the difference, we'll balance that another time. But give me your hand on the bargain; you are an honest fellow, Charles—I beg pardon, sir, for being so free. —Come, Moses.

Char: Egad, this is a whimsical old fellow! —But hark'ee[4], Premium, you'll prepare lodgings for these gentlemen.

Oliv: Yes, yes, I'll send for them in a day or two.

Char: But hold; do now send a genteel conveyance for them, for, I assure you, they were most of them used to ride in their own carriages.

Oliv: I will, I will—for all but Qliver.

Char: Ay, all but the little nabob.

Oliv: You're fixed on that?

Char: Peremptorily.

Oliv: [Aside] A dear extravagant rogue! —[Aloud] Good day! —Come, Moses. —[Aside] Let me hear now who dares call him profligate!

[Exit with Moses]

Care: Why, this is the oddest genius of the sort I ever met with!

Char: Egad, he's the prince of brokers, I think. I wonder how the devil Moses got acquainted with so honest a fellow. —Ha! Here's Rowley. —Do, Careless, say I'll join the company in a few moments.

Care: I will—but don't let that old blockhead persuade you to squander any of that money on old musty debts, or any such nonsense; for tradesmen, Charles, are the most exorbitant fellows.

Char: Very true, and paying them is only encouraging them.

Care: Nothing else.

Char: Ay, ay, never fear. —[Exit Careless] So! this was an odd old fellow, indeed. Let me see, two-thirds of these five hundred and thirty odd pounds are mine by right. 'Fore Heaven! I find one's ancestors are more valuable relations than I took them for! —Ladies and gentlemen, your most obedient and very grateful servant.

[Bows ceremoniously to the pictures. Enter Rowley] Ha! old Rowley! egad, you are just come in time to take leave of your old acquaintance.

Row: Yes, I heard they were a-going. But I wonder you can have such spirits under so many distresses.

Char: Why, there's the point! my distresses are so many, that I can't afford to part with my spirits; but I shall be rich and splenetic, all in good time. However, I suppose you are surprised that I am not more sorrowful at parting with so many near relations; to be sure, 'tis very affecting; but you see they never move a muscle, so why should I?

Row: There's no making you serious a moment.

Char: Yes, faith, I am so now. Here, my honest Rowley, here, get me this changed directly, and take a hundred pounds of it immediately to old Standley.

IV. The Restoration and the Eighteenth Century

Row: A hundred pounds! Consider only—

Char: Gad's life, don't talk about it! poor Standley's wants are pressing, and, if you don't make haste, we shall have some one call that has a better right to the money.

Row: Ah! There's the point! I never will cease dunning you with the old proverb—

Char: Be just before you're generous. —Why, so I would if I could; but Justice is an old hobbling beldame, and I can't get her to keep pace with generosity, for the soul of me.

Row: Yet, Charles, believe me, one hour's reflection—

Char: Ay, ay, it's very true; but, hark'ee, Rowley, while I have, by Heaven I'll give; so, damn your economy! and now for hazard.

Notes

1. the Conquest: Norman Conquest of England in 1066.
2. Raphaels: the four archangels named in Hebrew tradition.
3. Master Premium: Sir Pliver goes to Charles' house under this name.
4. hark'ee: listen to me.

Questions for Understanding

1. What makes Sir Oliver change his opinion about his nephew Charles Surface and decide that Charles will be his heir?
2. Joseph Surface always claims himself to be a man of sentiment. What is the significance of this self-proclaimed title and how is it ridiculed in the course of this act?
3. What is your impression of the major characters of the play, the two brothers, Sir and Lady Teazle?

Aspects of Appreciation

1. Theatrical art of Sheridan

Sheridan's greatness also lies in his theatrical art. He seems to have inherited from his parents a natural ability and inborn knowledge about the theater. Though his dramatic techniques are largely conventional, they are exploited to the best advantage.

2. The plot of the play

The plot is well organized, and the characters, either major or minor, are all sharply drawn. Sheridan's manipulation of such devices as disguise, mistaken identity and dramatic irony is masterly. Witty dialogues, neat and decent language also mark a characteristic of his plays.

Suggested Further Reading

Sheridan's play *The Rivals*.

Topics for Further Study

1. Sheridan is a male writer who writes about marriage and women in *The School for Scandal*. Research the role of women in London society and women's perspectives of marriage.
2. Try to find out Sheridan's witty use of language in *The School for Scandal*.

Knowledge of Literature

Comedies of manners

A comedy of manners is a comedy satirizing the attitudes and behavior of a particular social group, often of fashionable society. *The School for Scandal* emphasizes use of manners and conventions of sophisticated society.

V

The Age of Romanticism

Robert Burns
(1759~1796)

About the Author

Robert Burns (1759~1796), known as Scotland National Bard or the Ploughman Poet, was born into a poor tenant farmer's family in Ayreshire, Scotland. He is appreciated mainly for his songs written in the Scottish dialect on a variety of subjects. He wrote his own rural experiences as well as dealing with themes of love, friendship, patriotism, republicanism, class, poverty, inequalities, Scottish cultural identity and sexuality. As an 18th century poet, Burns wrote in most of the typical 18th century forms: satire, verse epistle and mock-heroic verse. Besides making original compositions, Burns was also devoted to collecting folk songs from across Scotland, editing, revising or adapting them. His often quoted poems and songs include "A Red, Red Rose" "A Man's A Man for A'That" "To a Louse" "To a Mouse" "Auld Lang Syne", and "Scots, Wha Hae". Unfortunately, he was carried off by falling health at the age of 37. Yet in that short time he has attained an almost mythical stature not only in his native land but around the world.

★ A Red, Red Rose

About the poem

It is one of Robert Burns's most famous love poems. The speaker compares his love to a blooming rose and a sweet melody, proclaims that his love will last forever. He then bids her farewell for a short time, but assures his beloved that he will love her even if the long distance separates them.

O my Luve's[1] like a red, red rose,
That's newly sprung in June;
O my Luve's like the melodie[2]
That's sweetly play'd in tune.

As fair art thou, my bonnie lass[3],
So deep in luve am I;
And I will luve thee still, my dear,
Till a'[4] the seas gang[5] dry.

Till a' the seas gang dry, my dear,
And the rocks melt wi' the sun:
I will luve thee still, my dear,
While the sands o' life shall run.

And fare thee weel[6], my only Luve!
And fare thee weel, a while!
And I will come again, my Luve,
Tho' it were ten thousand mile!

Notes

1. Luve: love.
2. melodie: melody.
3. bonnie lass: beautiful girl.

4. a': a shortened form of all.
5. gang: go.
6. fare thee weel: farewell for now, farewell for the time being.

Questions for Understanding

1. What are the figures of speech used in "A Red, Red Rose"? How do they help to emphasize the intense love between the lovers?
2. What are the natural images in this poem? What does nature have to do with love?
3. What does it really mean to compare love to a rose? To a "melodie"?
4. Why do you think the poem's first line—"my Luve is like a red, red rose"—has remained popular for so long?
5. What elements in this poem reflect Burn's own endless love for Scottish heritage of folk songs and ballads?

Aspects of Appreciation

The poem pieces together the traditional subject of love and the more complex implications of time as shown by the image of "the sands o' life". On the one hand, the poem elaborates a kind of love that will transcend time and outlast even the destruction of the earth—the evaporation of the seas and the melting of the rocks; on the other hand, however, it also reminds the reader of the fact that a "red, red rose"—the perfect symbol of love—is itself an object of an hour, "newly sprung" only "in June" and afterward subject to the decay of time.

★ John Anderson, My Jo[1]

About the Poem

This was originally a ballad, which Robert Burns turned into a charming verse about the enduring love of an old married couple. It has always been admired as one of Burns' most touching lyrics. Structurally well balanced, the poem contains pairs of contrasts between youth and old age, past and present, death and eternity. Meanwhile, it carries a spirit of romanticism, which would prevail as the main trend of English literature in the early 19th century.

John Anderson, my jo, John,
When we were first acquent[2];
Your locks were like the raven,
Your bonie[3] brow was brent[4];
But now your brow is beld[5], John,
Your locks are like the snaw[6];
But blessings on your frosty pow[7],
John Anderson, my jo.

John Anderson, my jo, John,
We clamb[8] the hill thegither[9];
And mony a cantie[10] day, John,
We've had wi' ane anither:
Now we maun[11] totter down, John,
And hand in hand we'll go,
And sleep thegither at the foot,
John Anderson, my jo.

Notes

1. jo: darling.
2. acquent: acquainted.
3. bonie: pretty, beautiful.
4. brent: smooth.
5. beld: bald.
6. snaw: snow.
7. pow: crown of your head.
8. clamb: climb.
9. thegither: together.
10. cantie: happy, cheerful.
11. maun: must.

Questions for Understanding

1. What are the contrasting words, phrases or images in "John Anderson, My Jo"? Why are they so effective in conveying the message of continuing love?

2. What does the hill in "John Anderson, My Jo" stands for? How do you explain the meaning of the old couple's climbing up and tottering down the hill?
3. What kind of a person do you think the speaker is in "John Anderson, My Jo"?
4. What is Robert Burns's philosophy of life reflected in this poem?

Aspects of Appreciation

1. Burns's love poems

Many of Burns's love poems and songs touchingly express human experience of love in all its phases: the sexual love of "The Fornicator"; the more mature love of "A Red, Red Rose"; and the happiness of a couple grown old together in "John Anderson, My Jo". Whatever the subject, a profound celebration of love and an irrepressible joy in living can be found in them. For example, in "John Anderson, My Jo", we have noticed an immediate sense of intimacy and tenderness created by the direct address of the opening lines and by the sound of the repeated [dʒ] consonant and the almost whispered "John" throughout this poem.

2. Poetic bilingualism

Many of Burns's poems are written in the Scottish dialect, which is made acceptable in elevated, serious poetry. The words of Scottish dialect in this poem such as "jo" "bonie" "thegither" "cantie" "maun", bring a stimulating and much-needed freshness and color, which along with Burns's observation and humor, have contributed to his enduring fame. More significantly, Burns judiciously mingled both English and Scottish here and secured a much wider audience than simply Scottish people.

★ My Heart's in the Highlands[1]

About the Poem

This poem was written after Robert Burns made a tour to the Scottish Highlands. The poet is greatly enchanted with its splendid scenery. The rugged wild terrain, snow-covered mountains, green valleys, gushing floods and local people's deer-chasing are all captured forever in this poem. The refrain of "My heart's in the Highlands" deepens the poet's strong attachment to the place and his reluctant departure.

Farewell to the Highlands, farewell to the North,
The birth-place of Valour[2], the country of Worth;
Wherever I wander, wherever I rove[3],
The hills of the Highlands for ever I love.

My heart's in the Highlands, my heart is not here;
My heart's in the Highlands a-chasing[4] the deer;
A-chasing the wild-deer, and following the roe[5],
My heart's in the Highlands wherever I go.

Farewell to the mountains high covered with snow;
Farewell to the straths[6] and green valleys below;
Farewell to the forests and wild-hanging woods[7];
Farewell to the torrents and loud-pouring floods.

My heart's in the Highlands, my heart is not here;
My heart's in the Highlands a-chasing the deer;
A-chasing the wild-deer, and following the roe,
My heart's in the Highlands wherever I go.

Notes

1. highlands: the mountainous Northern part of Scotland.
2. valour: great bravery.
3. rove: roam, wander.
4. a-chasing: chasing (a-prefix used before verbal), going after.
5. roe: also roe deer, a type of small deer.
6. strath: a flat, wide river valley.
7. wild-hanging woods: woods covering steep mountain slopes or reaching the edge of precipices.

Questions for Understanding

1. What are the poetic features of "My heart's in the Highlands"?
2. How does Burns use Scottish dialect to express his feelings in this poem?
3. The last four lines of this poem are the exact repetition of the very first four lines. How do you understand this?

4. How do you understand the human activity of chasing deer against the natural surroundings in "My heart's in the Highlands"?

Aspects of Appreciation

1. Use of refrain

Refrain is a repeated part of a poem, particularly when it comes either at the end of a stanza or between two stanzas. The use of the refrain in "My Heart's in the Highlands" helps a lot in enhancing their emotional appeal and songlike quality. It also helps to leave a deep impression on readers' mind, which will be easy for readers to remember.

2. Rural theme

Numerous are Burns' songs woven against the background of the Scottish rural countryside with such vividness and simplicity that they appeal directly to the reader's heart. Noticeably, his depiction of rural Scottish life and manners is a gesture of a radical departure from the stately and decorous subjects typical of eighteenth-century poetry.

Suggested Further Reading

Robert Burns's poems: "Auld Lang Syne" "To a Mouse" and "A Man's a Man for a'that".

Topics for Further Study

1. How can Robert Burns's poems be divided in terms of theme?
2. Both Robert Burns's sentimental poem "To a Mouse" and American poet Robert Frost's "The Exposed Nest" describe similar situations: men's inadvertent disturbance of the natural beings. Can you make a comparison between them?
3. The title of Burns's poem "A Man's a Man for a'that" has been featured on the Special Stamps issued by British Royal Mail in 2009 at the 250th anniversary of Burns's birth. What do you think has guaranteed the poem's everlasting charm?

Knowledge of Literature

Ballad

Ballads are a part of oral tradition. They celebrate a desirable attribute, tell a story, or herald a significant event and they often contain a refrain. The metrical and rhyming structure of ballads can take many forms. Usually it is arranged into four line stanzas that alternate between iambic tetrameter and iambic trimeter. The rhyme scheme is usually *abab* or *abcb*.

William Blake
(1757~1827)

About the Author

William Blake(1757~1827) is now regarded as a very original poet and artist in the Romantic Age with his prophetic poetry and visual art. He was influenced by the ideals of the French and American revolutions and kept an active interest in social and political events. Retaining the spirit of freedom for all his life, he was against oppressions of any type. Besides, from a young age, Blake claimed to have seen visions of God and angels.

As a poet, Blake is regarded as visionary, highly individual, creative, and much ahead of his time. He produced a diverse and rich corpus of poetry characterized by serious and somber themes, philosophical and political implications, rich imagery of religious and mythological connotations, symbolism, mysticism, lyrical beauty, and use of simple language.

Blake's most important poetic works are *Songs of Innocence* (1789) and *Songs of Experience* (1794), which form sharp contrast to each other, "showing the Two Contrary States of the Human Soul". The other works of his include *Poetical Sketches* (1783), *The Marriage of Heaven and Hell* (1790), *The Book of Thel* (1795), and *The Book of Los* (1795).

With a poetry more congenial to the 20th century, Blake looks more like a modern poet than a poet of his time and he exerted an enormous influence on the poets of later generations such as Walt Whitman, Allen Ginsberg and other beat poets of the 1950s as well as quite a few other modern writers.

★ The Tyger[1]

About the Poem

"The Tyger", from *Songs of Experience*, is one of Blake's best-known and most analyzed poems and it is usually considered as a companion piece to his "The Lamb" from *Songs of Innocence*. The poem is highly symbolic, and to some extent mystical, possible of different

V. The Age of Romanticism

interpretations. Therefore it has been the rich source of interpretations and literary criticism not long after its publication.

>Tyger! Tyger! burning bright
>In the forests of the night,
>What immortal hand or eye
>Could frame thy fearful symmetry?
>
>In what distant deeps[2] or skies
>Burnt the fire of thine eyes?
>On what wings dare he aspire[3]?
>What the hand dare sieze the fire[4]?
>
>And what shoulder, and what art,
>Could twist the sinews of thy heart?
>And when thy heart began to beat,
>What dread[5] hand? & what dread feet?
>
>What the hammer? what the chain?
>In what furnace was thy brain[6]?
>What the anvil? what dread grasp
>Dare its deadly terrors clasp?
>
>When the stars threw down their spears,
>And watered heaven with their tears,
>Did he smile his work to see?
>Did he who made the Lamb make thee?
>
>Tyger! Tyger! burning bright
>In the forests of the night,
>What immortal hand or eye
>Dare frame thy fearful symmetry?

※ ※

Notes

1. tyger: tiger. Blake's spelling "tyger" was common but slightly archaic at

the time. Thus, his choice of "tyger" might create an effect of exotic or alien quality of the animal.
2. deeps: depths of seas or of oceans.
3. aspire(archaic): rise or fly up.
4. Note the possible allusion to Prometheus in Greek Methology.
5. dread: dreadful.
6. In what furnace was thy brain: In what furnace was thy brain made.

Questions for Understanding

1. What does the phrase "burning bright" describe?
2. How do you understand "dread hand" and "dread feet"?
3. How do you understand "fearful symmetry"? What are the two aspects of the tiger involved in the poem?
4. What is the maker of the tiger compared to? Is this comparison appropriate?
5. What might be the allusions involved in the poem?
6. What might the tiger symbolize? Is the tiger good or evil or both?
7. Why does evil exist in a universe created and ruled by a benevolent God?
8. Is the poem more about the creator of the tiger or about the tiger itself? Or is this about man's understanding of the mystery of world?

Aspects of Appreciation

1. Meter

The poem is in trochaic tetrameter with catalexis(诗行最后音步音节缺失) at the end of each line. A tetrameter line usually consists of eight syllables. A trochaic foot is a unit of meter composed of a pair of syllables—a stressed syllable followed by an unstressed syllable. Catalexis is the absence of a syllable in the final foot in a line. In Blake's poem, an unstressed syllable is absent in the last trochaic foot of each line. Thus, every line has seven syllables, not the conventional eight.

```
        1         2          3         4
   TIger, | TIger, | BURN ing | BRIGHT
        1         2          3         4
   IN the | FOR ests | OF the | NIGHT
```

This irregularity in the trochaic pattern may strengthen the rhythm, allowing each line to end with an accented syllable that seems to mimic the beat of the maker's hammer on the anvil, creating the "anvil music".

2. Allusion

An allusion is a reference to a person, place, literary work, historical event, or anything else that lies outside the immediate context of a given literary work. This poem may have allusion to Daedalus in Greek Mythology who made wings with feathers and wax to fly away from King Minos's labyrinth in Crete with his son Icarus. But Icarus flew too high so that the heat of the sun melted the wax and he fell into the sea and got drowned. Besides, the poem may also allude to Prometheus story in Greek Mythology.

3. Symbols

The tiger in the poem can be a very complex symbol representing beauty as well as terror and strength, good as well as evil. It may also be a kind of mysterious and destructive force. Among other possibilities, distant deeps might mean Hell and skies may embody Heaven.

4. Other rhetorical devices

Alliteration: /b/(burning bright); /d/(distant deeps); /f/(frame ... fearful).

Consonance: /s/(distant deeps or skies).

Assonance: /ai/(Tyger! Tyger! burning bright).

Metaphor: Comparison of the tiger and his eyes to fire.

Anaphora(首语重复): Repetition of what is at the beginning of sentences or lines. (What dread hand and what dread feet? What the hammer? What the chain?)

★ The Sick Rose

About the Poem

The first publication of "The Sick Rose" was in 1794 when it was included in his collection *Songs of Experience*. The image of the rose in the poem is striking in that it goes quite beyond the conventional symbolic meaning in western literature and it is possible of quite a few different interpretations. The poem forms a contrast to "The Blossom" in the *Songs of Innocence*, perverting its images of spring-like growth into those of decay and disease.

O Rose, thou art sick!
The invisible worm

That flies in the night,
In the howling storm,

Has found out thy bed
Of crimson joy
And his dark secret love
Does thy life destroy.

Questions for Understanding

1. Which words let you know that neither the flower nor the worm is to be taken literally?
2. What is the conventional symbolic significance of a rose? How does this one differ?
3. What do worms usually symbolize? What added characteristics is the worm here given?
4. What might be allegorical implications of the poem?

Aspects of Appreciation

Possible interpretations of the poem: virginity destroyed by a wicked man, love destroyed by selfishness or jealousy, innocence destroyed by experience, mortal beauty destroyed by time, imagination destroyed by reason, among other things.

Suggested Further Reading

Some other poems by William Blake: "The Lamb" "London" "The Chimney's Sweepers" "The Blossom" "Ah Sun-Flower" and "A Poison Tree".

Topics for Further Study

1. Why is it significant that the tiger was created in "the forest of the night" rather than in the day? Why is it important that the worm flies in the night?
2. Possible politically allegorical implications of Blake's poems.
3. Understand "The Tyger" in comparison with "The Lamb" and "The Sick Rose" with "The Blosom", and note how the poems throw light upon the understanding of each other.
4. How do the poems in *Songs of Experience* differ from those in *Songs of*

Innocence? Blake's idea of contraries (oppositions) as reflected in his poems.
5. What might be the significance of Blake's poems as a reaction against the restraints and limitations of Neo-classicism and the Age of Reason?

Knowledge of Literature

1. Sound devices

Sound devices are rhetorical devices by use of sounds to create or strengthen poetic effect. Sound devices can include alliteration(头韵：use of identical initial consonant sounds in words in proximity), consonance(和声：use of identical consonant sounds in words in proximity), assonance(半韵：use of identical vowel sounds in words in proximity); and metrical devices include meter, end rhyme and internal rhyme etc.. The effect of sound devices depends upon the meaning or idea of the poem, that is, the sounds should be appropriate to, or in harmony with, the main idea or the general meaning of the poem. As Alexander Pope states, "The Sound must seem an echo to the Sense": "Soft is the strain when Zephyr gently blows", but "The hoarse, rough Verse should like the Torrent roar". The effective use of sound devices can heighten musicality, create aural imagery, and strengthen the meaning.

2. Conventional vs personal symbols

Symbols can be divided into conventional symbols and personal symbols. Conventional symbols have a shared traditional meaning for a particular culture, nation, or group. Personal symbols, on the other hand, rather than being commonly recognized, are unique to a given poem or poet. For instance, in western culture a rose may generally be understood as a symbol of love, beauty or a beautiful woman, so it is a conventional symbol. But in Blake's "The Sick Rose", the rose may have more connotations than are generally recognized, therefore it is Blake's personal symbol. When a conventional symbol acquires a more universally and permanently established meaning in a culture, it becomes an archetypal symbol, such as symbols of birth, life, death and rebirth.

William Wordsworth
(1770~1850)

About the Author

One of the Lake Poets and of the first generation of Romantic poets (the other two being S. T. Coleridge and Robert Southey), William Wordsworth (1770~1850), together with Coleridge, published *Lyrical Ballads* in 1798, which marked the break with Neoclassicism in literature and the beginning of English Romantic Movement. In his "Preface to *Lyrical Ballads*" of 1800 edition, called the "manifesto" of English Romantic criticism, Wordsworth gives his principles of poetry, among which are: (1) poetry should use language really used by men; (2) all good poetry is the spontaneous overflow of powerful feelings: it takes its origin from emotion recollected in tranquility; (3) the principal object of poetry is to choose incidents and situations from common life. Thus he is regarded as the chief spokesman of Romantic poetry.

Wordsworth was a practitioner of his own poetic principles. He uses simple language to describe the common incidents of life and simple-natured people. His poetry is marked by vivid images, beauty in simplicity (unadorned beauty) and the sincere feelings of his and the lyrical beauty of his poems always have strong appeal. Wordsworth had a strong love of nature. He emphasized the importance of the harmony between man and nature, and he believed that nature not only has a positive influence upon man's morality, spiritual well-being, in nature there is also a spirit or an audience waiting to hear man speak. So, a constant theme of his poetry is the growth of the human spirit in the natural environment. And in his descriptions of nature, there is also expression of moods and philosophical speculation.

Wordsworth's famous works include "Lines Composed a Few Miles Above Tintern Abbey" (1798), "We Are Seven" (1798), *The Prelude* (1850), "Lucy Poems" (1799), "To the Cuckoo" (1802), "My Heart Leaps Up" (1802), "Composed upon Westminster Bridge" (1802), "I Wandered Lonely as a Cloud" (1804), "The Solitary Reaper" (1805), "The World Is Too Much with Us" (1806) and "Ode: Intimations of Immortality" (1807).

★ She Dwelt among the Untrodden Ways

About the Poem

As the best known of Wordsworth's famous "Lucy" series of five poems, "She Dwelt among the Untrodden Ways" was written in 1798 and then printed in *Lyrical Ballads* in 1800 both as a meditation on his own feelings of loneliness, and as an ode to the beauty and dignity of a woman who lived unnoticed by all except by the poet himself. Many believe that Lucy in the poem was based upon a real woman, but as to whom she really was there are different opinions.

> She dwelt among the untrodden ways
> Beside the springs of Dove[1],
> A Maid whom there were none to praise
> And very few to love:
>
> A violet by a mossy stone
> Half hidden from the eye!
> Fair as a star, when only one
> Is shining in the sky.
>
> She lived unknown, and few could know
> When Lucy ceased to be;
> But she is in her grave, and, oh,
> The difference to me!

Notes

1. Dove: the name of several rivers in England.

Questions for Understanding

1. How do you understand the word "dwelt" and how effectively is it used?
2. What qualities are attributed to the girl by the "violet by a mosy stone" and the star at night?

3. How do you understand "ceased to be"? What effect is achieved by this expression?
4. What is the effect of the contrast between "none" and "very few" in the first stanza and "few" and "me" in the last?
5. What is the importance of the imagery in the poem?
6. What emotional impact is conveyed by the last line? Is there anything in the poem that has prepared you for the end of the poem or does it come as a surprise?

Aspects of Appreciation

1. The poem is in ballad stanza, four lines of iambic tetrameter in the first and third lines and iambic trimeter in the second and fourth lines, rhyming *abab* or *abcb* (in this poem).
2. The poem can be seen as an example of Wordsworth's practice of his own poetic principles: common incidents of life, common people, strong feelings and simple language are all there in the poem, which are what the poet advocated.
3. The effect of the poem mainly comes from several incongruities or contrasts. For instance, the incongruities between the girl's obscurity and her noble qualities; between the speaker's (or the poet's) strong feeling for her on the one hand, and her ignorance of it and the speaker's apparent unconcerned attitude to her on the other; between the poet's deliberate ambiguity, and thus the reader's assumption that she might be alive, and the final revelation that she was dead.
4. One of the most striking incongruities comes from the use of overstatement and understatement (低调陈述) in the same context. Overstatement (or hyperbole) is an exaggeration of emotion or content whereas understatement is the use of language that says less than the situation seems to call for. The examples of overstatement are "untrodden" "few could know" "none to praise"; examples of understatement are "ceased to be" (meaning "died") and "difference to me" (meaning "I felt heart-broken"). Both overstatement and understatement are forms of verbal irony, a mode of speech or writing in which the usual or expected meanings of words are in some way modified or reversed.
5. The poet is deliberately being ambiguous about Lucy's state of mortality by using the word "dwelt" (meaning "lived" or "was buried") so as to

keep the reader in suspense. When it is finally revealed that Lucy was dead, it comes as a surprise to the reader, achieving great emotional impact and poetic effect.

★ My Heart Leaps Up When I Behold

About the Poem

Written on March 26, 1802 and published in 1807 as an epigraph to "Ode: Intimations of Immortality", the poem "My Heart Leaps Up When I Behold" addresses the same theme of nature found in many other poems of Wordsworth's and expresses the speaker's or the poet's affinity to nature.

> My heart leaps up when I behold
> A rainbow in the sky:
> So was it when my life began;
> So is it now I am a man;
>
> So be it when I shall grow old,
> Or let me die!
> The Child is father of the Man;
> And I could wish my days to be
> Bound each to each by natural piety[1].

Notes

1. natural piety: piety for nature.

Questions for Understanding

1. How do you understand "My heart leaps up"?
2. How do you understand "The Child is father of the Man"?
3. In what way is a child related to nature? And to God?
4. What does the poet want to express in this poem?
5. What may "natural piety" mean? Can the word "natural" be understood in more than one way?

Aspects of Appreciation

1. The poem is about the poet's love for nature, relationship between child and man, child and nature. The following famous quotations can throw some light upon the understanding of the famous paradox in the poem "The Child is father of the Man", and for that matter, the understanding of the whole poem.

    (1) The childhood shews the man, as morning shews the day. (John Milton: *Paradise Regained*, iv. 220)

    (2) To carry on the feelings of childhood into the powers of manhood; to combine the child's sense of wonder and novelty with the appearances which every day perhaps for forty years had rendered familiar; ... this is the character and privilege of genius, ... (S. T. Coleridge: *Biographia Literaria*, iv.)

2. The rainbow can be an allusion to Genesis 9:8-17, in which the rainbow is God's promise to Noah that the earth and everything living on it would never again be destroyed by a flood. So the rainbow may signify the bond between man and God, giving the word "piety" religious connotation.

★ I Wandered Lonely as a Cloud

About the Poem

Written in 1804, first published in 1807, "I Wandered Lonely as a Cloud"(also commonly known as "Daffodils") is one of Wordsworth's most famous and often anthologised poems. The poem was inspired by an event in which Wordsworth and his sister, Dorothy, came across a "long belt" of daffodils in their walk around Glencoyne Bay, Ullsswater in the Lake District. The event was recorded on the same day in Dorothy's journal of Thursday, 15 April, 1802, which can throw much light upon the poem: "When we were in the woods beyond Gowbarrow Park, we saw a few daffodils close to the water side... But as we went along there were more, and yet more; and at last, under the boughs of the trees, we saw that there was a long belt of them along the shore, about the breadth of a country turnpike road. I never saw so beautiful daffodils. They grew among the mossy stones about and above them; some rested their heads upon these stones, as on a pillow for weariness;

V. The Age of Romanticism

and the rest tossed and reeled and danced, and seemed as if they verily laughed with the wind that blew upon them over the lake. They looked so gay ever dancing ever changing."

    I wandered lonely as a cloud
    That floats on high[1] o'er vales and hills,
    When all at once I saw a crowd,
    A host, of[2] golden daffodils;
    Beside the lake, beneath the trees,
    Fluttering and dancing in the breeze.

    Continuous[3] as the stars that shine
    And twinkle on the milky way,
    They stretched in never-ending line
    Along the margin of a bay:
    Ten thousand saw I at a glance,
    Tossing their heads in sprightly[4] dance.

    The waves beside them danced; but they
    Out-did[5] the sparkling waves in glee:
    A poet could not but be gay,
    In such a jocund[6] company:
    I gazed—and gazed—but little thought
    What wealth the show to me had brought:

    For oft, when on my couch I lie
    In vacant[7] or in pensive[8] mood,
    They flash upon that inward eye[9]
    Which is the bliss of solitude;
    And then my heart with pleasure fills,
    And dances with the daffodils.

Notes

1. on high: in the sky.
2. a crowd, a host of: a large number of.

3. continuous: continuously.
4. sprightly: lively.
5. out-did: did better than.
6. jocund: joyous, high-spirited.
7. vacant: empty, unthinking.
8. pensive: thinking deeply.
9. inward eye: mind.

Questions for Understanding

1. In what way is the simile in the title (also in the first line) used appropriately and effectively in view of the features of Romanticism?
2. How many words denoting happiness or joy are used and what are they?
3. What tenses are used and what is the significance of the change of tenses?
4. What are shown of the general qualities of Romanticism in the poem?
5. What are shown of special qualities of Wordsworth's poetry and his principles of poetry writing?
6. What is the relation between the poet and nature? What effect can nature have on the mind?

Aspects of Appreciation

1. The poem is in iambic tetrameter, rhyming *ababcc*.
2. The poem has quite a few characteristics of Romantic poetry: sense of loneliness and mood of melancholy, love of and closeness to nature which provides spiritual food for the mind.
3. The poem is a full realization of the poet's principles for poetry. Besides the simplicity of language, common incidents of life and spontaneous overflow of powerful feelings, what is most significant is that this emotion is recollected in tranquility. The present tense used in the last stanza forms a sharp contrast to the past tense used in the previous three stanzas, showing that the poet (speaker) is looking back from the present upon the event in the past with emotion.

Suggested Further Reading

William Wordsworth's other poems "Composed upon Westminster Bridge" "We Are Seven" "Lines Composed a Few Miles above Tintern Abbey" "London" and his "Preface to *Lyrical Ballads*" and more of Lucy poems.

Topics for Further Study

1. To some extent, the poem "I Wandered Lonely as a Cloud" is the short version of the long poem "Tintern Abbey" because it contains the main idea and some major elements of the longer poem. Try to find out the similarities and differences of the two poems.
2. One critic says that a sense of melancholy underlies Wordsworth's optimism and gives his best poetry its balance and subdued dignity. Try to find out if it is true of his poems we have discussed.
3. Comment on the similarities and differences between Wordsworth's poems and the poems of Coleridge.

Knowledge of Literature

1. Ambiguity(含混)

Ambiguity literally means "multiple meanings" and it can be a flaw in daily use of language, because it results in failure of clear expression and causes misunderstanding, as in the case of "We saw her play last night". However, in literature ambiguity is a required merit rather than a fault of imprecision, because it can be a source of poetic richness. In New Criticism, ambiguity becomes a central concept in the interpretation of poetry after William Empson, in his famous *Seven Types of Ambiguity* (1930), uses it as a key criterion to analyze and evaluate English poems. As a required quality of poetry, in New Critical terminology, ambiguity can bear resemblance to other concepts such as tension, paradox and irony.

2. Irony(反讽) as a quality of poetry

Traditionally irony can be divided into verbal irony in which what is said is contrary to what is meant, dramatic irony in which the audience knows more about a character's situation than the character does, and structural irony which involves the use of a naive hero or an unreliable narrator whose view of the world differs considerably from the knowledge of the author and the reader.

In New Critical terminology, irony has come to mean a quality in poetry that determines the value of a literary work. According to New Criticism, a poem's meaning is determined and created by the tension between the denotative meaning of the words and their connotations, which are, in turn, determined by the context of that poem. Irony, then, is "an equilibrium of opposing attitudes and evaluations", which ultimately determine the poem's meaning. In New Criticism, irony, tension, paradox and ambiguity are closely related and sometimes they are used as near synonyms. In the poem "She Dwelt among the Untrodden Ways" the incongruities and the use of overstatement and understatement are examples of irony as a quality of poetry.

Samuel Taylor Coleridge
(1772～1834)

About the Author

Samuel Taylor Coleridge(1772～1834), one of the Lake Poets and a literary critic, together with Wordsworth started the Romantic Movement in England with their *Lyrical Ballads*. Throughout his adult life, Coleridge suffered from bouts of anxiety and depression and in order to treat these episodes he became an addict to opium.

Coleridge is probably best known for his poems "The Rime of the Ancient Mariner"(1798), "Kubla Khan"(1816) and "Christabel"(1797～1800), and such conversation poems as "Frost at Midnight"(1798), "Fears in Solitude"(1798), "The Nightingale: A Conversation Poem"(1798) and "Dejection: An Ode"(1802). His poetic world is usually enchanting and dreamlike, full of mystery, fantasy and supernatural things. Mysticism, demonism, strong imagination and haunting music are distinctive features of his best poems. In many of his poems, he creates a strange and an exotic beauty by images. In some of his poems such as "The Ancient Mariner", "Christabel" and "Kubla Khan" there are elements of terror which are related to Gothic tradition in literature.

Coleridge is equally important as a critic mainly for his *Biographia Literaria* (1817), which contains the authors' lives, literary criticism, and a broad range of principles of literature ranging from Aristotle to Kant and Schelling, some original and insightful ideas about literature and literary criticism. He applied them to the poetry of his contemporaries such as William Wordsworth. Coleridge was one of the major influences, via Emerson, upon American Transcendentalism.

★ Kubla Khan

About the Poem

This poem was said to have been written in a dream when the poet had fallen into a nap at noon after taking some opium because of his pains. Coleridge claimed that he wrote several hundred lines in his dream, but his sleep was interrupted by a visitor and he forgot most of the poem and hence the fragment. In this poem the poet creates a world that is both wondrous and sinister by use of exotic images.

Kubla Khan[1]
OR, A VISION IN A DREAM.
A FRAGMENT.

In Xanadu[2] did Kubla Khan
A stately pleasure-dome[3] decree[4]:
Where Alph[5], the sacred river, ran
Through caverns measureless to man[6]
Down to a sunless sea.
So twice five miles[7] of fertile ground
With walls and towers were girdled round:
And there were gardens bright with sinuous rills[8],
Where blossomed many an incense-bearing tree;
And here were forests ancient as the hills,
Enfolding sunny spots of greenery.

But oh! that deep romantic chasm[9] which slanted
Down the green hill athwart[10] a cedarn[11] cover!
A savage place! As holy and enchanted
As e'er beneath a waning moon was haunted
By woman wailing for her demon-lover!
And from this chasm, with ceaseless turmoil seething,
As if this earth in fast thick pants[12] were breathing,
A mighty fountain momently[13] was forced:
Amid whose swift half-intermitted[14] burst
Huge fragments vaulted like rebounding hail,

Or chaffy grain beneath the thresher's flail:
And 'mid[15] these dancing rocks at once and ever
It flung up momently the sacred river.
Five miles meandering with a mazy motion
Through wood and dale the sacred river ran,
Then reached the caverns measureless to man,
And sank in tumult to a lifeless ocean:
And 'mid this tumult Kubla heard from far
Ancestral voices prophesying war!

The shadow[16] of the dome of pleasure
Floated midway on the waves;
Where was heard the mingled measure[17]
From the fountain and the caves.
It was a miracle of rare device,
A sunny pleasure-dome with caves of ice!

A damsel with a dulcimer[18]
In a vision once I saw:
It was an Abyssinian[19] maid,
And on her dulcimer she played,
Singing of Mount Abora[20].
Could I revive within me
Her symphony and song,
To such a deep delight 'twould win me[21],

That with music loud and long,
I would build that dome in air,
That sunny dome! those caves of ice!
And all who heard should see them there,
And all should cry, Beware! Beware!
His flashing eyes, his floating hair[22]!
Weave a circle round him thrice[23],
And close your eyes with holy dread,
For he on honey-dew hath fed,
And drunk the milk of Paradise.

V. The Age of Romanticism

Notes

1. Kubla Khan: Kubla(忽必烈, 1215?~1294), emperor of the Yuan Dynasty; Khan(汗), the title of a Mongolian monarch.
2. Xanadu: capital of the Yuan Dynasty, which might be 上都(what is Inner Mogolia today) or 大都(what is Beijing today).
3. pleasure-dome: great palace for entertainment.
4. decree: give order or command to build.
5. Alph: an imaginary river created by the poet.
6. measureless to man: too deep to be measured by man.
7. twice five miles: five miles both in length and in width.
8. sinuous rills: winding brooks.
9. chasm: deep opening or crack.
10. athwart: across.
11. cedarn: (poetic) of cedar(雪松的).
12. thick pants: gasping breaths in quick succession.
13. momently: every moment.
14. half-intermitted: half-interrupted.
15. 'mid: amid.
16. shadow: reflection.
17. mingled measure: harmonious music.
18. dulcimer: an ancient stringed musical instrument.
19. Abyssinian: of Abyssinia, now called Ethiopia.
20. Mount Abora: having vague allusion to Mount Amara in Milton's *Paradise Lost*.
21. To such a deep delight 'twould win me: it would bring me such a deep delight.
22. This line shows the poet as if inspired by the god of art like a person possessed by evil spirit.
23. This line shows a superstitious belief that a person possessed should be separated from other people by circling three times with his eye closed.

Questions for Understanding

1. How do you understand the two descriptive words "romantic"(Line 12) and "savage"(Line 14)?
2. What aspects of nature and human world are described in the poem?
3. What words or images contribute to the exotic and fantastic atmosphere

of the poem?
4. What elements contribute to the supernatural atmosphere of the poem?
5. What contribute(s) to the dreamy feature of the poem?
6. What are the opposing elements in the poem and what may be the significance of these opposing elements?

Aspects of Appreciation

1. Much of the effect of the poem lies in the exotic scene of beauty with a dreamy and supernatural atmosphere created by images and verbal music. The poem is written in variable iambic meter: iambic tetrameter and iambic pentameter.
2. Critics have suggested that the pleasure-dome may symbolize poetry and the sacred river, the flow of inspiration or instinctual life. As to other symbols such as ancestral voices and caves of ice, there seems less agreement, and students may be invited to venture their guesses.
3. The world of "Kubla Khan" is a world of oppositions and harmony between two opposites: cold and warm, dark and bright, human and non-human. It not only reveals the poet's view of the world, but also shows his belief in the power of imagination that can reconcile the opposites into an artistic unity.
4. It seems that Coleridge believed that the poet is inspired or possessed when he writes poems. The following quotation from Plato can throw light upon the understanding of the last part of "Kubla Khan":

> For all good poets, epic as well as lyric, compose their beautiful poems not by art, but because they are inspired and possessed. And as the Corybantian[女神西布莉随从（祭司）的] revellers when they dance are not in their right mind, so the lyric poets are not in their right mind when they are composing their beautiful strain. But when falling under the power of music and metre they are inspired and possessed; like Bacchic(酒神的) maidens who draw milk and honey from the rivers when they are under the influence of Dionysus(酒神) but not when they are in their right mind. (Plato: *Ion*, 534 a-b)

Suggested Further Reading

Samuel Taylor Coleridge's long poem "The Rime of the Ancient Mariner" and his literary criticism *Biographia Literaria*.

Topics for Further Study

1. Some critics claim that "Kubla Khan" is about the pleasures of art and the sinister forces that threaten it. Examine the evidence in the poem that would support this statement.
2. Robert Graves maintains that Coleridge is the finest poet in English in rendering the state of "entrancement". What makes the imaginative force of "Kubla Khan" so intense? How does Coleridge conceive the role of imagination in the poem?
3. Coleridge says in his *Biographia Literaria* that the supernatural in his poems get their "human interest and semblance of truth" by transference "from our inward nature". Try to provide psychological or psychoanalytical interpretations to the supernatural elements or elements of terror in "Kubla Khan" and/or "The Ancient Mariner".
4. Compare features of Coleridge's poems and those of Wordsworth's.
5. Compare "Kubla Khan" with Li Po's "A Dream of Tianmu Mountain" ("梦游天姥吟留别"). In what aspects are they similar and different?

Knowledge of Literature

Imagination

In general, imagination means the ability to make an image in one's mind or the mind's capacity to generate images of objects, states, or actions that have not been felt or experienced by the senses. Imagination was usually synonymous with fancy, commonly opposed to the faculty of reason prior to Romanticism. Coleridge's famous distinction between fancy and imagination in his *Biographia Literaria* emphasized the imagination's vitally creative power of dissolving and uniting images into new forms and of reconciling opposed qualities into a new unity. As Coleridge himself says, "This power [imagination]… reveals itself in the balance or reconcilement of opposite or discordant qualities; of sameness, with difference; of the general with the concrete; the idea with the image; the individual with the representative; the scene of novelty and freshness with old and familiar objects; a more than usual state of emotion with more than usual order…" This freely creative and transforming power of the imagination was a central principle of Romanticism.

George Gordon Byron
(1788~1824)

About the Author

George Gordon Byron(1788~1824) was a leading poet in Romanticism. Among Byron's best-known works are the short poems "She Walks in Beauty" "When We Two Parted" and "So, We'll Go No More", in addition to the narrative poems *Childe Harold's Pilgrimage* and *Don Juan*. He is regarded as one of the greatest British poets and remains widely read and influential, both in the English-speaking world and beyond. As a romantic poet, his main contribution to the romantic period is the Byronic Hero. Byron's poetic style is loose, fluent, and vivid. Ease and raciness are always characteristic of him. He is the master of cutting wit and biting repartee, and superior in imagery and diction. His cynicism and pessimism, his excessive individualism, and his continual posing as the hero in his own verse mar the true poetic qualities of his works.

Byron reveals his sympathy with the suffering people and raises his voice against the reaction that sets up in Europe after the defeat of Napoleon. He was called "Satanic" by Robert Southey because of his revolutionary spirit and his rebellion against society. Byron served as a regional leader of Italy's revolutionary organization, the Carbonari, in its struggle against Austria. He later travelled to fight against the Ottoman Empire in the Greek War of Independence, for which Greeks revered him as a national hero. He died from a fever contracted while in Messolonghi in Greece.

★ She Walks in Beauty

About the Poem

In this poem, Byron described a beautiful, elegant lady who wore in black. Some critics have said that Byron wrote this poem the morning after he had met his beautiful cousin, Mrs. Robert John Wilmot, who wore a black mourning gown brightened with spangles. He fell passionately in love with his cousin and wrote this poem for her. Thus,

V. The Age of Romanticism

seeing her in her modest black dress (hence the allusions to darkness, with the light referring to her beauty), Byron was greatly impressed by his cousin's delicate beauty and splendid grace. Maybe this poem is not necessarily a love poem, but more of a celebration of the subject's beauty.

> She walks in beauty—like the night
> Of cloudless climes and starry skies,
> And all that's best of dark and bright
> Meet[1] in her aspect[2] and her eyes;
> Thus mellowed to the tender light
> Which heaven to gaudy day denies[3].
>
> One shade the more, one ray the less,
> Had half impaired the nameless grace[4]
> Which waves in every raven tress[5]
> Or softly lightens o'er[6] her face—
> Where thoughts serenely sweet express
> How pure, how dear their dwelling place[7].
>
> And on that cheek and o'er that brow
> So soft, so calm yet eloquent[8],
> The smiles that win[9], the tints that glow
> But tell of days in goodness spent
> A mind at peace with[10] all below,
> A heart whose love is innocent.

Notes

1. Meet: get together.
2. aspect: appearance.
3. heaven refuses to give tender light to gaudy day. The light of the gaudy day can not be compared with the tender light of that lady.
4. Add one more shade or reduce one more light, it will damage the undescribable grace.
5. raven tress: a lock of black hair.

6. o'er: over.
7. dwelling place: the heart of the lady.
8. The facial expression can express her inner world and tell everything in her heart.
9. win: attract.
10. at peace with: in harmony with.

Questions for Understanding

1. Can you describe the image of the lady in your own words?
2. How is this image created?
3. How does the poet appreciate this lady?
4. What does "their dwelling place" refer to in the last line of the second stanza?
5. What does the lady's winning smiles indicate? How do they appear to the poet?
6. Is this a love poem? Why or why not?

Aspects of Appreciation

Alliteration occurs frequently to enhance the appeal of the poem to the ear. The most obvious examples of this figure of speech include the following:

cloudless climes, starry skies (line 2); day denies (line 6); Had half (line 8); Which waves (line 9); serenely sweet (line 11); So soft (line 14)

Suggested Further Reading

Byron's works *Childe Harold's Pilgrimage*, *Don Juan*, *Oriental Tales*.

Topics for Further Study

1. The Oedipus Complex showed in Byron's literary works.
2. Byron's "private conversation"—study on his private letters.

Percy Bysshe Shelley
(1792~1822)

About the Author

Percy Bysshe Shelley (1792~1822) was the most progressive among the English Romanticists. At nineteen, he co-authored a pamphlet titled *The Necessity of Atheism* and was expelled from Oxford for doing so. In the same year, he eloped to Scotland with Harriet Westbrook, sixteen, and married her later. His first long serious work, *Queen Mab: A Philosophical Poem* showed the influence from British philosopher William Godwin's freethinking Socialist philosophy. Later he became enamored of Godwin's daughter, Mary, later famous as the author of *Frankenstein*. In 1816 after Harriet committed suicide they got officially married. Shelley lost custody of his two children by Harriet because of his atheism and his adherence to the notion of free love. Many of his greatest works were written in the year of 1819, including "Ode to the West Wind", *Prometheus Unbound*, "The Mask of Anarchy" and "England in 1819". His other famous works are *The Revolt of Islam* (1818), "Ozymandias" (1818), "To a Skylark" (1820) "Adonaïs: An Elegy on the Death of John Keats" (1821) and *A Defense of Poetry* (1821) which is his most important prose work. Shortly before his thirtieth birthday, Shelley was drowned in a storm while sailing in Italy. He became an idol of the next three or four generations of poets, and has been admired by many famous writers and philosophers.

★ Ode to the West Wind[1]

About the Poem

"Ode to the West Wind" was written by Percy Bysshe Shelley in 1819, while he was an English expatriate in Italy. It is a brilliant fuse of Dante's terza rima and the Shakespearean sonnet. Many critics have interpreted the poem as the poet's wish to get united with nature, due to his own sense of powerlessness in face of intellectual and moral imprisonment of the world. He was feeling depressed owing to suffering from the loss of his son while being detached from his home land. Other critics have regarded shelley as a political, religious, and literary radical, because Shelley had always wanted to influence society and effect change. This is one of the poems in which he considers the role and power of the poet-prophet figure and expresses his wish to be free like the wind and to spread message of reform and revolution. This poem is regarded as one of the greatest works of art in the Romantic period.

Canto I

    O wild West Wind, thou[2] breath of Autumn's being,
    Thou, from whose unseen presence the leaves dead
    Are driven, like ghosts from an enchanter fleeing[3],

    Yellow, and black, and pale, and hectic red[4],
    Pestilence-stricken multitudes[5]: O thou,
    Who chariotest[6] to their dark wintry bed

    The winged seeds, where they lie cold and low,
    Each like a corpse within its grave, until
    Thine azure sister of the Spring[7] shall blow

    Her clarion[8] o'er the dreaming earth, and fill
    (Driving sweet buds like flocks to feed in air)
    With living hues and odours plain and hill:

    Wild Spirit, which art moving everywhere;
    Destroyer and preserver[9]; hear, oh hear!

Canto II

    Thou on whose stream, 'mid the steep sky's commotion[10],
    Loose clouds like earth's decaying leaves are shed,
    Shook from the tangled boughs of Heaven and Ocean,

    Angels of rain and lightning: there are spread[11]
    On the blue surface of thine airy surge,
    Like the bright hair uplifted from the head

    Of some fierce Maenad[12], even from the dim verge
    Of the horizon to the zenith's height,
    The locks[13] of the approaching storm. Thou dirge

    Of the dying year, to which this closing night
    Will be the dome of a vast sepulchre[14],
    Vaulted[15] with all thy congregated might

Of vapours, from whose solid atmosphere
Black rain, and fire, and hail will burst: oh hear!

Canto III
Thou who didst waken from his summer dreams
The blue Mediterranean, where he lay,
Lull'd by the coil[16] of his crystalline streams,

Beside a pumice isle in Baiae's bay[17],
And saw in sleep old palaces and towers
Quivering within the wave's intenser day,

All overgrown with azure moss and flowers
So sweet, the sense faints picturing them! Thou
For whose path the Atlantic's level powers

Cleave themselves into chasms, while far below
The sea-blooms and the oozy woods which wear
The sapless foliage of the ocean, know

Thy voice, and suddenly grow gray with fear,
And tremble and despoil themselves[18]: oh hear!

Canto IV
If I were a dead leaf thou mightest bear;
If I were a swift cloud to fly with thee;
A wave to pant beneath thy power, and share

The impulse of thy strength, only less free
Than thou, O uncontrollable! If even
I were as in my boyhood, and could be

The comrade of thy wanderings over Heaven[19],
As then, when to outstrip thy skiey speed[20]
Scarce seem'd a vision; I would ne'er have striven

As thus with thee in prayer in my sore need.

Oh, lift me as a wave, a leaf, a cloud!
I fall upon the thorns of life! I bleed!

A heavy weight of hours has chain'd and bow'd
One too like thee: tameless, and swift, and proud.

Canto V

Make me thy lyre[21], even as the forest is:
What if my leaves are falling like its own!
The tumult[22] of thy mighty[23] harmonies

Will take from both a deep autumnal[24] tone,
Sweet though in sadness. Be thou, Spirit fierce,
My spirit! Be thou me, impetuous one[25]!

Drive[26] my dead thoughts over the universe
Like withered[27] leaves, to quicken a new birth;
And, by the incantation[28] of this verse,

Scatter, as from an unextinguished hearth[29]
Ashes and sparks, my words among mankind!
Be through my lips to unawakened earth[30]

The trumpet of a prophecy! O Wind,
If Winter comes, can Spring be far behind?[31]

Notes

1. According to Shelley's own note, "this poem was conceived and chiefly written in a wood that skirts the Arno, near Florence, and on a day when that tempestuous wind, whose temperature is at once mild and animating, was collecting the vapors which pour down the autumnal rains. They began, as I foresaw, at sunset with a violent tempest of hail and rain, attended by that magnificent thunder and lightning peculiar to the Cisalpine regions".
2. Thou: you, the poet is personifying the West Wind. This rhetorical

V. The Age of Romanticism

device is called apostrophe.

3. Are driven … fleeting: souls of dead compared to fallen leaves driven by the wind is a traditional epic simile found in Homer, Vigil, Dante and Milton. However, here it is the leaves that are driven by the West Wind like ghosts.
4. Yellow, and black, and pale, and hectic red: G. M. Matthews notes they are the four colors of man—Mongoloid, Negroid, Caucasian and American Indian. "Hectic red" also means the complexion of those suffering from tuberculosis.
5. Pestilence-stricken multitudes: the great number of the dead leaves which are driven by pestilence(瘟疫).
6. Chariotest: chariot.
7. Thine azure sister of the spring: thine: your. Azure is the color of the sky. Sister of the spring probably refers to a goddess that represents generative force but is not a formal mythological figure.
8. clarion: a musical instrument; piercing, war-like trumpet.
9. Destroyer and preserver: Ian Lancashire notes the West Wind is perhaps like the Hindu gods Siva the destroyer and Vishnu the preserver, known to Shelley from Edward Moor's *Hindu Pantheon*, and the works of Sir William Jones (1746~1794). The West Wind is considered as both "destroyer" and "preserver".
10. mid the steep sky's commotion: amid the steep sky's great turbulence.
11. there are spread … the locks of the approaching storm: the basic sentence structure of the above several lines is "there be" (there are … the locks …).
12. Maenad: a participant in the rites of Dionysus (or Bacchus in Latin name), Greek god of wine and fertility (酒神的女祭司).
13. locks: cirrus clouds that look like curls of hair(卷云).
14. sepulcher: tomb.
15. vaulted: formed into an arch. The sky is usually referred to as the vault of heaven in poetry.
16. coil: encircling cables, referring to the ripples of the clear streams.
17. a pumice isle in Baiae's bay: Shelley had once taken a boat trip from Naples west to the Bay of Baiae in 1818 and had been impressed by its beauty. Baiae is the site of ruined underwater ancient Roman villas, a favorite resort of Italy. Pumice: lava cooled into a porous, foam-like stone (浮石).

18. While far below…and despoil themselves: "The phenomenon alluded to at the conclusion of the third stanza is well known to naturalists. The vegetation at the bottom of the sea, of rivers, and of lakes, sympathizes with that of the land in the change of seasons, and is consequently influenced by the winds which announce it." (Shelley's note) Despoil themselves: despoil themselves of the foliage.
19. The comrade of thy wanderings over Heaven: a loyal friend of your wanderings in the sky.
20. outstrip thy skiey speed: to surpass your speed through the sky.
21. lyre: it refers to Aeolian harp, a common metaphor in Romantic poetry. The Aeolian harp is a wind harp that you only have to place in the breeze and nature will play its own tunes (风弦琴,伊奥利亚竖琴).
22. tumult: big sound.
23. mighty: powerful.
24. autumnal: like autumn.
25. Be thou, Spirit fierce,/My spirit! Be thou me, impetuous one: I wish you, the violent evolutionary spirit, become my spirit! I wish you, the impulsive spirit, become my spirit! Note the rhetorical device of repetition.
26. drive: scatter, spread.
27. withered: dead.
28. incantation: magical power.
29. unextinguished hearth: burning fire.
30. unawakened earth: sleeping world.
31. If Winter comes, can Spring be far behind: this line contains the prophecy in the form of a rhetorical question, which expresses Shelley's hope for the future.

Questions for Understanding

1. Why does the speaker say the West Wind is a preserver as well as a destroyer?
2. What transformations does the poet hope the West Wind will help him to have? Why?
3. Why does the speaker describe his own thoughts as "dead"?
4. In his "Defence of Poetry" Shelley states that poets are the unacknowledged legislators of the World. Do you think this sentence underlies the thought of "Ode to the West Wind"?

5. Can you find any mythological references in this poem? What do they imply?

Aspects of Appreciation

1. The rhyme scheme and meter of "Ode to the West Wind"

By titling the poem "Ode to the West Wind", Shelley intended to write a very serious poem, dealing with some dignified and solemn themes, since an ode is a long, serious, meditative poem with an elaborate structure, praising or glorifying an event or individual.

But this poem is far more than an ordinary ode: it contains five 14-lined cantos of iambic pentameter, that is, five sonnets, with each made up of four tercets (three-line stanza) and a closing couplet; the rhyme scheme of every canto is *aba bcb cdc ded ee*, an interlocking three-line rhyme scheme. This work is a brilliant fuse of Dante's terza rima and the Shakespearean sonnet.

William Baer observes on the tercets of terza rima, "These interlocking rhymes tend to pull the listener's attention forward in a continuous flow … Given this natural tendency to glide forward, terza rima is especially well-suited to narration and description".

Shelley puts this function of terza rima into full use and produces an effect that is both auditory and visual: the constant blowing wind, embodied by the continuous flow of the interlocking rhymes without full stops, is seen sweeping forward over the land, in the sky and under the sea, as the cantos move on. The ending couplet of each canto sounds like the crescendo of the force of the wind in that place, as well as the climax of the speaker's emotion.

2. The outline of the poem and the way it develops

Odes are often divided into three general sections with two major shifts in tone. Generally speaking, the first section of an ode usually establishes one point; the second establishes a contrary point; the end of the poem brings them together. "Ode to the West Wind" fits this pattern perfectly.

Shelley's five cantos can be divided into three parts. The first part is from Canto Ⅰ to Canto Ⅲ, which employs a second-person tone.

In Canto Ⅰ, the speaker addresses the West Wind as "Thou, the breath of Autumn" and describes its activities over the land, sweeping away the multicolored dead leaves, carrying seeds to their graves to be revived by the spring wind. The West Wind is called "Destroyer and Preserver", for it brings the death of winter, and also makes possible the regeneration of spring.

Canto II describes the West Wind's movement in the sky. It brings a storm by spreading thunderclouds which look like wild locks of hair on a Maenad. It is addressed as "dirge of the dying year", and the night is going to be like a dark-domed tomb.

Canto III still begins with "Thou" and narrates that the Mediterranean has been woken by the West Wind and the Atlantic Ocean is also subservient to its powers.

Then the poem shifts to first-person at Canto IV, begins the second part of the poem. The speaker wishes he were a "dead leaf" or a "swift cloud" or "a wave" that would be lifted by the West Wind, since life has chained and bowed him and now he is not "tameless, and swift, and proud" like the West Wind itself any more.

Part IV, i.e. Canto V, moves on to consider the West Wind(you) and the speaker(me) together: at first the speaker wants the wind to turn him into its lyre and play its own music on him. Then he wants to unite with the wind's "fierce" spirit entirely and makes its spirit to become his; he wants the wind to drive his dead thoughts over the universe and scatter his words among mankind. Finally he asks the wind a seemingly simple question: "If Winter comes, can Spring be far behind?" According to some critics, the speaker asks whether or not a rebirth is always following the death and decay of something, and it is his hope for the future.

3. Shelley's style

Ian Lancashire points out Shelley belonged to a philosophical movement called "Neo-Platonism", which values idealism and that is why Shelley seems to like to leave the Earth entirely behind and soar up into the heavens. He cries out to the West Wind, "Be thou, Spirit fierce, / My spirit!" This audaciousness would have been scorned by traditional readers and the poets of the eighteenth century, but they would envy his courage to go out into the storm and shout like that. Some established British critics point out that today if someone wrote, "I fall upon the thorns of life! I bleed!" in a poem and sent it off to a prestigious magazine, its poetry editors would laugh at it, but Shelley is just exclaiming the hardships of life sincerely. His verse lines are passionate, smooth and very honest, which pour out straight from his heart. This use of natural imagery to express his abstract ideas in a concise way has impressed readers for many generations.

Suggested Further Reading

Percy Bysshe Shelley's poems "Ozymandias" "To a Skylark" "England in 1819", and "A Defense of Poetry".

Topics for Further Study

1. What is the relationship between man and the natural world? Does the speaker in this poem sound that he is praying to the West Wind?
2. What are the geographical elements in this poem? What do they imply?

Knowledge of Literature

1. Ode

An Ode is a long, serious, meditative poem dealing with dignified and solemn theme written in an elevated formal style. Odes first appeared in classical Greek which were originally poetic pieces accompanied by symphonic orchestras. This form has been used by a great many later poets, especially by English poets of the seventeenth and eighteenth centuries. Milton, Wordsworth, Coleridge, Keats, and Shelley all wrote odes that are still among the most famous poems in the English language. There are three typical forms of odes: the Pindaric, Horatian, and irregular. Odes are often divided into three general sections with two shifts in tone. The sections are called the "strophe" "antistrophe", and "epode".

2. Terza rima

It is a poetical form which consists of interlocking tercets (three-line stanzas). The middle rhyme of one tercet becomes the outside rhyme of the next one. Its rhyme scheme is *aba*, *bcb*, *cdc* and so on and it usually ends in a couplet. Terza rima is well-suited to narration and description. It is created by the Italian poet Dante and it is most famously used in his *The Divine Comedy*. Shelley's "Ode to the West Wind" also employs this form.

John Keats
(1795~1821)

About the Author

John Keats (1795 ~ 1821) was one of the key poets in the second generation of the Romantic movement along with Byron and Shelley, and his influence on poets such as Alfred Tennyson and Wilfred Owen was significant. He died in Rome of a very young age and the epitaph he wrote for himself was "Here lies one whose name was writ in water".

As his famous quotations go, "A thing of beauty is a joy forever;/ Its loveliness increases, it will never/Pass into nothingness" and "Beauty is truth; truth beauty", Keats was concerned with creating beauty and immortalizing the transient beauty of natural world into permanent work of art. His poetry is characterized by sensual imagery, musicality and melancholy mood, most notably in the series of odes mostly written from 1818 to 1820, which remain among the most popular and most treasured poems in English literature. The letters of Keats are also among the most celebrated in English literature.

John Keats's famous short lyrics are: "Ode to a Nightingale" "Ode on a Grecian Urn" "Ode on Melancholy" "To Autumn" "Ode to Psyche" "On First Looking into Chapman's Homer"(1816) and "On the Grasshopper and Cricket". His long poems include *Endymion*(1818), *Isabella*(1820), *The Eve of Saint Agnes*(1820) and *Hyperion*(1820).

★ Ode[1] on a Grecian Urn

About the Poem

What is described in the poem might be painted pictures or sculptured reliefs on an urn that may only have existed in Keats's imagination: Dionysian ecstasies, panting young lovers in flight and pursuit, a pastoral piper under spring foliage, and the quiet celebration of communal pieties. Existing in a frozen or suspended time, they cannot move or change, nor can their feelings change, yet the unknown painter or sculptor has succeeded in creating a sense of living passion and a world of lasting beauty.

Thou still[2] unravish'd[3] bride of quietness,
Thou foster-child of silence and slow time,
Sylvan[4] historian, who canst thus express
A flowery tale more sweetly than our rhyme[5]:
What leaf-fring'd legend[6] haunt about thy shape
Of deities or mortals, or of both,

In Tempe⁷ or the dales of Arcady⁸?
What men or gods are these? What maidens loth⁹?
What mad pursuit? What struggle to escape?
What pipes and timbrels? What wild ecstasy?

Heard melodies are sweet, but those unheard
Are sweeter; therefore, ye soft pipes, play on;
Not to the sensual ear¹⁰, but, more endear'd,
Pipe to the spirit ditties of no tone¹¹:
Fair youth, beneath the trees, thou canst not leave
Thy song, nor ever can those trees be bare;
Bold lover, never, never canst thou kiss,
Though winning near the goal-yet, do not grieve;
She cannot fade, though thou hast not thy bliss,
For ever wilt thou love, and she be fair!

Ah, happy, happy boughs! that cannot shed
Your leaves, nor ever bid the spring adieu¹²;
And, happy melodist, unwearied,
For ever piping songs for ever new;
More happy love! more happy, happy love!
For ever warm and still to be enjoy'd,
For ever panting, and for ever young;
All breathing human passion far above¹³,
That leaves a heart high-sorrowful and cloy'd¹⁴,
A burning forehead, and a parching tongue.

Who are these coming to the sacrifice?
To what green altar¹⁵, O mysterious priest,
Lead'st thou that heifer¹⁶ lowing at the skies,
And all her silken flanks with garlands drest¹⁷?
What little town by river or sea shore,
Or mountain-built with peaceful citadel¹⁸,
Is emptied of this folk, this pious morn?
And, little town, thy streets for evermore
Will silent be; and not a soul to tell
Why thou art desolate, can e'er return.

O Attic[19] shape! Fair attitude[20]! with brede[21]
Of marble men and maidens overwrought[22],
With forest branches and the trodden weed;
Thou, silent form, dost tease us out of thought[23]
As doth eternity: Cold Pastoral[24]!
When old age shall this generation waste,
Thou shalt remain, in midst of other woe[25]
Than ours, a friend to man, to whom thou say'st,
"Beauty is truth, truth beauty,"—that is all
Ye know on earth, and all ye need to know.

※ ※

Notes

1. ode: a long lyric poem, serious and dignified in subject, tone and style, sometimes with elaborate stanzaic structure, often written to celebrate an event or an individual.
2. still: There has been disputes as to the meaning of this word: an adverb meaning "as yet" or an adjective meaning "motionless".
3. unravish'd: (virginity of the bride) not taken away; pure.
4. sylvan: of forest; rustic, rural.
5. rhyme: this poem.
6. leaf-fring'd legend: rural scene on the urn decorated with a border of leaves and trees.
7. Tempe: a beautiful valley in Greece which has come to stand for supreme rural beauty.
8. Arcady: valleys of Arcadi, a state in ancient Greece now regarded as a symbol of the pastoral ideal.
9. loth: loath, reluctant.
10. sensual ear: ear of sense or physical ear (as opposed to "spiritual ear" or imagination).
11. This line means "Pipe ditties of no tone (short songs without tune) to the spirit (to imagination)".
12. bid the spring adieu: say good-bye to the spring.
13. The line means that (young lovers and their love on the urn) are far above the breathing human passion in that they are immune to sorrows. "breathing" here means "too strong" or "exciting".

14. cloy'd: annoyed (by too much of something).
15. altar: 祭坛。
16. heifer: young cow.
17. drest: dressed.
18. citadel: fortress on high ground overlooking and protecting a city or town.
19. Attic: delicate form of art in ancient Greece.
20. attitude: posture, position or shape.
21. brede: braid, pattern ornamented.
22. overwrought: interwoven.
23. tease us out of thought: make us think.
24. Cold Pastoral: the pastoral scene on the urn which lacks life and warmth.
25. woe: sorrow.

Questions for Understanding

1. What is the dramatic situation of the poem? What does the speaker see?
2. How do you understand "unravish'd bride of quietness" and "foster-child of silence and slow time" respectively?
3. What is suggested in the above expressions about the urn's relationship with time and change?
4. How do you understand "Heard melodies are sweet, but those unheard / are sweeter"?
5. How many aspects of life are described in the poem? What are they?
6. What types of art are mentioned in the poem besides the Grecian urn? What are the similarities of these forms of art? And the difference(s)?
7. How do you understand "Beauty is truth, truth beauty"?

Aspects of Appreciation

1. An ode usually has an elaborate stanzaic structure. This ode by Keats consists of 5 stanzas of 10 lines each, basically in iambic pentameter, the first seven lines of each stanza rhyming invariably *ababcde*, and the second three lines of the five stanzas rhyming respectively *dce*, *ced*, *cde*, *cde* and *dce*.
2. This poem is about beauty or charm and immortality of art or literature, superiority of art over life or reality, and transient beauty immortalized by art.

3. The most striking artistic features of the poem may be its sensuousness: the use of vivid and palpable images; different forms of art combined: poetry, music and painting. All these appeal to different senses.
4. "Ode on a Grecian Urn" is based on a series of paradoxes and opposites: the discrepancy between the urn with its frozen images and the dynamic life portrayed on the urn, the human and changeable versus the immortal and permanent, participation versus observation, and life versus art.
5. The Chinese saying "一瓷永寿,百代消亡" can throw some light on the understanding of theme of immortality of art and literature or poetry in particular. We can also benefit if we read this poem in light of the popular song sung by Zhou Jielun (Jay Chou) "Blue-and-White Porcelain Vase" (《青花瓷》) in which the artistic object the Porclain is dealt with in relation to a beautiful lass.

Suggested Further Reading

Helen Vendler says the odes "are a group of works in which the English language find ultimate embodiment". Read John Keats's odes and other poems "Ode to a Nightingale" "Ode on Melancholy" "To Autumn" "Ode to Psyche" "On First Looking into Chapman's Homer" and "On the Grasshopper and Cricket".

Topics for Further Study

1. What is the relationship between the urn and poetry? What functions better as "historian"?
2. Compare Keats's idea of the function of art with that of Shakespeare's as shown in his "Sonnet 18".
3. Contrast the depiction of nature in this poem with a depiction of nature in Shelley, Wordsworth or Coleridge. Compare different ways of creating beauty by different Romantic poets (Wordsworth, Coleridge, Byron, Shelley and Keats), or different characteristics of beauty in the poems of these Romantic writers.

Knowledge of Literature

Motif of immortality of art

Immortality of art or literature has been a common and frequent motif (namely theme, idea, image or situation frequently occuring in literary works, folktales or myths) in literature or poetry. Such writers as

Shakespeare, Keats and Yeats believed in the superiority of art and literature over life and reality. Shakespear in his sonnets, represented by his most famous "Sonnet 18", believes that his poetry can preserve his friend's youth and beauty; Keats in his "Ode on a Grecian Urn" holds that art can immortalize youth with their passions and their youthful beauty. Besides, art itself is long-lived and certain forms of art, e. g. painting, sculpture or porcelain can preserve other forms of art, say music or dancing. In his "Sailing to Byzantium" Yeats thinks that the world of art is superior to natural or sensual world because art is spiritual and therefore permanent.

Jane Austen
(1775~1817)

About the Author

Jane Austen was born in Hampshire, England, of a country clergyman's family and educated at home and unmarried. She began writing when she was still a little girl. As she published her works anonymously, she was not famous in her lifetime. Scott admired her talent for portraying ordinary life in a wonderful way. Her vision of real life as lived in a particular segment of society has placed her as part of the "Great Tradition" of the English novel, i. e. realism. She wrote six novels which are all about family life. Her novels are very different in style from the Romanticism favoured by her contemporaries. With trenchant observation and in meticulous detail, she presented the quiet, day-to-day country life of the upper-middleclass in England. Among her numerous strengths are her exquisite, compact prose, her moral judgment, her wit, and her character portrayal. Austen died quietly at Winchester in 1817.

★ Pride and Prejudice

About the Novel

Pride and Prejudice, a story of marriages of four young couples, centers around the love affair between Elizabeth and Darcy. Elizabeth is a lively young middle-class woman with a strong personality, whereas Darcy from a wealthy upper-class family is an apparently serious and unconsciously arrogant young man. He first offends Elizabeth with his haughty contempt for her inferior social position and the poor manners of her family members. On account of this, Elizabeth makes up her mind not to care about Darcy at all. However, Darcy reluctantly finds himself attracted by Elizabeth's lovely personality. As he proposes to Elizabeth, he cannot help showing his pride for his status. Elizabeth, in return, develops a strong dislike for and prejudice against Darcy and rejects Darcy's proposal flatly. Later, Darcy writes a letter explaining his past conducts to Elizabeth and frees himself from Elizabeth's charges against him. After a series of events, especially after Darcy reveals his virtues in helping solve the problem of Lydia's elopement with Wickham, reconciliation of the two comes. As Darcy renews his proposal to Elizabeth, he realizes that it was his pride that made him arrogant and insensitive. Elizabeth, in turn, accepts his offer with the knowledge that her prejudice caused her to mistake his real character. When they join their hands together, they find happiness and a better understanding of themselves.

Chapter I

It is a truth universally acknowledged that a single man in possession of a good fortune must be in want of a wife.

However little known the feelings or views of such a man may be on his first entering a neighbourhood, this truth is so well fixed in the minds of the surrounding families, that he is considered as the rightful property of some one or other of their daughters.

"My dear Mr. Bennet," said his lady to him one day, "have you heard that Netherfield Park[1] is let at last?"

Mr. Bennet replied that he had not.

"But it is," returned she; "for Mrs. Long[2] has just been here, and she told me all about it."

Mr. Bennet made no answer.

"Do you not want to know who has taken it?" cried his wife impatiently.

"You want to tell me, and I have no objection to hearing it."

This was invitation enough.

"Why, my dear, you must know, Mrs. Long says that Netherfield is taken by a young man of large fortune from the north of England; that he came down on Monday in a chaise and four[3] to see the place, and was so much delighted with it that he agreed with Mr. Morris[4] immediately; that he is to take possession before Michaelmas[5], and some of his servants are to be in the house by the end of next week."

"What is his name?"

"Bingley."

"Is he married or single?"

"Oh, single, my dear, to be sure! A single man of large fortune; four or five thousand a year. What a fine thing for our girls!"

"How so? How can it affect them?"

"My dear Mr. Bennet," replied his wife, "how can you be so tiresome! You must know that I am thinking of his marrying one of them."

"Is that his design in settling here?"

"Design? Nonsense, how can you talk so! But it is very likely that he may fall in love with one of them, and therefore you must visit him as soon as he comes".

"I see no occasion for that. You and the girls may go, or you may send them by themselves, which perhaps will be still better; for, as you are as handsome as any of them, Mr. Bingley might like you the best of the party."

"My dear, you flatter me. I certainly have had my share of beauty[6], but I do not pretend to be anything extraordinary now. When a woman has five grown up daughters, she ought to give over[7] thinking of her own beauty."

"In such cases, a woman has not often much beauty to think of."

"But, my dear, you must indeed go and see Mr. Bingley when he comes into the neighbourhood."

"It is more than I engage for[8], I assure you."

"But consider your daughters. Only think what an establishment it would be for one of them. Sir William and Lady Lucas[9] are determined to go, merely on that account, for in general, you know, they visit no new comer. Indeed you must go, for it will be impossible for us to visit him, if you do not."

"You are over-scrupulous, surely. I dare say Mr. Bingley will be very glad to see you; and I will send a few lines[10] by you to assure him of my hearty consent to his marrying whichever he chooses of the girls; though I must throw in a good word for my little Lizzy[11]."

"I desire you will do no such thing. Lizzy is not a bit better than the others; and I am sure she is not half so handsome as Jane[12], nor half so good humoured as Lydia[13]. But you are always giving her the preference."

"They have none of them much to recommend them," replied he, "they are all silly and ignorant like other girls; but Lily has something more of quickness than her sisters."

"Mr. Bennet, how can you abuse your own children in such a way? You take delight in vexing me. You have no compassion on my poor nerves."

"You mistake me, my dear. I have a high respect for your nerves. They are my old friends. I have heard you mention them with consideration these twenty years at least."

"Ah! You do not know what I suffer."

"But I hope you will get over it, and live to see many young men of four thousand a year come into the neighbourhood."

"It will be no use to us if twenty such should come, since you will not visit them."

"Depend upon it, my dear, that when there are twenty I will visit them all."

Mr. Bennet was so odd a mixture of quick parts[14], sarcastic humour, reserve, and caprice, that the experience of three-and-twenty years had been insufficient to make his wife understand his character. Her mind was less difficult to develop[15]. She was a woman of mean understanding, little information, and uncertain temper. When she was discontented, she fancied herself nervous. The business of her life was to get her daughters married; its solace was visiting and news.

Chapter II

Mr. Bennet was among the earliest of those who waited on Mr. Bingley. He had always intended to visit him, though to the last always assuring his wife that he should not go; and till the evening after the visit was paid, she had no knowledge of it. It was then disclosed in the following manner. Observing his second daughter employed in trimming a hat, he suddenly addressed her with,—

"I hope Mr. Bingley will like it, Lizzy."

"We are not in a way to know what Mr. Bingley likes," said her mother resentfully, "since we are not to visit."

"But you forget, mama," said Elizabeth, "that we shall meet him at the assemblies[16], and that Mrs. Long has promised to introduce him."

"I do not believe Mrs. Long will do any such thing. She has two nieces of her own. She is a selfish, hypocritical woman, and I have no opinion of her."

"No more have I," said Mr. Bennet; "and I am glad to find that you do not depend on her serving you."

Mrs. Bennet deigned not to make any reply; but, unable to contain herself, began scolding one of her daughters.

"Don't keep coughing so, Kitty[17], for heaven's sake! Have a little compassion on my nerves. You tear them to pieces."

"Kitty has no discretion in her coughs," said her father; "she times them ill[18]".

"I do not cough for my own amusement," replied Kitty fretfully.

"When is your next ball to be, Lizzy?"

"To-morrow fortnight."

"Ay, so it is," cried her mother, "and Mrs. Long does not come back till the day before; so it will be impossible for her to introduce him, for she will not know him herself."

"Then, my dear, you may have the advantage of your friend, and introduce Mr. Bingley to her."

"Impossible, Mr. Bennet, impossible, when I am not acquainted with him myself; how can you be so teasing?"

"I honour your circumspection. A fortnight's acquaintance is certainly very little. One cannot know what a man really is by the end of a fortnight. But if we do not venture[19], somebody else will; and after all, Mrs. Long and her nieces must stand their chance; and therefore, as she will think it an act of kindness, if you decline the office[20], I will take it on myself."

The girls stared at their father. Mrs. Bennet said only, "Nonsense, nonsense!"

"What can be the meaning of that emphatic exclamation?" cried he. "Do you consider the forms of introduction, and the stress that is laid on them, as nonsense? I cannot quite agree with you there. What say you, Mary[21]? For you are a young lady of deep reflection, I know, and read great books, and make extracts."

Mary wished to say something very sensible, but knew not how.

"While Mary is adjusting her ideas," he continued, "let us return to Mr. Bingley."

"I am sick of Mr. Bingley," cried his wife.

"I am sorry to hear that; but why did not you tell me so before? If I had known as much this morning, I certainly would not have called on him. It is very unlucky; but as I have actually paid the visit, we cannot escape the acquaintance now."

The astonishment of the ladies was just what he wished—that of Mrs. Bennet perhaps surpassing the rest—though when the first tumult of joy was over, she began to declare that it was what she had expected all the while.

"How good it was in you, my dear Mr. Bennet! But I knew I should persuade you at last. I was sure you loved our girls too well to neglect such an acquaintance. Well, how pleased I am! And it is such a good joke, too, that you should have gone this morning, and never said a word about it till now."

"Now, Kitty, you may cough as much as you choose," said Mr. Bennet, and, as he spoke, he left the room, fatigued with the raptures of his wife.

"What an excellent father you have, girls!" said she, when the door was shut. "I do not know how you will ever make him amends for his kindness; or me either[22], for that matter. At our time of life, it is not so pleasant, I can tell you, to be making new acquaintance every day; but for your sakes, we would do any thing. Lydia, my love, though you are the youngest, I dare say Mr. Bingley will dance with you at the next ball."

"Oh!" said Lydia stoutly, "I am not afraid; for though 1 am the youngest, I'm the tallest."

The rest of the evening was spent in conjecturing how soon he would return Mr. Bennet's visit, and determining when they should ask him to dinner.

Notes

1. Netherfield Park: the name of an estate in the neighbourhood of the home of the Bennets.
2. Mrs. Long: a neighhour of the Bennets.
3. a chaise and four: a lightweight carriage drawn by four horses.
4. Mr. Morris: the owner of Netherfield Park.
5. Michaelmas: September 29, church festival in honor of the Archangel Michael.
6. I certainly have had my share of beauty: I certainly was beautiful once.

7. give over: stop.
8. It is more than I engage for: I could not give my permission for this.
9. Sir William and Lady Lucas: Sir William Lucas and his wife, neighbours of the Bennets.
10. a few lines: short note, a short letter.
11. Lizzy: Mr. Bennet's second daughter.
12. Jane: Mr. Bennet's eldest daughter.
13. Lydia: Mr. Bennet's youngest daughter.
14. quick parts: wit.
15. Her mind was less difficult to develop: It was easier to understand her mind.
16. the assemblies: the balls.
17. Kitty: Mr. Bennet's fourth daughter.
18. she times them ill: She does not cough at the right time.
19. But if we do not venture: But if we do not venture to introduce Mr. Bingley to her.
20. office: service.
21. Mary: Mr. Bennet's third daughter.
22. or me either: neither can you make me amends.

Questions for Understanding

1. The opening sentence of this novel is probably one of the most famous sentences found in fiction. What has this sentence to do with the tone of the whole novel? What are the implied meanings of this sentence?
2. In the last paragraph of Chapter I, the author summarizes the character of Mr. and Mrs. Bennet. How is their character revealed in the selection you have read? Find examples. Can you say anything more about their character besides what the author summarizes?
3. What is Mr. Bennet's attitude towards his wife? What kind of relationship do the couple have between them?
4. What is Jane Austen's chief technique in characterization in this selection?
5. Jane Austen's novels are mostly concerned with young men and women's social growth and self-discovery. Nearly all of them explore a consistent theme that maturity is achieved through the loss of illusions. Faults of character displayed by the people of her novels are corrected when, through various trials and misunderstandings, lessons are learned. Is the statement right when we understand the theme of *Pride and Prejudice*?

How do you interpret the conflict between Elizabeth and Darcy? What do you learn from the process of their courtship?

Aspects of Appreciation

1. Perspectives of class and gender

Almost all of the characters in Jane Austen's novels are members of England's middle to upper-middle class. Although they share a similar lifestyle, there are significant differences in income and social prestige between them. These differences play a critical role in the relationship between Darcy and Elizabeth. Darcy's inordinate pride is based on his extreme class-consciousness. Austen is often critical of the assumptions and prejudices of upper-class England. She distinguishes between internal merit, goodness of individual, and external merit, rank and possessions, and criticizes an overemphasis on class.

Austen also describes different socially regimented ideas of appropriate behaviour for each gender. While social advancement for young men lay in the military, church, or law, the chief method of self-improvement for women was the acquisition of wealth. Women could only accomplish this goal through successful marriage, which explains the ubiquity of matrimony as a goal and topic of conversation in the works.

Class division and gender differences make up much of the tension in her novels, arising from balancing financial necessity against other concerns: love, friendship, honour and self-respect. Austen sets brilliant example to integrate observations on the human condition within a convincing love story.

2. Irony in the novel

Pride and Prejudice is a model of Jane Austen's successful employment of irony. Irony plays a decisive part in characterization as well as in plot development. The verbal irony in the dialogues and the situational or dramatic irony here are especially note-worthy. By saying one thing but meaning another, we see the stupidity of Mrs. Bennet and Elizabeth's derision of Darcy's pride. And in terms of plot, the whole story seems to be composed of ironies. With a negative start on both sides at the beginning of the story, we watch with anxiety the gradual development of love between Darcy and Elizabeth. One ironical event leads to another where mutual repulsion is turned into mutual attraction, verbal quarrels turned into confessions, intended riddance turned into unexpected but nonetheless welcoming meetings, the proud turned into the humbled and the prejudiced turned into the repentant. With other characters too, irony abounds. Mr. Collins proposes to one but marries another; Miss Bingley tries to engage the heart of her beloved by speaking ill of her rival but only to arouse his greater interest in the latter; Wickham's lies lead to the exposure of his true nature, and Lady de Bourgh's intervention between Elizabeth and Darcy only brings hope and the final union of the two, etc. The irony helps to bring the conscious criticism of the author to the reader and makes it fun to read the novel.

Suggested Further Reading

1. Jane Austen's other novels.
2. Howard S. Babb. *Jane Austen's Novels: The Fabric of Dialogue*, 1967.
3. Lloyd W. Brown. *Bits of Ivory: Narrative Techniques in Jane Austen's Fiction*, 1973.

Topics for Further Study

1. What do you think of the title of the novel? What is your opinion about Darcy's pride and Elizabeth's prejudice?
2. Give examples to show the author's skill of irony.

VI

Age of Realism (The Victorian Age)

Charlotte Brontë
(1816～1855)

About the Author

  Charlotte Brontë, born on April 21, 1816, was the third child of a poor clergyman at a small village of Haworth, Yorkshire, in northern England. When she was only five, her mother died, leaving five daughters and a son. In 1824 Charlotte and her sisters except Anne, the youngest, were sent to a charity school at Cowan's Bridge. They were cruelly treated and her two elder sisters died of tuberculosis. She and Emily were thus withdrawn from the school to be educated by their father. In 1831 Charlotte went to another boarding school at Roehead, and she worked as a teacher there between 1835～1838. She was a governess twice in rich families. With the idea of establishing a school of her own, she went with Emily in 1842 to study French and German in Brussels, and was employed as a teacher there in 1843. But poor health compelled her to return home the following year. Her project of starting a private school was never carried out.

  In 1845 Charlotte discovered by chance the manuscript of Emily's poems and was surprised by their quality, though each of the sisters was aware that the others had written poems for some time. They decided to put into effect their long-cherished hope of becoming professional writers. A year later a volume of verse was published at their own cost under the title of *Poems by Currer, Ellis and Acton Bell*, the pseudonyms of Charlotte, Emily and Anne. But only two copies were sold. Next they tried their hands at writing novels. Anne's *Agnes Grey* and Emily's *Wuthering Heights* were both accepted for publication while her novel *The Professor* was refused by several publishers. She was cast down by this failure, but she kept on writing. Her next novel *Jane Eyre* came out in 1847, just a few months after her sister's novels. It became immediately popular. But fresh sorrows befell her when her brother died in September 1848, which was followed in quick succession by the deaths of her two sisters Emily (who died in December 1848) and Anne (who died in May 1849). However, with restless energy, she wrote two more novels, *Shirley* (1849) and *Villette* (1853). The former deals with the life of the English workers at the time of the Luddite Movement in the early 19th century, while the latter is an account of her experience at a boarding school in Brussels. Her first rejected novel, *The Professor*, was published posthumously in 1857.

In 1854 Charlotte married her father's curate Arthur Bell Nicholls, but she died in childbirth on March 31, 1855.

Charlotte Brontë was an impressive presence on the literary scene of her time. She was generally praised for her depth of feeling and her courageous realism, and her works continue to hold high popularity and critical esteem.

★ Jane Eyre

About the Novel

Jane Eyre tells a fascinating story of suffering, love and growth. The major character, Jane Eyre, an orphan who stays with her aunt, suffers immensely from neglect and malice of her aunt's family. She experiences a nervous breakdown and an emotional outburst, and is sent to a mental institution, where she becomes a teacher eventually. Then having taken a job offer as a governess, she falls in love with Rochester, the owner of the Thornfield manor. Their marriage is interrupted by Rochester's insane wife's brother. The sorely disappointed Jane leaves in disgust and despair, almost dies, and is picked up by the pious St. John Rivers and his sisters. Jane finds herself in an emotional tug of war: torn between her love for Rochester and St. John. Then just as she is about to accept St. John's proposal and gets ready to go with him to India, she seems to hear a call coming across space from Rochester and goes back to Thornfield, only to find Rochester's manor all devastated in a fire his mad wife has set on it and Rochester blinded in his attempt to save his wife from death. Jane and Rochester reunite, and begin a new chapter in their lives.

Chapter 23

A splendid Midsummer shone over England: skies so pure, suns so radiant as were then seen in long succession, seldom favour, even singly[1], our wave-girt land[2]. It was as if a band of Italian days had come from the South, like a flock of glorious passenger birds, and lighted to rest them on the cliffs of Albion[3]. The hay was all got in; the fields round Thornfield were green and shorn; the roads white and baked; the trees were in their dark prime; hedge and wood, full-leaved and deeply tinted, contrasted well with the sunny hue of the cleared meadows between.

On Midsummer-eve, Adele[4], weary with gathering wild strawberries in Hay Lane half the day, had gone to bed with the sun. I watched her drop asleep, and when I left her, I sought the garden.

It was now the sweetest hour of the twenty-four: "day its fervid fires had wasted"[5], and dew fell cool on panting plain and scorched summit[6]. Where the sun had gone down in simple state—pure of the pomp of clouds[7]—spread a solemn purple, burning with the light of red jewel and furnace flame at one point, on one hill—peak, and extending high and wide, soft and still softer, over half heaven. The east had its own charm of fine, deep blue, and its own modest gem[8], a rising and solitary star: soon it would boast the moon[9]; but she was yet beneath the horizon.

I walked a while on the pavement; but a subtle, well-known scent-that of a cigar-stole from some window; I saw the library casement open a handbreadth; I knew I might be watched thence; so I went apart into the orchard. No nook in the grounds more sheltered and more Eden-like; a very high wall shut it out from the court on one side; on the other a beech avenue screened it from the lawn. At the bottom was a sunk fence, its, sole separation from lonely fields; a winding walk, bordered with laurels and terminating in a giant horse-chestnut, circled at the base by a seat, led clown to the fence. Here one could wander unseen. While such honeydew fell, such silence reigned, such gloaming gathered, I felt as if I could haunt such shade for ever; but in treading the flower and fruit parterres at the upper part of the enclosure, enticed there by the light the now rising moon cast on this more open quarter, my step is stayed—not by sound, not by light, but once more by a warning fragrance.

Sweet-brier and southern-wood, jasmine, pink, and rose have long been yielding their evening sacrifice of incense: this new scent is neither of shrub nor flower; it is—I know it well—it is Mr. Rochester's cigar. I look round and listen. I see trees laden with ripening fruit. I hear a nightingale warbling in a wood half a mile off: no moving form is visible, no coming step audible; but that perfume increases: I must flee. I make for the wicket leading to the shrubbery, and I see Mr. Rochester entering. I step aside into the ivy recess; he will not stay long: he will soon return whence he came, and if I sit still he will never see me.

But no-eventide is as pleasant to him as to me, and this antique garden as attractive; and he strolls on, now lifting the gooseberry-tree branches to look at the fruit, large as plums, with which they are laden; now taking a ripe cherry from the wall; now stooping towards a knot of flowers either to inhale their fragrance or admire the dew-beads on their petals. A great moth goes humming by me; it alights on a plant at Mr. Rochester's foot: he sees it, and bends to examine it.

"Now he has his back towards me," thought I, "and he is occupied too; perhaps, if I walk softly, I can slip away unnoticed."

I trod on an edging of turf that[10] the crackle of the pebbly gravel might not betray me: he was standing among the beds at a yard or two distant from where I had to pass; the moth apparently engaged him. "I shall get by very well," I meditated. As I crossed his shadow, thrown long over the garden by the moon, not yet risen high, he said quietly, without turning—

"Jane, come and look at this fellow."

I had made no noise: he had not eyes behind—could his shadow feel? I started at first, and then I approached him.

"Look at his wings," said he, "he reminds me rather of a West Indian insect; one does not often see so large and gay a night-rover in England; there! He is flown."

The moth roamed away, I was sheepishly retreating also; but Mr. Rochester followed me, and when we reached the wicket he said—

"Turn back: on so lovely a night it is a shame to sit in the house; and surely no one can wish to go to bed while sunset is thus at meeting with moonrise."

It is of my faults, that though my tongue is sometimes prompt enough at answer, there are times when it sadly fails me in framing an excuse; and always the lapse occurs at some crisis, when a facile word of plausible pretext is specially wanted to get me out of painful embarrassment. I did not like to walk at this hour alone with Mr. Rochester in the shadowy orchard: but I could not find a reason to allege for leaving him. I followed with lagging step, and thoughts busily bent on discovering a means of extrication[11]: but he himself looked so composed and so grave also, I became ashamed of feeling any confusion: the evil—if evil existent or prospective there was[12]—seemed to lie with me only; his mind was unconscious and quiet.

"Jane," he recommenced, as we entered the laurel walk and slowly strayed down in the direction of the sunk fence and the horse chestnut, "Thornfield is a pleasant place in summer, is it not?"

"Yes sir."

"You must have become in some degree attached to the house-you who have an eye for natural beauties[13], and a good deal of the organ of Adhesiveness[14]?"

"I am attached to it, indeed."

"And though I don't comprehend how it is, I perceive you have acquired a degree of regard for that foolish little child Adele, too; and even for simple Dame Fairfax?"

"Yes, sir; in different ways, I have an affection for both."

"And would be sorry to part with them?"

"Yes,"

"Pity!" he said, and sighed and paused.

"It is always the way of events in this life," he continued presently: "no sooner have you got settled in a pleasant resting-place, than a voice calls out to you to rise and move on, for the hour of repose is expired."

"Must I move on, sir?" I asked. "Must I leave Thornfield?"

"I believe you must, Jane. I am sorry, Janet, but I believe indeed you must."

This was a blow: but I did not let it prostrate me.

"Well, sir, I shall be ready when the order to march comes."

"It is come now—I must give it to-night."

"Then you are going to be married, sir?"

"Ex-act-ly-pre-cise-ly: with your usual acuteness, you have hit the nail straight on the head."

"Soon, sir?"

VI. Age of Realism (The Victorian Age)

"Very soon, my-that is, Miss Eyre: and you'll remember, Jane, the first time I, or Rumour, plainly intimated to you that it was my intention to put my old bachelor's neck into the sacred noose, to enter into the holy state of matrimony[15]—to take Miss Ingram to my bosom, in short (she's an expensive armful: but that's not to the point—one can't have too much of such a very, excellent thing as my beautiful Blanche): well, as I was saying—listen to me, Jane! You're not turning your head to look after more moths, are you? That was only a lady-clock, child; 'flying away home'. I wish to remind you that it was you who first said to me, with that discretion[16] I respect in you—with that foresight, prudence, and humility[17] which befit your responsible and dependent position—that in case I married Miss Ingram, both you and Adele had better trot forthwith. I pass over the sort of slur conveyed in this suggestion on the character of my beloved; indeed, when you are far away, Jane, I'll try to forget it: I shall notice only its wisdom; which is such that I have made it my law of action. Adele must go to school; and you, Miss Eyre, must get a new situation."

"Yes, sir, I will advertise immediately: and meantime, I suppose"—I was going to say, "I suppose I may stay here, till I find another shelter to betake myself to": but I stopped, feeling it would not do to risk a long sentence, for my voice was not quite under command.

"In about a month I hope to be a bridegroom," continued Mr. Rochester; "and in the interim, I shall myself look out for employment and an asylum for you."

"Thank you, sir; I am sorry to give—"

"Oh, no need to apologize! I consider that when a dependent does her duty as well as you have done yours, she has a sort of claim upon her employer for any little assistance he can conveniently render her; indeed, I have already, through my future mother-in-law, heard of a place that I think will suit: it is to undertake the education of the five daughters of Mrs. Dionysius O'Gall of Bitternutt Lodge, Connaught, Ireland. You'll like Ireland, I think: they're such warm-hearted people there, they say."

"It is a long way off, sir."

"No matter—a girl of your sense will not object to the voyage or the distance."

"Not the voyage but the distance: and then the sea is a barrier".

"From what, Jane?"

"From England and from Thornfield: and—"

"Well?"

"From *you*, sir."

I said this almost involuntarily, and with as little sanction of free will, my tears gushed out. I did not cry. so as to be heard, however; I avoided sobbing. The thought of Mrs. O'Gall and Bitternutt Lodge struck cold on my heart; and colder the thought of all the brine and foam[18] destined, as it seemed, to rush between me and the master at whose side I now walked; and coldest the remembrance of the wider ocean—wealth, caste, custom—intervened between me and what I naturally and inevitably loved.

"It is a long way," I again said.

"It is, to be sure; and when you get to Bitternutt Lodge, Connaught, Ireland, I shall never see you again, Jane: that's morally certain. I never go over to Ireland, not having myself much of a fancy for the country. We have been good friends, Jane; have we not?"

"Yes, sir."

"And when friends are on the eve of separation, they like to spend the little time that remains to them close to each other. Come! We'll talk over the voyage and the parting quietly, half an hour or so, while the stars enter into their shining life up in heaven yonder: here is the chestnut-tree; here is the bench at its old roots. Come, we will sit there in peace to-night, though we should never more be destined to sit there together."

He seated me and himself.

"It is a long way to Ireland, Jane, and I am sorry to send my little friend on such weary travels: but if I can't do better, how is it to be helped? Are you anything akin to me, do you think, Jane?"

I could risk no sort of answer by this time: my heart was still.

"Because," he said, "I sometimes have a queer feeling with regard to you—especially when you are near to me as now: it is as if I had a string somewhere under my left fibs, tightly and inextricably knotted to a similar string situated in the corresponding quarter of your little frame. And if that boisterous Channel, and two hundred miles or so of land, come broad between us, I am afraid that cord of communion will be snapped; and then I've a nervous notion I should take to bleeding inwardly. As for you—you'd forget me."

"Jane, do you hear that nightingale singing in the wood? Listen!"

In listening, I sobbed convulsively; for I could repress what I endure no longer; I was obliged to yield and I was shaken from head to foot with acute distress. When I did speak, it was only to express an impetuous wish that I had never been born, or never come to Thornfield.

"Because you are sorry to leave it?"

The vehemence of emotion, stirred by grief and love within me, was claiming mastery, and struggling for full sway, and asserting a right to predominate, to overcome, to live, rise, and reign at last: yes—and to speak.

"I grieve to leave Thornfield; I love Thornfield; I love it, because I have lived in it a full and delightful life—momentarily at least. I have not been buried with inferior minds[19], and excluded from every glimpse of communion with what is bright and energetic and high. I have talked, face to face, with what I reverence, with what I delighted in—with an original, a vigorous, an expanded mind. I have known you, Mr. Rochester; and it strikes me with terror and anguish to feel I absolutely must be torn from you for ever. I see the necessity of departure; and it is like looking on the necessity of death."

"Where do you see the necessity?" he asked suddenly.

"Where? You, sir, have placed it before me."

"In what shape?"

"In the shape of Miss Ingram; a noble and beautiful woman-your bride."

"My bride! What bride? I have no bride!"

"But you will have."

"Yes,-I will!" he set his teeth.

"Then I must go—you have said it yourself."

"No: you must stay! I swear it—and the oath shall be kept."

"I tell you I must go!" I retorted, roused to something like passion. "Do you think I can stay to become nothing to you? Do you think I am an automaton? A machine without feelings? And can bear to have my morsel of bread snatched from my lips, and my drop of living water dashed from my cup? Do you think, because I am poor, obscure, plain, and little, I am soulless and heartless? You think wrong! —I have as much soul as you-and full as much heart! And if God had gifted me with some beauty and much wealth, I should have made it as hard for you to leave me, as it is now for me to leave you. I am not talking to you now through the medium of custom, conventionalities, nor even of mortal flesh[20]: it is my spirit that addressees your spirit; just as if both had passed through the grave, and we stood at God's feet, equal—as we are!"

"As we are!" repeated Mr. Rochester— "so," he added, enclosing me in his arms, gathering me to his breast, pressing his lips to my lips: "so, Jane!"

"Yes, so, sir," I rejoined: "and yet not so: for you are a married man—or as good as a married man, and wed to one inferior to you—to one with whom you have no sympathy—whom I do not believe you truly love; for I have seen and heard you sneer at her. I would scorn such a union: therefore I am better than you—let me go!"

"Where, Jane? To Ireland?"

"Yes—to Ireland. I have spoken my mind, and can go anywhere now."

"Jane, be still; don't struggle so, like a wild frantic bird that is rending its own plumage in its desperation."

"I am no bird; and no net ensnares me; I am a free human being with an independent will, which I now expect to leave you."

Another effort set me at liberty, and I stood erect before him.

"And your will shall decide your destiny," he said. "I offer you my heart, my hand, and a share of all my possessions."

"You play a farce, which I merely laugh at."

"I ask you to pass through life at my side—to be my second self, and best earthly companion."

"For that fate you have already made your choice, and must abide by it."

"Jane, be still a few moments, you are over-excited: I will be still too."

A waft of wind came sweeping down the laurel-walk, and trembled through the boughs of the chestnut: it wandered away-away-to an indefinite distance—it died. The nightingale's song was then the only voice of the hour: in listening to it I again went. Mr. Rochester sat quiet, looking at me gently and seriously. Some time passed before he spoke; he at last said—

"Come to my side, Jane, and let us explain and understand one another."

"I will never again come to your side: I am torn away now, and cannot return."

"But, Jane, I summon you as my wife: it is you only I intended to marry."

I was silent: I thought he mocked me.

"Come, Jane—come hither."

VI. Age of Realism (The Victorian Age)

"Your bride stands between us."

He rose, and with a stride reached me.

"My bride is here," he said, again drawing me to him, "because my equal is here, and my likeness. Jane, will you marry me?"

Still I did not answer, and still I writhed myself from his grasp: for I was still incredulous.

"Do you doubt me, Jane?"

"Entirely!"

"You have no faith in me?"

"Not a whit."

"Am I a liar in your eyes?" he asked passionately. "Little sceptic, you *shall* be convinced. What love have I for Miss Ingram? None: and that you know. What love has she for me? None: as I have taken pains to prove: I caused a rumour to reach her that my fortune was not a third of what was supposed, and after that I presented myself to see the result; it was coldness both from her and her mother. I would not—I could not—marry Miss Ingram. You—you strange, you almost unearthly thing!—I love you as my own flesh. You-poor and obscure, and small and plain as you are—I entreat to accept me as a husband."

"What, me!" I ejaculated, beginning in his earnestness—and especially in his incivility—to credit his sincerity: "me who have not a friend in the world but you—if you are my friend! not a shilling but what you have given me?"

"You, Jane, I must have you for my own-entirely my own. Will you be mine? Say yes, quickly."

"Mr. Rochester, let me look at your face: turn to the moonlight."

"Why?"

"Because I want to read your countenance—turn!"

"There! You will find it scarcely more legible than a crumpled, scratched page. Read on: only make haste, for I suffer."

His face was very much agitated and very much flushed, and there were strong workings in the features[21], and strange gleams in the eyes.

"Oh, Jane, you torture me!" he exclaimed. "With that searching and yet faithful and generous look, you torture me!"

"How can I do that? If you are true, and your offer real, my only feelings to you must be gratitude and devotion-they cannot torture."

"Gratitude!" he ejaculated; and added wildly—"Jane, accept me quickly. Say, Edward—give me my name—Edward—I will marry you."

"Are you in earnest? Do you truly love me? Do you sincerely wish me to be your wife?"

"I do; and if an oath is necessary to satisfy, I swear it."

"Then, sir, I will marry you."

"Edward-my little wife!"

"Dear Edward!"

"Come to me-come to me entirely now," said he; and added in his deepest tone, speaking in my ear as his cheek was laid on mine, "Make my happiness—I will make yours."

"God pardon me!" he subjoined ere long; "and man meddle not with me; I have her, and will hold her."

"There is no one to meddle, sir. I have no kindred to interfere."

"No—that is the best of it," he said. And if I had loved him less I should have thought his accent and look of exultation savage; but sitting by him, mused from the nightmare of parting—called to the paradise of union—I thought only of the bliss given me to drink in so abundant a flow. Again and again he said, "Are you happy, Jane?" And again and again I answered, "Yes." After which he murmured, "It will atone[22]—it will atone. Have I not found her friendless, and cold, and comfortless? Will I not guard, and cherish, and solace her? Is there no love in my heart, and constancy in my resolves? It will expiate at God's tribunal[23]. I know my Maker sanctions[24] what I do. For the world's judgment—I wash my hands thereof[25]. For man's opinion—I defy it."

But what had befallen the night? The moon was not yet set, and we were all in shadow: I could scarcely see my master's face, near as I was. And what ailed the chestnut tree? it writhed and groaned; while wind roared in the laurel walk, and came sweeping over us.

"We must go in," said Mr. Rochester, "the weather changes, I could have sat with thee till morning, Jane."

"And so," thought I, "could I with you." I should have said so, perhaps, but a livid, vivid spark leapt out of a cloud at which I was looking, and there was a crack, a crash, and a close rattling peal; and I thought only of hiding my dazzled eyes against Mr. Rochester's shoulder.

The rain rushed down. He hurried me up the walk, through the grounds, and into the house; but we were quite wet before we could pass the threshold. He was taking off my shawl in the hall, and shaking the water out of my loosened hair, when Fairfax emerged from her room. I did not observe her at first, nor did Mr. Rochester. The lamp was lit. The clock was on the stroke of twelve.

"Hasten to take off your wet things," said he; "and before you go, good-night-good-night, my darling."

He kissed me repeatedly. When I looked up, on leaving his arms, there stood the widow, pale, grave, and amazed. I only smiled at her, and ran upstairs. 'Explanation will do for another time,'thought I. Still, when I reached my chamber, I felt a pang at the idea she should even temporarily misconstrue what she had seen. But joy soon effaced every other feeling; and loud as the wind blew, near and deep as the thunder crashed, fierce and frequent as the lightning gleamed, cataract-like as the rain fell during a storm of two hours' duration, I experienced no fear and little awe. Mr. Rochester came thrice to my door in the course of it, to ask if I was safe and tranquil: and that was comfort, that was strength for anything.

Before I left my bed in the morning, little Adele came running in to tell me that the great horse- chestnut, at the bottom of the orchard had been struck by lightning in the night, and half of it split away.

※ ※

Notes

1. even singly: even for a single day.
2. our wave-girt land: referring to Great Britain, which is surrounded by sea on all sides. The word "girt" is the past participle of "gird", meaning surrounded.
3. Albions:Britain as called by the Greeks and Romans. "Albion" is derived from the Latin word "Albus", meaning "white".
4. Adele: Jane's pupil, who is deserted by her mother Adela Varens, Rochester's former mistress.
5. day its fervid fires had wasted = day had wasted its fervid fires: cf. Thomas Campbell, *The Turkish Lady*: Day her sultry fires had wasted/ Calm and sweet the moonlight rose.
6. summit: top of a hill.
7. pure of the pomp of clouds: meaning cloudless.
8. gem: a thing regarded as specially good or valuable.
9. soon it would boast the moon: soon it would boast to the moon about its

brightness.
10. I trod on an edging of turf that: "that" = so that.
11. a means of extrication: an excuse to get away from him.
12. if evil existent or prospective there was = if there was evil existent or prospective. "Evil" here refers to Jane's fear that Rochester might have an ill intention in asking her to take a walk with him.
13. have an eye for natural beauties: have an ability to notice and appreciate natural beauties.
14. the organ of Adhesiveness: meaning natural inclination or tendency to be mixed with others.
15. to put my old bachelor's neck into the sacred noose, to enter into the holy state of matrimony: a humorous way of saying "to cease to be a bachelor and get married".
16. discretion: the ability to decide what is most suitable to be done.
17. humility: humbleness.
18. All the brine and foam: referring to the sea that separates England from Ireland.
19. inferior minds: referring here to the housemaids.
20. nor even of mortal flesh = nor even through the medium of mortal flesh; nor even bodily.
21. strong workings in the features: deep wrinkles on the face.
22. It will atone: "It" refers to Rochester's purpose in marrying Jane. Rochester was here trying to defend himself. He argued that it was not just for his own interests but also for the sake of Jane that he decided to marry her.
23. It will expiate at God's tribunal: It (his good intention to marry Jane) will make up for his marrying Jane at God's court of justice. In other words, he thought that if God took into consideration his intention to marry Jane, he might not punish him.
24. sanction: agree with.
25. For the world's judgment—I wash my hands thereof: would not care what other people might say about the marriage.

Questions for Understanding

1. What do you think of the setting of this chapter?
2. What is Rochester's state of mind after Jane Eyre accepted his proposal?
3. Is there any meaning implied in the sudden change of the weather—the

wind, the rain, the thunder and lightning that struck the chestnut tree?

Aspects of Appreciation

1. The interpretation of *Jane Eyre*, as a novel, can be focused on its autobiographical elements, the Gothic elements, significance of social criticism, the form of a Bildungsroman, that is, a novel that tells the story of Jane's growth from childhood to adulthood.
2. One of the attractions of *Jane Eyre* is its central theme of a plain orphan girl's struggle for independence and true love. The story is romantic in nature with realistic reflections of Victorian values and social problems. In recent years, critics pay more attention to its central images and fairy-tale sub-structures and its reference to the Bible and other literary works. For instance, Jane's marriage to Rochester, a wealthy man from a higher class, is suggestive of the fairy tale Cinderella.
3. Feminist critics approve Jane's self-respect and pursuit of equality and independence. They further explore, for example, the power struggle between men and women shown in the love and marriage of Rochester and Jane. They see in Jane and Rochester's match the struggle of conquering and being conquered, and the mad woman is interpreted by some as a psychological representation of Jane's. She reveals the frustration and persecution every woman experiences in this or that phase of her life; and her setting fire to the mansion is representative of the possible inner rage of all women including Jane, and their secret wish to give vent to it. Modern readings, therefore, have greatly enriched our understanding of this novel and enabled us to better appreciate it as an artistic piece.

Suggested Further Reading

1. Charlotte Brontë. *Villette* (1853).
2. M. Allot ed. *Charlotte Brontë: Jane Eyre and Villette, A Casebook*, 1973.
3. Mike Edwards. *Charlotte Bronte: the Novels*, 1999.

Topics for Further Study

1. Share your reading experience of *Jane Eyre* and discuss with your classmates. List the qualities you admire in Jane Eyre.
2. In what ways might *Jane Eyre* be considered as a feminist novel? What

points does the novel make about the treatment and position of women in Victorian society? With particular attention to the treatment of marriage in the novel, is there any way in which it might be considered anti-feminist?
3. Compare and contrast some of the characters who serve as foils throughout *Jane Eyre*: Blanche to Jane, St. John to Rochester, and perhaps Bertha to Jane. Also think about the points of comparison between the Reed and Rivers families. How do these contrasts add to the development of the themes of the novel?
4. Search for information on the Internet about the life experiences of the author Charlotte Brontë and compare them with Jane Eyre's.

Charles Dickens
(1812~1870)

About the Author

Dickens came from a poor background. When he was young, his father was imprisoned for debt, and he had to leave school and work in a nightmarish blacking factory. Thus he had little formal education, but managed to make up for the deficiency through avid and extensive reading on his own. Still later he learned the shorthand and became a reporter on parliamentary proceedings. Then he wrote for a pictorial book, *The Pickwick Papers*(1837), which became immediately popular and started him off on his lifelong writing career. Dickens was a prolific writer. He wrote 20-odd novels, not to say the host of his other writings that came out in print. Reading him is always an enjoyable experience. His effect on the readers can be such big that they feel instantly that they are in the presence of greatness.

Dickens died of a stroke on June 9, 1870, with his last novel *The Mysteries of Edwin Drood* left unfinished. He was buried in the Poets' Corner in Westminster Abbey, near Geoffrey Chaucer and other fellow writers.

Dickens was the foremost English novelist of the Victorian Age and one of the greatest writers of the English language. He was acclaimed for his rich storytelling and memorable characters, and he achieved massive worldwide popularity both in his lifetime and afterwards.

VI. Age of Realism (The Victorian Age)

★ Great Expectations

About the Novel

The novel *Great Expectations* is set in Kent in the years about between 1810 and 1830. It tells of the growth of Pip from boyhood to manhood. Pip is a poor orphan, who is left under the care of his sister Mrs. Joe Gargery. One day he meets on the marshes a convict who has escaped from a nearby prison-ship. Early the next morning, he steals some food and a file from his home, and gives them to the convict as he is threatened to. With the file the convict cuts his leg-iron but is soon recaptured.

There lives in the neighboring town a rich lady named Miss Havisham, who was deserted by her faithless lover on her wedding day many years ago and has since shut herself inside the house. At twelve Pip receives an invitation from her, and so he often goes to visit her. In the meantime, he becomes infatuated with a beautiful girl of his own age by the name of Estella, whom Miss Havisham adopts as her daughter and has reared to be cruel and distant as her revenge upon the male sex. His visits cease when, at the age of fourteen, Pip is apprenticed to Joe Gargery, a blacksmith and his brother-in-law. Then, about four years later, he is informed by a lawyer that he has "great expectations" from a mysterious benefactor, who wishes him to be educated as a gentleman. He owes this to Miss Havisham and that she intends him to marry Estella.

Pip goes to London for his education, and snobbishly neglects his childhood friends. He lives idly and unhappily, and is constantly snubbed by Estella although he does everything possible to court her. When he is twenty-three, his true benefactor appears, who turns out to be the very convict named Magwitch he met when he was a small boy of seven. Pip is greatly disappointed. But gradually he changes his snobbish attitude towards the convict and tries desperately to save him from the punishment which his home-coming from Australia has caused. Unfortunately Magwitch is betrayed by Compeyson, a villain and his personal enemy, and is retaken and put to death. Pip learns his lessons and becomes a changed man.

Chapter 58

The tidings[1] of my high fortunes having had a heavy fall, had got down to my native place and its neighborhood, before I got there. I found the Blue Boar[2] in possession of the intelligence, and I found that it made a great change in the Boar's demeanor[3]. Whereas the Boar had cultivated my good opinion with warm assiduity[4] when I was coming into property, the Boar was exceedingly cool on the subject now that I was going out of property.

It was evening when I arrived, much fatigued by the journey I had so often made so easily. The Boar could not put me into my usual bedroom, which was engaged(probably by someone who had expectations), and could only assign me a very indifferent chamber among the pigeons and post-chaises up the yard. But, I had as sound a sleep in that lodging as in the most superior accommodation the Boar could have given me, and the quality of my dreams was about the same as in the best bedroom.

Early in the morning while my breakfast was getting ready, I strolled round by Satis House[5]. There were printed bills on the gate, and on bits of carpet hanging out of the windows, announcing a sale by auction of the Household Furniture and Effects, next week. The House itself was to be sold as old building materials and pulled down. LOT[6] 1 was marked in whitewashed knock-knee letters on the brew house; LOT 2 on that part of the main building which had been so long shut up. Other lots were marked off on other parts of the structure, and the ivy had been torn down to make room for the inscriptions, and much of it trailed low in the dust and was withered already. Stepping in for a moment at the open gate and looking around me with the uncomfortable air of a stranger who had no business there, I saw the auctioneer's clerk walking on the casks and telling them off for the information of a catalogue compiler, pen in hand, who made a temporary desk of the wheeled chair I had so often pushed along to the tune of Old Clem.

When I got back to my breakfast in the Boar's coffee-room, I found Mr. Pumblechook[7] conversing with the landlord. Mr. Pumblechook(not improved in appearance by his late nocturnal adventure) was waiting for me, and addressed me in the following terms.

"Young man, I am sorry to see you brought low. But what else could be expected! What else could be expected!"

As he extended his hand with a magnificently forgiving air, and as I was broken by illness and unfit to quarrel, I took it.

VI. Age of Realism (The Victorian Age)

"William," said Mr. Pumblechook to the waiter, "put a muffins[8] on table. And has it come to this! Has it come to this!"

I frowningly sat down to my breakfast. Mr. Pumblechook stood over me and poured out my tea—before I could touch the teapot—with the air of a benefactor who was resolved to be true to the last.

"William," said Mr. Pumblechook, mournfully, "put the salt on. In happier times," addressing me, "I think you took sugar. And did you take milk? You did. Sugar and milk. William, bring a watercress[9]."

"Thank you," said I, shortly, "but I don't eat watercresses."

"You don't eat' em," returned Mr. Pumblechook, sighing and nodding his head several times, as if he might have expected that, and as if abstinence from watercresses were consistent with my downfall. "True. The simple fruits of the earth. No. You needn't bring any, William."

I went on with my breakfast, and Mr. Pumblechook continued to stand over me, staring fishily and breathing noisily, as he always did.

"Little more than skin and bone!" mused Mr. Pumblechook, aloud. "And yet when he went from here (I may say with my blessing), and I spread afore him my humble store, like the Bee, he was as plump as a Peach!"

This reminded me of the wonderful difference between the servile manner in which he had offered his hand in my new prosperity, saying, "May I?" and the ostentatious clemency[10] with which he had just now exhibited the same fat five fingers.

"Hah!" he went on, handing me the bread-and-butter. "And air you a-going to Joseph[11]?"

"In heaven's name," said I, firing in spite of myself, "what does it matter to you where I am going? Leave that teapot alone."

It was the worst course I could have taken[12], because it gave Pumblechook the opportunity he wanted.

"Yes, young man," said he, releasing the handle of the article in question, retiring a step or two from my table, and speaking for the behoof of the landlord and waiter at the door, "I will leave that teapot alone. You are right, young man. For once, you are right. I forgit myself when I take such an interest in your breakfast, as to wish your frame, exhausted by the debilitating effects of prodigygality, to be stimilated by the 'olesome nourishment of your forefathers. And yet," said Pumblechook, turning to the landlord and waiter, and pointing me out at arm's length, "this is him as

I ever sported with in his days of happy infancy! Tell me not it cannot be; I tell you this is him!"

A low murmur from the two replied. The waiter appeared to be particularly affected. "This is him," said Pumblechook, "as I have rode in my shaycart[13]. This is him as I have seen brought up by hand. This is him untoe the sister of which I was uncle by marriage, as her name was Georgiana M'ria[14] from her own mother, let him deny it if he can!"

The waiter seemed convinced that I could not deny it, and that it gave the case a black look. "Young man," said Pumblechook, screwing his head at me in the old fashion, "you air a-going to Joseph. What does it matter to me, you ask me, where you air a-going? I say to you, Sir, you air a-going to Joseph."

The waiter coughed, as if he modestly invited me to get over that.

"Now," said Pumblechook, and all this with a most exasperating[15] air of saving in the cause of virtue what was perfectly convincing and conclusive, "I will tell you what to say to Joseph. Here is Squires of the Boar present, known and respected in this town, and here is William, which his father's name was Potkins if I do not deceive myself."

"You do not, sir," said William.

"In their presence," pursued Pumblechook, "I will tell you, young man, what to say to Joseph. Says you, 'Joseph, I have this day seen my earliest benefactor and the founder of my fortun's. I will name no names, Joseph, but so they are pleased to call him up-town, and I have seen that man.'"

"I swear I don't see him here," said I.

"Say that likewise," retorted Pumblechook. "Say you said that, and even Joseph will probably betray surprise."

"There you quite mistake him," said I. "I know better."

"Says you," Pumblechook went on, "Joseph, I have seen that man, and that man bears you no malice and bears me no malice. He knows your character, Joseph, and is well acquainted with your pig-headedness and ignorance; and he knows my character, Joseph, and he knows my want of gratitoode[16]. Yes, Joseph, says you," here Pumblechook shook his head and hand at me, "he knows my total deficiency of common human gratitoode. He knows it, Joseph, as none can. You do not know it, Joseph, having no call to know it, but that man do."

Windy donkey[17] as he was, it really amazed me that he could have the face to talk thus to mine.

"Says you, 'Joseph, he gave me a little message, which I will now repeat. It was, that in my being brought low, he saw the finger of Providence. He knowed that finger when he saw it, Joseph, and he saw it plain. It pinted out this writing, Joseph. Reward of ingratitoode to his earliest benefactor, and founder of fortun's. But that man said he did not repent of what he had done, Joseph. Not at all. It was right to do it, it was kind to do it, it was benevolent to do it, and he would do it again.'"

"It's pity," said I, scornfully, as I finished my interrupted breakfast, "that the man did not say what he had done and would do again."

"Squires of the Boar!" Pumblechook was now addressing the landlord, "and William! I have no objections to your mentioning, either up-town or down-town, if such should be your wishes, that it was right to do it, kind to do it, benevolent to do it, and that I would do it again."

With those words the Impostor[18] shook them both by the hand, with an air, and left the house; leaving me much more astonished than delighted by the virtues of that same indefinite "it". I was not long after him in leaving the house too, and when I went down the High-street I saw him holding forth(no doubt to the same effect) at his shop door to a select group, who honored me with very unfavorable glances as I passed on the opposite side of the way.

But, it was only the pleasanter to turn to Biddy[19] and to Joe[20], whose great forbearance shone more brightly than before, if that could be, contrasted, with this brazen pretender. I went towards them slowly, for my limbs were weak, but with a sense of increasing relief as I drew nearer to them, and a sense of leaving arrogance and untruthfulness further and further behind.

The June weather was delicious. The sky was blue, the larks were soaring high over the green corn, I thought all that countryside more beautiful and peaceful by far than I had ever known it to be yet. Many pleasant pictures of the life that I would lead there, and of the change for the better that would come over my character when I had a guiding spirit at my side whose simple faith and clear home-wisdom I had proved, beguiled my way. They awakened a tender emotion in me; for, my heart was softened by my return, and such a change had come to pass, that I felt like one who was toiling home barefoot from distant travel, and whose wanderings had lasted many years.

The schoolhouse where Biddy was mistress, I had never seen; but, the little roundabout lane by which I entered the village for quietness' sake, took me past it. I was disappointed to find that the day was a holiday; no children were there, and Biddy's house was closed. Some hopeful notion of seeing her busily engaged in her daily duties, before she saw me, had been in my mind and was defeated.

But, the forge was a very short distance off, and I went towards it under the sweet green limes, listening for the clink of Joe's hammer. Long after I ought to have heard it, and long after I had fancied I heard it and found it but a fancy, all was still. The limes were there, and the white thorns were there, and the chestnut-trees were there, and their leaves rustled harmoniously when I stopped to listen; but, the clink of Joe's hammer was not in the midsummer wind.

Almost fearing, without knowing why, to come in view of the forge, I saw it at last, and saw that it was closed. No gleam of fire, no glittering shower of sparks, no roar of bellows; all shut up, and still.

But, the house was not deserted, and the best parlor seemed to be in use, for there were white curtains fluttering in its window, and the window was open and gay with flowers. I went softly towards it, meaning to peep over the flowers, when Joe and Biddy stood before me, arm in arm.

At first Biddy gave a cry, as if she thought it was my apparition[21], but in another moment she was in my embrace. I wept to see her, and she wept to see me; I, because she looked so fresh and pleasant; she, because I looked so worn and white.

"But dear Biddy, how smart you are!"

"Yes, dear Pip."

"And Joe, how smart you are!"

"Yes, dear old Pip, old chap."

I looked at both of them, from one to the other, and then—

"It's my wedding-day," cried Biddy, in a burst of happiness, "and I am married to Joe!"

They had taken me into the kitchen, and I had laid my head down on the old deal table. Biddy held one of my hands to her lips, and Joe's restoring touch was on my shoulder. "Which he wasn't strong enough, my dear, fur to be surprised," said Joe. And Biddy said, "I ought to have thought of it, dear Joe, but I was too happy". They were both so overjoyed to see me, so proud to see me, so touched by my coming to them, so

VI. Age of Realism (The Victorian Age)

delighted that I should have come by accident to make their day complete!

My first thought was one of great thankfulness that I had never breathed this last baffled hope to Joe. How often, while he was with me in my illness, had it risen to my lips. How irrevocable would have been his knowledge of it, if he had remained with me but another hour!

"Dear Biddy," said I, "you have the best husband in the whole world, and if you could have seen him by my bed you would have—But no, you couldn't love him better than you do."

"No, I couldn't indeed," said Biddy.

"And, dear Joe, you have the best wife in the whole world, and she will make you as happy as even you deserve to be, you dear, good, noble Joe!"

Joe looked at me with a quivering lip, and fairly put his sleeve before his eyes.

"And Joe and Biddy both, as you have been to church today, and are in charity and love with all mankind, receive my humble thanks for all you have done for me and all I have so ill repaid! And when I say that I am going away within the hour, for I am soon going abroad, and that I shall never rest until I have worked for the money with which you have kept me out of prison, and have sent it to you, don't think, dear Joe and Biddy, that if I could repay it a thousand times over, I suppose I could cancel a farthing of the debt I owe you, or that I would do so if I could!"

They were both melted by these words, and both entreated me to say no more.

"But I must say more. Dear Joe, I hope you will have children to love, and that some little fellow will sit in this chimney corner of a winter night, who may remind you of another little fellow gone out of it for ever. Don't tell him, Joe, that I was thankless; don't tell him, Biddy, that I was ungenerous and unjust; only tell him that I honored you both, because you were both so good and true, and that, as your child, I said it would be natural to him to grow up a much better man than I did."

"I ain't a-going," said Joe, from behind his sleeve, "to tell him nothink o' that natur, Pip. Nor Biddy ain't. Nor yet no one ain't."

"And now, though I know you have already done it in your own kind hearts, pray tell me, both, that you forgive me! Pray let me hear you say the words, that I may carry the sound of them away with me, and then I shall be able to believe that you can trust me, and think better of me, in the time to come!"

"O dear old Pip, old chap," said Joe. "God knows as I forgive you, if I have anythink to forgive!"

"Amen! And God knows I do!" echoed Biddy.

Now let me go up and look at my old little room, and rest there a few minutes by myself, and then when I have eaten and drunk with you, go with me as far as the fingerpost, dear Joe and Biddy, before we say good-bye!"

I sold all I had, and put aside as much as I could, for a composition[22] with my creditors—who gave me ample time to pay them in full—and I went out and joined Herbert[23]. Within a month, I had quitted England, and within two months I was clerk to Clarriker and Co.[24], and within four months I assumed my first undivided responsibility.

For, the beam across the parlor ceiling at Mill Pond Bank, had then ceased to tremble under old Bill Barley's growls and was at peace, and Herbert had gone away to marry Clara, and I was left in sole charge of the Eastern Branch until he brought her back.

Many a year went round, before I was a partner in the House; but, I lived happily with Herbert and his wife, and lived frugally, and paid my debts, and maintained a constant correspondence with Biddy and Joe. It was not until I became third in the Firm, that Clarriker betrayed me to Herbert; but, he then declared that the secret of Herbert's partnership had been long enough upon his conscience, and he must tell it. So, he told it, and Herbert was as much moved as amazed, and the dear fellow and I were not the worse friends for the long concealment. I must not leave it to be supposed that we were ever a great house, or that we made mints of money. We were not in a grand way of business, but we had a good name, and worked for our profits, and did very well. We owed so much to Herbert's ever cheerful industry and readiness, that I often wondered how I had conceived that old idea of his inaptitude, until I was one day enlightened by the reflection, that perhaps the inaptitude had never been in him at all, but had been in me.

Chapter 59

For eleven years, I had not seen Joe nor Biddy with my bodily eyes—though they had both been often before my fancy in the East—when, upon an evening in December, an hour or two after dark, I laid my hand softly on the latch of the old kitchen door. I touched it so softly that I was not heard, and looked in unseen. There, smoking his pipe in the old place by the kitchen firelight, as hale and as strong as ever though a little gray, sat Joe; and there, fenced into the corner with Joe's leg, and sitting on my own little stool looking at the fire, was—I again!

"We give him the name of Pip for your sake, dear old chap," said Joe, delighted when I took another stool by the child's side (but I did not rumple his hair), "and we hoped he might grow a little bit like you, and we think he do."

I thought so too, and I took him out for a walk next morning, and we talked immensely, understanding one another to perfection. And I took him down to the churchyard, and set him on a certain tombstone there, and he showed me from that elevation which stone was sacred to the memory of Philip Pirrip[25], late of this Parish, and Also Georgiana, Wife of the Above.

"Biddy," said I, when I talked with her after dinner, as her little girl lay sleeping in her lap, "you must give Pip to me, one of these days; or lend him, at all events."

"No, no," said Biddy, gently. "You must marry."

"So Herbert and Clara say, but I don't think I shall, Biddy. I have so settled down in their home, that it's not at all likely. I am already quite an old bachelor."

Biddy looked down at her child, and put its little hand to her lips, and then put the good matronly hand with which she had touched it, into mine. There was something in the action and in the light pressure of Biddy's wedding-ring, that had a very pretty eloquence in it.

"Dear Pip," said Biddy, "you are sure you don't fret for her[26]?"

"O no—I think not, Biddy."

"Tell me as an old, old friend. Have you quite forgotten her?"

"My dear Biddy, I have forgotten nothing in my life that ever had a foremost place there, and little that ever had any place there. But that poor dream, as I once used to call it, has all gone by, Biddy, all gone by!"

Nevertheless, I knew while I said those words, that I secretly intended to revisit the site of the old house that evening, alone, for her sake. Yes even so. For Estella's sake.

I had heard of her as leading a most unhappy life, and as being separated from her husband, who had used her with great cruelty, and who had become quite renowned as a compound of pride, avarice, brutality, and meanness. And I had heard of the death of her husband, from an accident consequent on his ill-treatment of a horse. This release had befallen her some two years before; for anything I knew, she was married again.

The early dinner-hour at Joe's, left me abundance of time, without hurrying my talk with Biddy, to walk over to the old spot before dark. But, what with loitering[27] on the way, to look at old objects and to think of old times, the day had quite declined when I came to the place.

There was no house now, no brewery, no building whatever left, but the wall of the old garden. The cleared space had been enclosed with a rough fence, and, looking over it, I saw that some of the old ivy had snuck root anew, and was growing green on low quiet mounds of ruin. A gate in the fence standing ajar, I pushed it open, and went in.

A cold silvery mist had veiled the afternoon, and the moon was not yet up to scatter it. But, the stars were shining beyond the mist, and the moon was coming, and the evening was not dark. I could trace out where every part of the old house had been, and where the brewery had been, and where the gate, and where the casks. I had done so, and was looking along the desolate garden walk, when I beheld a solitary figure in it.

The figure showed itself aware of me, as I advanced. It had been moving towards me, but it stood still. As I drew nearer, I saw it to be the figure of a woman. As I drew nearer yet, it was about to turn away, when it stopped, and let me come up with it. Then, it faltered as if much surprised, and uttered my name, and I cried out:

"Estella!"

"I am greatly changed. I wonder you know me."

The freshness of her beauty was indeed gone, but its indescribable majesty and its indescribable charm remained. Those attractions in it, I had seen before; what I had never seen before, was the saddened softened light of the once proud eyes; what I had never felt before, was the friendly touch of the once insensible hand.

We sat down on a bench that was near, and I said, "After so many years, it is strange that we should thus meet again, Estella, here where our first meeting was! Do you often come back?"

"I have never been here since."

"Nor I."

The moon began to rise, and I thought of the placid look at the white ceiling, which had passed away. The moon began to rise, and I thought of the pressure on my hand when I had spoken the last words he had heard on earth.

Estella was the next to break the silence that ensued[28] between us.

"I have very often hoped and intended to come back, but have been prevented by many circumstances. Poor, poor old place!"

The silvery mist was touched with the first rays of the moonlight, and the same rays touched the tears that dropped from her eyes. Not knowing that I saw them, and setting herself to get the better of them, she said quietly,

"Were you wondering, as you walked along, how it came to be left in this condition?"

"Yes, Estella."

"The ground belongs to me. It is the only possession I have not relinquished[29]. Everything else has gone from me, little by little, but I have kept this. It was the subject of the only determined resistance I made in all the wretched years."

"Is it to be built on?"

"At last it is. I came here to take leave of it before its change. And you," she said, in a voice of touching interest to a wanderer, "you live abroad still?"

"Still."

"And do well, I am sure?"

"I work pretty hard for a sufficient living, and therefore—Yes, I do well."

"I have often thought of you," said Estella.

"Have you?"

"Of late, very often. There was a long hard time when I kept far from me, the remembrance, of what I had thrown away when I was quite ignorant of its worth. But, since my duty has not been incompatible with the admission of that remembrance, I have given it a place in my heart."

"You have always held your place in my heart," I answered.

And we were silent again, until she spoke.

"I little thought," said Estella, "that I should take leave of you in taking leave of this spot. I am very glad to do so."

"Glad to part again, Estella? To me, parting is a painful thing. To me, the remembrance of our last parting has been ever mournful and painful."

"But you said to me," returned Estella, very earnestly, "'God bless you, God forgive you!' And if you could say that to me then, you will not hesitate to say that to me now—now, when suffering has been stronger than all other teaching, and has taught me to understand what your heart used to be. I have been bent and broken, but—I hope—into a better shape. Be as considerate and good to me as you were, and tell me we are friends."

"We are friends," said I, rising and bending over her, as she rose from the bench.

"And will continue friends apart," said Estella.

I took her hand in mine, and we went out of the ruined place; and, as the morning mists had risen long ago when I first left the forge, so the evening mists were rising now, and in all the broad expanse of tranquil light they showed to me, I saw no shadow of another parting from her.

Notes

1. tidings: news.
2. Blue Boar: a hotel at Pip's hometown.
3. demeanor: the way someone behaves or looks that gives you a general idea of his or her character.
4. assiduity: the quality or state marked by careful unremitting attention or persistent application; solicitous or obsequious attention to a person.
5. Satis House: Miss Havisham's manor where Pip once worked as a boy.
6. LOT: something to be sold, especially at an auction; and the things on sale at auction are marked with numbers.
7. Mr. Pumblechook: Pip's pompous, arrogant uncle.
8. muffin: a small thick round kind of bread, usually eaten hot with butter.
9. watercress: a small plant with strong tasting green leaves that grows in water.
10. clemency: disposition to be merciful and especially to moderate the severity of punishment due.
11. "And air you a-going to Joseph": And are you going to Joseph? (Notice the local dialect used by Mr. Pumblechook. You will find more in the following part.)
12. It was the worst course I could have taken: It was the worst thing Pip could have said.
13. shaycart: four-wheel horse carriage.
14. Georgiana M'ria: Pip's mother who died when Pip was very young.
15. exasperating: extremely annoying.
16. gratitoode: gratitude.

17. windy donkey: bombastic fool.
18. Impostor: someone who pretends to be someone else in order to trick people.
19. Biddy: A simple, kindhearted country girl. Biddy first befriends Pip when they attend school together. After Mrs. Joe is attacked and becomes an invalid, Biddy moves into Pip's home to care for her. Throughout most of the novel, Biddy represents the opposite of Estella; she is plain, kind, moral, and of Pip's own social class.
20. Joe: Joe Gargery, Pip's brother-in-law, the village blacksmith. Joe stays with his overbearing, abusive wife—known as Mrs. Joe—solely out of love for Pip. Joe's quiet goodness makes him one of the few completely sympathetic characters in *Great Expectations*. Although he is uneducated and unrefined, he acts solely for the benefit of those he loves and suffers in silence when Pip treats him coldly.
21. apparition: something that you imagine you can see, especially the spirit of a dead person.
22. composition: mutual settlement or agreement.
23. Herbert: Herbert Pocket, whom Pip first meets in the garden of Satis House. Years later, they meet again in London, and Herbert becomes Pip's best friend and key companion after Pip's elevation to the status of gentleman. Herbert is the son of Matthew Pocket, Miss Havisham's cousin, and hopes to become a merchant so that he can afford to marry Clara Barley.
24. Clarriker and Co.: the company for which Pip works.
25. Philip Pirrip: here referring to Pip's father.
26. her: here referring to Estella.
27. loiter: to move or travel slowly, or to keep stopping when you should keep moving.
28. ensued: happened as a result of something.
29. relinquish: to let someone else have position, power, or rights, especially unwillingly.

Questions for Understanding

1. How do the townspeople treat Pip when he returns to his hometown?
2. What does Pip beg Joe and Biddy to do?
3. Why does Pip notice the ivy growing on the ruins of the house? Is it in any way significant for him?

4. Estella remarks that they "will continue friends apart". Pip also says that he still works abroad, and "does well". Why, then, does Pip say at the end of the chapter that he "saw no shadow of another parting from her"?

Aspects of Appreciation

1. Money in the novel

Great Expectations recounts the development of the character of the narrator, showing how money corrupts people's minds, causing people to be lost in integrity, and how people learn their lessons and regain themselves after adversity.

When Pip falls in love with Estella, he begins to feel ashamed of his life and his position in the society because he believes that it will ruin his hopes of Estella loving him. When he is informed of the "great expectations", his ego grows tremendously, and he looks down upon his friends. When he finally learns that Abel Magwitch is his benefactor, his expectations start to fade, and his good nature begins to overcome the negative traits that he had developed. Pip has finally accepted responsibility for his lie. He also looks at others in a new light.

2. The ending

Dickens originally devised a sad ending for Pip's love affair with Estella. It had Estella remarried to a doctor, meeting Pip once on a London street but she has not changed at all and he, in return, feels none of the old feelings for her. Later, Dickens took the advice of a novelist friend, Bulwer Lytton, and changed the ending to give Pip, Estella, and the readers a chance for a happy conclusion.

The first ending, though much more depressing, seems more true to the theme of the story. The second ending, however, is ambiguous and no one is certain if the "shadow of no parting" means that they would stay together or not.

The argument is that Pip must come to obtain happiness through his own internal process and not through some external situation such as position or wealth, or persons like Estella. According to this, there is some justice in Estella and Pip finally finding love in each other, since both of them seem to have realized what it means to be happy and therefore are ready for a healthy relationship with each other. Although Estella's transformation from ice queen to sensitive lady is not directly presented, she is a true victim of society's values, and therefore, her suffering is worthy of sympathy.

Suggested Further Reading

1. Charles Dickens. *Oliver Twist*, *David Copperfield*.
2. Steven Conner. ed. *Charles Dickens*, Harlow: Longman, 1996.

Topics for Further Study

1. What significance does the novel's title, *Great Expectations*, have for the story? In what ways does Pip have "great expectations"?
2. *Great Expectations* is the story of Pip, his initial dreams and resulting disappointments that eventually lead to his becoming a genuinely good man. In this sense, it is said that the self-losing and self-regaining makes the process of Pip's character development, and helps to establish the central theme of the novel. What is your interpretation?
3. Think about the novel's two endings: the "official" version in which Pip and Estella are reunited in the garden and the earlier version in which they merely speak briefly on the street and go their separate ways. Which version do you prefer? Which version seems more true to the thematic development of the novel? Why?

William Makepeace Thackeray
(1811~1863)

About the Author

William Makepeace Thackeray was born on July 18, 1811, in Calcutta, India, the son of an official of the East India Company. After his father's death and his mother's remarriage, young Thackeray went to London for his schooling at Charterhouse. He then entered Cambridge University. The failure of Indian bank where he had deposited his inherited fortune forced him to end his university days. He left Cambridge in 1830 without taking a degree. These disasters, however, turned into a good thing, since they obliged him to work seriously and take stock of his literary talents. Thackeray tried his hand at drawing and painting at first; it was only after his marriage to Isabella Shawe in 1836 that he turned seriously to literature. Thereupon followed a decade of brilliant writing in the minor literary forms that brought in ready money. *Vanity Fair* was in serial form (1847~1848), and it established his reputation. It was followed by other novels such as *Pendennis* (1850) and *The Newcomes* (1855). However, with *The Virginians* (1857~1858), his fiction declined in popularity. He died in London on December 24, 1863.

Thackeray is now recognized as a major author of the Victorian Age. Compared with Dickens, Thackeray was less interested in direct social criticism. He was mainly concerned with showing people's vanity and their deluded efforts to achieve wealth and social status. His greatest skill lay in creating characters who display various facets of human nature and are at the same time highly individualized and real. He had a remarkable way of telling a story and commenting on it. His fiction offered both theme and method to later novelists.

★ Vanity Fair

About the Novel

Vanity Fair is Thackeray's masterpiece. The subtitle of the novel is "*A Novel Without a Hero*". The writer's intention was not to portray individuals, but the bourgeois and aristocratic society as a whole. The title of the novel was taken from John Bunyan's *The Pilgrim's Progress*. This can show Thackeray's opinion of the English bourgeois and aristocratic society, and he intended to draw a picture of the life of the upper class of England.

The main plot centers on the story of two women, Amelia Sedley and Rebecca Sharp. Both of them are typical women in a bourgeois society, in sharply different ways. Amelia Sedley is simple, sentimental, weak, but good at heart. The story begins with the departure of the two girls from their school in a London suburb, where they have studied for six years. Amelia is the daughter of a wealthy merchant, and Rebecca (Becky) is an orphan. Becky is determined to worm her way into upper society at all costs. First she attempts to entrap Amelia's brother, Joseph for a husband, but she fails. Then she manages to become governess in Sir Pitt Crawley's family. She soon gains favour from her master, who is so captivated by her charm that he proposes to her after his wife dies. But Becky has to give up this good chance, because she has been already secretly married to the old man's younger son Rawdon, who has the bright prospect of inheriting his aunt's property. But Rawdon's aunt disinherits him on account of his marriage with a dowryless girl. So Becky's hopes of being married to a rich man are dashed.

Amelia is married to a light-minded young lieutenant called George Osborne. When British troops are sent to the Continent, George goes to war, and is killed in the battle of Waterloo.

A few years later, Rebecca meets her former friend Amelia again. Amelia still holds the dear memory of her dead husband George. But Becky discloses an old secret. She shows Amelia a letter written to her by George. In his letter, George asks Becky to elope with him on the eve of the battle of Waterloo. Amelia feels very disappointed. Then she is married to a man who has a lifelong affection for her. Becky now lives with Amelia's brother, Joseph, until he dies in the West Indies, leaving his property to her. Then she returns to England and tries to live like a lady, but her son by Rawdon, now a baronet, refuses to acknowledge her.

In this novel, Thackeray describes the life of the upper class of England in the early decades of the 19th century, and attacks the social relationship of the bourgeois world by satirizing the individual in the different strata of the upper society. It is a world where money grubbing is the main motive for all members of the upper class. Becky Sharp is a classic example of this money-grubbing instinct. Everyone wishes to gain something in Vanity Fair and acts almost in the same manner as Becky. The character Becky Sharp is drawn with admirable skill.

Chapter 36
How to Live Well on Nothing a Year

...

On nothing per annum[1], then, and during a course of some two or three years, of which we can afford to give but a very brief history, Crawley and his wife lived very happily and comfortably at Paris. It was in this period that he quitted the Guards, and sold out of the army[2]. When we find him again, his mustachios and the title of colonel on his card are the only relics of his military profession.

It has been mentioned that Rebecca, soon after her arrival in Paris, took a very smart and leading position in the society of that capital, and was welcomed at some of the most distinguished houses of the restored French nobility[3]. The English men of fashion in Paris courted her, too, to the disgust of the ladies, their wives, who could not bear the parvenue[4]. For some months the salons of the Faubourg St. Germain[5], in which her place was secured, and the splendors of the new Court, where she was received with much distinction, delighted, and perhaps a little intoxicated Mrs. Crawley who may have been disposed during this period of elation to slight the people—honest young military men mostly—who formed her husband's chief society.

But the colonel yawned sadly among the duchesses and great ladies of the Court. The old women who played écarté[6] made such a noise about a five-franc piece, that it was not worth Colonel Crawley's while to sit down at a card-table. The wit of their conversation he could not appreciate, being ignorant of their language. And what good could his wife get, he urged, by making curtsies every night to a whole circle of princesses? He left Rebecca presently to frequent these parties alone; resuming his own simple pursuits and amusements amongst the amiable friends of his own choice.

The truth is, when we say of a gentleman that he lives elegantly on nothing a year, we use the word "nothing" to signify something unknown; meaning simply, that we don't know how the gentleman in question defrays the expenses of his establishment[7]. Now, our friend the colonel had a great aptitude for all games of chance; and exercising himself, as he continually did, with the cards, the dice-box, or the cue, it is natural to suppose that he attained a much greater skill in the use of these articles than men can possess who only occasionally handle them. To use a cue at billiards well is like using a pencil, or a German flute, or a small-sword—you can not master any one of these implements at first, and it is only by repeated study and perseverance, joined to a natural taste, that a man can excel in the handling of either. Now, Crawley, from being only a brilliant amateur had grown to a consummate master of billiards. Like a great general, his genius used to rise with the danger, and when the luck had been unfavorable to him for a whole gang, and the bets were consequently against him, he would, with consummate skill and boldness, make some prodigious hits which would restore the battle, and come a victor at the end, to the astonishment of everybody—of everybody, that is, who was a stranger to his play. Those who were accustomed to see it were cautious how they staked their money against a man of such sudden resources, and brilliant and overpowering skill.

At games of cards he was equally skillful; for though he would constantly lose money at the commencement of an evening, playing so carelessly and making such blunders, that newcomers were often inclined to think meanly of his talent; yet when roused to action, and awakened to caution by repeated small losses, it was remarked that Crawley's play became quite different, and that he was pretty sure of beating his enemy thoroughly before the night was over. Indeed, very few men could say that they ever had the better of him[8].

His successes were so repeated that no wonder the envious and the vanquished spoke sometimes with bitterness regarding them. And as the French say of the Duke of Wellington[9], who never suffered a defeat, that only an astonishing series of lucky accidents enabled him to be an invariable winner; yet even they allow that he cheated at Waterloo, and was enabled to win the last great trick[10]; so it was hinted at head quarters in England, that some foul play must have taken place in order to account for the continuous successes of Colonel Crawley.

Though Frascati and the Salon[11] were open at that time in Paris, the mania for play was so widely spread, that the public gambling-rooms did not suffice for the general ardor, and gambling went on in private houses as much as if there had been no public means for gratifying the passion. At Crawley's charming little reunions of an evening this fatal amusement commonly was practiced—much to good-natured little Mrs. Cawley's annoyance[12]. She spoke about her husband's passion for dice with the deepest grief; she bewailed it to everybody who came to her house. She besought the young fellows never, never to touch a box; and when young Green of the Rifles[13], lost a very considerable sum of money, Rebecca passed a whole night in tears, as the servant told the unfortunate young man, and actually went on her knees to her husband to beseech him to remit the debt[14], and burn the acknowledgment. How could he? He had lost just as much himself to Blackstone of the Hussars[15], and Count Punter of the Hanoverian Cavalry[16]. Green might have any decent time; but pay? —of course he must pay; to talk of burning IOU's[17] was child's play.

Other officers, chiefly young—for the young fellows gathered round Mrs. Crawley—came from her parties with long faces, having dropped more or less money at her fatal card-tables. Her house began to have an unfortunate reputation. The old hands warned the less experienced of their danger. Colonel O'dowd, of the-th regiment, one of those occupying in Paris, warned Lieutenant Spooney of that corps. A loud and violent fracas[18] took place between the infantry-colonel and his lady, who were dining at the Cafe de Paris, and Colonel and Mrs. Crawley who were also taking their meal there. The ladies engaged on both sides. Mrs. O'dowd snapped her fingers in Mrs. Crawley's face[19], and called her husband "no better than a blackleg[20]," Colonel Crawley challenged Colonel O'dowd, C. B.[21] The commander-in-chief hearing of the dispute sent for Colonel Crawley, who was getting ready the same pistols, "which he shot Captain Marker," and had such a conversation with him that no duel took place. If Rebecca had not gone on her knees to General Tufto[22], Crawley would have been sent back to England; and he did not play, except with civilians, for some weeks after.

But in spite of Rawdon's undoubted skill and constant successes, it became evident to Rebecca, considering these things, that their position was but a precarious one, and that, even although they paid scarcely anybody, their little capital would end one day by dwindling into zero. "Gambling," she would say, "dear, is good to help your income, but not as an income itself. Some day people may be tired of play, and then where are we?" Rawdon acquiesced in the justice of her opinion[23]; and in truth he had remarked that after a few nights of his little suppers, etc., gentlemen were tired of play with him, and, in spite of Rebecca's charms, did not present themselves very eagerly.

Easy and pleasant as their life at Paris was, it was after all only an idle dalliance and amiable trifling; and Rebecca saw that she must push Rawdon's fortune in their own country. She must get him a place or appointment at home or in the colonies; and she determined to make a move upon England as soon as the way could be cleared for her. As a first step she had made Crawley sell out of the Guards, and go on half-pay. His function as aide de camp[24] to General Tufto had ceased previously. Rebecca laughed in all companies at that officer, at his toupee[25] (which he mounted on coming to Paris), at his waistband, at his false teeth, at his pretensions to be a lady-killer above all, and his absurd vanity in fancying every woman whom he came near was in love with him. It was Mrs. Brent, the beetle-browed[26] wife of Mr. Commissary Brent, to whom the general transferred his attentions now—his bouquets, his dinners at the restaurateurs', his opera-boxes, and his knick-knacks[27]. Poor Mrs. Tufto was no more happy than before, and had still to pass long evenings alone with her daughters,

VI. Age of Realism (The Victorian Age)

knowing that her general was gone off scented and curled to stand behind Mrs. Brent's chair at the play. Becky had a dozen admirers in his place to be sure; and could cut her rival to pieces with her wit. But as we have said, she was growing tired of this idle social life: opera-boxes and restaurateur dinners palled upon her: nosegays could not be laid by as a provision for future years; and she could not live upon knick-knacks, laced handkerchiefs, and kid gloves. She felt the frivolity of pleasure, and longed for more substantial benefits.

At this juncture news arrived which was spread among the many creditors of the Colonel at Paris, and which caused them great satisfaction. Miss Crawley, the rich aunt from whom he expected his immense inheritance, was dying; the Colonel must haste to her bedside, Mrs. Crawley and her child would remain behind until he came to reclaim them. He departed for Calais[28], and having reached that place in safety, it might have been supposed that he went to Dover; but instead he took the diligence[29] to Dunkirk[30], and thence traveled to Brussel, for which place he had a former predilection. The fact is, he owed more money at London than at Paris; and he preferred the quiet little Belgian city to either of the more noisy capitals.

Her aunt was dead. Mrs. Crawley ordered the most intense mourning for herself and little Rawdon. The Colonel was busy arranging the affairs of the inheritance. They could take the premier[31] now, instead of the little entresol[32] of the hotel which they occupied. Mrs. Crawley and the landlord had a consultation about the new hangings, an amicable wrangle about the carpets, and a final adjustment of everything except the bill. She went off in one of his carriages; her French bonne[33] with her; the child by her side; the admirable landlord and landlady smiling farewell to her from the gate. General Tufto was furious when he heard she was gone, and Mrs. Brent furious with him for being furious; Lieutenant Spooney cut to the heart; and the landlord got ready his best apartments previous to the return of the fascinating little woman and her husband. He serre'd[34] the trunks which she left in his charge with the greatest care. They were not, however, found to be particularly valuable when opened some time later.

But before she went to join her husband in the Belgic[35] capital, Mrs. Crawley made an expedition into England, leaving behind her little son upon the Continent, under the care of her French maid.

The parting between Rebecca and the little Rawdon did not cause either party much pain. She had not, to say truth, seen much of the young gentleman since his birth. After the amiable fashion of French mothers, she had placed him out at nurse in a village in the neighborhood of Paris, where little Rawdon passed the first months of his life, not unhappily, with a numerous family of foster-brothers in wooden shoes. His father would ride over many a time to see him here, and the elder Rawdon's paternal heart glowed to see him rosy and dirty, shouting lustily, and happy in the making of mudpies under the superintendence of the gardener's wife, his nurse.

Rebecca did not care much to go and see the son and heir. Once he spoiled a new dove-colored pelisse[36] of hers. He preferred his nurse's caresses to his mamma's, and when finally he quitted that jolly nurse and almost parent, he cried loudly for hours. He was only consoled by his mother's promise that he should return to his nurse the next day; indeed the nurse herself, who probably would have been pained at the parting too, was told that the child would immediately be restored to her, and for some time awaited quite anxiously his return.

In fact, our friends may be said to have been among the first of that brood of hardy English adventurers who have subsequently invaded the Continent and swindled in all the capitals of Europe. The respect in those happy days of 1817~1818 was very great for the wealth and honor of Britons. They had not then learned, as I was told, to haggle for bargains with the pertinacity which now distinguishes them. The great cities of Europe had not been as yet open to the enterprise of our rascals. And whereas there is now hardly a town of France or Italy in which you shall not see some noble countryman of our own, with that happy swagger and insolence of demeanor which we carry everywhere, swindling inn-landlords, passing fictitious cheques upon credulous bankers, robbing coach-makers of their carriages, goldsmiths of their trinkets, easy travelers of their money at cards, even public libraries of their books—thirty years ago you needed but to be a Milor Anglais[37], traveling in a private carriage, and credit was at your hand[38] wherever you chose to seek it, and gentlemen, instead of cheating, were cheated. It was not for some weeks after the Crawleys' departure that the landlord of the hotel which they occupied during their residence at Paris found out the losses which he had sustained: not until Madame Marabou, the milliner, made repeated visits with her little bill for articles supplied to Madame Crawley; not until Monsieur Didelot from Boule d'Or[39] in the Palais Royal[40] had asked half a dozen times whether cette charmante Miladi[41] who had bought watches and bracelets of him was de retour[42]. It is a fact that even the poor gardener's wife, who had nursed madame's child, was never paid after the first six months for that supply of the milk of human kindness with which she had furnished the lusty and healthy little Rawdon. No, not even the nurse was paid—the Crawleys were in too great a hurry to remember their trifling debt to her. As for the landlord of the hotel, his curses against the English nation were violent for the rest of his natural life. He asked all travelers whether they knew a certain Colonel Lor Crawley—avec sa femme[43] une petite dame, tres spirituelle[44]. "Ah, Monsieur!" he would add—"ils m'ont affreusement volé."[45] It was melancholy to hear his accents as he spoke of that catastrophe".

Rebecca's object in her journey to London was to effect a kind of compromise with her husband's numerous creditors, and by offering them a dividend of nine-pence or a shilling in the pound, to secure a return for him into his own country. It does not become us to trace the steps which she took in the conduct of this most difficult negotiation; but, having shown them to their satisfaction, that the sum which she was empowered to offer was all her husband's available capital, and having convinced them that Colonel Crawley would prefer a perpetual retirement on the Continent to a residence in this country with his debts unsettled; having proved to them that there was no possibility of money accruing to him from other quarters, and no earthly chance of their getting a larger dividend than that which she was empowered to offer, she brought the Colonel's creditors, unanimously to accept her proposals, and purchased with fifteen hundred pounds of ready money more than ten times that amount of debts.

Mrs. Crawley employed no lawyer in the transaction. The matter was so simple, to have or to leave, as she justly observed, that she made the lawyers of the creditors themselves do the business. And Mr. Lewis representing Mr. Davids, of Red Lion Square, and Mr. Moss acting for Mr. Manasseh of Cursitor Street(chief creditors of the Colonel's), complimented his lady upon the brilliant way in which she did business, and declared that there was no professional man who could beat her.

Rebecca received their congratulations with perfect modesty; ordered a bottle of sherry and a bread cake to the little dingy lodgings where she dwelt, while conducting the business, to treat the enemy's lawyers: shook hands with them at parting, in excellent good humor, and returned straightway to the Continent, to rejoin her husband and son and acquaint the former with the glad news of his entire liberation. As for the latter, he had been considerably neglected during his mother's absence by Mademoiselle Genevieve, her French maid; for that young woman, contracting an attachment for a soldier in the garrison of Calais, forgot her charge in the society of this militaire, and little Rawdon very narrowly escaped drowning on Calais sands at this period, where the absent Genevieve had left and lost him.

And so, Colonel and Mrs. Crawley came to London; and it is at their house in Curzon Street, May Fair, that they really showed the skill which must be possessed by those who would live on the resources above named.

Notes

1. per annum: every year.
2. sold out of the army: left the army by selling the commission.
3. the restored French nobility: after the defeat of Napoleon in 1815, the French aristocrats were restored to power.
4. parvenue: (French) a person of low social origin who has obtained wealth or position; an upstart.
5. Faubourg St. Germain: a residential district for aristocrats.
6. écarté: (French) a card game between two people.
7. defrays the expenses of his establishment: pays the expenses of his household.
8. had the better of him: defeated him.
9. Duke of Wellington: Duke of Wellington(1769~1852) was the commander-in-chief of the allied army and defeated Napoleon at the Battle of Waterloo in 1815.
10. the last great trick: referring to the Battle of Waterloo.
11. Frascati and the Salon: two gambling houses in Paris.
12. much to good-natured little Mrs. Crawley's annoyance: It suggests the trick Becky played to cheat people out of their money.
13. young Green of the Rifles: a certain young officer named Green in the infantry.
14. to remit the debt: to cancel the debt.
15. Blackstone of the Hussars: an officer named Blackstone in the regiment of Hussars.

VI. Age of Realism (The Victorian Age)

16. Count Punter of the Hanoverian Cavalry: Count Punter, an officer in the regiment of the Hanoverian Cavalry.
17. IOU: "I Owe You", a receipt for a loan.
18. fracas: a French word for "a noisy quarrel".
19. snapped her fingers in Mrs. Crawley's face: a sign of contempt.
20. blackleg: cheater.
21. C. B. : abbreviations for "Companion of the Bath", an order of knighthood.
22. General Tufto: Captain Rawdon's superior who flirted with Becky.
23. Rawdon acquiesced in the justice of her opinion: Rawdon agreed with his wife in her judgment.
24. aide de camp:(French) an officer who carries the order of a general and acts as secretary.
25. toupee: a wig with a top-knot.
26. beetle-browed: with overhanging or prominent brows.
27. knick-knacks: small, trifling ornamental articles.
28. Calais: seaport in northern France, from which ships cross the English Channel for Britain.
29. diligence:(French) a public stage-coach in France carrying passengers and luggage.
30. Dunkirk: a seaport town in North France.
31. the premier:(French) the first floor in a hotel.
32. entresol:(French) the low-ceilinged storey between the first and the ground floors. It was a sign of greater prosperity and wealth to move from the entresol to the first floor.
33. bonne:(French) maidservant.
34. serré'd:(French) packed, stowed away.
35. Belgic: Belgium.
36. pelisse:(French) a lady's long mantle.
37. Milor Anglais: (French) my English lord.
38. credit was at your hand: You can easily gain the trust of the merchants and buy things on credit.
39. Boule d'Or:(gold ball) the name of a jeweler's shop.
40. Palais Royal: a large building with shops on the ground floor in Paris.
41. cette charmante Miladi:(French) that charming lady.
42. de retour:(French) to return.
43. avec sa femme:(French) with his wife.

44. une petite dame, tres spirituelle: (French) a very small lady, very lively.
45. ils m'ont affreusement volé: (French) they have robbed me dreadfully.

Questions for Understanding

1. How is Rebecca received in the Paris upper-class society?
2. Why does Rebecca want to push Rawdon's fortune in their own country?
3. How does Rebecca manage to make Rawdon's debtors in London receive him?
4. How do Rebecca and Rawdon manage to live well on nothing in Paris?

Aspects of Appreciation

1. The subtitle of the novel *Vanity Fair* is "A Novel Without a Hero". This subtitle helps to reinforce the title and the themes of the novel and it is very significant. From it, readers are enlightened about the world the novel depicts. As a novel without a hero, it can mean first in this novel there are no exactly positive characters. That is to say, this is a world full of bad or faulty people. No one here is really good enough to be a hero as the world or society here is corrupted. Second, this is a novel not about some particular person but about a society, the upper-middle-class society. The social manners, made up of individual behaviors, become the predominant concern, and the general impression is that of noisy, whirling commotion. Third, it can be a novel about women instead of men. Evidence is found in the absolute domination of the stage by the major characters: Becky Sharp and her foil, Amelia. They, particularly Becky, are the heroines at the centre of life while the male characters are but means and tools in their climb or search for position and money.
2. Most characters in this novel are portrayed through contrast. The young, graceful but weak-minded, unfaithful George is set in contrast to his friend, the reliable and faithful though humbly-born and large-footed Dobbin, and the blindly faithful good-for-nothing Rawdon; the careless but kind-hearted old Sedley to his ungrateful, unsympathetic, shrewd friend, old Osborne; the impotent yet arrogant old Sir Pitt Crawley to the corrupted yet clever Lord Steyne, etc. The major contrast, however, is to be found in the characterization of the two heroines, Becky and Amelia.
3. Satire is the most distinguishing feature of the novel. The reader can find satire everywhere: from the title to the description and portrayal of characters, from

the author's comments to the narration of the characters' life. The writer achieves satire by use of certain names, such as Miss Toady, Mr. Flower Dew, Mrs. High Flyer, etc; by giving humourous situations and by creating irony.

Suggested Further Reading

Gordon N. Ray. *The Buried Life: A Study of the Relations Between Thackery's Fiction and His Personal History*, Oxford University Press, 1952.

Topics for Further Study

1. What do you think is the intention of the author in his use of "Vanity Fair" as the title of the novel?
2. In what kind of tone is the novel written? Give examples to support your argument. And then, give instances to show the author's use of humor and satire.
3. How does the author portray Amelia and Rebecca respectively? What techniques of characterization are used?

Alfred, Lord Tennyson
(1809~1892)

About the Author

Alfred, Lord Tennyson succeeded William Wordsworth as Poet Laureate in 1850. Tennyson inherited the Romantic tradition—Wordsworth, Byron, especially Keats and there is a sense of melancholy and a sensuousness in his poetry like those in Keats's. Therefore he is usually regarded as the poet of the third generation of Romanticism with Robert Browning. He used a variety of materials and resorted to the world of romances: classical, medieval and English. He is best noted for his lyric gift for musicality with a perfect control of the sound and cadence of English, a good taste and a consummate choice in words. His poems are characterized by metrical variety, rich imagery, and exquisite verbal melodies. Besides, he was also skilled in the dramatic monologue. As the most popular poet of the Victorian age, Tennyson often dealt with the doubts and uncertainties of the age and sometimes there is a note of subdued sadness in his poems. Yet there is also a serenity, a kind of nobility, a feeling of reassurance in his best poems. Tennyson's major works are *Poems*(1842), *The Princess*(1847), *In Memoriam*(1850), *Maud*(1855), *Enoch Arden*(1864) and *Idylls of the King*(1859~1885).

★ The Eagle

About the Poem

First published in 1851, "The Eagle: A Fragment" personifies the eagle as a lonely and romantic human. As with the best of the poet's works, this short poem displays great lyricism with strong musicality and consummate choice of words.

> He clasps the crag with crooked hands;
> Close to the sun in lonely lands,
> Ringed with[1] the azure world, he stands.
>
> The wrinkled sea beneath him crawls;
> He watches from his mountain walls,
> And like a thunderbolt he falls.

Notes

1. Ringed with: circled by.

Questions for Understanding

1. What does "the azure world" refer to?
2. What might "being close to the sun" imply as to the position and also quality of the eagle?
3. How do you understand the word "falls"?
4. What might be the symbolic meaning of the sea which crawls?
5. What qualities are attributed to the eagle?
6. How effectively are the sound devices used in the poem?

Aspects of Appreciation

1. This is a poem in memory of his friend Hallam, in praise of his noble

personality and a hymn of independence and free spirit.
2. Form and devices
   (1) The single rhyme in each stanza may symbolize the singleness and aloneness or uniqueness of the eagle.
   (2) Alliteration in the first line: the hard consonant /k/ in the three words may suggest hardness of the rock and firmness of the bird.
   (3) Imagery or symbolism: the eagle may be symbolic of a noble person or free spirit. Besides, the wrinkled sea may stand for the masses or ordinary people and the sun may represent truth.
   (4) The motionlessness of the first stanza forms the sharp contrast to the thunderbolt-like action in the second stanza.

★ Break, Break, Break

About the Poem

Written during early 1835 and published in 1842, "Break, Break, Break" is a lyric elegy for the death of the poet's best friend Arthur Hallam, a fellow poet.

Break, break, break,
On thy cold gray stones, O Sea!
And I would[1] that my tongue could utter
The thoughts that arise in me.

O, well for[2] the fisherman's boy,
That he shouts with his sister at play!
O, well for the sailor lad,
That he sings in his boat on the bay!

And the stately ships go on
To their haven under the hill;
But O for[3] the touch of a vanished hand[4],
And the sound of a voice that is still!

Break, break, break,
At the foot of thy crags, O Sea!

But the tender grace[5] of a day that is dead
Will never come back to me.

Notes

1. I would: I wish.
2. O, well for: O it would be well for(那该多好啊).
3. O for: How I wish for.
4. a vanished hand: a dead person's hand(which is impossible to touch).
5. tender grace: tender feelings, kindness or friendship.

Questions for Understanding

1. What does "the cold gray stones" convey to you? How is the image relative to the theme or the mood of the poem?
2. What might be the "thoughts" that arise in the speaker (Stanza 1)?
3. What might the images of the fisherman's boy, his sister and the sailor lad symbolize (Stanza 2)? In what way does the second stanza contribute to the theme of the poem?
4. What might the stately ships symbolize?
5. What is the figure of speech used in "a vanished hand" and what is the effectiveness?
6. In what ways can "break, break, break" be understood?

Aspects of Appreciation

1. The poem is about the speaker's or the poet's grief over the death of his friend and over the loss of youth, innocence and happiness.
2. Nature is indifferent to man and it continues to function according to its rhythms and cycles regardless of what happens to human beings. The sea will rise and fall in a defiant, unrelenting manner that refuses to acknowledge tragedy in the everyday life of men.
3. Metrical features: the poem uses alternately anapestic, iambic, spondaic meter, achieving a variety of rhythms and creating the effect of the sounds of the sea waves breaking. The insistent beat of "Break, break, break" emphasizes the relentless note of sadness. Besides, the use of long vowels slows down the pace of the poem and creates the suitable mood for the poem.

VI. Age of Realism (The Victorian Age)

4. Other rhetorical devices are also used, such as apostrophe in which the sea is addressed directly, personification in which the sea is regarded as a human being, alliteration ("boat on the bay" and "day that is dead"), paradox ("Touch of a vanished hand" and "sound of a voice that is still"), images and symbols.

★ Crossing the Bar

About the Poem

This is an 1889 poem by Tennyson and is traditionally the last poem in collections of his work. It seems that Tennyson meant it to be his own elegy, as the poem has a tone of finality about it. The poem uses an extended metaphor comparing death to crossing the "sandbar" between the tide or river of life and the ocean that lies beyond death.

Sunset and evening star,
And one clear call for me!
And may there be no moaning of the bar[1],
When I put out to sea.

But such a tide as moving seems asleep,
Too full for sound and foam,
When that which drew from out the boundless deep
Turns again home!

Twilight and evening bell,
And after that the dark!
And may there be no sadness of farewell,
When I embark;

For though from out our bourn[2] of Time and Place
The flood may bear me far,
I hope to see my Pilot face to face
When I have crossed the bar.

Notes

1. moaning of the bar: mournful sound of the ocean beating on a sand bar at the mouth of a harbour.
2. bourn: boundary.

Questions for Understanding

1. What images of life and of death can you find in the poem?
2. What are the images which may have religious implications?
3. What might be the tone of the poem?
4. How are the sound devices effectively used in the poem?

Aspects of Appreciation

1. The wavelike quality of the long-and-short lines parallels the content of the poem.
2. The whole poem depends upon an extended metaphor of "crossing of bar" meaning crossing the demarcation line between life and eternity that is death. An extended metaphor is a figure of speech which develops through a number of lines or a whole poem. In this poem, all the metaphors such as the sea, bar, boundless deep, sound and foam, bourn, flood and Pilot, namely God, are related and they centre on the key metaphor "the bar" to make a central and unified meaning.

Suggested Further Reading

Other poems by Tennyson: "Ulysses" and "Tears, Idle Tears".

Topics for Further Study

1. Critics have pointed out that the major influence on Tennyson was Keats, whom he resembles in mood and technique. Comment on the similarities of the two poets in terms of mood and technique.
2. It is suggested by critics that in his life time Tennyson was regarded as a great poet, but his reputation as a great poet declined after his death. Try to explain this phenomenon by taking into account the quality of his poetry and the moral mood of his time and the literary trend in modern period.

VI. Age of Realism (The Victorian Age)

Knowledge of Literature

Sound and Meaning

In spite of the fact that language is basically conventional, that is, there is not correspondence between the formation of the words(sound) and their meanings, however in some cases, this correspondence does exist. For instance, in case of onomatopoeia. Besides, some linguists find also an interesting set of phoneme combinations which do not constitute specific morphemes, yet are experienced by speakers of English as having a common, though very loose-boundaried, area of meaning. Examples are the initial sounds represented by "fl-" in the set of words "flash, flare, flame, flicker, flimmer", all of which signify a kind of moving light; while in the set "fly, flip, flap, flop, flit, flutter", the same initial sounds all signify a kind of movement in air. The terminal sounds represented by "-ash", as they occur in the set "bash, crash, clash, dash, flash, gash, mash, slash", have an overlapping significance of sudden or violent movement. Such combinations of phonemes are sometimes called "phonetic intensives", or else instances of sound-symbolism, exploited especially by poets, in which the sounds of the words seem peculiarly appropriate to their significance.

Geoffrey N. Leech has also noted the relationship between the sound and the sense and he divides consonant sounds into hard consonants(硬辅音) and soft consonants(软辅音). The hard consonants include plosives(爆破音)(/b, p, d, k, g/), affricates(塞擦音)(/ts, dz/); the soft consonants include liquids(流音)(/l, r/), nasals(鼻音)(/m, n, ŋ/), sibilants(咝音)(/s, z/)and fricatives(擦音)(/f, s, d, v/). Poets often make use of sound devices and Keats and Tennyson are skillful in using soft sounds in their poems to achieve certain effect. Two famous examples are "For summer has o'er-brimm'd their clammy cells" in Keats's "To Autumn" "The moan of doves in immemorial elms" and "murmuring of innumerable bees" in Tennyson's "Come down O maid from yonder mountain height". They make use of soft consonants, onomatopoeia, assonance and alliteration to achieve musicality and convey ideas. On the other hand, the three hard consonants /k/ in the first line of Tennyson's "The Eagle" may suggest hardness of the rock and firmness of the bird's hold.

Robert Browning
(1812~1889)

About the Author

Robert Browning(1812~1889), an English poet and a playwright, was raised in a family with an environment of literature and art: his father had a library of around 6,000 books and his mother was a talented musician.

Browning took fancy to Renaissance Italy and drew upon the materials of this period for his writings. His fame and literary contribution mainly lie in his dramatic monologues, in which he places his characters before the reader at some revealing moments of their life and lets them speak for themselves. The character will unwittingly give away about himself and his true nature in the process of rationalizing his past actions, or "special-pleading" his case to a silent but an identifiable audience in the poem.

Browning's major works are *Paracelsus* (1835), *Strafford* (1837), *Pippa Passes* (1841), *Dramatic Lyrics* (1842), *Dramatic Romances and Lyrics* (1845), *Men and Women* (1855), *Dramatic Personae* (1855) and *The Ring and the Book* (1868). Browning's modern and experimental style owes much to John Donne's poems with their abrupt openings, colloquial phrasing and irregular rhythms. In spirit he was more of a Shelley's descendant than of any other poet.

★ My Last Duchess[1]

About the Poem

This is one of the most characteristic and perhaps most frequently cited examples of the poet's dramatic monologues in which a jealous tyrant Duke shows to the match-maker a picture of his late wife drawn by a monk artist. The picture caught her smile that brought about her death.

The attentive reader discovers the most horrific example of a character that is very cold and cruel in spite of his eloquence. The duchess is revealed to be murdered and reduced to an object of art in the Duke's collection of paintings and statues.

Ferrara[2]

That's my last Duchess painted on the wall,
Looking as if she were alive. I call
That piece a wonder, now: Fra Pandolf's[3] hands
Worked busily a day, and there she stands.
Will't please you sit and look at her? I said
"Fra Pandolf" by design[4], for never read
Strangers like you that pictured countenance[5],
The depth and passion of its earnest glance[6],
But to myself they turned (since none puts by
The curtain I have drawn for you, but I)
And seemed as they would ask me, if they durst[7],
How such a glance came there; so, not the first
Are you to turn and ask thus. Sir, 'twas not
Her husband's presence only, called[8] that spot
Of joy[9] into the Duchess' cheek: perhaps
Fra Pandolf chanced to say "Her mantle laps
Over my lady's wrist too much," or "Paint
Must never hope to reproduce the faint
Half-flush that dies along her throat[10]": such stuff[11]
Was courtesy, she thought, and cause enough
For calling up[12] that spot of joy. She had
A heart—how shall I say? —too soon made glad,
Too easily impressed; she liked whate'er
She looked on, and her looks went everywhere.
Sir, 'twas all one[13]! My favour at her breast[14],
The dropping of the daylight in the West,
The bough of cherries some officious[15] fool
Broke in the orchard for her, the white mule
She rode with round the terrace—all and each
Would draw from her alike the approving speech,
Or blush, at least. She thanked men,—good! but thanked
Somehow—I know not how—as if she ranked
My gift of a nine-hundred-years-old name[16]
With anybody's gift. Who'd stoop[17] to blame
This sort of trifling? Even had you skill
In speech—(which I have not)—to make your will

Quite clear to such an one[18], and say, "Just this
Or that in you disgusts me; here you miss[19],
Or there exceed the mark[20]"—and if she let
Herself be lessoned so[21], nor plainly set
Her wits to yours[22], forsooth[23], and made excuse,
—E'en then would be some stooping[24]; and I choose
Never to stoop. Oh sir, she smiled, no doubt,
Whene'er I passed her; but who passed without
Much the same smile? This grew[25]; I gave commands;
Then all smiles stopped together[26]. There she[27] stands
As if alive. Will't please you rise? We'll meet
The company below[28], then. I repeat,
The Count your master's known munificence[29]
Is ample warrant[30] that no just pretence[31]
Of mine for dowry will be disallowed[32];
Though his fair daughter's self, as I avowed
At starting, is my object. Nay, we'll go
Together down, sir. Notice Neptune[33], though,
Taming a sea-horse, thought a rarity[34],
Which Claus of Innsbruck[35] cast in bronze for me!

Notes

1. Scholars have conjectured that the poem is based on incidents in the life of Alfonso Ⅱ, Duke of Ferrara, whose first wife died in 1561 under mysterious circumstances. The Duke negotiated his second marriage to the daughter of the Count of Tyrol through an agent.
2. Ferrara: a city near Venice.
3. Fra Pandolf: a fictitious name invented by Browning; the painter is represented as a member of a monastic order ("Fra" means "Brother").
4. by design: on purpose, deliberately.
5. for never read … pictured countenance: inverted sentence meaning that strangers like you never understood that pictured countenance (read: understand).
6. The whole line serves as the appositive (同位语) of "that pictured countenance".

VI. Age of Realism (The Victorian Age)

7. durst: dare.
8. called: caused.
9. spot of joy: smile or blush.
10. "her" "my lady's" etc. : used to address the late Duchess, meaning "your" for respect; Half-flush that dies along her throat: the delicate shades of blush gradually disappear along her throat.
11. such stuff: such nonsensical talk.
12. calling up: causing.
13. 'twas all one: it was all the same.
14. my favour at her breast: my gift(love gift, such as a ribbon or a jewel) worn by her at her breast.
15. officious: 好管闲事的,献殷勤的。
16. a nine-hundred-years-old name: the tittle of the Duchess of Ferrara I gave her through marriage.
17. stoop: lower oneself (to do something).
18. such an one: such a person, referring to the Duchess(Note the Duke's contemptuous tone).
19. miss: not do enough.
20. exceed the mark: go too far.
21. let herself be lessoned so: accept the instruction or blame or criticism from the Duke.
22. nor plainly set her wits to yours: not openly argue with you.
23. forsooth: indeed.
24. E'en then would be some stooping: Even then there would be some stooping(for me).
25. grew: became worse.
26. Then all smiles stopped together: it implies that the Duke silenced her or killed her.
27. she: her picture.
28. The company below: people downstairs.
29. munificence: generosity.
30. ample warrant: adequate guarantee.
31. pretence: claim.
32. disallowed: refused.
33. Neptune: Roman god of the sea.
34. a rarity: a rare and precious thing.
35. Claus of Innsbruck: an imaginary sculptor.

Questions for Understanding

1. What is the dramatic situation? Who is the speaker and to whom is he speaking?
2. What is he talking about and what may his intention be in talking this way?
3. What is the speaker's "last duchess" like? What is the speaker like?
4. Is there any discrepancy between the speaker's view of his late wife and of himself on the one hand, and the reader's opinion of these two characters on the other?
5. What might be inferred about the character of the listener or addressee in the poem?

Aspects of Appreciation

1. This dramatic monologue has the form similar to heroic couplet (iambic pentameter rhyming *aa bb cc dd* …)
2. The major characters in the poem are the duke who is revealed to be a cruel, despotic, jealous, hypocritical, selfish and narrow-minded person; and his late wife the duchess who through the duke's account the reader discovers to be gentle, kind, beautiful, noble-minded and democratic. The silent listener, the marriage agent, can be inferred to be clever, silver-tongued and eloquent. There is discrepancy between the duke's opinion of himself and the reader's opinion of him, his opinion of his late wife and the reader's opinion of her. In his own opinion, he is powerful, noble, benevolent, but in fact he is despotic and cruel. He thinks of his late wife as frivolous, but the reader knows that she was noble-minded and the duke is selfish and jealous.
3. Irony, created by discrepancies of different kinds, abounds in this poem. The duke's opinions and the reader's constitute discrepancies. The word "last" in the title and the duke's eagerness in getting a new marriage form another contrast or irony. Besides, the duke's intention in gilding himself and belittling his late duchess only brings about the opposite results.
4. The frequent use of caesura, the pause within a line of poetry, throughout the poem emphasizes the duke's desire to control: control over the conversation, over everything including his wife. The use of caesura can create variety of rhythm, give emphasis, and reveal the personality of the duke of an absolute tyrant. Besides, the poet's

deliberate omission of the necessary transition between "I gave commands" and "Then all smiles stopped together" strengthens the duke's power and cruelty.

Suggested Further Reading

Robert Browning's other poems "Home Thoughts, from Abroad" "Meeting at Night" "Parting at Morning" "Pippa's Song"("The Year's at the Spring") and Mrs. Browning's poem "How Do I Love Thee".

Topics for Further Study

1. Compare Robert Browning's dramatic monologue with those of Alfred Tennyson's.
2. Analyze the way in which this dramatic monologue is structured around the gradual revelation of the speaker's personality.
3. A critic, Leonard Nathanson, writes that "the Duke performs the very act he asserts to be the most repugnant to his nature; after sacrificing his wife rather than his dignity, he sacrifices that dignity" What other instances and varieties of irony do you detect in the poem?

Knowledge of Literature

Dramatic monologue

Dramatic monologue is a type of lyric poem that was perfected by Robert Browning. In its fullest form, as represented in Browning's "My Last Duchess" and other poems, the dramatic monologue has the following features. (1) A single person, who is patently not the poet, utters the speech that makes up the whole of the poem, in a specific situation at a critical moment. (2) This person addresses and interacts with one or more other people; but we know of the auditors' presence, and what they say and do, only from clues in the discourse of the single speaker. (3) The main principle controlling the poet's formulation of what the lyric speaker says is to reveal to the reader, in a way that enhances its interest, the speaker's temperament and character. The third feature of self-revelation distinguishes a dramatic monologue with its near relation, the dramatic lyric, which is also a monologue uttered in an identifiable situation at a dramatic moment, but which only focuses upon the argument of the speaker's itself rather than upon revealing the character of the speaker inadvertently. John Donne's poems such as "The Flea" and Wordsworth's "Tintern Abbey" are dramatic lyrics rather than dramatic monologues. Tennyson's "Ulysses" and T. S. Eliot's "The Love Song of J. Alfred Prufrock" are famous dramatic monologues.

Matthew Arnold
(1822~1888)

About the Author

Matthew Arnold(1822~1888) was an English poet and cultural critic. He was the son of Thomas Arnold, the famed headmaster of Rugby School, and brother to both Tom Arnold, literary professor, and William Delafield Arnold, novelist and colonial administrator. Matthew Arnold's poetry is elevated and meditative, with a tone of regret, disillusionment and melancholy. He usually records his own experiences, his own feelings of loneliness and isolation and his wish for an unattainable serenity. Matthew Arnold has been characterized as a sage writer, a type of writer who chastises and instructs the reader on contemporary social issues. Arnold is called the third great Victorian poet, along with Alfred Tennyson and Robert Browning.

★ Dover Beach

About the Poem

"Dover Beach" is a short lyric poem first published in 1867 in the collection *New Poems*. The title locale and subject of the poem's descriptive opening lines is the shore of the English ferry port of Dover, facing France at the narrowest part of the English Channel, where Arnold honeymooned in 1851. "Dover Beach" depicts a nightmarish world from which the old religious verities have receded. It is sometimes held up as an early, if not the first, example of the modern sensibility. Some consider Arnold to be the bridge between Romanticism and Modernism. His use of symbolic landscapes is typical of the Romantic era, while his skeptical and pessimistic perspective is typical of the Modern era.

The sea is calm to-night.
The tide is full, the moon lies fair

Upon the straits; on the French coast the light
Gleams and is gone; the cliffs of England stand;
Glimmering and vast, out in the tranquil bay.
Come to the window, sweet is the night-air!
Only, from the long line of spray
Where the sea meets the moon-blanched land,
Listen! you hear the grating roar
Of pebbles which the waves draw back, and fling,
At their return, up the high strand,
Begin, and cease, and then again begin,
With tremulous cadence slow, and bring
The eternal note of sadness in.

Sophocles[1] long ago
Heard it on the Aegean, and it brought
Into his mind the turbid ebb and flow
Of human misery; we
Find also in the sound a thought,
Hearing it by this distant northern sea.

The Sea of Faith
Was once, too, at the full, and round earth's shore
Lay like the folds of a bright girdle furled.
But now I only hear
Its melancholy, long, withdrawing roar,
Retreating, to the breath
Of the night-wind, down the vast edges drear
And naked shingles of the world.

Ah, love, let us be true
To one another! for the world, which seems
To lie before us like a land of dreams,
So various, so beautiful, so new,
Hath really neither joy, nor love, nor light,
Nor certitude, nor peace, nor help for pain;
And we are here as on a darkling plain
Swept with confused alarms of struggle and flight,

Where ignorant armies clash by night.

Notes

1. Sophocles(496B. C. ~406B. C.): Greek playwright, who wrote tragedies of fate and the will of gods.

Questions for Understanding

1. How does the poet describe time, place and personal relationships in the poem?
2. When the author said "Ah, love, let us be true/ To one another/", what did he want to show?
3. What is the relationship between the poem's setting and the imagery in last three lines?
4. What is the author's attitude toward life and faith?

Aspects of Appreciation

1. The poem "Dover Beach" consists of some rhymed stanzas. The stanzas are uneven and the rhyme scheme is irregular. The poem reflects the mental distress of the late Victorians who lost their faith in religion and became pessimistic about the future of mankind.
2. The poem begins with a naturalistic description of the nightly Dover sea, with a series of images of sight and sound, of light and darkness: the calm sea full to the brim; the moon on the straits as personified in "lies fair"; the light on the French coast, gleaming, and then gone; the Dover cliffs standing "glimmering and vast". The fullness of the tide and the calmness of the sea suggest a contrast to the moral-spiritual vacuum as much as to the state of unrest in Arnold's contemporary Victorian England that the elegy aims to lament. If the gleaming light on the French coast is a sign of hope, its fast disappearance suggests the gloom of hopelessness. The vast and glimmering cliffs of Dover furthers the suggestion of dimness.

Suggested Further Reading

Matthew Arnold's *Poems*, *New Poems* and *Essays in Criticism*.

Topics for Further Study

1. The romantic and modern features in Arnold's poems.
2. Arnold's philosophy in his poems.

Thomas Hardy
(1840~1928)

About the Author

Thomas Hardy was the last important novelist of the Victorian Age. In his Wessex novels, he vividly and truthfully described the tragic lives of the tenants in the last decade of the 19th century.

Hardy was born in Dovsetshire, a county in the south of England. His birthplace was later used as the setting of his novels and he called it "Wessex", which suggests the mysterious past of England during the Anglo-Saxon period. For it was here that the Wessex kingdom once prospered under King Alfred and the prehistorical Stonehenge is located. The place is rich in its legend, folk customs and superstitions—all these would play their roles in Hardy's Wessex novels.

Born in an architect's family, he was expected to become an architect. He did become an architect, but his real interest was in literature. His most famous novels are *Tess of the D'Urbervilles* (1891) and *Jude the Obscure* (1896).

Hardy was pessimistic in his view of life. His philosophy was that everything in the universe is determined by the Immanent Will, which is present in all parts of the universe and is impartially hostile towards human beings' desire for joy and happiness. The dominant theme of his novels is the futility of man's effort to struggle against cruel and unintelligible Fate, Chance, and Circumstances, which are all predetermined by the Immanent Will. Although there is a humorous and attractive side to life, the prevailing mood in his novels is tragic. Since love is the most intense expression of human desire for happiness, it is in love that conflict between the efforts of human beings and the relentless force of the Immanent Will is most acute.

From 1896 Hardy turned to poetry writing. He wrote 918 poems altogether, published in eight collections. Besides, he also wrote a great epic-drama, *The Dynasts*, which was published in three parts (1904, 1906,

1908).

Hardy married his first wife in 1874. Their marriage lasted until her death in 1912. In 1914, he married his second wife. He died on January 11, 1928 and was buried with impressive ceremonies in the Poet's Corner in Westminster Abbey, but his heart was brought back to his birthplace.

★ Tess of the D'Urbervilles

About the Novel

Tess of the D'Urbervilles is the most pastoral of Hardy's novels. Its plot centers on the tragic occurrences of its heroine Tess's life. Tess is the daughter of a poor villager who at the beginning of the novel discovers that he is the descendant of the ancient family of the D'Urbervilles. However, the family is very poor and unfortunately their horse is killed by accident. So Tess is encouraged by her parents to seek out the old noble family. However, she is seduced by Alec D'Urberville whom they believe to be her cousin, and has an illegitimate child by him. The child dies soon after its birth, and she is considered a sinful woman. Trying to build a new life for herself, Tess goes to a dairy farm far to the south to be a dairymaid. There she meets the son of a parson, Angel Clare, who comes to work just for the experience of work, and who falls in love with Tess. He proposes to her and they arrange to get married. On their wedding night, after Angel tells her of his past relations with a bad woman, Tess tells her whole story about Alec. Angel deserts her and goes to live abroad. After a period of extreme hardship, she encounters her seducer again, who persuades her to live with him as his wife. When Angel returns to tell her that he has forgiven her and that he still loves her, he finds her with Alec again. Seeing that Alec's relations with her prevents her from going back to live happily with Angel, Tess hates him for ruining her life and kills him. When Tess tells Angel what she has done, Angel forgives her, but she is caught and hanged.

Phase Seven: Fulfillment

Chapter 57

Meanwhile Angel Clare had walked automatically along the way by

VI. Age of Realism (The Victorian Age)

which he had come, and, entering his hotel, sat down over the breakfast, staring at nothingness. He went on eating and drinking unconsciously till on a sudden he demanded his bill; having paid which he took his dressing-bag in his hand, the only luggage he had brought with him, and went out.

At the moment of his departure a telegram was handed to him-a few words from his mother, stating that they were glad to know his address, and informing him that his brother Cuthbert[1] had proposed to and been accepted by Mercy Chant.

Clare crumpled up the paper, and followed the route to the station; reaching it, he found that there would be no train leaving for an hour and more. He sat down to wait, and having waited a quarter of an hour felt that he could wait there no longer. Broken in heart and numbed, he had nothing to hurry for; but he wished to get out of a town which had been the scene of such an experience, and turned to walk to the first station onward, and let the train pick him up there.

The highway that he followed was open, and at a little distance dipped into[2] a valley, across which it could be seen running from edge to edge. He had traversed the greater part of this depression, and was climbing the western acclivity[3], when, pausing for breath, he unconsciously looked back. Why he did so he could not say, but something seemed to impel him to the act. The tape-like surface of the road diminished in his rear as far as he could see, and as he gazed a moving spot intruded on the white vacuity[4] of its perspective.

It was a human figure running. Clare waited, with a dim sense that somebody was trying to overtake him.

The form descending the incline was a woman's, yet so entirely was his mind blinded to the idea of his wife's following him that even when she came nearer he did not recognize her under the totally changed attire in which he now beheld her. It was not till she was quite close that he could believe her to be Tess.

"I saw you—turn away from the station—just before I got there—and I have been following you all this way!"

She was so pale, so breathless, so quivering in every muscle, that he did not ask her a single question, but seizing her hand, and pulling it within his arm, he led her along. To avoid meeting any possible wayfarers[5] he left the high road, and took a footpath under some fir-trees. When they were deep among the moaning boughs he stopped and looked at her inquiringly.

"Angel," she said, as if waiting for this, "do you know what I have been running after you for? To tell you that I have killed him!" A pitiful white smile lit her face as she spoke.

"What!" said he, thinking from the strangeness of her manner that she was in some delirium[6].

"I have done it—I don't know how," she continued. "Still, I owed it to you, and to myself, Angel. I feared long ago, when I struck him on the mouth with my glove, that I might do it some day for the trap he set for me in my simple youth, and his wrong to you through me. He has come between us and ruined us, and now he can never do it any more. I never loved him at all, Angel, as I loved you. You know it, don't you? You believe it? You didn't come back to me, and I was obliged to go back to him. Why did you go away—why did you—when I loved you so? I can't think why you did it. But I don't blame you; only, Angel, will you forgive me my sin against you, now I have killed him? I thought as I ran along that you would be sure to forgive me now I have done that. It came to me as a shining light that I should get you back that way. I could not bear the loss of you any longer-you don't know how entirely I was unable to bear your not loving me! Say you do now, dear, dear husband; say you do, now I have killed him!"

"I do love you, Tess—O, I do—it is all come back!" he said, tightening his arms round her with fervid pressure. "But how do you mean—you have killed him?"

"I mean that I have," she murmured in a reverie.

"What, bodily? Is he dead?"

"Yes. He heard me crying about you, and he bitterly taunted me; and called you by a foul name; and then I did it. My heart could not bear it. He had nagged me about you before. And then I dressed myself and came away to find you."

By degrees he was inclined to believe that she had faintly attempted, at least, what she said she had done; and his horror at her impulse was mixed with amazement at the strength of her affection for himself, and at the strangeness of its quality, which had apparently extinguished her moral sense altogether. Unable to realize the gravity of her conduct she seemed at last content; and he looked at her as she lay upon his shoulder, weeping with happiness, and wondered what obscure strain in the D'Urbervilles blood had led to this aberration[7]—if it were an aberration. There momentarily flashed through his mind that the family tradition of the coach and murder might have arisen because the D'Urbervilles had been known to do these things. As well as his confused and excited ideas could reason, he supposed that in the moment of mad grief of which she spoke her mind had lost its balance, and plunged her into this abyss.

It was very terrible if true; if a temporary hallucination, sad. But, anyhow, here was this deserted wife of his, this passionately-fond woman, clinging to him without a suspicion that he would be anything to her but a protector. He saw that for him to be otherwise was not, in her mind, within the region of the possible. Tenderness was absolutely dominant in Clare at last. He kissed her endlessly with his white lips, and held her hand, and said—

"I will not desert you! I will protect you by every means in my power, dearest love, whatever you may have done or not have done!"

They then walked on under the trees, Tess turning her head every now and then to look at him. Worn and unhandsome as he had become, it was plain that she did not discern the least fault in his appearance. To her he was, as of old, all that was perfection, personally and mentally. He was still her Antinous[8], her Apollo even; his sickly face was beautiful as the morning to her affectionate regard on this day no less than when she first beheld him; for was it not the face of the one man on earth who had loved her purely, and who had believed in her as pure!

With an instinct as to possibilities he did not now, as he had intended, make for the first station beyond the town, but plunged still farther under the firs, which here abounded for miles. Each clasping the other round the waist they promenaded[9] over the dry bed of fir-needles, thrown into a vague intoxicating atmosphere at the consciousness of being together at last, with no living soul between them; ignoring that there was a corpse.

Thus they proceeded for several miles till Tess, arousing herself, looked about her, and said, timidly—

"Are we going anywhere in particular?"

"I don't know, dearest. Why?"

"I don't know."

"Well, we might walk a few miles further, and when it is evening find lodgings somewhere or other—in a lonely cottage, perhaps. Can you walk well, Tessy?"

"O yes! I could walk for ever and ever with your arm round me!"

Upon the whole it seemed a good thing to do. Thereupon they

quickened their pace, avoiding high roads, and following obscure paths tending more or less northward. But there was an unpractical vagueness in their movements throughout the day; neither one of them seemed to consider any question of effectual escape, disguise, or long concealment. Their every idea was temporary and unforefending[10], like the plans of two children.

At mid-day they drew near to a roadside inn, and Tess would have entered it with him to get something to eat, but he persuaded her to remain among the trees and bushes of this half-woodland, half-moorland part of the country, till he should come back. Her clothes were of recent fashion; even the ivory-handled parasol that she carried was of a shape unknown in the retired spot to which they had now wandered; and the cut of such articles would have attracted attention in the settle of a tavern. He soon returned, with food enough for half-a-dozen people and two bottles of wine—enough to last them for a day or more, should any emergency arise.

They sat down upon some dead boughs and shared their meal. Between one and two o'clock they packed up the remainder and went on again.

"I feel strong enough to walk any distance," said she.

"I think we may as well steer in a general way towards the interior of the country, where we can hide for a time, and are less likely to be looked for than anywhere near the coast," Clare remarked. "Later on, when they have forgotten us, we can make for some port."

She made no reply to this beyond that of grasping him more tightly, and straight inland they went. Though the season was an English May, the weather was serenely bright, and during the afternoon it was quite warm. Through the latter miles of their walk their footpath had taken them into the depths of the New Forest, and towards evening, turning the corner of a lane, they perceived behind a brook and bridge a large board on which was painted in white letters, "This desirable Mansion to be Let Furnished"; particulars following, with directions to apply to some London agents. Passing through the gate they could see the house, an old brick building of regular design and large accommodation.

"I know it," said Clare. "It is Bramshurst Court. You can see that it is shut up, and grass is growing on the drive."

"Some of the windows are open," said Tess.

"Just to air the rooms, I suppose."

"All these rooms empty, and we without a roof to our heads!"

"You are getting tired, my Tess!" he said. "We'll stop soon." And kissing her sad mouth he again led her onwards.

He was growing weary likewise, for they had wandered a dozen or fifteen miles, and it became necessary to consider what they should do for rest. They looked from afar at isolated cottages and little inns, and were inclined to approach one of the latter, when their hearts failed them, and they sheered off[11]. At length their gait dragged, and they stood still.

"Could we sleep under the trees?" she asked.

He thought the season insufficiently advanced.

"I have been thinking of that empty mansion we passed," he said. "Let us go back towards it again."

They retraced their steps, but it was half an hour before they stood without the entrance-gate as earlier. He then requested her to stay where she was, whilst he went to see who was within.

She sat down among the bushes within the gate, and Clare crept towards the house. His absence lasted some considerable time, and when he returned Tess was wildly anxious, not for herself, but for him. He had found out from a boy that there was only an old woman in charge as caretaker, and she only came there on fine days, from the hamlet near, to open and shut the windows. She would come to shut them at sunset. "Now, we can get in through one of the lower windows, and rest there," said he.

Under his escort she went tardily forward to the main front, whose shuttered windows, like sightless eyeballs, excluded the possibility of watchers. The door was reached a few steps further, and one of the windows beside it was open. Clare clambered in, and pulled Tess in after him.

Except the hall the rooms were all in darkness, and they ascended the staircase. Up here also the shutters were tightly closed, the ventilation being perfunctorily done, for this day at least, by opening the hall-window in front and an upper window behind. Clare unlatched the door of a large chamber, felt his way across it, and parted the shutters to the width of two or three inches. A shaft of dazzling sunlight glanced into the room, revealing heavy, old-fashioned furniture, crimson damask hangings, and an enormous four-post bedstead, along the head of which were carved running figures, apparently Atalanta's race[12].

"Rest at last!" said he, setting down his bag and the parcel of viands.

They remained in great quietness till the caretaker should have come to shut the windows: as a precaution, putting themselves in total darkness by barring the shutters as before, lest the woman should open the door of their chamber for any casual reason. Between six and seven o'clock she came, but did not approach the wing they were in. They heard her close the windows, fasten them, lock the door, and go away. Then Clare again stole a chink of light from the window, and they shared another meal, till by-and-by they were enveloped in the shades of night which they had no candle to disperse.

Chapter 58

The night was strangely solemn and still. In the small hours she whispered to him the whole story of how he had walked in his sleep with her in his arms across the Froom stream, at the imminent risk of both their lives, and laid her down in the stone coffin at the ruined abbey. He had never known of that till now.

"Why didn't you tell me next day?" he said. "It might have prevented much misunderstanding and woe."

"Don't think of what's past!" said she. "I am not going to think outside of now. Why should we! Who knows what tomorrow has in store[13]?"

But it apparently had no sorrow. The morning was wet and foggy, and Clare, rightly informed that the caretaker only opened the windows on fine days, ventured to creep out of their chamber, and explore the house, leaving Tess asleep. There was no food on the premises, but there was water, and he took advantage of the fog to emerge from the mansion, and fetch tea, bread, and butter from a shop in a little place two miles beyond, as also a small tin kettle and spirit-lamp, that they might get fire without smoke. His re-entry awoke her; and they breakfasted on what he had brought.

They were indisposed[14] to stir abroad, and the day passed, and the night following, and the next, and next; till, almost without their being aware, five days had slipped by in absolute seclusion, not a sight or sound of a human being disturbing their peacefulness, such as it was. The changes of the weather were their only events, the birds of the New Forest their only company. By tacit consent they hardly once spoke of any incident of the past subsequent to their wedding-day. The gloomy intervening time seemed to sink into chaos, over which the present and prior times closed as if it never had been. Whenever he suggested that they should leave their shelter, and go forwards towards Southampton or London, she showed a strange unwillingness to move.

"Why should we put an end to all that's sweet and lovely!" she deprecated[15], "What must come will come." And, looking through the shutter-chink: "All is trouble outside there; inside here content."

He peeped out also. It was quite true; within was affection, union, error forgiven: outside was the inexorable[16].

"And—and," she said, pressing her cheek against his, "I fear that what you think of me now may not last. I do not wish to outlive your present feeling for me. I would rather not. I would rather be dead and buried when the time comes for you to despise me, so that it may never be known to me that you despised me."

"I cannot ever despise you."

"I also hope that. But considering what my life had been I cannot see why any man should, sooner or later, be able to help despising me… How wickedly mad I was! Yet formerly I never could bear to hurt a fly or a worm, and the sight of a bird in a cage used often to make me cry."

They remained yet another day. In the night the dull sky cleared, and the result was that the old caretaker at the cottage awoke early. The brilliant sunrise made her unusually brisk; she decided to open the contiguous mansion immediately, and to air it thoroughly on such a day. Thus it occurred that, having arrived and opened the lower rooms before six o'clock, she ascended to the bedchambers, and was about to turn the handle of the one wherein they lay. At that moment she fancied she could hear the breathing of persons within. Her slippers and her antiquity had rendered her progress a noiseless one so far, and she made for instant retreat; then, deeming that her hearing might have deceived her, she turned anew to the door and softly tried the handle. The lock was out of order, but a piece of furniture had been moved forward on the inside, which prevented her opening the door more than an inch or two. A stream of morning light through the shutter-chink fell upon the faces of the pair, wrapped in profound slumber, Tess's lips being parted like a half-opened flower near his cheek. The caretaker was so struck with their innocent appearance, and with the elegance of Tess's gown hanging across a chair, her silk stockings beside it, the pretty parasol, and the other habits in which she had arrived because she had none else, that her first indignation at the effrontery[17] of tramps and vagabonds gave way to a momentary sentimentality over this genteel elopement, as it seemed. She closed the door, and withdrew as softly as she had come, to go and consult with her neighbors on the odd discovery.

Not more than a minute had elapsed after her withdrawal when Tess woke, and then Clare. Both had a sense that something had disturbed them, though they could not say what; and the uneasy feeling which it engendered grew stronger. As soon as he was dressed he narrowly scanned the lawn through the two or three inches of shutter-chink.

"I think we will leave at once," said he. "It is a fine day. And I cannot help fancying somebody is about the house. At any rate, the woman will be sure to come today."

She passively assented, and putting the room in order they took up the few articles that belonged to them, and departed noiselessly. When they had got into the Forest she turned to take a last look at the house.

"Ah, happy house—goodbye!" she said. "My life can only be a question of a few weeks. Why should we not have stayed there?"

"Don't say it, Tess! We shall soon get out of this district altogether. We'll continue our course as we've begun it, and keep straight north. Nobody will think of looking for us there. We shall be looked for at the Wessex ports if we are sought at all. When we are in the north we will get to a port and away."

Having thus persuaded her, the plan was pursued, and they kept a bee-line northward[18]. Their long repose at the manor-house lent them walking power now; and towards mid-day they found that they were approaching the steepled city of Melchester, which lay directly in their way. He decided to rest her in a clump of trees during the afternoon, and push onward under cover of darkness. At dusk Clare purchased food as usual, and their night march began, the boundary between Upper and Mid-Wessex being crossed about eight o'clock.

To walk across country, without much regard to roads was not new to Tess, and she showed her old agility in the performance. The intercepting city, ancient Melchester, they were obliged to pass through in order to take advantage of the town bridge for crossing a large river that obstructed them. It was about midnight when they went along the deserted streets, lighted fitfully by the few lamps, keeping off the pavement that it might not echo their footsteps. The graceful pile of cathedral architecture rose dimly on their left hand, but it was lost upon them now. Once out of the town they followed the turnpike-road, which after a few miles plunged across an open plain.

Though the sky was dense with cloud a diffused light from some fragment of a moon had hitherto helped them a little. But the moon had now sunk, the clouds seemed to settle almost on their heads, and the night grew as dark as a cave. However, they found their way along, keeping as much on the tuff as possible that their tread might not resound, which it was easy to do, there being no hedge or fence of any kind. All around was open loneliness and black solitude, over which a stiff breeze blew.

They had proceeded thus gropingly two or three miles further when on a sudden Clare became conscious of some vast erection[19] close in his front, rising sheer from the grass. They had almost struck themselves against it.

"What monstrous place is this?" said Angel.

"It hums," said she, "Hearken!"

He listened. The wind, playing upon the edifice, produced a booming tune, like the note of some gigantic one-stringed harp. No other sound came from it, and lifting his hand and advancing a step or two, Clare felt the vertical surface of the structure. It seemed to be of solid stone, without joint or molding. Carrying his fingers onward he found that what he had come in contact with was a colossal rectangular pillar; by stretching out his left hand he could feel a similar one adjoining. At an indefinite height overhead something made the black sky blacker, which had the semblance of a vast architrave uniting the pillars horizontally. They carefully entered beneath and between; the surfaces echoed their soft rustle; but they seemed to be still out of doors. The place was roofless. Tess drew her breath fearfully, and Angel, perplexed, said—

"What can it be?"

Feeling sideways they encountered another tower-like pillar, square and uncompromising as the first; beyond it another and another. The place was all doors and pillars, some connected above by continuous architraves[20].

"A very Temple of the Winds," he said.

The next pillar was isolated; others composed a trilithon[21]; others were prostrate, their flanks forming a causeway wide enough for a carriage and it was soon obvious that they made up a forest of monoliths[22] grouped upon the grassy expanse of the plain. The couple advanced further into this pavilion of the night till they stood in its midst.

"It is Stonehenge[23]!" said Clare.

"The heathen temple, you mean?"

"Yes. Older than the centuries; older than the D'Urbervilles! Well, what shall we do, darling? We may find shelter further on."

But Tess, really tired by this time, flung herself upon an oblong slab that lay close at hand, and was sheltered from the wind by a pillar. Owing to the action of the sun during the preceding day the stone was warm and dry, in comforting contrast to the rough and chill grass around, which had damped her skirts and shoes.

"I don't want to go any further, Angel," she said, stretching out her hand for his. "Can't we bide here?"

"I fear not. This spot is visible for miles by day, although it does not seem so now."

"One of my mother's people was a shepherd hereabouts, now I think of it. And you used to say at Talbothays[24] that I was a heathen. So now I am at home".

He knelt down beside her outstretched form, and put his lips upon hers.

"Sleepy are you, dear? I think you are lying on an altar."

"I like very much to be here," she murmured. "It is so solemn and lonely—after my great happiness—with nothing but the sky above my face. It seems as if there were no folk in the world but we two; and I wish there were not—except 'Liza-Lu[25]."

Clare thought she might as well rest here till it should get a little lighter, and he flung his overcoat upon her, and sat down by her side.

"Angel, if anything happens to me, will you watch over 'Liza-Lu for my sake?" she asked, when they had listened a long time to the wind among the pillars.

"I will."

"She is so good and simple and pure. O, Angel—I wish you would marry her if you lose me, as you will do shortly. O, if you would!"

"If I lose you I lose all! And she is my sister-in-law."

"That's nothing, dearest. People marry sister-laws continually about Marlott[26]; and 'Liza-Lu is so gentle and sweet, and she is growing so beautiful. O, I could share you with her willingly when we are spirits[27]! If you would train her and teach her, Angel, and bring her up for your own self! ... She had all the best of me without the bad of me; and if she were to become yours it would almost seem as if death had not divided us... Well, I have said it. I won't mention it again."

She ceased, and he fell into thought. In the far north-east sky he could see between the pillars a level streak of light. The uniform concavity of black cloud was lifting bodily like the lid of a pot, letting in at the earth's edge the coming day, against which the towering monoliths and trilithons began to be blackly defined.

"Did they sacrifice to God here?" asked she.

"No," said he.

"Who to?"

"I believe to the sun. That lofty stone set away by itself is in the direction of the sun, which will presently rise behind it."

"This reminds me, dear," she said. "You remember you never would interfere with any belief of mine before we were married? But I knew your mind all the same, and I thought as you thought—not from any reasons of my own, but because you thought so. Tell me now, Angel, do you think we shall meet again after we are dead? I want to know."

He kissed her to avoid a reply at such a time.

"O, Angel—I fear that means no!" said she, with a suppressed sob. "And I wanted so to see you again—so much, so much! What—not even you and I, Angel, who love each other so well?"

Like a greater than himself, to the critical question at the critical time he did not answer; and they were again, silent. In a minute or two her breathing became more regular, her clasp of his hand relaxed, and she fell asleep. The band of silver paleness along the east horizon made even the distant parts of the Great Plain appear dark and near; and the whole enormous landscape bore that impress of reserve, taciturnity, and hesitation which is usual just before day. The eastward pillars and their architraves stood up blackly against the light, and the great flame-shaped Sun-stone beyond them; and the Stone of Sacrifice midway. Presently the night wind died out, and the quivering little pools in the cup-like hollows of the stones lay still. At the same time something seemed to move on the verge of the dip eastward—a mere dot. It was the head of a man approaching them from the hollow beyond the Sun-stone. Clare wished they had gone onward, but in the circumstances decided to remain quiet. The figure came straight towards the circle of pillars in which they were.

He heard something behind him, the brush of feet. Turning, he saw over the prostrate columns another figure; then before he was aware, another was at hand on the right, under a trilithon, and another on the left. The dawn shone full on the front of the man westward, and Clare could discern from this that he was tall, and walked as if trained. They all closed in with evident purpose. Her story then was true! Springing to his feet, he looked around for a weapon, loose stone, means of escape, anything. By this time the nearest man was upon him.

"It is no use, sir," he said. "There are sixteen of us on the Plain, and the whole country is reared."

"Let her finish her sleep!" he implored in a whisper of the men as they gathered round.

When they saw where she lay, which they had not done till then, they showed no objection, and stood watching her, as still as the pillars around. He went to the stone and bent over her, holding one poor little hand; her breathing now was quick and small, like that of a lesser creature than a woman. All waited in the growing light, their faces and hands as if they were silvered, the remainder of their figures dark, the stones glistening green-gray, the Plain still a mass of shade. Soon the light was strong, and a ray shone upon her unconscious form, peering under her eyelids and waking her.

"What is it, Angel?" she said, starting up. "Have they come for me?"

"Yes, dearest," he said. "They have come."

"It is as it should be," she murmured. "Angel, I am almost glad—yes, glad! This happiness could not have lasted. It was too much. I have had enough; and now I shall not live for you to despise me!"

She stood up, shook herself, and went forward, neither of the men having moved. "I am ready," she said quietly.

※ ※

Notes

1. Cuthbert: Cuthbert Clare, one of Angel's older brothers.
2. dipped into: went downward into.
3. acclivity: an ascending slope.
4. vacuity: a lack of intelligent, interesting, or serious thought.
5. wayfarers: a traveler who walks from one place to another.
6. delirium: a state in which some one is delirious, especially because they are very ill.
7. aberration: an action or event that is different from what usually happens or what someone usually does.
8. Antinous: a youth of remarkable beauty, who was a favorite of the Emperor Hadrian. He was drowned in the Nile in A.D. 122.

VI. Age of Realism (The Victorian Age)

9. promenaded: walked in a leisurely way.
10. unforefending: not taking cautious or protecting measures.
11. sheered off: changed direction suddenly, especially in order to avoid something.
12. Atalanta's race: In Greek myth, a maiden challenged each of her suitors to a footrace and was eventually married to Hippomenes who defeated her by dropping on the course three golden apples which she stopped to pick up.
13. what tomorrow has in store: what would happen tomorrow; "in store": something unexpected is about to happen.
14. indisposed: not willing to do something.
15. deprecate: strongly disapprove of.
16. inexorable: a situation or process that cannot be stopped.
17. effrontery: behavior that you think someone should be ashamed of, although they do not seem to be.
18. kept a bee-line northward: kept going quickly and directly toward the north.
19. vast erection: huge structure that has been built.
20. architraves: the molding around a rectangular opening (as a door).
21. trilithon: very large and tall three-part block of stone.
22. monoliths: a huge block of stone, especially one that was put in place in ancient times.
23. Stonehenge: It is Britain's most important prehistoric monument. Probably used as a temple, the history of Stonehenge spans about 15 centuries from about 3050 B.C. to 1600 B.C. Stonehenge exudes a powerful sense of mystery which has enthralled successive generations.
24. Talbothays: the Talbothays Dairy in the Froom Valley, where Tess worked as a dairymaid and met Angel.
25. 'Liza-Lu: Tess's younger sister who travels to Flintcomb-Ash to request that her sister return home when her parents are ill.
26. Marlott: Tess's home village where she was born and grew up.
27. when we are spirits: when Tess and Angel both died and were united to live in another world.

Questions for Understanding

1. How did Angel feel after he left Tess and was on the way to the railway station?

2. What drove her to kill Alec, according to Tess? What drove Tess to kill Alec in your opinion?
3. Why is it significant that Tess was arrested while she was sleeping on the altar slab at Stonehenge?
4. Why is Tess ready to die at the end of the novel?

Aspects of Appreciation

1. Hardy is noted for his pessimistic novels of life. Living at the turn of the century, Hardy is often regarded as a transitional writer, influenced by both the Victorian and the modern. In his novels, there is an apparent nostalgic touch in his description of the primitive rural life, which was gradually declining and disappearing as England was marching fast into an industrial country. And he was always sympathetic with those traditional characters and mourned over their failure and misfortune.

   In his works, man is shown driven by a combined force of "nature", both inside and outside. His inherent nature may prompt him to go and search for some specific happiness or success and set him in conflict with the environment. The outside environment produces mistimed actions and unfortunate coincidences. Man proves impotent before his ordained destiny. This pessimistic view of life predominates most of his works and earns him a reputation as a writer of naturalism.

   Though naturalism plays an important part in some of his works, Hardy is never far away from the real life and the existing society. Most of his works are devoted to a realistic presentation of life, and there is often bitter and sharp criticism and even open defiance of the wicked, hypocritical and corrupted Victorian institution, convention and morality which strangle the individual will and destroy natural human emotions and relationships. The conflict between the traditional and the modern, between the old rural value of respectability and honesty and the new utilitarian commercialism, between the old, false social moral and the natural human passion, etc., are all closely set in a realistic background.

2. All of Tess's life is the result of either an accident, fate, or the intervention of other forces. As an insecure and inferior being, she can never love in a genuine and generous way. She is not the master of her own life. She is exploited, preyed upon, then humiliated and abandoned. The novel ends, "Justice was done, and the President of the Immortals had ended his sport with Tess." The last words highlight Hardy's

critical attitude toward the unjust treatment of women and his denunciation of the hypocrisy of the social structures and moral codes of Victorian England.

On the one hand, Tess's fate is personal, because she happens to be so beautiful, pure, innocent, obedient and poor, and because she happens to get involved with the two men who, though apparent rivals, actually join their forces in bringing about her destruction. On the other hand, her fate is a social one, representing the tenants who are driven out of their land and home, and forced to seek somewhere else for sustenance.

Suggested Further Reading

1. Thomas Hardy. *Jude the Obscure*, 1896.
2. Florence Harvey. *The Complete Critical Guide to Thomas Hardy*, 2003.

Topics for Further Study

1. Discuss the differences found in Angel Clare and Alec D'Urbervilles.
2. Discuss the character of Tess. To what extent is she a helpless victim?
3. What does the author mean when he entitles the part "Phase the Seventh: Fulfillment"? Do you think Tess's life is a fulfilled one? Why or why not?

VII
Modern Age

W. B. Yeats
(1865~1939)

About the Author

William Butler Yeats(1865~1939), a poet and a dramatist, is regarded with T. S. Eliot as one of the two important and influential writers in modern poetry. Their revolt against the imprecise language and sentimentalism of the Victorian poets led to the modernist movement in literature.

Born of Irish parents in Dublin and influenced by his family, Yeats developed a love of Ireland and its culture, and he was devoted to the cause of Irish nationalism and to the Celtic Revival Movement, promoting the literary heritage of Ireland. Deep-rooted in Irish culture with its folklore, legends, music and magic, Yeats drew wisdom and inspiration from, and wrote about, the traditions and history of the Irish nation. His early poetry was marked by dreamy romanticism with clarity, imagery and musicality that show his indebtedness to Edmund Spenser and Shelley. In his later years he found a metaphysical and French symbolistic approach to poetry and wrote on the great, eternal subject of time and change, love and age, life and art. His poetry was characterized by disillusion, bitter satire, strong symbolism and the combination of colloquial and formal language. He believed that all history and life follow a circular, spiral pattern consisting of long cycles which repeat themselves over and over on different levels. So, symbols like winding stairs, spinning tops, gyres and spirals are frequent and important in his poems. There is profound beauty and also mysticism in his poetry.

Yeats's major poetic works include *The Wanderings of Oisin and Other Poems* (1889), *The Wind among the Reeds* (1899), *The Responsibilities* (1914), *The Wild Swans at Coole* (1919), *The Tower* (1928), *The Winding Stair and Other Poems* (1933) and *New Poems* (1938). His important dramatic works are *The Hour Glass* (1901), *The Land of Heart's Desire* (1894) and *The Shadowy Waters* (1900). *A Vision* (1925~1926) is a book of philosophy which shows his mysticism. Yeats won Nobel Prize in 1923.

★ The Second Coming[1]

About the Poem

Yeats wrote "The Second Coming" in 1919 when Europe and much of the rest of the world were trying to recover from World War I. The poem expresses Yeats's belief that history was cyclic, and that his age represented the end of the cycle that began with the rise of Christianity. The poem presents a picture of turmoil and tribulation in the world, and sings of a dirge for the decline of European civilisation.

> Turning and turning in the widening gyre[2]
> The falcon cannot hear the falconer;
> Things fall apart; the centre cannot hold;
> Mere anarchy is loosed upon the world,
> The blood-dimmed tide is loosed, and everywhere
> The ceremony of innocence is drowned;
> The best lack all conviction, while the worst[3]
> Are full of passionate intensity[4].
>
> Surely some revelation is at hand;
> Surely the Second Coming is at hand.
> The Second Coming! Hardly are those words out
> When[5] a vast image out of Spiritus Mundi[6]
> Troubles my sight: somewhere in sands of the desert
> A shape with lion body and the head of a man[7],
> A gaze blank and pitiless as the sun,
> Is moving its slow thighs, while all around it

Reel shadows of the indignant desert birds.
The darkness drops again; but now I know
That twenty centuries of stony sleep[8]
Were vexed to nightmare by a rocking cradle,
And what rough beast, its hour come round at last,
Slouches towards Bethlehem[9] to be born?

Notes

1. The term "second coming" was traditionally used to refer to expectations of the return of Jesus for the salvation of believers, as described in Mark 13, Matthew 24, Luke 21, Revelation etc. Yeats believed that human history could be measured in cycles of approximately 2,000 years. In this cycle, the birth of Jesus had ended the Greco-Roman cycle, and in 1919 when Yeats wrote this poem, it seemed to him that the Christian period was ending and a new era was about to take its place, and this new era would be taken over by an anti-Christ or evil force.
2. gyre: a radiating spiral, cone etc., usually used by Yeats to symbolize a cycle of history. Here it literally means the widening spiral of a falcon's flight and the near end of a cycle of history.
3. The best: the best people; the worst: the worst people.
4. Lines 4-8 may refer to World War II, the turmoil in Ireland and Russian Revolution of 1917.
5. Hardly…/When…: As soon as these words are spoken out/Then…
6. Spiritus Mundi (世界之灵): the Spirit or Soul of the Universe, a collective human unconscious which Yeats believed furnish writers and thinkers with a common fund of images and symbols.
7. A shape with lion body and the head of a man: a sphinx, because of whose pre-Christian origin, this image is given qualities associated with a monstrous, superhuman, Satanic figure.
8. twenty centuries of stony sleep: twenty centuries since the birth of Jesus.
9. Bethlehem: 伯利恒。

Questions for Understanding

1. What images of turning are used and what might be the symbolic meanings of these images?

2. What might "the best" and "the worst" specifically refer to respectively?
3. What might "the falcon" and "the falconer" symbolize respectively? And what might "the falcon" and "desert birds" stand for respectively?
4. What may "the ceremony of innocence" refer to?
5. What attributes might the sphinx figure have that is revealed as a "rough beast"? What may be the significance of his going "to Bethlehem to be born"?
6. In what way is the biblical allusion used and what does the poet want to express?

Aspects of Appreciation

1. Yeats's concept of history and philosophical idea Order is breaking down and communication becomes impossible.
2. Symbolism of Yeats's poetry, cycles, the widening gyre etc.
3. Use of biblical allusions of seconding coming, Jesus Christ, cradle, Bethlehem, etc.

Suggested Further Reading

W. B. Yeats's other poems "When You Are Old" "A Deep-Sworn Vow" "Leda And the Swan" "Sailing to Byzantium" "The Lake Isle Of Innisfree" and "The Wild Swans at Coole".

Topics for Further Study

1. The poem "The Second Coming" is representative of Yeats's style of later period. Try to compare it with his poems of the early period, say, "The Lake Isle of Innisfree", to see their differences.
2. W. B. Yeats and T. S. Eliot are regarded as two important representatives of modern poetry. Try to find the similarities and differences of their poems and specify the general features of modern poetry.

Knowledge of Literature

Spiritus Mundi and collective unconscious(集体无意识)

Spiritus Mundi is Yeats's system of images or symbols which in his belief, "is a general storehouse of images", to which all human minds are connected. He thought that all people preserve the memory of the human race deep in their sub-conscious and this is the source of symbols for the poet. Yeats's idea bears some resemblance to the theory of collective unconscious proposed by Carl Jung(1875~1961), one of the key figures in myth and archetypal criticism in the early of 20th century. Jung believed that collective unconscious is the inborn racial memory which is the primitive source of the archetypes or universal symbols found in legends, poetry, and dreams.

Bernard Shaw
(1856~1950)

About the Author

George Bernard Shaw(1856~1950)is an Irish dramatist, literary critic, socialist spokesman, and a leading figure in the 20th century theater. Shaw was a free thinker, a supporter of women's rights and an advocate of equality of income. In 1925, he was awarded the Nobel Prize for Literature. Shaw accepted the honor, but refused the money. His *Widower's Houses* and *Mrs. Warren's Profession* savagely attack social hypocrisy, while in plays such as *Arms and the Man* and *The Man of Destiny* the criticism is less fierce. Shaw's radical rationalism, his utter disregard of conventions, his keen dialectic interest and verbal wit often turn the stage into a forum of ideas. Shaw's greatest success came between the years of 1904~1907, when *Man and Superman*, *Major Barbara*, and *The Doctor's Dilemma* were all produced.

★ Major Barbara

About the Play

Major Barbara was first performed at the Royal Court Theatre in 1905 and published in 1907. Like the characters in Shaw's other plays, the members of the Undershaft family, together with the suitors of the two daughters are all passionate people, obsessed by their intellectual and moral passions. The dramatic conflict of the play lies between two principal characters: Barbara, a major in the Salvation Army, and her father, Andrew Undershaft, a millionaire and cannon manufacturer, embodying spiritual and worldly forces respectively. The events in the play are centered around one single action: conversations. Although there is not too much action in the play, Shaw's ideas are conveyed to his audience and readers through the lengthy talks of his characters.

Act III (Excerpt)

Mot: [At the door] Mr. Undershaft.

[Undershaft comes in. Morrison goes out]

Und: Alone! How fortunate!

Lady: [Rising] Don't be sentimental, Andrew. Sit down. [She sits on the settee; he sits besides her, on her left. She comes to the point before he has time to breathe] Sarah must have 800 pounds a year until Charles Lomax comes into his property. Barbara will need more, and need it permanently, because Adolphus hasn't any property.

Und: [Resignedly] Yes, my dear. I will see to it. Anything else? for yourself, for instance?

Lady: I want to talk to you about Stephen.

Und: [Rather wearily] Don't my dear. Stephen doesn't interest me.

Lady: He does interest me. He is our son.

Und: Do you really think so? He has induced us to bring him into the world; but he chose his parents very incongruously, I think. I see nothing of myself in him, and less of you.

Lady: Andrew, Stephen is an excellent son, and a most steady, capable, high-minded young man. You are simply trying to find an excuse for disinheriting him.

Und: My dear Biddy, the Undershaft tradition disinherits him. It would be dishonest of me to leave the cannon foundry to my son.

Lady: It would be most unnatural and improper of you to leave it to anyone else, Andrew. Do you suppose this wicked and immoral tradition can be kept up for ever? Do you pretend that Stephen could not carry on the foundry just as well as all the other sons of the big business houses?

Und: Yes, he could learn the office routine without understanding the business, like all the other sons; and the firm would go on by its own momentum until the real Undershaft—probably an Italian or a German—would invent a new method and cut him out.

Lady: There is nothing that any Italian or German could do that Stephen could not do. And Stephen at least has breeding.

Und: The son of a foundling! Nonsense!

Lady: My son, Andrew! And even you may have good blood in your veins for all you know.

Und: True. Probably I have. That is another argument in favour of a foundling.

Lady: Andrew, don't be aggravating. And don't be wicked. At present you are both.

Und: This conversation is part of the Undershaft tradition, Biddy. Every Undershaft's wife has treated him to it ever since the house was founded. It is mere waste of breath. If the tradition be ever broken it will be for an abler man than Stephen.

Lady: [Pouting] Then go away.

Und: [Deprecatory] Go away!

Lady: Yes, go away. If you will do nothing for Stephen, you are not wanted here. Go to your foundling, whoever he is; and look after him.

Und: The fact is, Biddy—

Lady: Don't call me Biddy. I don't call you Andy.

Und: I will not call my wife Britomart, it is not good sense. Seriously, my love, the Undershaft tradition has landed me in a difficulty. I am getting on in years; and my partner Lazarus has at last made a stand and insisted that the succession must be settled one way or the other; and of course he is quite right. You see, I haven't found a fit successor yet.

Lady: [Obstinately] There is Stephen.

Und: That's just it. All the foundlings I can find are exactly like Stephen.

Lady: Andrew!!

Und: I want a man with no relations and no schooling: that is, a man who would be out of the running altogether if he were not a strong man. And I can't find him. Every blessed foundling nowadays is snapped up in his infancy by Barnardo[1] homes or School Board officers, or Boards of Guardians; and if he shews the least ability, he is fastened on by schoolmasters; trained to win scholarships like a racehorse; crammed with secondhand ideas; drilled and disciplined in docility and what they call good taste; and lamed for life so that he is fit for nothing but teaching. If you want to keep the foundry in the family, you had better find an eligible foundling and marry him to Barbara.

Lady: Ah! Barbara! Your pet! You would sacrifice Stephen for Barbara.

Und: Cheerfully. And you, my dear, would boil Barbara to make soup for Stephen.

Lady: Andrew, this is not a question of our likings and dislikings: it is a question of duty. It is your duty to make Stephen your successor.

Und: Just as much as it is your duty to submit to your husband. Come, Biddy! these tricks of the governing class are of no use with me. I am one of the governing class myself; and it is waste of time giving tracts to a missionary. I have the power in this matter; and I am not to be humbugged into using it for your purposes.

Lady: Andrew, you can talk my head off; but you can't change wrong into right. And your tie is all on one side. Put it straight.

Und: [Disconcerted] It won't stay unless it's pinned—[He fumbles at it with childish grimaces]

[Stephen comes in]

Ste: [At the door] I beg your pardon. [About to retire]

Lady: No, come in, Stephen. [Stephen comes forward to his mother's writing table.]

Und: [Not very cordially] Good afternoon.

Ste: [Coldly] Good afternoon.

Und: [To Lady Britomart] He knows all about the tradition, I suppose?

Lady: Yes. [To Stephen] It is what I told you last night, Stephen.

Und: [Sulkily] I understand you want to come into the cannon business.

Ste: I go into trade! Certainly not.

Und: [Opening his eyes, greatly eased in mind and manner.] Oh! in that case—

Lady: Cannons are not trade, Stephen. They are enterprise.

Ste: I have no intention of becoming a man of business in any sense. I have no capacity for business and no taste for it. I intend to devote myself to politics.

Und: [Rising] My dear boy: this is an immense relief to me. And I trust it may prove an equally good thing for the country. I was afraid you would consider yourself disparaged and slighted. [He moves towards Stephen as if to shake hands with him.]

Lady: [Rising and interposing] Stephen, I cannot allow you to throw away an enormous property like this.

Ste: [Stiffly] Mother, there must be an end of treating me as a child, if you please. [Lady Britomart recoils, deeply wounded by his tone] Until last night I did not take your attitude seriously, because I did not think you meant it seriously. But I find now that you left me in the dark as to matters which you should have explained to me years ago. I am extremely hurt and offended. Any further discussion of my intentions had better take place with my father, as between one man and another.

Lady: Stephen! [She sits down again, her eyes filling with tears.]

Und: [With grave compassion] You see, my dear, it is only the big men who can be treated as children.

Ste: I am sorry, mother, that you have forced me—

Und: [Stopping him] Yes, yes, yes, yes, that's all right, Stephen. She won't interfere with you any more. Your independence is achieved. You have won your latchkey. Don't rub it in; and above all, don't apologize. [He resumes his seat] Now what about your future, as between one man and another—I beg your pardon, Biddy, as between two men and a woman.

Lady: [Who has pulled herself together strongly.] I quite understand, Stephen. By all means go your own way if you feel strong enough. [Stephen sits down magisterially in the chair at the writing table with an air of affirming his majority.]

Und: It is settled that you do not ask for the succession to the cannon business.

Ste: I hope it is settled that I repudiate the cannon business.

Und: Come, come! Don't be so devilishly sulky. It's boyish. Freedom should be generous. Besides, I owe you a fair start in life in exchange for disinheriting you. You can't become prime minister all at once. Haven't you a turn for something? What about literature, art, and so forth?

Ste: I have nothing of the artist about me, either in faculty or character, thank Heaven!

Und: A philosopher, perhaps? Eh?

Ste: I make no such ridiculous pretension.

Und: Just so. Well, there is the army, the navy, the Church, the Bar. The Bar requires some ability. What about the Bar?

Ste: I have not studied law. And I am afraid I have not the necessary push—I believe that is the name barristers give to their vulgarity—for success in pleading.

Und: Rather a difficult case, Stephen. Hardly anything left but the stage, is there? [Stephen makes an impatient movement.] Well, come! is there anything you know or care for?

Ste: [Rising and looking at him steadily.] I know the difference between right and wrong.

Und: [Hugely tickled] You don't say so! What! no capacity for business, no knowledge of law, no sympathy with art, no pretension to philosophy; only a simple knowledge of the secret that has puzzled all the philosophers, baffled all the lawyers, muddled all the men of business, and ruined most of the artists, the secret of right and wrong. Why, man, you're a genius, a master of masters, a god! At twenty-four, too!

Ste: [Keeping his temper with difficulty] You are pleased to be facetious. I pretend to nothing more than any honourable English gentleman claims as his birthright. [He sits down angrily.]

Und: Oh, that's everybody's birthright. Look at poor little Jenny Hill, the Salvation lassie! she would think you were laughing at her if you asked her to stand up in the street and teach grammar or geography or mathematics or even drawing room dancing; but it never occurs to her to doubt that she can teach morals and religion. You are all alike, you respectable people. You can't tell me the bursting strum of a ten inch gun, which is a very simple matter; but you all think you can tell me the bursting strain of a man under temptation. You daren't handle high explosives; but you're all ready to handle honesty and truth and justice and the whole duty of man, and kill one another at that game. What a country! What a world!

Lady: [Uneasily] What do you think he had better do, Andrew?

Und: Oh, just what he wants to do. He knows nothing and he thinks he knows everything. That points clearly to a political career. Get him a private secretaryship to someone who can get him an Under Secretaryship; and then leave him alone. He will find his natural and proper place in the end on the Treasury Bench.

Ste: [Springing up again] I am sorry, sir, that you force me to forget the respect due to you as my father. I am an Englishman and I will not hear the Government of my country insulted. [He thrusts his hands in his pockets, and walks angrily across to the window.]

Und: [With a touch of brutality] The government of your country! I am the government of your country, I, and Lazarus. Do you suppose that you and half a dozen amateurs like you, sitting in a row in that foolish gabble shop, can govern Undershaft and Lazarus? No, my friend, you will do what pays us. You will make war when it suits us, and keep peace when it doesn't. You will find out that trade requires certain measures when we have decided on those measures. When I want anything to keep my dividends up, you will discover that my want is a national need. When other people want something to keep my dividends down, you will call out the police and military. And in return you shall have the support and applause of my newspapers, and the delight of imagining that you are a great statesman. Government of your country! Be off with you, my boy, and play with your caucuses and leading articles and historic parties and great leaders and burning questions and the rest of your toys. I am going back to my counting house to pay the piper and call the tune.

Ste: [Actually smiling, and putting his hand on his father's shoulder with indulgent patronage] Really, my dear father, it is impossible to be angry with you. You don't know how absurd all this sounds to me. You are very properly proud of having been industrious enough to make money; and it is greatly to your credit that you have made so much of it. But it has kept you in circles where you are valued for your money and deferred to for it, instead of in the doubtless very old-fashioned and behind-the-times public school and university where I formed my habits of mind. It is natural for you to think that money governs England; but you must allow me to think I know better.

Und: And what does govern England, pray?

Ste: Character, father, character.

Und: Whose character? Yours or mine?

Ste: Neither yours nor mine, father, but the best elements in the English national character.

Und: Stephen: I've found your profession for you. You're a born journalist. I'll start you with a hightoned weekly review. There! [Before Stephen can reply Sarah, Barbara, Lomax, and Cusins come in ready for walking. Barbara crosses the room to the window and looks out. Cusin drifts amiably to the armchair. Lomax remains near the door, whilst Sarah comes to her mother. Stephen goes to the smaller writing table and busies himself with his letters.]

Sar: Go and get ready, mamma. The carriage is waiting. [Lady Britomart leaves the room]

Und: [To Sarah] Good day, my dear. Good afternoon, Mr. Lomax.

Lom: [Vaguely] Ahdedoo.

Und: [To Cusins] Quite well after last night, Euripides[2], eh?

Cus: As well as can be expected.

Und: That's right. [To Barbara] So you are coming to see my death and devastation factory, Barbara?

Bar: [At the window] You came yesterday to see my salvation factory. I promised you a return visit.

Lom: [Coming forward between Sarah and Undershaft] You'll find it awfully interesting. I've been through the Woolwich Arsenal; and it gives you a ripping feeling of security, you know, to think of the lot of beggars we could kill if it came to fighting. [To Undershaft, with sudden solemnity] Still, it must be rather an awful reflection for you, from the religious point of view as it were. You're getting on, you know, and all that.

Sar: You don't mind Cholly's imbecility, papa, do you?

Lom: [Much taken aback.] Oh I say!

Und: Mr. Lomax looks at the matter in a very proper spirit, my dear.

Lom: Just so. That's all I meant, I assure you.

Sar: Are you coming, Stephen?

Ste: Well, I am rather busy—er—[Magnanimously] Oh well, yes: I'll come. That is, if there is room for me.

Und: I can take two with me in a little motor I am experimenting with for field use. You won't mind its being rather unfashionable. It's not painted yet; but it's bullet proof.

Lom:[Appalled at the prospect of confronting Wilton Crescent in an unpainted motor.] Oh I say!

Sar: The carriage for me, thank you. Barbara doesn't mind what she's seen in.

Lom: I say, Dolly old chap: do you really mind the car being a guy[3]? Because of course if you do I'll go in it. Still—

Cus: I prefer it.

Lom: Thanks awfully, old man. Come, ownest. [He hurries out to secure his seat in the carriage. Sarah follows him.]

Cus: [Moodily walking across to Lady Britomart's writing table] Why are we two coming to this Works Department of Hell? that is what I ask myself.

Bar: I have always thought of it as a sort of pit where lost creatures with blackened faces stirred up smoky fires and were driven and tormented by my father, is it like that, dad?

Und: [Scandalized] My dear! It is a spotlessly clean and beautiful hillside town.

Cus: With a Methodist chapel? Oh do say there's a Methodist chapel.

Und: There are two: a Primitive one and a sophisticated one. There is even an Ethical Society; but it is not much patronized, as my men are all strongly religious. In the High Explosives Sheds they object to the presence of Agnostics as unsafe.

Cus: And yet they don't object to you!

Bar: Do they obey all your orders?

Und: I never give them any orders. When I speak to one of them it is "Well, Jones, is the baby doing well? and has Mrs. Jones made a good recovery?" "Nicely, thank you, sir." And that's all.

Cus: But Jones has to be kept in order. How do you maintain discipline among your men?

Und: I don't. They do. You see, the one thing Jones won't stand is any rebellion from the man under him, or any assertion of social equality between the wife of the man with 4 shillings a week less than himself, and Mrs. Jones! Of course they all rebel against me, theoretically. Practically, every man of them keeps the man just below him in his place. I never meddle with them. I never bully them. I don't even bully Lazarus. I say that certain things are to be done; but I don't order anybody to do them. I don't say, mind you, that there is no ordering about and snubbing and even bullying. The men snub the boys and order them about; the carmen snub the sweepers; the artisans snub the unskilled labourers; the foremen drive and bully both the labourers and artisans; the assistant engineers find fault with the foremen; the chief engineers drop on the assistants; the departmental managers worry the chiefs; and the clerks have tall hats and hymn-books and keep up the social tone by refusing to associate on equal terms with anybody. The result is a colossal profit, which comes to me.

Cus: [Revolted] You really are a—well, what I was saying yesterday.

Bar: What was he saying yesterday?

Und: Never mind, my dear. He thinks I have made you unhappy. Have I?

Bar: Do you think I can be happy in this vulgar silly dress? I! who have worn the uniform. Do you understand what you have done to me? Yesterday I had a man's soul in my hand. I set him in the way of life with his face to salvation. But when we took your money he turned back to drunkenness and derision. [With intense conviction] I will never forgive you that. If I had a child, and you destroyed its body with your explosives—if you murdered Dolly with your horrible guns—I could forgive you if my forgiveness would open the gates of heaven to you. But to take a human soul from me, and turn it into the soul of a wolf! that is worse than any murder.

Und: Does my daughter despair so easily? Can you strike a man to the heart and leave no mark on him?

Bar: [Her face lighting up] Oh, you are right. He can never be lost now. Where was my faith?

Cus: Oh, clever clever devil!

Bar: You may be a devil; but God speaks through you sometimes. [She takes her father's hands and kisses them.] You have given me back my happiness: I feel it deep down now, though my spirit is troubled.

Und: You have learnt something. That always feels at first as if you had lost something.

Bar: Well, take me to the factory of death; and let me learn something more. There must be some truth or other behind all this frightful irony. Come, Dolly. [She goes out.]

Cus: My guardian angel! [To Undershaft] Avaunt! [He follows Barbara.]

Ste: [Quietly, at the writing table] You must not mind Cusins, father. He is a very amiable good fellow; but he is a Greek scholar and naturally a little eccentric.

Und: Ah, quite so. Thank you, Stephen. Thank you. [He goes out.]

[Stephen smiles patronizingly; buttons his coat responsibly; and crosses the room to the door. Lady Britomart, dressed for out-of-doors, opens it before he reaches it. She looks round for the others; looks at Stephen; and turns to go without a word.]

Ste: [Embarrassed] Mother—

Lady: Don't be apologetic, Stephen. And don't forget that you have out-grown your mother. [She goes out.]

[Perivale St Andrews lies between two Middlesex hills, half climbing the northern one. It is an almost smokeless town of white walls, roofs of narrow green slates or red titles, tall trees, domes, campaniles, and slender chimney shafts, beautifully situated and beautiful in itself. The best view of it is obtained from the crest of a slope about half a mile to the east, where the high explosives are dealt with. The foundry lies hidden in the depths between, the tops of its chimneys sprouting like high skittles into the middle distance. Across the crest runs an emplacement of concrete, with a firestep, and a parapet which suggests a fortification, because there is a hugh cannon of the obsolete Woolwich Infant pattern peering across it at the town. The cannon is mounted on an experimental gun carriage: possibly the original model of the Undershaft disappearing rampart gun alluded to by Stephen. The firestep, being a convenient place to sit, is furnished here and there with straw disc cushions; and at one place there is the additional luxury of a fur rug. Barbara is standing on the firestep, looking over the parapet towards the town. On her right is the cannon; on her left the end of a shed raised on piles, with a ladder of three of four steps up to the door, which opens outwards and has a little wooden landing at the threshold, with a fire bucket in the corner of the landing. Several dummy soldiers more or less mutilated, with straw protruding from their gashes, have been shoved out of the way under the landing. A few others are nearly upright against the shed; and one has fallen forward and lies, like a grotesque corpse, on the emplacement. The parapet stops short of the shed, leaving a gap which is the beginning of the path down the hill through the foundry to the town. The rug is on the firestep near this gap. Down on the emplacement behind the cannon is a trolley carrying a huge conical bombshell with a red band painted on it. Further to the right is the door of an office, which, like the sheds, is of the lightest possible construction. Cusins arrives by the path from the town.]

Bar: Well?

Cus: Not a ray of hope. Everything perfect! wonderful! real! It only needs a cathedral to be a heavenly city instead of a hellish one.

Bar: Have you found out whether they have done anything for old Peter Shirley[4]?

Cus: They have found him a job as gatekeeper and timekeeper. He's frightfully miserable. He calls the timekeeping brain-work, and says he isn't used to it; and his gate lodge is so splendid that he's ashamed to use the rooms, and skulks in the scullery.

Bar: Poor Peter!

[Stephen arrives from the town. He carries a field-glass.]

Ste: [Enthusiastically] Have you two seen the place? Why did you leave us?

Cus: I wanted to see everything I was not intended to see; and Barbara wanted to make the men talk.

VII. Modern Age

Ste: Have you found anything discreditable?

Cus: No. They call him Dandy Andy and are proud of his being a cunning old rascal; but it's all horribly, frightfully, immorally, unanswerably perfect.

[Sarah arrives.]

Sar: Heavens! what a place! [She crosses to the trolley.] Did you see the nursing home!? [She sits down on the shell.]

Ste: Did you see the libraries and schools!?

Sar: Did you see the ball room and the banqueting chamber in the Town Hall!?

Ste: Have you gone into the insurance fund, the pension fund, the building society, the various applications of cooperation!?

[Undershaft comes from the office, with a sheaf of telegrams in his hand]

Und: Well, have you seen everything? I'm sorry I was called away. [Indicating the telegrams] Good news from Nanchuria[5].

Ste: Another Japanese victory?

Und: Oh, I don't know. Which side wins does not concern us here. No, the good news is that the aerial battleship is a tremendous success. At the first trial it has wiped out a fort with three hundred soldiers in it.

Cus: Dummy soldiers?

Und: [Striding across to Stephen and kicking the prostrate dummy brutally out of his way.] No: the real thing.

[Cusins and Barbara exchange glances. Then Cusins sits on the step and buries his face in his hands. Barbara gravely lays her hand on his shoulder. He looks up at her in whimsical desperation]

Und: Well, Stephen, what do you think of the place?

Ste: Oh, magnificent. A perfect triumph of modern industry. Frankly, my dear father, I have been a fool: I had no idea of what it all meant: of the wonderful forethought, the power of organization, the administrative capacity, the financial genius, the colossal capital it represents. I have been repeating to myself as I came through your streets "Please hath her victories no less renowned that War." I have only one misgiving about it all.

Und: Out with it.

Ste: Well, I cannot help thinking that all this provision for every want of your workmen may sap their independence and weaken their sense of responsibility. And greatly as we enjoyed our tea at that splendid restaurant—how they gave us all that luxury and cake and jam and cream for threepence I really cannot imagine! —still you must remember that restaurants break up home life. Look at the continent, for instance! Are you sure so much pampering is really good for the men's characters?

Und: Well you see, my dear boy, when you are organizing civilization you have to make up your mind whether trouble and anxiety are good things or not. If you decide that they are, then, I take it, you simply don't organize civilization; and there you are, with trouble and anxiety enough to make us all angels! But if you decide the other way, you may as well go through with it. However, Stephen, our characters are safe here. A sufficient dose of anxiety is always provided by the fact that we may be blown to smithereens[6] at any moment.

Sar: By the way, papa, where do you make the explosives?

Und: In separate little sheds, like that one. When one of them blows up, it costs very little; and only the people quite close to it are killed.

[Stephen, who is quite close to it, looks at it rather scaredly, and moves away quickly to the cannon. At the same moment the door of the shed is thrown abruptly open; and a foreman in overalls and list slippers comes out on the little landing and holds the door for Lomax, who appears in the doorway.]

Lom: [With studied coolness] My good fellow: you needn't get into a state of nerves. Nothing's going to happen to you; and I suppose it wouldn't be the end of the world if anything did. A little bit of British pluck is what you want, old chap. [He descends and strolls across to Sarah.]

Und: [To the foreman] Anything wrong, Bilton?

Bil: [With ironic calm] Gentleman walked into the high explosives shed and lit a cigaret, sir; that's all.

Und: Ah, quite so. [Going over to Lomax] Do you happen to remember what you did with the match?

Lom: Oh come! I'm not a fool. I took jolly good care to blow it out before I chucked it away.

Bil: The top of it was red hot inside, sir.

Lom: Well, suppose it was! I didn't chuck it into any of your messes.

Und: Think no more of it, Mr. Lomax. By the way, would you mind lending me your matches?

Lom: [Offering his box] Certainly.

Und: Thanks. [He pockets the matches.]

Lom: [Lecturing to the company generally] You know, these high explosives don't go off like gunpowder, except when they're in a gun. Then they're spread loose, you can put a match to them without the least risk: they just burn quietly like a bit of paper.

[Warming to the scientific interest of the subject] Did you know that, Undershaft? Have you ever tried?

Und: Not on a large scale, Mr. Lomax. Bilton will give you a sample of gun cotton when you are leaving if you ask him. You can experiment with it at home. [Bilton looks puzzled.]

Sar: Bilton will do nothing of the sort, papa. I suppose it's your business to blow up the Russians and Japs; but you might really stop short of blowing up poor Cholly. [Bilton gives it up and retires into the shed.]

Lom: My ownest, there is no danger. [He sits beside her on the shell.]

[Lady Britomart arrives from the town with a bouquet.]

Lady: [Impetuously] Andrew, you shouldn't have let me see this place.

Und: Why, my dear?

Lady: Never mind why, you shouldn't have. That's all. To think of all that [Indicating the town] being yours! and that you have kept it to yourself all these years!

Und: It does not belong to me. I belong to it. It is the Undershaft inheritance.

Lady: It is not. Your ridiculous cannons and that noisy banging foundry may be the Undershaft inheritance; but all that plate and linen, all that furniture and those houses and orchards and gardens belong to us. They belong to me. They are not a man's business. I won't give them up. You must be out of your senses to throw them all away; and if you persist in such folly, I will call in a doctor.

Und: [Stooping to smell the bouquet] Where did you get the flowers, my dear?

Lady: Your men presented them to me in your William Morris Labor Church[7].

Cus: Oh! It needed only that. ALabor Church! [He mounts the firestep distractedly, and leans with his elbows on the parapet, turning his back to them.]

Lady: Yes, with Morris's words in mosaic letters ten feet high round the dome. NO MAN IS GOOD ENOUGH TO BE ANOTHER MAN's MASTER. The cynicism of it!

Und: It shocked the men at first, I am afraid. But now they take no more notice of it than of the ten commandments in church.

Lady: Andrew, you are trying to put me off the subject of the inheritance by profane jokes. Well, you shan't. I don't ask it any longer for Stephen: he has inherited far too much of your perversity to be fit for it. But Barbara has rights as well as Stephen. Why should not Adolphus succeed to the inheritance? I could manage the town for him; and he can look after the cannons, if they are really necessary.

Und: I should ask nothing better if Adolphus were foundling. He is exactly the sort of new blood that is wanted in English business. But he's not a foundling; and there's an end of it. [He makes for the office door.]

Cus: [Turning to them] Not quite. [They all turn and stare at him] I think—Mind! I am not committing myself in any way as to my future course—but I think the foundling difficulty can be got over. [He jumps down to the emplacement.]

Und: [Coming back to him] What do you mean?

Cus: Well, I have something to say which is in the nature of a confession.

Sar, Lady, Bar, Ste, Confession!

Lom: Oh I say!

Cus: Yes, a confession. Listen, all. Until I met Barbara I thought myself in the main an honorable, truthful man, because I wanted the approval of my conscience more than I wanted anything else. But the moment I saw Barbara, I wanted her far more than the approval of my conscience.

Lady: Adolphus!

Cus: It is true. You accused me yourself, Lady Brit, of joining the Army to worship Barbara; and so I did. She bought my soul like a flower at a street corner, but she bought it for herself.

Und: What! Not for Dionysos or another?

Cus: Dionysos and all the others are in herself. I adored what was divine in her, and was therefore a true worshiper. But I was romantic about her too. I thought she was a woman of the people, and that a marriage with a professor of Greek would be far beyond the wildest social ambitions of her rank.

Lady: Adolphus!!

Lom: Oh I say!!!

Cus: When I learnt the horrible truth—

Lady: What do you mean by the horrible truth, pray?

Cus: That she was enormously rich; that her grandfather was an earl; that her father was the Prince of Darkness—

Und: Chut!

Cus: —and that I was only an adventurer trying to catch a rich wife, then I stooped to deceive her about my birth.

Bar: [Rising] Dolly!

Lady: Your birth! Now Adolphus, don't dare to make up a wicked story for the sake of these wretched cannons. Remember: I have seen photographs of your parents; and the Agent General for South Western Australia knows them personally and has assured me that they are most respectable married people.

Cus: So they are in Australia; but here they are outcasts. Their marriage is legal in Australia, but not in England. My mother is my father's deceased wife's sister; and in this island I am consequently a foundling. [Sensation]

Bar: Silly! [She climbs to the cannon, and leans, listening, in the angle it makes with the parapet.]

Cus: Is the subterfuge good enough, Machiavelli[8]?

Und: [Thoughtfully] Biddy, this may be a way out of the difficulty.

Lady: Stuff! A man can't make cannons any the better for being his own cousin instead of his proper self. [She sits down on the rug with a bounce that expresses her downright contempt for their casuistry]

Und: [To Cusins] You are an educated man. That is against the tradition.

Cus: Once in ten thousand times it happens that the schoolboy is a born master of what they try to teach him. Greek has not destroyed my mind: it has nourished it. Besides, I did not learn it at an English public school.

Und: Hm! Well, I cannot afford to be too particular: you have cornered the foundling market. Let it pass. You are eligible, Euripides, you are eligible.

Bar: Dolly: yesterday morning, when Stephen told us all about the tradition, you became very silent; and you have been strange and excited ever since. Were you thinking of your birth then?

Cus: When the finger of Destiny suddenly points at a man in the middle of his breakfast, it makes him thoughtful.

Und: Aha! You have had your eye on the business, my young friend, have you?

Cus: Take care! There is abyss of moral horror between me and your accursed aerial battleships.

Und: Never mind the abyss for the present. Let us settle the practical details and leave your final decision open. You know that you will have to change your name. Do you object to that?

Cus: Would any man named Adolphus—any man called Dolly!—object to be called something else?

Und: Good. Now, as to money! I propose to treat you handsomely from the beginning. You shall start at a thousand a year.

Cus: [With sudden heat, his spectacles twinkling with mischief.] A thousand! You dare offer a miserable thousand to the son-in-law of a millionaire! No, by Heavens, Machiavelli! You shall not cheat me. You cannot do without me; and I can do without you. I must have two thousand five hundred a year for two years. At the end of that time, if I am a failure, I go. But if I am a success, and stay on, you must give me the other five thousand.

Und: What other five thousand?

Cus: To make the two years up to five thousand a year. The two thousand five hundred is only half pay in case I should turn out a failure. The third year I must have ten percent on the profits.

Und: [Taken aback] Ten percent! Why, man, do you know what my profits are?

Cus: Enormous, I hope. Otherwise I shall require twenty-five percent.

Und: But, Mr. Cusins, this is a serious matter of business. You are not bringing any capital into the concern.

Cus: What! no capital! Is my mastery of Greek no capital? Is my access to the subtlest thought, the loftiest poetry yet attained by humanity, no capital? My character! my intellect! my life! my career! What Barbara calls my soul! Are these no capital? Say another word; and I double my salary.

Und: Be reasonable—

Cus: [Peremptorily] Mr. Undershaft: you have my terms. Take them or leave them.

Und: [Recovering himself] Very well. I note your terms; and I offer you half.

Cus: [Disgusted] Half!

Und: [Firmly] Half.

Cus: You call yourself a gentleman; and you offer me half!

Und: I do not call myself a gentleman; but I offer you half.

Cus: This to your future partner! Your successor! Your son-in-law!

Bar: You are selling your own soul, Dolly, not mine. Leave me out of the bargain, please.

Und: Come! I will go a step further for Barbara's sake. I will give you three fifths; but that is my last word.

Cus: Done!

Lom: Done in the eye! Why, I get only eight hundred, you know.

Cus: By the way, Mac, I am a classical scholar, not an arithmetical one. Is three fifths more than half of less?

Und: More, of course.

Cus: I would have taken two hundred and fifty. How you can succeed in business when you are willing to pay all that money to a University don who is obviously not worth a junior clerk's wages! —well! What will Lazarus say?

Und: Lazarus is a gentle romantic Jew who cares for nothing but string quartets and stalls at fashionable theatres. He will be blamed for your rapacity in money matters, poor fellow! As he has hitherto been blamed for mine. You are a shark of the first order, Euripides. So much the better for the firm!

Bar: Is the bargain closed, Dolly? Does your soul belong to him now?

Cus: No, the price is settled: that is all. The real tug of war is still to come. What about the moral question?

Lady: There is no moral question in the matter at all, Adolphus. You must simply sell cannons and weapons to people whose cause is right and just, and refuse them to foreigners and criminals.

Und: [Determinedly] No, none of that. You must keep the true faith of an Armorer, or you don't come in here.

Cus: What on earth is the true faith of an Armorer?

Und: To give arms to all men who offer an honest price for them, without respect of persons or principles, to aristocrat and republican, to Nihilist and Tsar[9], to Capitalist and Socialist, to Protestant and Catholic, to burglar and policeman, to black man, white man and yellow man, to all sorts and conditions, all nationalities, all faiths, all follies, all causes and all crimes. The first Undershaft wrote up in his shop IF GOD GAVE THE HAND, LET NOT MAN WITHHOLD THE SWORD. The second wrote up ALL HAVE THE RIGHT TO FIGHT: NONE HAVE THE RIGHT TO JUDGE. The third wrote up TO MAN THE WEAPON: TO HEAVEN THE VICTORY. The fourth had no literary turn; so he did not write up anything; but he sold cannons to Napoleon under the nose of George the Third. The fifth wrote up PEACE SHALL NOT PREVAIL SAVE WITH A SWORD IN HER HAND. The sixth, my master, was the best of all. He wrote up NOTHING IS EVER DONE IN THIS WORLD UNTIL MEN ARE PREPARED TO KILL ONE ANOTHER IF IT IS NOT DONE. After that, there was nothing left for the seventh to say. So he wrote up, simply, UNASHAMED.

Cus: My good Machiavelli, I shall certainly write something up on the wall; only as I shall write it in Greek, you won't be able to read it. But as to your Armorer's faith, if I take my neck out of the noose of my own morality I am not going to put it into the noose of yours. I shall sell cannons to whom I please and refuse them to whom I please. So there!

Und: From the moment when you become Andrew Undershaft, you will never do as you please again. Don't come here lusting for power, young man.

Cus: If power were my aim I should not come here for it. You have no power.

Und: None of my own, certainly.

Cus: I have more power than you, more will. You do not drive this place: it drives you. And what drives the place?

Und: [Enigmatically] A will of which I am a part.

Bar: [Startled] Father! Do you know what you are saying; or are you laying a snare for my soul?

Cus: Don't listen to his metaphysics, Barbara. The place is driven by the most rascally part of society, the money hunters, the pleasure hunters, the military promotion hunters; and he is their slave.

Und: Not necessarily. Remember the Armorer's Faith. I will take an order from a good man as cheerfully as from a bad one. If you good people prefer preaching and shirking to buying my weapons and fighting the rascals, don't blame me. I cannot make courage and conviction. Bah! you tire me, Euripides, with your morality mongering. Ask Barbara, she understands.

[He suddenly reaches up and takes Barbara's hands, looking powerfully into her eyes] Tell him, my love, what power really means.

Bar: [Hypnotized] Before I joined the Salvation Army, I was in my own power; and the consequence was that I never knew what to do with myself. When I joined it, I had not time enough for all the things I had to do.

Und: [Approvingly] Just so. And why was that, do you suppose?

Bar: Yesterday I should have said, because I was in the power of God. [She resumes her self-possession, withdrawing her hands from his with a power equal to his own.] But you came and shewed me that I was in the power of Bodger and Undershaft. Today I feel—oh! How can I put it into words? Sarah: do you remember the earthquake at Cannes, when we were little children? —how little the surprise of the first shock mattered compared to the dread and horror of waiting for the second? That is how I feel in this place today. I stood on the rock I thought eternal; and without a word of warning it reeled and crumbled under me. I was safe with an infinite wisdom watching me, an army marching to Salvation with me; and in a moment, at a stroke of your pen in a cheque book, I stood alone; and the heavens were empty. That was the first shock of the earthquake: I am waiting for the second.

Und: Come, come, my daughter! don't make too much of your little tinpot tragedy. What do we do here when we spend years of work and thought and thousands of pounds of solid cash on a new gun or an aerial battleship that turns out just a hairsbreadth wrong after all? Scrap it. Scrap it without wasting another hour or another pound on it. Well, you have made for yourself something that you call a morality or a religion or what not. It doesn't fit the facts. Well, scrap it. Scrap it and get one that does fit. That is what is wrong with the world at present. It scraps its obsolete steam engines and dynamos; but it won't scrap its old prejudices and its old moralities and its old religions and its old political constitutions. What's the result? In machinery it does very well; but in morals and religion and politics it is working at a loss that brings it nearer bankruptcy every year. Don't persist in that folly. If your old religion broke down yesterday, get a newer and a better one for tomorrow.

Bar: Oh how gladly I would take a better one to my soul! But you offer me a worse one. [Turning on him with sudden vehemence] Justify yourself, shew me some light through the darkness of this dreadful place, with its beautifully clean workshops, and respectable workmen, and model homes.

Und: Cleanliness and respectability do not need justification, Barbara; they justify themselves. I see no darkness here, no dreadfulness. In your Salvation shelter I saw poverty, misery, cold and hunger. You gave them bread and treacle and dreams of heaven. I give from thirty shillings a week to twelve thousand a year. They find their own dreams; but I look after the drainage.

Bar: And their souls?

Und: I save their souls just as I saved yours.

Bar: [Revolted] You saved my soul! What do you mean?

Und: I fed you and clothed you and housed you. I took care that you should have money enough to live handsomely—more than enough; so that you could be wasteful, careless, generous. That saved your soul from the seven deadly sins[10].

Bar: [Bewildered] The seven deadly sins!

Und: Yes, the deadly seven. [Counting on his fingers] Food, clothing, firing, rent, taxes, respectability and children. Nothing can lift those seven millstones from Man's neck but money; and the spirit cannot soar until the millstones are lifted. I lifted them from your spirit. I enabled Barbara to become Major Barbara; and I save her from the crime of poverty.

Cus: Do you call poverty a crime?

Und: The worst of crimes. All the other crimes are virtues beside it: all the other dishonors are chivalry itself by comparison. Poverty blights whole cities; spreads horrible pestilences; strikes dead the very souls of all who come within sight, sound or smell of it. What you call crime is nothing: a murder here and a theft there, a blow now and a curse then: what do they matter? They are only the accidents and illnesses of life: there are not fifty genuine professional criminals in London. But there are millions of poor people, abject people, dirty people, ill fed, ill clothed people. They poison us morally and physically: they kill the happiness of society; they force us to do away with our own liberties and to organize unnatural cruelties for fear they should rise against us and drag us down into their abyss. Only fools fear crime: we all fear poverty. Pah! [Turning on Barbara] You talk of your half-saved ruffian in West Ham[11]: you accuse me of dragging his soul back to perdition. Well, bring him to me here; and I will draw his soul back again to salvation for you. Not by words and dreams; but by thirty-eight shillings a week, a sound house in a handsome street, and a permanent job. In three weeks he will have a fancy waistcoat; in three months a tall hat and a chapel sitting; before the end of the year he will shake hands with a duchess at a Primrose League meeting[12], and join the Conservative Party.

Bar: And will he be the better for that?

Und: You know he will. Don't be a hypocrite, Barbara. He will be better fed, better housed, better clothed, better behaved; and his children will be pounds heavier and bigger. That will be better than an American cloth mattress in a shelter, chopping firewood, eating bread and treacle, and being forced to kneel down from time to time to thank heaven for it. Knee drill, I think you call it. It is cheap work converting starving men with a Bible in one hand and a slice of bread in the other. I will undertake to convert West Ham to Mahometanism on the same terms. Try your hand on my men: their souls are hungry because their bodies are full.

Bar: And leave the east end to starve?

Und: [His energetic tone dropping into one of bitter and brooding remembrance] I was an east ender. I moralized and starved until one day I swore that I would be full-fed free man at all costs—that nothing should stop me except a bullet, neither reason nor morals nor the lives of other men. I said "Thou shalt starve ere I starve"; and with that word I became free and great. I was a dangerous man until I had my will: now I am a useful, beneficent, kindly person. That is the history of most self-made millionaires, I fancy. When it is the history of every Englishman we shall have an England worth living in.

Lady: Stop making speeches, Andrew. This is not the place for them.

Und: [Punctured] My dear, I have no other means of conveying my ideas.

Lady: Your ideas are nonsense. You got on because you were selfish and unscrupulous.

Und: Not at all. I had the strongest scruples about poverty and starvation. Your moralists are quite unscrupulous about both: they make virtues of them. I had rather be a thief than a pauper. I had rather be a murderer than a slave. I don't want to be either; but if you force the alternative on me, then, by Heaven, I'll choose the braver and more moral one. I hate poverty and slavery worse than any other crimes whatsoever. And let me tell you this. Poverty and slavery have stood up for centuries to your sermons and leading articles. They will not stand up to my machine guns. Don't preach at them; don't reason with them. Kill them.

Bar: Killing. Is that your remedy for everything?

Und: It is the final test of conviction, the only lever strong enough to overturn a system, the only way of saying Must. Let six hundred and seventy fools loose in the street; and three policemen can scatter them. But huddle them together in a certain house in Westminster; and let them go through certain ceremonies and call themselves certain names until at last they get the courage to kill; and your six hundred and seventy fools become a government. Your pious mob fills up ballot papers and imagines it is governing its masters; but the ballot paper that really governs is the paper that has a bullet wrapped up in it.

Cus: That is perhaps why, like most intelligent people, I never vote.

Und: Vote! Bah! When you vote, you only change the names of the cabinet. When you shoot, you pull down governments, inaugurate new epochs, abolish old orders and set up new. Is that historically true, Mr. Learned Man, or is it not?

Cus: It is historically true. I loathe having to admit it. I repudiate your sentiments. I abhor your nature. I defy you in every possible way. Still, it is true. But it ought not to be true.

Und: Ought! ought! ought! ought! Are you going to spend your life saying ought, like the rest of our moralists? Turn your oughts into shalls, man. Come and make explosives with me. Whatever can blow men up can blow society up. The history of the world is the history of those who had courage enough to embrace this truth. Have you the courage to embrace it, Barbara?

Notes

1. Barnardo: the philanthropist Thomas John Barnardo(1845～1905), who founded the East End Juvenile Mission for Destitute Children, which later developed into a large organization for homeless children.
2. Euripides: Cusins is a professor of Greek, hence he is addressed by Andrew Undershaft with the name of the famous Greek dramatist.
3. guy: ridiculous-looking, laughable.
4. Perter Shirley: an unemployed coal-worker, who comes to the Salvation Army shelter in Act II.

5. This line carries a reference to the Russian-Japanese war at the end of the nineteenth century.
6. smithereens: bits, fragments.
7. William Morris(1834~1896), an English poet, artist, and socialist.
8. Machiavelli: an Italian statesman and political philosopher(1469~1527), known for his cunning, duplicity, and bad faith.
9. Nihilist: a member of a 19th century Russian organization advocating revolutionary reform and using terrorism and assassination.
10. Conventionally the "seven deadly sins" refer to pride, covetousness, lust, anger, gluttony, envy, and sloth.
11. West Ham: the location of the Salvation Army shelter.
12. Primrose League: a conservative organization named after the favorite flower of Prime Minister Benjamin Disraeli.

Questions for Understanding

1. How does Andrew Undershaft define his relation with the cannon enterprise? Does his definition have any symbolic meaning as far as his (or Shaw's) concept of the world is concerned?
2. How do the different members of the family react to the moral question of the armament industry?
3. To Andrew Undershaft, the worst of the crimes in the world is poverty. Do Barbara and Cusins accept this notion? What is your opinion?
4. In the course of conversation, Undershaft lectures on a number of social issues: voting, change of government, justice of war, etc. Do these ideas reflect the belief of the dramatist?
5. How do Barbara, Cusins and Undershaft explain their understandings of saving the soul?

Aspects of Appreciation

Conflict in the play

The tension between Barbara and her father moves the whole mechanics of the play forward. The most ironical point is that Barbara, who once regarded money as the origin of sins, grows up with the support from it for her generous and decent life. Shaw is purposefully inverting everything. The Salvation Army, set to offer spiritual console, is hellishly dark and damp, while the ammunition foundry, resembling spiritual destruction, appears heavenly and delightful. It can be a conflict between poverty as the root of crimes and a way of economic salvation.

Suggested Further Reading

Bernard Shaw's *Widowers' Houses*, *Man and Superman* and *The Doctor's Dilemma*.

Topics for Further Study

The use of dialect in the scenes at the Salvation Army shelter.

Knowledge of Literature

Drama

Drama is the specific mode of fiction represented in performance. The term comes from a Greek word meaning "action", which is derived from "to do". The enactment of drama in theatre, performed by actors on a stage before an audience, presupposes collaborative modes of production and a collective form of reception. The structure of dramatic texts, unlike other forms of literature, is directly influenced by this collaborative production and collective reception. The early modern tragedy *Hamlet* by Shakespeare and the classical Athenian tragedy *Oedipus the King* by Sophocles are among the supreme masterpieces of the art of drama.

E. M. Forster
(1879~1970)

About the Author

E. M. Forster was born in London in 1879. His father was an architect, and died shortly after Forster was born. Forster was educated at Tonbridge School and Cambridge. At Tonbridge, he witnessed the tribulations of a day boy at a boarding school, which was responsible for a good deal of his later criticism of the English public school system. Cambridge turned out to be nurturing, and the friends he made and the intellectual companionship he found there influenced his entire life. He visited Greece and spent some time in Italy in 1901, which also had a permanent influence on him. Both Greek mythology and Italian Renaissance art opened up to him a world of spontaneity, which was in sharp contrast to the stuffy, hypocritical, and distorted modern world. Forster began his writing by working as a contributor for a magazine, and in 1905 published his first novel, *Where Angels Fear to Tread*. Forster visited India twice. The first trip was made in 1912, and the second in 1922. During World War I, he was engaged in civilian work in Alexandria, Egypt. In 1946, he was awarded an honorary fellowship at King's College, Cambridge. He spent his later years at Cambridge writing and teaching, and died at Coventry, England, in 1970.

Forster was an important member of the Bloomsbury Group, which included some liberal-minded intellectuals who made free discussions and criticisms of the social, religious, and moral issues of the then English society. Forster strongly criticized the coldness, narrow-mindedness, and hypocrisy of the middle class manners and morals in England. Meanwhile, he spoke out for spontaneity of feeling, and for the natural warmth and simplicity of the coarse, uneducated people. By satirizing the English officials and their ill-treatment of the natives in the colonies, Forster expressed his passionate hatred of colonialism and imperialism. Forster held a liberal, humanistic view towards life and human relation. He demanded a personal connection between inner feeling and outer action, and between body and soul. He concentrated his effort on exploring the possibilities of realizing natural and harmonious relationship between man and man in a suppressing and decaying world.

As both the traditional and modernistic elements can be found in Forster's works, critics disagree as to whether to categorize him as a traditional writer or a modernist. Forster's modernistic trend is shown in his themes, in his major concerns with personal relationships and in his use of poetic style and symbolism. But compared with the modernistic masters like James Joyce or Virginia Woolf, Forster is a less experimental writer in forms and techniques. Basically, he follows the traditional pattern of realistic novels from Defoe to Meredith. The fine traditions of realism and the new modernistic trend are well balanced in this writer of the transitional age.

★ A Passage to India

About the Novel

A Passage to India is a straightforward story exploring the possibilities of establishing true friendship between Englishmen and Indians under the British colonialist rule. The story develops mainly around the relations of Aziz, a Muslim Indian doctor, and Cyril Fielding, an English humanist, who works in India as the principal of the Government College. It covers a period of approximately two and a half years.

Mrs. Moore and Miss Adela Quested come recently to India to visit Ronny Heaslop, the city magistrate of Chandrapore, who is Mrs. Moore's son and Miss Quested's fiancé. Both women have strong liberal ideas and are eager to meet Indians on an equal position. A chance meeting at the mosque strikes a mutual like between Mrs. Moore and Dr. Aziz. At the tea party given by Mr. Fielding, Dr. Aziz warmly invites the newly-arrived ladies and Fielding to visit the local Marabar Caves, a prehistoric site 20 miles away from the city. As Fielding has missed the train, Aziz accompanies the two ladies to visit the caves. Mrs. Moore is soon tired by the heat and the stuffy, echoing caves and stays behind, leaving Adela and Aziz with a guide to continue "the slightly tedious expedition". While visiting one of the caves, Adela seems to be overcome by some traumatic experience and rushes down the hill alone. Later Aziz is accused of insulting Miss Adela and arrested by police. Adela's accusation brings the already strained relations between the British and the Indians to a crisis. The only Englishman who believes Aziz innocent is Fielding. During the stormy trial, Adela recovers from her hysteria. With her words "I have made a mistake—Dr. Aziz never followed me into the cave" declared in court, the crisis is resolved, and Dr. Aziz is set free. While the Indians are celebrating their victory, Adela is dropped by all the British community except Fielding who helps her back to England.

Fielding comes back to India again after two years and meets Aziz. They are somewhat reconciled; but Aziz clearly expresses his opinion that there will be no true friendship between the two peoples before India gets complete independence.

Chapter 24(Excerpt)

...

(Dr. Aziz is standing trial, at which Adela withdraws her charge.)
Presently the case was called.

Their chairs preceded them into the Court, for it was important that they should look dignified. And when the chuprassies[1] had made all ready, they filed into the ramshackle room with a condescending air, as if it was a booth at a fair. The Collector[2] made a small official joke as he sat down, at which his entourage smiled, and the Indians, who could not hear what he said, felt that some new cruelty was afoot, otherwise the sahibs[3] would not chuckle.

The Court was crowded and of course very hot, and the first person Adela noticed in it was the humblest of all who were present, a person who had no bearing officially upon the trial: the man who pulled the punkah[4]. Almost naked, and splendidly formed, he sat on a raised platform near the back, in the middle of the central gangway, and he caught her attention as she came in, and he seemed to control the proceedings. He had the strength and beauty that sometimes come to flower in Indians of low birth. When that strange race nears the dust and is condemned as untouchable, then nature remembers the physical perfection that she accomplished elsewhere, and throws out a god—not many, but one here and there, to prove to society how little its categories impress her. This man would have been notable anywhere; among the thin-hammed, flat-chested mediocrities of Chandrapore[5] he stood out as divine, yet he was of the city, its garbage had nourished him, he would end on its rubbish heaps. Pulling the rope towards him, relaxing it rhythmically, sending swirls of air over others, receiving none himself, he seemed apart from human destinies, a male fate, a winnower of souls. Opposite him, also on a platform, sat the little assistant magistrate, cultivated, self-conscious, and conscientious. The punkah wallah[6] was none of these things; he scarcely knew that he existed and did not understand why the Court was fuller than usual, indeed he did not know that it was fuller than usual, didn't even know he worked a fan, though he thought he pulled a rope. Something in his aloofness impressed the girl from middle-class England, and rebuked the narrowness of her sufferings. In virtue of what had she collected this roomful of people together? Her particular brand of opinions, and the suburban Jehovah[7] who sanctified them—by what right did they claim so much importance in the world, and assume the title of civilization? Mrs. Moore—she looked round, but Mrs. Moore was far away on the sea; it was the kind of question they might have discussed on the voyage out, before the old lady had turned disagreeable and queer.

While thinking of Mrs. Moore she heard sounds, which gradually grew more distinct. The epoch-making trial had started, and the Superintendent of Police was opening the case for the prosecution.

Mr. McBryde[8] was not at pains to be an interesting speaker; he left eloquence to the defence who would require it. His attitude was, "Everyone knows the man's guilty, and I am obliged to say so in public before he goes to the Andamans[9]". He made no moral or emotional appeal, and it was only by degrees that the studied negligence of his manner made itself felt, and lashed part of the audience to fury. Laboriously did he describe the genesis of the picnic. The prisoner had met Miss Quested at an entertainment given by the Principal of Government College, and had there conceived his intentions concerning her: prisoner was a man of loose life, as documents found upon him at his arrest would testify, also his fellow-assistant, Dr Parma Lal, was in a position to throw light on his character, and Major Callendar himself would speak. Here Mr. McBryde paused. He wanted to keep the proceedings as clean as possible, but Oriental Pathology, his favourite theme, lay around him, and he could not resist it. Taking off his spectacles, as was his habit before enunciating a general truth, he looked into them sadly, and remarked that the darker races are physically attracted by the fairer, but not vice versa—not a matter for bitterness this, not a matter for abuse, but just a fact which any scientific observer will confirm.

"Even when the lady is so uglier than the gentleman?"

The comment fell from nowhere, from the ceiling perhaps. It was the first interruption, and the Magistrate felt bound to censure it. "Turn that man out," he said. One of the native policemen took hold of a man who had said nothing, and turned him out roughly. Mr. McBryde resumed his spectacles and proceeded. But the comment had upset Miss Quested. Her body resented being called ugly, and trembled.

"Do you feel faint, Adela?" asked Miss Derek[10], who tended her with loving indignation.

"I never feel anything else, Nancy. I shall get through, but it's awful,

VII. Modern Age

awful."

This led to the first of a series of scenes. Her friends began to fuss around her, and the Major[11] called out, "I must have better arrangements than this made for my patient; why isn't she given a seat on the platform? She gets no air."

Mr. Das[12] looked annoyed and said, "I shall be happy to accommodate Miss Quested with a chair up here in view of the particular circumstances of her health." The chuprassies passed up not one chair but several, and the entire party followed Adela on to the platform, Mr. Fielding being the only European who remained in the body of the hall.

"That's better," remarked Mrs. Turton[13], as she settled herself.

"Thoroughly desirable change for several reasons," replied the Major.

The Magstrate knew that he ought to censure this remark, but did not dare to. Callendar saw that he was afraid, and called out authoritatively, "Right, McBryde, go ahead now sorry to have interrupted you."

"Are you all right yourselves?" asked the Superintendent.

"We shall do, we shall do."

"Go on, Mr. Das, we are not here to disturb you," said the Collector patronizingly. Indeed, they had not so much disturbed the trial as taken charge of it.

While the prosecution continued, Miss Quested examined the hall—timidly at first, as though it would scorch her eyes. She observed to left and right of the punkah man many a half-known face. Beneath her were gathered all the wreckage of her silly attempt to see India—the people she had met at the Bridge Party[14], the man and his wife who hadn't sent their carriage, the old man who would lend his car, various servants, villagers, officials, and the prisoner himself. There he sat—strong, neat little Indian with very black hair, and pliant hands. She viewed him without special emotion. Since they last met, she had elevated him into a principle of evil, but now he seemed to be what he had always been—a slight acquaintance. He was negligible, devoid of significance, dry like a bone, and though he was "guilty" no atmosphere of sin surrounded him. "I suppose he is guilty. Can I possibly have made a mistake?" she thought. For this question still occurred to her intellect, though since Mrs. Moore's departure it had ceased to trouble her conscience.

Pleader Mahmoud Ali[15] now arose, and asked with ponderous and ill-judged irony whether his client could be accommodated on the platform too:

even Indians felt unwell sometimes, though naturally Major Callendar did not think so, being in charge of a Government Hospital. "Another example of their exquisite sense of humour," sang Miss Derek. Ronny looked at Mr. Das to see how he would handle the difficulty, and Mr. Das became agitated and snubbed Pleader Mahmoud Ali severely.

"Excuse me—" It was the turn of the eminent barrister from Calcutta: He was a fine-looking man, large and bony, with grey closely cropped hair. "We object to the presence of so many European ladies and gentlemen upon the platform," he said in an Oxford voice. "They will have the effect of intimidating our witnesses. Their place is with the rest of the public in the body of the hall. We have no objection to Miss Quested remaining on the platform, since she has been unwell; we shall extend every courtesy to her throughout, despite the scientific truths revealed to us by the District Superintendent of Police; but we do object to the others."

"Oh, cut the cackle and let's have the verdict," the Major growled.

The distinguished visitor gazed at the Magistrate respectfully.

"I agree to that," said Mr. Das, hiding his face desperately in some papers. "It was only to Miss Quested that I gave permission to sit up here. Her friends should be so excessively kind as to climb down."

"Well done, Das, quite sound," said Ronny with devastating honesty.

"Climb down, indeed, what incredible impertinence!" Mrs. Turton cried.

"Do come quietly, Mary," murmured her husband.

"Hi! My patient can't be left unattended."

"Do you object to the Civil Surgeon remaining, Mr. Amritrao?"

"I should object. A platform confers authority."

"Even when it's one foot high; so come along all," said the Collector, trying not to laugh.

"Thank you very much, sir," said Mr. Das, greatly relieved. "Thank you, Mr. Heaslop, thank you, ladies all."

And the party, including Miss Quested, descended from its rash eminence. The news of their humiliation spread quickly, and people jeered outside. Their special chairs followed them. Mahmoud Ali(who was quite silly and useless with hatred) objected even to these; by whose authority had special chairs been introduced, why had the Nawab Babadur[16] not been given one, etc. People began to talk all over the room, about chairs ordinary and special, strips of carpet, platforms one foot high.

But the little excursion had a good effect on Miss Quested's nerves. She felt easier now that she had seen all the people who were in the room. It was like knowing the worst. She was sure now that she should come through "all right"—that is to say without spiritual disgrace, and she passed the good news on to Ronny and Mrs. Turton. They were too much agitated with the defeat to British prestige to be interested. From where she sat, she could see the renegade Mr. Fielding. She had had a better view of him from the platform, and knew that an Indian child perched on his knee. He was watching the proceedings, watching her. When their eyes met, he turned his away, as if direct intercourse was of no interest to him.

The Magistrate was also happier. He had won the battle of the platform, and gained confidence. Intelligent and impartial, he continued to listen to the evidence, and tried to forget that later on he should have to pronounce a verdict in accordance with it. The Superintendent trundled steadily forward: he had expected these outbursts of insolence—they are the natural gestures of an inferior race, and he betrayed no hatred of Aziz, merely an abysmal contempt.

The speech dealt at length with the "prisoner's dupes," as they were called—Fielding, the servant Antony, the Nawab Bahadur. This aspect of the case had always seemed dubious to Miss Quested, and she had asked the police not to develop it. But they were playing for a heavy sentence, and wanted to prove that the assault was premeditated. And in order to illustrate the strategy, they produced a plan of the Marabar Hills[17], showing the route that the party had taken, and the "Tank of the Dagger," where they had camped.

The Magistrate displayed interest in archaeology.

An elevation of a specimen cave was produced; it was lettered "Buddhist Cave".

"Not Buddhist, I think, Jain[18] ... "

"In which cave is the offence alleged, the Buddhist or the Jain?" asked Mahmoud Ali, with the air of unmasking a conspiracy.

"All the Marabar caves are Jain."

"Yes, sirs; then in which Jain cave?"

"You will have an opportunity of putting such questions later."

Mr. McBryde smiled faintly at their fatuity. Indians invariably collapse over some such point as this. He knew that the defense had some wild hope of establishing an alibi, that they had tried (unsuccessfully) to identify the guide, and that Fielding and Hamidullah[19] had gone out to the Kawa Dol and paced and measured all one moonlit night. "Mr. Lesley[20] says they're Buddhist, and he ought to know if anyone does. But may I call attention to the shape?" And he described what had occurred there. Then he spoke of Miss Derek's arrival, of the scramble down the gully, of the return of the two ladies to Chandrapore, and of the document Miss Quested signed on her arrival, in which mention was made of the field-glasses. And then came the culminating evidence: the discovery of the field-glasses on the prisoner. "I have nothing to add at present," he concluded, removing his spectacles. "I will now call my witnesses. The facts will speak for themselves. The prisoner is one of those individuals who have led a double life. I dare say his degeneracy gained upon him gradually. He has been very cunning at concealing, as is usual with the type, and pretending to be a respectable member of society, getting a Government position even. He is now entirely vicious and beyond redemption, I am afraid. He behaved most cruelly, most brutally, to another of his guests, another English lady. In order to get rid of her, and leave him free for his crime, he crushed her into a cave among his servants. However, that is by the way."

But his last words brought on another storm, and suddenly a new name, Mrs. Moore, burst on the court like a whirlwind. Mahmoud Ali had been enraged, his nerves snapped; he shrieked like a maniac, and asked whether his client was charged with murder as well as rape, and who was this second English lady.

"I don't propose to call her."

"You don't because you can't, you have smuggled her out of the country; she is Mrs. Moore, she would have proved his innocence, she was on our side, she was poor Indians' friend."

"You could have called her yourself," cried the Magistrate. "Neither side called her, neither must quote her as evidence."

"She was kept from us until too late—I learn too late—this is English justice, here is your British Raj[21]. Give us back Mrs. Moore for five minutes only, and she will save my friend, she will save the name of his sons; don't rule her out, Mr. Das; take back those words as you yourself are a father; tell me where they have put her, oh, Mrs. Moore…"

"If the point is of any interest my mother should have reached Aden," said Ronny dryly; he ought not to have intervened, but the onslaught had startled him.

"Imprisoned by you there because she knew the truth." He was almost out of his mind, and could be heard saying above the tumult: "I ruin my career, no matter; we are all to be ruined one by one."

"This is no way to defend your case," counseled the Magistrate.

"I am not defending a case, nor are you trying one. We are both of us slaves."

"Mr. Mahmoud Ali, I have already warned you, and unless you sit down I shall exercise my authority."

"Do so, this trial is a farce, I am going." And he handed his papers to Amritrao and left, calling from the door histrionically yet with intense passion, "Aziz, Aziz—farewell for ever." The tumult increased, the invocation of Mrs. Moore continued, and people who did not know what the syllables meant repeated them like a charm. They became Indianized into Esmiss Esmoor, they were taken up in the street outside. In vain the Magistrate threatened and expelled. Until the magic exhausted itself, he was powerless.

"Unexpected," remarked Mr. Turton.

Ronny furnished the explanation. Before she sailed, his mother had taken to talk about the Marabar in her sleep, especially in the afternoon when servants were on the veranda, and her disjointed remarks on Aziz had doubtless been sold to Mahmoud Ali for a few annas[22]: that kind of thing never ceases in the East.

"I thought they'd try something of the sort. Ingenious." He looked into their wide-open mouths. "They get just like that over their religion," he added calmly. "Start and can't stop. I'm sorry for your old Das, he's not getting much of a show."

"Mr. Heaslop, how disgraceful dragging in your dear mother," said Miss Derek, bending forward.

"It's just a trick, and they happened to pull it off. Now one sees why they had Mahmoud Ali—just to make a scene on the chance. It is his speciality." But he disliked it more than he showed. It was revolting to hear his mother travestied into Esmiss Esmoor, a Hindu goddess.

"Esmiss Esmoor
Esmiss Esmoor
Esmiss Esmoor
Esmiss Esmoor…"

"Ronny—"

"Yes, old girl?"

"Isn't it all queer?"

"I'm afraid it's very upsetting for you."

"Not the least. I don't mind it."

"Well, that's good."

She had spoken more naturally and healthily than usual. Bending into the middle of her friends, she said: "Don't worry about me, I'm much better than I was; I don't feel the least faint, I shall be all right, and thank you all, thank you, thank you for your kindness." She had to shout her gratitude, for the chant, Esmiss Esmoor, went on.

Suddenly it stopped. It was as if the prayer had been heard, and the relics exhibited. "I apologize for my colleague," said Mr. Amritrao, rather to everyone's surprise. "He is an intimate friend of our client, and his feelings have carried him away."

"Mr. Mahmoud Ali will have to apologize in person," the Magistrate said.

"Exactly, sir, he must. But we had just learnt that Mrs. Moore had important evidence which she desired to give. She was hurried out of the country by her son before she could give it; and this unhinged Mr. Mahmoud Ali—coming as it does upon an attempt to intimidate our only other European witness, Mr. Fielding. Mr. Mahmoud Ali would have said nothing had not Mrs. Moore been claimed as a witness by the police." He sat down.

"An extraneous element is being introduced into the case," said the Magistrate. "I must repeat that as a witness Mrs. Moore does not exist. Neither you, Mr. Amritrao, nor Mr. McBryde, you, have any right to surmise what that lady would have said. She is not here, and consequently she can say nothing."

"Well, I withdraw my reference," said the Superintendent wearily. "I would have done so fifteen minutes ago if I had been given the chance. She is not of the least importance to me."

"I have already withdrawn it for the defense." He added with forensic humour: "Perhaps you can persuade the gentlemen outside to withdraw it too," for the refrain in the street continued.

"I am afraid my powers do not extend so far," said Das, smiling.

So peace was restored, and when Adela came to give her evidence the atmosphere was quieter than it had been since the beginning of the trial.

Experts were not surprised. There is no stay in your native. He blazes up over a minor point, and has nothing left for the crisis. What he seeks is a grievance, and this he had found in the supposed abduction of an old lady. He would now be less aggrieved when Aziz was deported.

But the crisis was still to come.

Adela had always meant to tell the truth and nothing but the truth, and she had rehearsed this as a difficult task—difficult, because her disaster in the cave was connected, though by a thread, with another part of her life, her engagement to Ronny. She had thought of love just before she went in, and had innocently asked Aziz what marriage was like, and she supposed that her question had roused evil in him. To recount this would have been incredibly painful, it was the one point she wanted to keep obscure; she was willing to give details that would have distressed other girls, but this story of her private failure she dared not allude to, and she dreaded being examined in public in case something came out. But as soon as she rose to reply, and heard the sound of her own voice, she feared not even that. A new and unknown sensation protected her, like magnificent armour. She didn't think what had happened, or even remember in the ordinary way of memory, but she returned to the Marabar Hills, and spoke from them across a sort of darkness to Mr. McBryde. The fatal day recurred, in every detail, but now she was of it and not of it at the same time, and this double relation gave it indescribable splendour. Why had she thought the expedition "dull"? Now the sun rose again, the elephant waited, the pale masses of the rock flowed round her and presented the first cave, she entered and a match was reflected in the polished walls—all beautiful and significant, though she had been blind to it at the time. Questions were asked, and to each she found the exact reply; yes, she had noticed the "Tank of the Dagger", but not known its name, yes, Mrs. Moore had been tired after the first cave and sat in the shadow of a great rock, near the dried-up mud. Smoothly the voice in the distance proceeded, leading along the paths of truth, and the airs from the punkab behind her wafted her on…

"… the prisoner and the guide took you on to the Kawa Dol, no one else being present?"

"The most wonderfully shaped of those hills. Yes." As she spoke, she created the Kawa Dol, saw the niches up the curve of the stone, and felt the heat strike her face. And something caused her to add. "No one else was present to my knowledge. We appeared to be alone."

"Very well, there is a ledge half-way up the hill, or broken ground rather, with caves scattered near the beginning of a mullah."

"I know where you mean."

"You went alone into one of those caves?"

"That is quite correct."

"And the prisoner followed you."

"Now we've got'im," from the Major.

She was silent. The court, the place of question, awaited her reply. But she could not give it until Aziz entered the place of answer.

"The prisoner followed you, didn't he?" he repeated in the monotonous tones that they both used; they were employing agreed words throughout, so that this part of the proceedings held no surprises.

"May I have half a minute before I reply to that, Mr. McBryde?"

"Certainly."

Her vision was of several caves. She saw herself in one, and she was also outside it, watching its entrance, for Aziz to pass in. She failed to locate him. It was the doubt that had often visited her, but solid and attractive, like the hills, "I am not-" Speech was more difficult than vision. "I am not quite sure."

"I beg your pardon?" said the Superintendent of Police.

"I cannot be sure…"

"I didn't catch that answer." He looked scared, his mouth shut with a snap. "You are on that landing, or whatever we term it, and you have entered a cave. I suggest to you that the prisoner followed you."

She shook her head.

"What do you mean, please?"

"No," she said in a flat, unattractive voice. Slight noises began in various parts of the room, but no one yet understood what was occurring except Fielding. He saw that she was going to have a nervous breakdown and that his friend was saved.

"What is that, what are you saying? Speak up, please." The Magistrate bent forward.

"I'm afraid I have made a mistake."

"What nature of mistake?"

"Dr. Aziz never followed me into the cave."

The Superintendent slammed down his papers, then picked them up and said calmly. "Now, Miss Quested, let us go on. I will read you the words of the deposition which you signed two hours later in my bungalow."

"Excuse me, Mr. McBryde, you cannot go on. I am speaking to the witness myself. And the public will be silent. If it continues to talk, I have the court cleared. Miss Quested, address your remarks to me, who am the Magistrate in charge of the case, and realize their extreme gravity. Remember you speak on oath, Miss Quested."

"Dr. Aziz never-"

"I stop these proceedings on medical grounds," cried the Major on a word from Turton, and all the English rose from their chairs at once, large white figures behind which the little magistrate was hidden. The Indians rose too, hundreds of things went on at once, so that afterwards each person gave a different account of the catastrophe.

"You withdraw the charge? Answer me," shrieked the representative of Justice.

Something that she did not understand took hold of the girl and pulled her through. Though the vision was over, and she had returned to the insipidity of the world, she remembered what she had learnt. Atonement and confession they could wait. It was in hard prosaic tones that she said, "I withdraw everything."

"Enough—sit down. Mr. McBryde, do you wish to continue in the face of this?"

The Superintendent gazed at his witness as if she was a broken machine, and said, "Are you mad?"

"Don't question her, sir; you have no longer the right."

"Give me time to consider-"

"Sahib, you will have to withdraw; this becomes a scandal," boomed the Nawab Bahadur suddenly from the back of the court.

"He shall not," shouted Mrs. Turton against the gathering tumult. "Call the other witnesses; we're none of us safe-" Ronny tried to check her, and she gave him an irritable blow, then screamed insults at Adela.

The Superintendent moved to the support of his friends, saying nonchalantly to the Magistrate as he did so, "Right, I withdraw."

Mr. Das rose, nearly dead with the strain. He had controlled the case, just controlled it. He had shown that an Indian can preside. To those who could hear him he said, "The prisoner is released without one stain on his character; the question of costs will be decided elsewhere."

And then the flimsy framework of the court broke up, the shouts of derision and rage culminated, people screamed and cursed, kissed one another, wept passionately. Here were the English, whom their servants protected, there Aziz fainted in Hamidullah's arms. Victory on this side, defeat on that—complete for one moment was the antithesis. Then life returned to its complexities, person after person struggled out of the room to their various purposes, and before long no one remained on the scene of the fantasy but the beautiful naked god. Unaware that anything unusual had occurred, he continued to pull the cord of his punkah, to gaze at the empty dais and the overturned special chairs, and rhythmically to agitate the clouds of descending dust.

※※※※※※※※※※※※※※※※※※※※※※※※※※※※

Notes

1. chuprassies: official messengers or servants.
2. Collector: administrative head of a district in some provinces of British India.
3. sahib: Indian title for a European.
4. punkah: a large fan.
5. Chandrapore: fictitious name.
6. punkah wallah: fan operator.
7. Jehovah: God.
8. Mr. McBryde: the British superintendent of police.
9. Andamans: Andaman islands, India.
10. Miss Derek: a visiting British woman.
11. the Major: Major Callendar, the civil surgeon, Aziz's superior at the hospital.
12. Mr. Das: Ronny's Indian Assistant and the presiding magistrate of the trial.
13. Mrs. Turton: wife of Mr. Turton who is the highest ranking British official in India.
14. the Bridge Party: the party held for Mrs. Moore to meet and talk with native Indians.
15. Pleader Muhmound Ali: a friend of Aziz's, a Muslim lawyer.
16. Nawab Bahadur: rich local Muslim landowner.
17. the Marabar Hills: hills where the Marabar Caves are located.
18. Jain: a believer or follower of an ascetic religion of India.

19. Hamidullah: a friend of Aziz's.
20. Mr. Lesley: a minor character.
21. British Raj: British rule.
22. anna: former copper coin of India and Pakistan.

Questions for Understanding

1. Why does Ronny Heaslop send his mother back to England before the trial? And why is Mrs. Moore worshipped by the Indians?
2. Why does Adela accuse Aziz? What causes Adela's breakdown?
3. How does Adela's accusation affect Aziz's life?
4. What qualities enable Adela to admit the truth at the trial?
5. What can you understand about the relationship between the British people and the Indian people through this trial scene?

Aspects of Appreciation

1. The modernistic and traditional elements

It is, sometimes, difficult to decide whether E. M. Forster should be labeled as a traditional writer or a modernist; for both traditional and modernistic elements can be found in his works. Forster's modernistic trend is shown in his themes, in his major concerns with personal relationships and in his use of poetic style and symbolism. Forster has a close affinity to Virginia Woolf in points of view and in writing style. For they both belong to the Bloomsbury group and both write about "nice" people (the middle-class people) in a "nice" manner with a "nice" style (the poetic style). Forster also shares with D. H. Lawrence a similar view on personal relationships. They both concentrate their efforts on exploring the possibilities of realizing natural harmonious relationships between man and man in a suppressing and decaying world.

But compared with the modernistic masters like Joyce or Woolf, Forster is a less experimental writer in forms or techniques. Basically, he follows the traditional pattern of realistic novels from Defoe to Meredith. His novels have well-organized, sometimes melodramatic, plots with considerable complexity in structure; his stories are told in a masterly way with incident after incident in a series of pictures, which are easily, vividly and economically drawn; his insight into certain aspects of character is acute with microscopic exactness; he traces and analyses the blended course of thought and feeling and the changing mood of his characters. By using the third-person omniscient narrative, Forster, like Fielding and Thackeray, presents subtle comments on his characters. Influenced by Samuel Butler and Thomas Hardy, Forster shows great concerns with the social and moral issues. In order to expose the "undeveloped heart" of the English middle class, Forster makes a skillful use of the cosmic satire inherited from Jane Austen.

2. The subtle use of symbolism

In order to express a moral and spiritual interpretation of human experience, Forster makes subtle use of symbolism. In his novels, the images, metaphors, and the details of descriptions and actions are all woven into such an organic pattern that each of them seems to have carried a certain symbolic meaning. The more obvious symbols in his works are those names of places and characters. Sawston, Howards End, Greece, Italy and Cambridge are typical place names which carry strong symbolic meanings. And there is usually a character in each of his novels, such as Old Mr. Emerson, Stephen Wanham, Gino, Mr. Wilcox and Mrs. Moore, who stands broadly either for vitality or for saintliness and who symbolically exerts a strong influence over the development of the story. The more conventional symbols like the blood on the photographs or unexpected blood relationships in his early novels lead up to the more imposing symbolism of *Howards End* and *A Passage to India* in which the whole story seems to be moved by symbols. The characters mean more than they say; the plots and structures suggest more than they are actually there.

Suggested Further Reading

E. M. Forster. *A Room with a View* (1908), and *Aspects of the Novel* (1949).

Topics for Further Study

1. Describe the effect of the incident at the Marabar caves on Mrs. Moore and Adela Quested.
2. How is Mrs. Moore able to be accepted in both Indian and English cultures? What do Fielding, Adela Quested, and Ronny lack in comparison to Mrs. Moore?
3. The Marabar case remains to be a mystery though the trial is over. What do you think could be the possibilities?
4. As briefly as possible, explain the themes of the novel. Justify your

choice of the theme.

D. H. Lawrence
(1885～1930)

About the Author

    D. H. Lawrence was born at a mining village in Nottinghamshire. His father was a coal miner with little education; but his mother, once a school teacher, was from a somewhat higher class, who came to think that she had married beneath her and desired to raise the cultural level of her sons so as to help them escape from the life of coal miners. The conflict between the earthy, coarse, energetic but often drunk father and the refined, strong-willed and up-climbing mother is vividly presented in his autobiographical novel, *Sons and Lovers* (1913). As a boy, Lawrence was quiet, clever and rather religious. He won a scholarship to Nottingham High School at the age of 13. He also showed his talent in painting. After high school, he went to work as a pupil teacher for a few years, and then he went on to take a teacher-training course at Nottingham University College for two years. After completing it, Lawrence began to work as a regular teacher.

    While teaching, Lawrence began writing novels and poems. His first novel, *The White Peacock* was published in 1911. Lawrence gave up teaching after his mother's death and his own suffering from a serious illness. The first version of *Sons and Lovers* was written in this period.

    In 1912, Lawrence went to see his former French teacher, Professor Weekley, at Nottingham University College, in the hope of getting a job as an English Lecturer in a German university. At Weekley's house, Lawrence met Frieda, the Professor's wife, who was a daughter of a German baron, mother of 3 children. They fell in love and eloped to the Continent. They got married in 1914 after Frieda had been divorced.

    During the First World War, Lawrence was suspected as a spy and watched by the police because of his anti-war attitude and his wife's German origin. His important novel, *Rainbow*, was published in 1915, but was banned as a danger to public morality.

    When the war was over, the Lawrences left England to Italy. He traveled far and wide, from Italy to Ceylon, Australia, New Zealand, the South Seas, America, Mexico and back to England, Italy, and finally died of tuberculosis in the south of France in 1930.

During all these years of wandering about, Lawrence kept on writing. With strong endurance of pain and enormous power of creation, he produced a large number of poems, stories, travel books, critical essays, and several novels.

Lawrence is regarded as one of the few 20th century figures who have altered the quality of human life and thought. He is traditional in narrative form but poetic and emotional in his style, and daring in his subject matter.

★ Sons and Lovers

About the Novel

Sons and Lovers, begun in 1911 and published in 1913, is the most successful among Lawrence's early novels. The first draft was called *Paul Morel*. Like some of his other novels, it also has Nottingham as its setting. To a very large extent, it is an autobiography. The Morel family is the counterpart of his own, and Paul Morel is his own shadow. The story is like this: Gertrude Coppard, who comes of a good burgher family, is married to Walter Morel, a coal miner. She is soon disillusioned with her husband, for the latter is coarse-mannered and often gets drunk. Thus she centres all her expectations and love on her sons, especially on the second son Paul after the first son William dies. Paul leaves school early and begins to work at 13 for a firm of surgical appliances in order to help support the family. He toils under terrible working conditions. A few years later he falls in love with a young girl Miriam and then with a married woman Clara. Thereafter he is confronted with a conflict of love between his mother and his two lovers. Finally his mother dies of cancer, which, sort of, releases him. But his soul can not leave her wherever she is. And regarding marriage as a bondage, he leaves his two lovers and drifts away aimlessly on the sea of life.

Chapter 9
Defeat of Miriam

Paul was dissatisfied with himself and with everything. The deepest of his love belonged to his mother. When he felt he had hurt her, or wounded his love for her, he could not bear it¹. Now it was spring and there was battle between him and Miriam. This year he had a good deal against her. She was vaguely aware of it. The old feeling that she was to be a sacrifice to this love, which she had had when she prayed, was mingled in all her emotions. She did not at the bottom believe she ever would have him. She did not believe in herself primarily: doubted whether she could ever be what he would demand of her. Certainly she never saw herself living happily through a lifetime with him. She saw tragedy, sorrow, and sacrifice ahead. And in sacrifice she was proud, in renunciation she was strong, for she did not trust herself to support everyday life. She was prepared for the big things and the deep things, like tragedy. It was the sufficiency of the small day-life she could not trust².

The Easter holidays³ began happily. Paul was his own frank self. Yet she felt it would go wrong. On the Sunday afternoon she stood at her bedroom window, looking across at the oak-trees of the wood, in whose branches a twilight was tangled, below the bright sky of the afternoon. Grey-green rosettes of honeysuckle leaves hung before the window, some already, she fancied, showing bud. It was spring, which she loved and dreaded⁴.

Hearing the clack of the gate she stood in suspense. It was a bright grey day⁵. Paul came into the yard with his bicycle, which glittered as he walked. Usually he rang his bell and laughed towards the house. Today he walked with shut lips and cold, cruel bearing, that had something of a slouch and a sneer in it. She knew him well by now, and could tell from keen-looking, aloof young body of his what was happening inside him. There was a cold correctness in the way he put his bicycle in its place, that made her heart sink.

She came downstairs nervously. She was wearing a new net blouse that she thought became her. It had a high collar with a tiny ruff, reminding her of Mary, Queen of Scots⁶, and making her, she thought, look wonderfully a woman, and dignified. At twenty she was full-breasted and luxuriously formed. Her face was still like a soft rich mask, unchangeable. But her eyes, once lifted, were wonderful. She was afraid of him. He would notice her new blouse⁷.

He, being in a hard, ironical mood, was entertaining the family to a description of a service given in the Primitive Methodist Chapel, conducted by one of the well-known preachers of the sect⁸. He sat at the head of the table, his mobile face, with the eyes that could be so beautiful, shining with tenderness or dancing with laughter, now taking on one expression and then another, in imitation of various people he was mocking. His mockery always hurt her; it was too near the reality. He was too clever and cruel. She felt that when his eyes were like this, hard with mocking hate, he would spare neither himself nor anybody else. But Mrs. Leivers, was wiping her eyes with laughter, and Mr. Leivers[9], just awake from his Sunday nap, was rubbing his head in amusement. The three brothers sat with ruffled, sleepy appearance in their shirt-sleeves, giving a guffaw from time to time. The whole family loved a "take-off"[10] more than anything.

He took no notice of Miriam. Later, she saw him remark her new blouse, saw that the artist approved, but it won from him not a spark of warmth[11]. She was nervous, could hardly reach the teacups from the shelves.

When the men went out to milk[12], she ventured to address him personally.

"You were late," she said.

"Was I?" he answered.

There was silence for a while.

"Was it rough riding?" she asked.

"I didn't notice it."

She continued quickly to lay the table. When she had finished—

"Tea won't be for a few minutes. Will you come and look at the daffodils?" she said.

He rose without answering. They went out into their back garden under the budding damson-trees. The hills and the sky were clean and cold. Everything looked washed, rather hard. Miriam glanced at Paul. He was pale and impassive. It seemed cruel to her that his eyes and brows, which she loved, could look so hurting.

"Has the wind made you tired?" she asked. She detected an underneath feeling of weariness about him.

"No, I think not," he answered.

"It must be rough on the road—the wood moans so."

"You can see by the clouds it's a south-west wind; that helps me here."

"You see, I don't cycle, so I don't understand," she murmured.

"Is there need to cycle to know that?" he said.

She thought his sarcasms were unnecessary. They went forward in silence. Round the wild, tussock lawn at the back of the house was a thorn hedge, under which daffodils were craning forward from among their sheaves of grey-green blades. The cheeks of the flowers were greenish with cold. But still some had burst, and their gold ruffled and glowed. Miriam went on her knees before one cluster, took a wild-looking daffodil between her hands, turned up its face of gold to her, and bowed down, caressing it with her mouth and cheeks and brow. He stood aside, with his hands in his pocket, watching her. One after another she turned up to him the faces of the yellow, bursten flowers appealingly, fondling them lavishly all the while[13].

"Aren't they magnificent?" she murmured.

"Magnificent? It's a bit thick—they're pretty!"

She bowed again to her flowers at his censure of her praise. He watched her crouching, sipping the flowers with fervid kisses.

"Why must you always be fondling things!" he said irritably.

"But I love to touch them," she replied, hurt.

"Can you never like things without clutching them as if you wanted to pull the heart out of them? Why don't you have a bit more restraint or reserve, or something[14]?"

She looked up at him full of pain, then continued slowly to stroke her lips against a ruffled flower. Their scent, as she smelled it, was so much kinder than he; it almost made her cry.

"You wheedle the soul out of things," he said. "I would never wheedle—at any rate, I'd go straight."

He scarcely knew what he was saying. These things came from him mechanically. She looked at him. His body seemed one weapon, firm and hard against her.

"You're always begging things to love you," he said, "as if you were a beggar for love. Even the flowers, you have to fawn on them—"

Rhythmically, Miriam was swaying and stroking the flower with her mouth, inhaling the scent which ever after made her shudder as it came to her nostrils.

"You don't want to love—your eternal and abnormal craving is to be loved. You aren't positive, you're negative. You absorb, absorb, as if you must fill yourself up with love, because you've got a shortage somewhere."

She was stunned by his cruelty, and did not hear. He had not the faintest notion of what he was saying. It was as if his fretted, tortured soul, run hot by thwarted passion, jetted off these sayings like sparks from electricity. She did not grasp anything he said. She only sat crouched beneath his cruelty and his hatred of her. She never realized in a flash. Over everything she brooded and brooded.

After tea he stayed with Edgar and the brothers, taking no notice of Miriam. She, extremely unhappy on this looked-for holiday, waited for him. And at last he yielded and came to her. She was determined to track this mood of his to its origin. She counted it not much more than a mood.

"Shall we go through the wood a little way?" she asked him, knowing he never refused a direct request.

They went down to the warren. On the middle path they passed a trap, a narrow horseshoe hedge of small fir-boughs, baited with the guts of a rabbit. Paul glanced at it frowning. She caught his eye.

"Isn't it dreadful?" she asked.

"I don't know! Is it worse than a weasel with its teeth in a rabbit's throat? One weasel or many rabbits? One or the other must go."

He was taking the bitterness of life badly. She was rather sorry for him.

"We will go back to the house," he said. "I don't want to walk out."

They went past the lilac-tree, whose bronze leaf-buds were coming unfastened. Just a fragment remained of the haystack, a monument squared and brown, like a pillar of stone. There was a little bed of hay from the last cutting.

"Let us sit here a minute," said Miriam.

He sat down against his will, resting his back against the hard wall of hey. They faced the amphitheatre of round hills that glowed with sunset, tiny white farms standing out, the meadows golden, the woods dark and yet luminous, tree-tops folded over tree-tops, distinct in the distance. The evening had cleared, and the east was tender with a magenta flush under which the land lay still and rich.

"Isn't it beautiful?" she pleaded.

But he only scowled. He would rather have had it ugly just then.

At that moment a big bull-terrier came rushing up, open-mouthed, pranced his two paws on the youth's shoulders, licking his face. Paul drew back, laughing. Bill was a great relief to him. He pushed the dog aside, but it came leaping back.

"Get out," said the lad, "or I'll dot thee one."

But the dog was not to be pushed away. So Paul had a little battle with the creature, pitching poor Bill away from him, who, however, only floundered tumultuously back again, wild with joy. The two fought together, the man laughing grudgingly, the dog grinning all over. Miriam watched them. There was something pathetic about the man. He wanted so badly to love, to be tender. The rough way he bowled the dog over was really loving. Bill got up, panting with happiness, his brown eyes rolling in his white face, and lumbered back again. He adored Paul. The lad frowned.

"Bill, I've had enough o'thee," he said.

But the dog only stood with two heavy paws, that quivered with love, upon his thigh, and flickered a red tongue at him. He drew back.

"No," he said—"no—I've had enough."

And in a minute the dog trotted off happily, to vary the fun.

He remained staring miserably across at the hills, whose still beauty he begrudged. He wanted to go and cycle with Edgar. Yet he had not the courage to leave Miriam.

"Why are you sad?" she asked humbly.

"I'm not sad; why should I be," he answered. "I'm only normal."

She wondered why he always claimed to be normal when he was disagreeable.

"But what is the matter?" she pleaded, coaxing him soothingly.

"Nothing!"

"Nay!" she murmured.

He picked up a stick and began to stab the earth with it.

"You'd far better not talk," he said.

"But I wish to know—" she replied.

He laughed resentfully.

"You always do," he said.

"It's not fair to me," she murmured.

He thrust, thrust, thrust at the ground with the pointed stick, digging up little clods of earth as if he were in a fever of irritation. She gently and firmly laid her hand on his wrist.

"Don't!" she said. "Put it away."

He flung the stick into the currant-bushes, and leaned back. Now he was bottled up.

"What is it?" she pleaded softly.

He lay perfectly still, only his eyes alive, and they full of torment.

"You know," he said at length, rather wearily-"you know—we'd better break off."

It was what she dreaded. Swiftly everything seemed to darken before her eyes.

"Why!" she murmured. "What has happened?"

"Nothing has happened. We only realize where we are. It's no good—"

She waited in silence, sadly, patiently. It was no good being impatient with him. At any rate, he would tell her now what ailed him.

"We agreed on friendship," he went on in a dull, monotonous voice. "How often have we agreed for friendship! And yet—it neither stops there, nor gets anywhere else."

He was silent again. She brooded. What did he mean? He was so wearying. There was something he would not yield. Yet she must be patient with him.

"I can only give friendship—it's all I'm capable of—it's a flaw in my make-up. The thing overbalances to one side—I hate a toppling balance. Let us have done."

There was warmth of fury in his last phrases. He meant she loved him more than he her. Perhaps he could not love her. Perhaps she had not in herself that which he wanted. It was the deepest motive of her soul, this self-mistrust. It was so deep she dared neither realize nor acknowledge. Perhaps she was deficient. Like an infinitely subtle shame, it kept her always back. If it were so, she would do without him. She would never let herself want him. She would merely see.

"But what has happened?" she said.

"Nothing—it's all in myself—it only comes out just now. We're always like this towards Easter-time."

He groveled so helplessly, she pitied him. At least she never floundered in such a pitiable way. After all, it was he who was chiefly humiliated.

"What do you want?" she asked him.

"Why—I mustn't come often—that's all. Why should I monopolize you when I'm not—You see, I'm deficient in something with regard to you—"[15]

He was telling her he did not love her, and so ought to leave her a chance with another man. How foolish and blind and shamefully clumsy he was! What were other men to her! What were men to her at all! But he, ah! She loved his soul. Was he deficient in something? Perhaps he was.

"But I don't understand," she said huskily. "Yesterday—"

The night was turning jangled and hateful to him as the twilight laded. And she bowed under her suffering.

"I know," he cried, "you never will! You'll never believe that I can't—can't physically, any more than I can fly up like a skylark—"

"What?" she murmured. Now she dreaded.

"Love you."

He hated her bitterly at that moment because he made her suffer. Love her! She knew he loved her. He really belonged to her. This about not loving her, physically, bodily, was a mere perversity on his part[16], because he knew she loved him. He was stupid like a child. He belonged to her. His soul wanted her. She guessed somebody had been influencing him. She felt upon him the hardness, the foreignness of another influence[17].

"What have they been saying at home?" she asked.

"It's not that," he answered.

And then she knew it was. She despised them for their commonness, his people. They did not know what things were really worth.

He and she talked very little more that night. After all he left her to cycle with Edgar.

He had come back to his mother. Hers was the strongest tie in his life. When he thought round, Miriam shrank away. There was a vague, unreal feel about her, and nobody else mattered. There was one place in the world that stood solid and did not melt into unreality: the place where his mother was. Everybody else could grow shadowy, almost non-existent to him, but she could not. It was as if the pivot and pole of his life, from which he could not escape, was his mother.

And in the same way she waited for him. In him was established her life now. After all, the life beyond offered very little to Mrs. Morel. She saw that our chance for doing is here, and doing counted with her. Paul was going to prove that she had been right; he was going to make a man whom nothing should shift off his feet; he was going to alter the face of the earth in some way which mattered. Wherever he went she felt her soul went with him. Whatever he did she felt her soul stood by him, ready, as it were, to hand him his tools. She could not bear it when he was with Miriam. William[18] was dead. She would fight to keep Paul[19].

And he came back to her. And in his soul was a feeling of the satisfaction of self-sacrifice because he was faithful to her. She loved him first; he loved her first. And yet it was not enough. His new young life, so strong and imperious, was urged towards something else[20]. It made him mad with restlessness. She saw this, and wished bitterly that Miriam had been a woman who could take this new life of his, and leave her the roots. He fought against his mother almost as he fought against Miriam[21].

It was a week before he went again to Willey Farm. Miriam had suffered a great deal, and was afraid to see him again. Was she now to endure the ignominy of his abandoning her? That would only be superficial and temporary. He would come back. She held the keys to his soul. But, meanwhile, how he would torture her with his battle against her. She shrank from it.

……

She fretted him to the bottom of his soul. There she remained—sad, pensive, a worshipper. And he caused her sorrow. Half the time he grieved for her, half the time he hated her. She was his conscience; and he felt, somehow, he had got a conscience that was too much for him. He could not leave her, because in one way she did hold the best of him. He could not stay with her because she did not take the rest of him, which was three-quarters. So he chafed himself into rawness over her.

When she was twenty-one he wrote her a letter which could only have been written to her.

"May I speak of our old, worn love, this last time. It, too, is changing, is it not? Say, has not the body of that love died, and left you its invulnerable soul? You see, I can give you a spirit love, I have given it you this long, long time; but not embodied passion. See, you are a nun[22]. I have given you what I would give a holy nun—as a mystic monk to a mystic nun. Surely you esteem it best. Yet you regret—no, have regretted—the other. In all our relations no body enters. I do not talk to you through the senses—rather through the spirit. That is why we cannot love in the common sense. Ours is not an everyday affection. As yet we are mortal, and to live side by side with one another would be dreadful, for somehow with you I cannot long be trivial, and, you know, to be always beyond this mortal state would be to lose it. If people marry, they must live together as affectionate humans, who may be commonplace with each other without feeling awkward—not as two souls. So I feel it.

"Ought I to send this letter? —I doubt it. But there—it is best to understand. *Au revoir*[23]."

Miriam read this letter twice, after which she sealed it up. A year later she broke the seal to show her mother the letter.

"You are a nun—you are a nun." The words went into her heart again and again. Nothing he ever had said had gone into her so deeply, fixedly, like a mortal wound.

She answered him two days after the party.

"Our intimacy would have been all-beautiful but for one little mistake," she quoted. "Was the mistake mine?"

Almost immediately he replied to her from Nottingham, sending her at the same time a little "Omar Khayyam"[24].

"I am glad you answered; you are so calm and natural you put me to shame. What a ranter I am! We are often out of sympathy. But in fundamentals we may always be together I think."

"I must thank you for your sympathy with my painting and drawing. Many a sketch is dedicated to you. I do look forward to your criticisms, which, to my shame and glory, are always grand appreciations. It is a lovely joke, that *Au revoir*".

This was the end of the first phase of Paul's love affair…

※ ※

Notes

1. The mother is an overwhelming power existing everywhere to influence Paul's choice and decision. Paul is in the dilemma between his love for his mother and his love for Miriam. Of the two loves, the former is dominating and prohibiting him from loving the latter.
2. Miriam feels uncertain and even frustrated in her love with Paul. In one way, she as a grown-up young girl, loves Paul; in another, she fears this love because of her religious belief, according to which, love is something "small". Therefore, she'd rather regard her love more like a sacrifice in spirit.
3. The Easter holidays: a Christian holy day in March or April when Christians remember the death of Christ and his return to life.
4. This is a vivid description of Miriam's feeling for Paul. Like spring, which unavoidably comes as a natural phenomenon, this explains her love as a young girl for a young man like Paul, which is spontaneous and normal. However, when she is in love, she has fear resulting from Paul's uncertain attitude toward her, and her own religious sense. Therefore,

she enjoys her love and at the same time she fears it.
5. "In suspense" expresses both Miriam's uncertain feeling at the clack of the gate and her feeling for Paul's love. The next sentence "It was a bright and grey day" means the same: glad and gloomy, cheerful and somewhat fearful.
6. Mary, Queen of Scots (1542~1587): the daughter of the Scottish King James V. She became Queen of Scotland when she was one week old, but in 1568 she was forced to give up her position, and she escaped to England.
7. This is a wonderful description of a girl in love. She dresses herself carefully, and is aware of her beauty and charm as a young lady, expecting her lover's praise and admiration.
8. Paul was low-spirited but he amused the family well with his imitation of a serious service. Methodist: someone who belongs to a Christian religious group that follows the ideas of John Wesley.
9. Mrs. Leivers and Mr. Leivers: the Parents of Miriam. "The three brothers": sons of Mr. and Mrs. Leivers. They all are kind and generous to Paul and welcome him on their farm.
10. "take-off": exaggerated imitation.
11. Paul praised Miriam's new blouse as an artist appreciating a fine piece of art without any warmth of a lover. Miriam is disappointed with his indifference. The novel is a story of Paul as a lover involved in affection contradiction and that of Paul as an artist keeping himself from life in a distance.
12. milk: to take milk.
13. Here is a suggestion that Miriam could restrain her love no more, she poured out her inner passion to daffodils. In the view of psychological analysis, "she turned up to him the faces of the yellow, bursten flowers appealingly" is showing her love to Paul, and her behavior of "fondling" the flower suggests that her love is repressed too deeply and receives no response, that she transfers her love to Daffodil and expresses her feeling in a different way. Daffodil is a kind of beautiful flower with long green leaves, usually symbolizing love, life and nature.
14. In the eyes of Paul, Miriam is too eager when she expresses her love and asks for love.
15. I'm deficient in something with regard to you: Paul embraced by the maternal love, admitted that he could not love Miriam with all his heart

and soul. That "He fought against his mother almost as he fought against Miriam" "it's a flaw in my make-up" "I can't—can't physically…love you", all express Paul's dilemma and incoherence in his heart and soul.

16. This about not loving her, physically, bodily, was a mere perversity on his part: It is abnormal for him not to be able to love her physically and bodily.
17. She felt upon him the hardness, the foreignness of another influence: This indicates Miriam felt the mother's influence upon Paul.
18. William: Paul's elder brother, who died in the first part of the novel. Feeling disappointed with her husband, Mrs. Morel initially pours all her energy into giving William expectations and ambition. She refuses to allow him to go down the pit and sets him on the road that leads from the local co-op to a responsible job in London. William fulfills part of Mrs. Morel's expectations. William's brief life has double meanings: its wider social significance is that it emphasizes the danger, pain and cost of upward mobility and social emancipation; the personal significance is that his life is a prefiguration of Paul's, an anticipatory illustration of the dangers as well as the triumphs of ambitious mother-love.
19. She would fight to keep Paul: this is a sentence to show the mother's possessive love of the son. Compare the following sentences: "She loved him first; he loved her first." There are many sentences to express the abnormal love of the mother and the son.
20. His new young life, so strong and imperious, was urged towards something else: As a young man, mere maternal love is not sufficient, it is natural for Paul to love a woman of his own age.
21. He fought against his mother almost as he fought against Miriam: This shows Paul's dilemma in the two inadequate loves of the mother and Miriam, as neither gives him a full feeling. The mother's is too possessive while Miriam's too spiritual, so when he falls in love with one, he spontaneously feels the demanding of the other. He wants to escape from both and finds new experience but cannot.
22. You're a nun: Paul's comments mean their love remains only in spiritual sense, but lacks physical attraction. This makes Miriam very sad and confused, and she feels greatly hurt. In fact, her physical presence is fully realized in a warm, sensuous, even exuberant manner. Her hair is free and unrestrained, her lips open, and her complexion glows with

healthy vitality. She yearns for Paul openly while he retracts in fear. Compare the previous description of her: "At twenty she was full-breasted and luxuriously formed." The novel describes the image of Miriam totally from Paul's view, thus fails to reveal the root of Miriam's problem and loveliness.

23. *Au revoir*: (French interjection) goodbye.
24. Omar Khayyam: a collection of poems by the poet Omar Khayyam.

Questions for Understanding

1. What is Miriam's view about religion, love and sex?
2. Why does the author say Miriam is defeated? Who is(are) the real loser (losers) in the love affair?
3. Why is Paul not able to accept Miriam's love?
4. What do flowers symbolize in the selection? What do Miriam and Paul's reactions towards flowers in spring reveal about them?
5. How would you describe Mrs. Morel's feeling toward Miriam? Can you explain why it is so?

Aspects of Appreciation

1. *Sons and Lovers* is a novel of growing up. It is evident that the central character is Paul Morel. It follows his growth and development from infancy to young manhood. It is his emotional, intellectual, social and, above all, psychological development that the novel portrays. *Sons and Lovers* is an unusual version of a common form of novel, namely, the education novel, or a Bildungsroman, of which many of the best examples are German. *Wieland's Agathon* is usually thought of as the first example of the genre, but the best and most imitated was Goethe's *Wilhelm Meister's Apprenticeship*. Wilhelm provides the model of innocent, inexperienced, well-meaning, but often foolish and erring, young man who sets out in life with either no aim in mind or the wrong one. By a series of false starts and mistakes and with the help from well-disposed friends he makes in the course of his experiences, he finally reaches maturity and finds his proper profession. The famous English novels of this genre include *Jane Eyre*, *A Portrait of the Artist as a Young Man*, *Sons and Lovers*, etc., all of which focus on the growth to maturity of a young person.
2. The relation between the mother and son is always central in the novel,

while the earlier part of the novel is about Paul's all but futile attempt to break free from the mother and find a fulfilling relationship with another woman. Obviously, Paul's mother influenced his life immeasurably. The novel describes Paul's unnatural devotion to his mother. He hates his father and dreams of living exclusively with his mother. In this sense, the novel is considered a classic example of the Oedipus complex. Sigmund Freud, the founder of psychoanalysis, derived the term from Sophocle's Greek tragedy *Oedipus the King*, whose protagonist has unknowingly killed his father and married his mother. But Lawrence himself claimed not to have read Freud before writing the novel, and dismissed the theory of complexes as "vicious half-statements of Freudians".

Suggested Further Reading

1. D. H. Lawrence. *The Rainbow* (1915), *Lady Chatterley's Lover* (1960).
2. Fiona Becket. *The Complete Critical Guide to D. H. Lawrence*, 2002.

Topics for Further Study

1. Why does Lawrence use the plural form in the title of *Sons and Lovers*? What wider significance does the author want to achieve?
2. Analyze the different expectations for love by Paul, Miriam and Mrs. Morel' and explain respectively their problems.
3. As one of the best Bildungsromans of the 20th century, *Sons and Lovers* records Paul's difficult journey of growing up. Discuss the strong influence of his family, especially his mother, on his life and his relationship with other women.

James Joyce
(1882~1941)

About the Author

James Joyce was born in a Catholic family on February 2, 1882 in Dublin, Ireland. With the intention of becoming a priest, he then entered Dublin's University College where he studied modern languages. He refused to take part in the nationalist movement, but became passionately interested in literature. He lost his faith in religion and was an ardent anti-Catholic.

He exiled himself to Europe. From 1904 to 1914, Joyce earned his living by teaching English in Switzerland and Italy. After that, his life was marked by continual struggles to publish his works. He settled down in Paris in 1920, and wrote his books there until the Second World War broke out. With the fall of France in December of 1940, he was forced to move again to Zurich. He died of a stomach ulcer in Zurich shortly afterwards on January 13, 1941.

Joyce's great literary works include: *Dubliners* (1914), a collection of 15 short stories; *A Portrait of the Artist as a Young Man* (1916), a novel which is largely autobiographical, about a boy growing up in Dublin; *Ulysses* (1922) and *Finnegan's Wake* (1939).

Joyce is celebrated as one of the great literary pioneers of the 20th century. He was one of the first writers to make extensive and convincing use of the stream of consciousness. And he is also noted for another stylistic technique, the epiphany, a moment in which a character makes a sudden, profound realization (whether prompted by an external object or a voice from within) that creates a change in his or her perception of the world.

★ Araby[1]

About the Work

"Araby" is the third story in *Dubliners*. The narrator, a young boy, tells the story of a childhood infatuation in urban Dublin. The boy lives in a world apart from adults, although he fantasizes about a neighbor's sister. She asks if he is going to Araby, an upcoming local bazaar. The boy, full of romantic notions, promises to bring her a gift from the bazaar if he goes. He takes a deserted train to the bazaar just as it is closing. Only a few stalls are open. The goods are far too expensive for him. The lights are being shut off, and the boy despairs: "Gazing up into the darkness I saw myself as a creature driven and derided by vanity; and my eyes burned with anguish and anger."

The story of the frustrated quest for beauty in the midst of drabness is both meticulously realistic in its handling of details of Dublin life and the Dublin scene, and highly symbolic in that almost every image and incident suggests some particular aspect of the theme.

North Richmond Street[2], being blind[3], was a quiet street except at the hour when the Christian Brothers' School set the boys free[4]. An uninhabited house of two storeys stood at the blind end, detached from its neighbors in a square ground. The other houses of the street, conscious of decent lives within them, gazed at one another with brown[5] imperturbable faces.

The former tenant of our house, a priest, had died in the back drawing-room. Air, musty from having been long enclosed, hung in all the rooms, and the waste room behind the kitchen was littered with old useless papers. Among these I found a few paper-covered books, the pages of which were curled and damp: *The Abbot*, by Walter Scott, *The Devout Communicant*, and *The Memoirs of Vidocq*[6]. I liked the last best because its leaves were yellow. The wild garden behind the house contained a central apple-tree and a few straggling bushes, under one of which I found the late tenant's rusty bicycle-pump. He had been a very charitable priest; in his will he had left all his money to institutions and the furniture of his house to his sister.

When the short days of winter came, dusk fell before we had well eaten our dinners. When we met in the street the houses had grown somber. The space of sky above us was the color of ever-changing violet and towards it the lamps of the street lifted their feeble lanterns. The cold air stung us and we played till our bodies glowed. Our shouts echoed in the silent street. The career of our play brought us through the dark muddy lanes behind the houses, where we ran the gantlet[7] of the rough tribes from the cottages, to the back doors of the dark dripping gardens where odors arose from the ashpits, to the dark odorous stables where a coachman smoothed and combed the horse or shook music from the buckled harness. When we returned to the street, light from the kitchen windows had filled the areas. If my uncle was seen turning the corner, we hid in the shadow[8] until we had seen him safely housed. Or if Mangan's sister[9] came out on the doorstep to call her brother in to his tea, we watched her from our shadow peer up and down the street. We waited to see whether she would remain or go in and, if she remained, we left our shadow and walked up to Mangan's steps resignedly. She was waiting for us, her figure defined by the light from the half-opened door. Her brother always teased her before he obeyed, and I stood by the railings looking at her. Her dress swung as she moved her body, and the soft rope of her hair tossed from side to side.

Every morning I lay on the floor in the front parlor watching her door. The blind was pulled down to within an inch of the sash so that I could not be seen. When she came out on the doorstep my heart leaped. I ran to the hall, seized my books and followed her. I kept her brown figure always in my eye and, when we came near the point at which our ways diverged, I quickened my pace and passed her. This happened, morning after morning. I had never spoken to her, except for a few casual words, and yet her name was like a summons to all my foolish blood.

Her image accompanied me even in places the most hostile to romance. On Saturday evenings when my aunt went marketing I had to go to carry some of the parcels. We walked through the flaring streets, jostled by drunken men and bargaining women, amid the curses of laborers, the shrill litanies of shop-boys who stood on guard by the barrels of pigs' cheeks, the nasal chanting of street-singers, who sang a *come-all-you about O'Donovan Rossa*[10], or a ballad about the troubles in our native land. These noises converged in a single sensation of life for me: I imagined that I bore my chalice safely through a throng of foes. Her name sprang to my lips at moments in strange prayers and praises which I myself did not understand. My eyes were often full of tears(I could not tell why) and at times a flood from my heart seemed to pour itself out into my bosom. I thought little of the future. I did not know whether I would ever speak to her or not or, if I spoke to her, how I could tell her of my confused adoration. But my body was like a harp and her words and gestures were like fingers running upon the wires.

One evening I went into the back drawing-room in which the priest had died. It was a dark rainy evening and there was no sound in the house. Through one of the broken panes I heard the rain impinge upon the earth, the fine incessant needles of water playing in the sodden beds. Some distant lamp or lighted window gleamed below me. I was thankful that I could see so little. All my senses seemed to desire to veil themselves and, feeling that I was about to slip from them, I pressed the palms of my hands together until they trembled, murmuring: "O love! O love!" many times.

At last she spoke to me[11]. When she addressed the first words to me I was so confused that I did not know what to answer. She asked me was I going to Araby. I forgot whether I answered yes or no. It would be a splendid bazaar; she said she would love to go.

—And why can't you? I asked.

While she spoke she turned a silver bracelet round and round her wrist. She could not go, she said, because there would be a retreat[12] that week in her convent. Her brother and two other boys were fighting for their caps, and I was alone at the railings.

She held one of the spikes, bowing her head towards me. The light from the lamp opposite our door caught the white curve of her neck, lit up her hair that rested there and, falling, lit up the hand upon the railing. It fell over one side of her dress and caught the white border of a petticoat, just visible as she stood at ease.

—It's well for you, she said.

—If I go, I said, I will bring you something.

What innumerable follies laid waste my waking and sleeping thoughts after that evening! I wished to annihilate the tedious intervening days. I chafed against the work of school. At night in my bedroom and by day in the classroom her image came between me and the page I strove to read. The syllables of the word Araby were called to me through the silence in which my soul luxuriated and cast an Eastern enchantment over me. I asked for leave to go to the bazaar on Saturday night. My aunt was surprised, and hoped it was not some Freemason affair[13]. I answered few questions in class. I watched my master's face pass from amiability to sternness; he hoped I was not beginning to idle. I could not call my wandering thoughts together. I had hardly any patience with the serious work of life which, now that it stood between me and my desire, seemed to me child's play, ugly monotonous child's play.

On Saturday morning I reminded my uncle that I wished to go to the bazaar in the evening. He was fussing at the hallstand, looking for the hat-brush, and answered me curtly:

—Yes, boy, I know.

As he was in the hall I could not go into the front parlor and lie at the window. I felt the house in bad humor and walked slowly towards the school. The air was pitilessly raw and already my heart misgave me.

When I came home to dinner my uncle had not yet been home. Still it was early. I sat staring at the clock for some time and, when its ticking began to irritate me, I left the room. I mounted the staircase and gained the upper part of the house. The high cold empty gloomy rooms liberated me and I went from room to room singing. From the front window I saw my companions playing below in the street. Their cries reached me weakened and indistinct and, leaning my forehead against the cool glass, I looked over at the dark house where she lived. I may have stood there for an hour, seeing nothing but the brown-clad figure cast by my imagination, touched discreetly by the lamplight at the curved neck, at the hand upon the railings and at the border below the dress.

When I came downstairs again I found Mrs. Mercer sitting at the fire. She was an old garrulous woman, a pawnbroker's widow, who collected used stamps for some pious purpose. I had to endure the gossip of the tea-table. The meal was prolonged beyond an hour and still my uncle did not come. Mrs. Mercer stood up to go: she was sorry she couldn't wait any longer, but it was after eight o'clock and she did not like to be out late, as the night air was bad for her. When she had gone I began to walk up and down the room, clenching my fists. My aunt said:

—I'm afraid you may put off your bazaar for this night of Our Lord.

At nine o'clock I heard my uncle's latchkey in the hall door. I heard him talking to himself and heard the hallstand rocking when it had received the weight of his overcoat. I could interpret these signs. When he was midway through his dinner I asked him to give me the money to go to the bazaar. He had forgotten.

—The people are in bed and after their first sleep now, he said.

I did not smile. My aunt said to him energetically:

—Can't you give him the money and let him go? You've kept him late enough as it is.

My uncle said he was very sorry he had forgotten. He said he believed in the old saying: "All work and no play makes Jack a dull boy." He asked me where I was going and, when I told him a second time, he asked me did I know *The Arab's Farewell to His Steed*[14]. When I left the kitchen he was about to recite the opening lines of the piece to my aunt.

I held a florin[15] tightly in my hand as I strode down Buckingham Street towards the station. The sight of the streets thronged with buyers and glaring with gas recalled to me the purpose of my journey. I took my seat in a third-class carriage of a deserted train. After an intolerable delay the train moved out of the station slowly. It crept onward among ruinous houses and over the twinkling river. At Westland Row Station a crowd of people pressed to the carriage doors; but the porters moved them back, saying that it was a special train for the bazaar. I remained alone in the bare carriage. In a few minutes the train drew up beside an improvised wooden platform. I passed out on to the road and saw by the lighted dial of a clock that it was ten minutes to ten. In front of me was a large building which displayed the magical name.

I could not find any sixpenny entrance and, fearing that the bazaar would be closed, I passed in quickly through a turnstile, handing a shilling to a weary-looking man. I found myself in a big hall girded at half its height by a gallery. Nearly all the stalls were closed and the greater part of the hall was in darkness. I recognized a silence like that which pervades a church after a service. I walked into the center of the bazaar timidly. A few people were gathered about the stalls which were still open. Before a curtain, over which the words "*Café Chantant*"[16] were written in colored lamps, two men were counting money on a salver[17]. I listened to the fall of the coins.

Remembering with difficulty why I had come I went over to one of the stalls and examined porcelain vases and flowered tea-sets. At the door of the stall a young lady was talking and laughing with two young gentlemen. I remarked their English accents and listened vaguely to their conversation.

—O, I never said such a thing!

—O, but you did!

—O, but I didn't!

—Didn't she say that?

—Yes. I heard her.

—O, there's a ... fib!

Observing me, the young lady came over and asked me did I wish to buy anything. The tone of her voice was not encouraging; she seemed to have spoken to me out of a sense of duty. I looked humbly at the great jars that stood like eastern guards at either side of the dark entrance to the stall and murmured:

—No, thank you.

The young lady changed the position of one of the vases and went back to the two young men. They began to talk of the same subject. Once or twice the young lady glanced at me over her shoulder.

I lingered before her stall, though I knew my stay was useless, to make my interest in her wares seem the more real. Then I turned away slowly and walked down the middle of the bazaar. I allowed the two pennies to fall against the sixpence in my pocket. I heard a voice call from one end of the gallery that the light was out. The upper part of the hall was now completely dark.

Gazing up into the darkness I saw myself as a creature driven and derided by vanity; and my eyes burned with anguish and anger.

Notes

1. Araby: a term used to express the romantic view of the east that had been popular since Napoleon's triumph over Egypt. And, of course, the story is about Romantic Irony, for the unnamed boy has a romantic view of the world.
2. North Richmond Street: In 1894 little Jimmy Joyce was 12, and lived at 17 North Richmond Street.
3. being blind: referring to the street having a dead end. But this also describes the condition of the boy's relation to reality.
4. set the boys free: Joyce uses this neat phrase to suggest that religion has imprisoned the boys.
5. brown: the most frequently used color in Dubliners. We note how quickly Joyce has been able to set a nearly hopeless and discouraged mood. In *Stephen Hero*, Joyce writes: "... one of those brown brick houses which seem the very incarnation of Irish paralysis."
6. *The Abbot*, by Walter Scott, *The Devout Communicant*, and *The Memoirs of Vidocq*: historical tale, a manual of religious instruction, and the recollections of a French adventure, respectively.
7. gantlet: an archaic spelling of "gauntlet."
8. shadow: Note the repetition of "shadow" (three times) in this paragraph. People of Dublin are not living, but ghost-like; the boys, who are very much alive, are surrounded by shades of people.
9. Mangan's sister: Here Joyce makes the connection with the popular, but sentimental and romantic 19th century Irish poet, James Clarence Mangan (1803～1849). Mangan was himself fond of writing about "Araby", and even though he knew no Arabic he claimed that some of his poems were translations from Arabic. Joyce's use of "Mangan" is one of the strongest supports for the theme of romanticism in the story, while at the same time it serves to strengthen previous instances of hypocrisy and false sentiment.
10. *come-all-you* about O'Donovan Rossa: street ballad, so called from its opening words. This one was about the 19th-century Irish nationalist Jeremiah Donovan, popularly known as O'Donovan Rossa.
11. she spoke to me: Here is a good example of an important modernist technique: "Show, do not tell."
12. retreat: period of seclusion from ordinary activities devoted to religious

exercises.
13. Freemason affair: international secret service society, also called the Free and Accepted Masons. His aunt shares her church's distrust of the Freemansons.
14. "*The Arab's Farewell to His Steed*": popular 19th century poem, which tells about an Arab boy who sells for gold coins the thing that he loves most in the world, his horse, however, as the horse is being led away the boy changes his mind and rushes after the man to return the money and reclaim his love.
15. a florin: a former two-shilling coin. It was a considerable amount of money for this boy. The florin originated in Florence during the Renaissance and had a likeness of the Virgin Mary on one side and that of St. John the Baptist on the other.
16. "*Café Chantant*": a French coffee house where musical entertainment is provided.
17. salver: tray, usually used for serving food.

Questions for Understanding

1. What kind of environment is the boy in?
2. How does the boy describe his feelings for Mangan's sister?
3. Why does the boy want to go to the bazaar?
4. Why does he arrive so late?
5. What do you think of the ending? How do you explain the word "vanity"?

Aspects of Appreciation

1. This story deals with longing for adventure and escape, though this longing finds a focus in the object of the narrator's desire. The title itself, "Araby" also suggests escape. To the 19th century European mind, the Islamic lands of North Africa, the Near East, and the Middle East symbolized decadence, exotic delights, escapism, and a luxurious sensuality. The boy's erotic desires for the girl become joined to his fantasies about the wonders that will be offered in the bazaar.
2. Frustration is another theme of the story. The protagonist has a series of romantic ideas about the girl and the wondrous event that he will attend on her behalf. But on the night when he awaits his uncle's return so that he can go to the bazaar, the boy's frustration mounts. When he finally does arrive, the bazaar is more or less over. His fantasies about the

bazaar and buying a great gift for the girl are revealed as ridiculous. The bazaar is a rather tawdry shadow of the boy's dreams. Though his anticipation of the event has provided him with pleasant daydreams, reality is much harsher. He remains a prisoner of his modest means and his city.
3. Unlike the structure of traditional novels, an epiphany is presented in this story. Faced with the vulgar adult world, the boy comes up with a painful epiphany. The boy has caught a glimpse of the truth, not only of the outside world but his own inner world as well.

Suggested Further Reading

1. James Joyce. *Dubliners*, 1914.
2. Clive Hart. ed. *James Joyce's Dubliners: Critical Essays*, 1969.
3. Matthew John Caldwell Hodgart. *James Joyce: A Student's Guide*, London: Routledge & K. Paul, 1978.

Topics for Further Study

1. What is the significance of the title of the story?
2. The story is an initiation story, meaning that the boy experiences growth or a rite of passage, from one stage of his life (e. g. childhood) to another (young adulthood). What do you think the boy has learned?
3. What is the nature of the boy's sudden realization? How does the author help prepare the reader for this sudden realization?

Virginia Woolf
(1882~1941)

About the Author

Virginia Woolf was born in London to Sir Leslie Stephen, a famous scholar, critic and biographer. Virginia and her sister grew up at home, educating themselves in their father's library. Although she lacked formal education, she was, in her early years, much influenced by the famous intellectuals who visited her father.

As early as her childhood she suffered from periods of nervous depression. In 1912, Virginia married Leonard Woolf, who encouraged her to write fiction and helped her by editing her work. In 1915 her first novel

The Voyage Out was published and received enthusiastic welcome from the public. Her second novel, *Night and Day* came out in 1919. She then began experimenting with new ways of writing. Her experimental novels include *Jacob's Room* (1922), *Mrs. Dalloway*(1925), *To The Lighthouse* (1927), *Orlando* (1928) and *The Waves* (1931). These books are noted for their special style that, while limiting the story to a short span of time, combines a stream of consciousness with the accumulation of many details and thus creates a strong feeling of intensity. In her last two novels, *The Years* (1937) and *Between the Acts* (1941), Woolf returned to the realistic world. In her last years of life, Woolf continued to suffer from mental depression. In 1941, she took her own life by drowning in the River Ouse near her home.

Woolf is now generally regarded as one of the greatest innovative novelists of the 20th century, and her techniques, such as the stream of consciousness and interior monologues, have been absorbed into the mainstream of fiction.

★ The Mark on the Wall[1]

About the Story

In this story the narrative seems to be a kind of web, which has captured the stream of thought of the narrator in all its randomness and flights of fancy, in its moment-to-moment consciousness. The narrator is sitting in a chair. She spots a mark on the wall, above the mantelpiece, and she wonders what it might be. She can easily get up and solve the mystery, but from where she is sitting, the mark might be anything. Virginia Woolf was fascinated with the interplay between surface and depth. Thought patterns of consciousness are so various and variegated that each is like a mark on a wall—you can't actually pin it down to any one thing, and trying to come to terms with each of them is like trying to decipher a mark which is just outside of your vision and comprehension.

The static mark and the daydreamer's inactivity are juxtaposed to the mental motion of reflection—covering several pages—on history, reality, society, art, writing, and life itself—incited by the flimsy ruse of an ontological inquiry. The irony of this juxtaposition intensifies at the end of the story, when the mark on the wall is revealed to be a snail, symbol of slow and measured existence.

　　Perhaps it was the middle of January in the present that I first looked up and saw the mark on the wall. In order to fix a date it is necessary to remember what one saw. So now I think of the fire; the steady film of yellow light upon the page of my book; the chrysanthemums[2] in the round glass bowl on the mantelpiece. Yes, it must have been the winter time, and we had just finished our tea, for I remember that I was smoking a cigarette when I looked up and saw the mark on the wall for the first time. I looked up through the smoke of my cigarette and my eye lodged for a moment upon the burning coals, and that old fancy of the crimson flag flapping from the castle tower came into my mind, and I thought of the cavalcade[3] of red knights riding up the side of the black rock. Rather to my relief the sight of the mark interrupted the fancy, for it is an old fancy, an automatic fancy, made as a child perhaps. The mark was a small round mark, black upon the white wall, about six or seven inches above the mantelpiece.

　　How readily our thoughts swarm upon a new object, lifting it a little way, as ants carry a blade of straw so feverishly, and then leave it... If that mark was made by a nail, it can't have been for a picture, it must have been for a miniature—the miniature of a lady with white powdered curls, powder-dusted cheeks, and lips like red carnations[4]. A fraud of course, for the people who had this house before us would have chosen pictures in that way—an old picture for an old room. That is the sort of people they were—very interesting people, and I think of them so often, in such queer places, because one will never see them again, never know what happened next. They wanted to leave this house because they wanted to change their style of furniture, so he said, and he was in process of saying that in his opinion art should have ideas behind it when we were torn asunder, as one is torn from the old lady about to pour out tea and the young man about to hit the tennis ball in the back garden of the suburban villa as one rushes past in the train.

　　But as for that mark, I'm not sure about it; I don't believe it was made by a nail after all; it's too big, too round, for that. I might get up, but if I got up and looked at it, ten to one I shouldn't be able to say for certain; because once a thing's done, no one ever knows how it happened. Oh! dear me, the mystery of life; The inaccuracy of thought! The ignorance of humanity! To show how very little control of our possessions we have—what an accidental affair this living is after all our civilization—let me just count over a few of the things lost in one lifetime, beginning, for that seems always the most mysterious of losses—what cat would gnaw, what rat would nibble—three pale blue canisters[5] of book-binding tools? Then there were the bird cages, the iron hoops, the steel skates, the Queen Anne coal-scuttle[6], the bagatelle[7] board, the hand organ—all gone, and jewels, too. Opals and emeralds, they lie about the roots of turnips. What a scraping paring affair it is to be sure! The wonder is that I've any clothes on my back, that I sit surrounded by solid furniture at this moment. Why, if one wants to compare life to anything, one must liken it to being blown through the Tube[8] at fifty miles an hour—landing at the other end without a single hairpin in one's hair! Shot out at the feet of God entirely naked! Tumbling head over heels in the asphodel meadows[9] like brown paper parcels pitched down a shoot in the post office! With one's hair flying back like the tail of a race-horse. Yes, that seems to express the rapidity of life, the perpetual waste and repair; all so casual, all so haphazard.

But after life. The slow pulling down of thick green stalks so that the cup of the flower, as it turns over, deluges one with purple and red light. Why, after all, should one not be born there as one is born here, helpless, speechless, unable to focus one's eyesight, groping at the roots of the grass, at the toes of the Giants? As for saying which are trees, and which are men and women, or whether there are such things, that one won't be in a condition to do for fifty years or so. There will be nothing but spaces of light and dark, intersected by thick stalks, and rather higher up perhaps, rose-shaped blots of an indistinct color-dim pinks and blues—which will, as time goes on, become more definite, become—I don't know what…

And yet that mark on the wall is not a hole at all. It may even be caused by some round black substance, such as a small rose leaf, left over from the summer, and I, not being a very vigilant housekeeper—look at the dust on the mantelpiece, for example, the dust which, so they say, buried Troy three times over, only fragments of pots utterly refusing annihilation, as one can believe.

The tree outside the window taps very gently on the pane… I want to think quietly, calmly, spaciously, never to be interrupted, never to have to rise from my chair, to slip easily from one thing to another, without any sense of hostility, or obstacle. I want to sink deeper and deeper, away from the surface, with its hard separate facts. To steady myself, let me catch hold of the first idea that passes… Shakespeare… Well, he will do as well as another. A man who sat himself solidly in an arm-chair, and looked into the fire, so—A shower of ideas fell perpetually from some very high Heaven down through his mind. He leant his forehead on his hand, and people, looking in through the open door,—for this scene is supposed to take place on a summer's evening—But how dull this is, this historical fiction! It doesn't interest me at all. I wish I could hit upon a pleasant track of thought, a track indirectly reflecting credit upon myself, for those are the pleasantest thoughts, and very frequent even in the minds of modest mouse-colored people, who believe genuinely that they dislike to hear their own praises. They are not thoughts directly praising oneself; that is the beauty of them; they are thoughts like this:

"And then I came into the room. They were discussing botany. I said how I'd seen a flower growing on a dust heap on the site of an old house in Kingsway[10]. The seed, I said, must have been sown in the reign of Charles the First. What flowers grew in the reign of Charles the First?" I asked—(but, I don't remember the answer). Tall flowers with purple tassels[11] to them perhaps. And so it goes on. All the time I'm dressing up the figure of myself in my own mind, lovingly, stealthily, not openly adoring it, for if I did that, I should catch myself out, and stretch my hand at once for a book in self-protection. Indeed, it is curious how instinctively one protects the image of oneself from idolatry[12] or any other handling that could make it ridiculous, or too unlike the original to be believed in any longer. Or is it not so very curious after all? It is a matter of great importance. Suppose the looking glass smashes, the image disappears, and the romantic figure with the green of forest depths all about it is there no longer, but only that shell of a person which is seen by other people—what an airless, shallow, bald, prominent world it becomes! A world not to be lived in. As we face each other in omnibuses and underground railways we are looking into the mirror that accounts for the vagueness, the gleam of glassiness, in our eyes. And the novelists in future will realize more and more the importance of these reflections, for of course there is not one reflection but an almost infinite number; those are the depths they will explore, those the phantoms they will pursue, leaving the description of reality more and more out of their stories, taking a knowledge of it for granted, as the Greeks did and Shakespeare perhaps—but these generalizations are very worthless. The military sound of the word is enough. It recalls leading articles, cabinet ministers—a whole class of things indeed which as a child one thought the thing itself, the standard thing, the real thing, from which one could not depart save at the risk of nameless damnation. Generalizations bring back somehow Sunday in London, Sunday afternoon walks, Sunday luncheons, and also ways of speaking of the dead, clothes, and habits—like the habit of sitting all together in one room until a certain hour, although nobody liked it. There was a rule for everything. The rule for tablecloths at that particular period was that they should be made of tapestry with little yellow compartments marked upon them, such as you may see in photographs of the carpets in the corridors of the royal palaces. Tablecloths of a different kind were not real tablecloths. How shocking, and yet how wonderful it was to discover that these real things, Sunday luncheons, Sunday walks, country houses, and tablecloths were not entirely real, were indeed half phantoms, and the damnation which visited the disbeliever in them was only a sense of illegitimate freedom. What now takes the place of those things I wonder, those real standard things? Men perhaps, should you be a woman; the masculine point of view which governs our lives, which sets the standard, which establishes Whitaker's Table of Precedency[13], which has become, I suppose, since the war half a phantom to many men and women, which soon—one may hope, will be laughed into the dustbin where the phantoms go, the mahogany[14] sideboards and the Landseer[15] prints, Gods and Devils, Hell and so forth, leaving us all with an intoxicating sense of illegitimate freedom—if freedom exists…

In certain lights that mark on the wall seems actually to project from the wall. Nor is it entirely circular. I cannot be sure, but it seems to cast a perceptible shadow, suggesting that if I ran my finger down that strip of the wall it would, at a certain point, mount and descend a small tumulus, a smooth tumulus like those barrows[16] on the South Downs which are, they say, either tombs or camps. Of the two I should prefer them to be tombs, desiring melancholy like most English people, and finding it natural at the end of a walk to think of the bones stretched beneath the turf… There must be some book about it. Some antiquary must have dug up those bones and given them a name… What sort of a man is an antiquary, I wonder? Retired Colonels for the most part, I daresay, leading parties of aged laborers to the top here, examining clods of earth and stone, and getting into correspondence with the neighboring clergy, which, being opened at breakfast time, gives them a feeling of importance, and the comparison of arrow-heads necessitates cross-country journeys to the county towns, an agreeable necessity both to them and to their elderly wives, who wish to make plum jam or to clean out the study, and have every reason for keeping that great question of the camp or the tomb in perpetual suspension, while the Colonel himself feels agreeably philosophic in accumulating evidence on both sides of the question. It is true that he does finally incline to believe in the camp; and, being opposed, indites a pamphlet which he is about to read at the quarterly meeting of the local society when a stroke lays him low, and his last conscious thoughts are not of wife or child, but of the camp and that arrowhead there, which is now in the case at the local museum, together with the foot of a Chinese murderess, a handful of Elizabethan nails, a great many Tudor clay pipes, a piece of Roman pottery, and the wine-glass that Nelson drank out of—proving I really don't know what.

No, no, nothing is proved, nothing is known. And if I were to get up at this very moment and ascertain that the mark on the wall is really—what shall we say? —the head of a gigantic old nail, driven in two hundred years ago, which has now, owing to the patient attrition[17] of many generations of housemaids, revealed its head above the coat of paint, and is taking its first view of modern life in the sight of a white-walled fire-lit room, what should I gain? —Knowledge? Matter for further speculation? I can think sitting still as well as standing up. And what is knowledge? What are our learned men save the descendants of witches and hermits who crouched in caves and in woods brewing herbs, interrogating shrew-mice and writing down the language of the stars? And the less we honor them as our superstitions dwindle and our respect for beauty and health of mind increases… Yes, one could imagine a very pleasant world. A quiet, spacious world, with the flowers so red and blue in the open fields. A world without professors or specialists or house-keepers with the profiles of policemen, a world which one could slice with one's thought as a fish slices the water with his fin, grazing the stems of the water-lilies, hanging suspended over nests of white sea eggs… How peaceful it is drown here, rooted in the center of the world and gazing up through the gray waters, with their sudden gleams of light, and their reflections—if it were not for Whitaker's Almanack—if it were not for the Table of Precedency!

I must jump up and see for myself what that mark on the wall really is—a nail, a rose-leaf, a crack in the wood?

Here is nature once more at her old game of self-preservation. This train of thought, she perceives, is threatening mere waste of energy, even some collision with reality, for who will ever be able to lift a finger against Whitaker's Table of Precedency? The Archbishop of Canterbury is followed by the Lord High Chancellor; the Lord High Chancellor is followed by the Archbishop of York. Everybody follows somebody, such is the philosophy of Whitaker; and the great thing is to know who follows whom. Whitaker knows, and let that, so Nature counsels, comfort you, instead of enraging you; and if you can't be comforted, if you must shatter this hour of peace, think of the mark on the wall.

I understand Nature's game—her prompting to take action as a way of ending any thought that threatens to excite or to pain. Hence, I suppose, comes our slight contempt for men of action—men, we assume, who don't think. Still, there's no harm in putting a full stop to one's disagreeable thoughts by looking at a mark on the wall.

Indeed, now that I have fixed my eyes upon it, I feel that I have grasped a plank in the sea; I feel a satisfying sense of reality which at once turns the two Archbishops and the Lord High Chancellor to the shadows of shades. Here is something definite, something real. Thus, waking from a midnight dream of horror, one hastily turns on the light and lies quiescent, worshipping the chest of drawers, worshipping solidity, worshipping reality, worshipping the impersonal world which is a proof of some existence other than ours. That is what one wants to be sure of... Wood is a pleasant thing to think about. It comes from a tree; and trees grow, and we don't know how they grow. For years and years they grow, without paying any attention to us, in meadows, in forests, and by the side of rivers—all things one likes to think about. The cows swish their tails beneath them on hot afternoons; they paint rivers so green that when a moorhen dives one expects to see its feathers all green when it comes up again. I like to think of the fish balanced against the stream like flags blown out; and of water-beetles slowly raiding domes of mud upon the bed of the river. I like to think of the tree itself:—first the close dry sensation of being wood; then the grinding of the storm; then the slow, delicious ooze of sap. I like to think of it, too, on winter's nights standing in the empty field with all leaves close-furled, nothing tender exposed to the iron bullets of the moon, a naked mast upon an earth that goes tumbling, tumbling, all night long. The song of birds must sound very loud and strange in June; and how cold the feet of insects must feel upon it, as they make laborious progresses up the creases of the bark, or sun themselves upon the thin green awning of the leaves, and look straight in front of them with diamond-cut red eyes... One by one the fibers snap beneath the immense cold pressure of the earth, then the last storm comes and, falling, the highest branches drive deep into the ground again. Even so, life isn't done with; there are a million patient, watchful lives still for a tree, all over the world, in bedrooms, in ships, on the pavement, lining rooms, where men and women sit after tea, smoking cigarettes. It is full of peaceful thoughts, happy thoughts, this tree. I should like to take each one separately-but something is getting in the way... Where was I? What has it all been about? A tree? A river? The Downs? Whitaker's Almanack? The fields of asphodel? I can't remember a thing. Everything's moving, falling, slipping, vanishing... There is a vast upheaval of matter. Someone is standing over me and saying—

"I'm going out to buy a newspaper."

"Yes?"

"Though it's no good buying newspapers... Nothing ever happens... Curse this war; God damn this war! ... All the same, I don't see why we should have a snail on our wall."

Ah, the mark on the wall! It was a snail.

Notes

1. This is a classic example of a modernist short story. On the simplest of pretexts, a mark on a wall, the narrator presents us with an organized narrative about how it got there or its significance but with an account of the reflections induced by it, most of which seem to be unrelated to the mark or its meaning.
2. chrysanthemums: a kind of flower.
3. cavalcade: a procession of riders or horse-drawn carriages.
4. carnations: any of numerous cultivated forms of a perennial plant having showy, variously colored, usually double, often fragrant flowers with fringed petals.
5. canister: a box or can of thin metal or plastic used for holding dry cooking ingredients, such as flour, sugar, or tea.
6. scuttle: a small opening or hatch with a movable lid in the deck or hull of a ship or in the roof, wall, or floor of a building.
7. bagatelle: a game played on an oblong table with a cue and balls.

8. Tube: London underground railway.
9. asphodel meadows: here referring to heaven, the next world (in Greek mythology, asphodel flowers grow in the Elysian fields).
10. Kingsway: a street in London.
11. tassel: a bunch of loose threads or cords bound at one end and hanging free at the other, used as an ornament on curtains or clothing, for example.
12. idolatry: worship of idols.
13. Whitaker's Table of Precedency: Whitaker's Almanack, an annual compendium of information, prints a "Table of Precedency", which shows the order in which the various ranks in public life and society proceed on formal occasions.
14. mahogany: the wood of any of these mahogany trees, used in making furniture.
15. Landseer: Edwin Henry Landseer, 19th century animal painter, reproductions of whose "Stag at Bay" "Monarch of the Glen" and similar painting were often found in Victorian homes.
16. barrows: mounds of earth or stones erected by prehistoric peoples, usually as burial places; the South Downs are a range of low hills in southeastern England.
17. attrition: a rubbing away or wearing down by friction.

Questions for Understanding

1. What do you learn about the narrator's past and her own feeling of the past?
2. The narrator says "Everything's moving, falling, slipping, vanishing... There is a vast upheaval of matter". What does she refer to? How do you understand the idea?
3. The narrator says "What an accidental affair this living is after all our civilization..." What does she mean by this statement in the context of her narrative?
4. What is the "moment of being" in this story? What does the mark on the wall turn out to be? Why is this significant?

Aspects of Appreciation

1. "The Mark on the Wall" is a classic example of a modernist short story. On one level, it is a humorous record of one mildly eccentric woman's

thoughts as she sits by the fire on a winter's day. Yet on another level, the thoughts this woman has and more importantly, the way she thinks of them, amount to a manifesto for modern literature. In Woolf's view, traditional narrative form cannot do justice to the tumultuous randomness of life. A novel that commences cleanly, unfolds a sequence of events logically and evenly, and concludes unambiguously, is too similar in its structure to "Whitaker's Almanack" with its "Table of Precedency" that explains the various ranks of society must comport themselves in public life.

On the simplest of pretexts, a mark on a wall, the narrator presents us not with an organized account of the reflections induced by it, most of which seem to be unrelated to the mark or its meaning. Throughout the story, Woolf has violated standard fictional techniques of coherence and logic, the most obvious violation being the lack of plot structure. That is, in this story, Woolf attempts to "distance the reader from codes of expected narrative and from patterns of response that had seemed to command universal or natural status".

2. Virginia Woolf is recognized as one of the great innovators of modern fiction. Her experiments with point of view and her use of stream of consciousness have influenced many writers that follow her. But one particular interesting technique that does not seem to receive much attention is her use of the "moment of being".

Woolf never explicitly defines what she means by the "moment of being". For Woolf, a moment of being is a moment when an individual is fully conscious of his experience, a moment when he is not only aware of himself but catches a glimpse of his connection to a larger pattern hidden behind the opaque surface of daily life. Unlike the moment of non-being, when the individual lives and acts without awareness, performing acts as if asleep, the moment of being opens up a hidden reality.

The moment of being can be found throughout Woolf's fiction. These are often moments of intense power and beauty. Unlike Joyce's epiphanies, these moments do not lead to decisive revelations for her characters. But they provide moments of energy and awareness that allow the character who experiences them to see life more clearly and more fully, if only briefly. And some of the characters try to share the vision that they glimpse, making the work of art that is life visible to others.

For Woolf, the significance of moments of being is: they reveal to the individual who experiences them the pattern behind the woolly curtain of existence; and the existence of a pattern reveals the possibility of connection to other people. When one experiences a moment with full consciousness, one experiences the true intensity of life. These moments of being can be read as brief poems hidden among the trivial details of life that some characters are fortunate enough to experience.

3. Themes in Virginia Woolf's works include gender relations, class hierarchy and the consequences of war. In her expression, she often moves away from the use of plot and structure to experiment with stream of consciousness, the underlying psychological as well as emotional motives of characters, and the various possibilities of fractured narrative and chronology to emphasize the psychological aspects of her characters. *Mrs. Dalloway* and *To the Lighthouse* are brilliant examples of novels of modernism.

Suggested Further Reading

1. Virginia Woolf. *Mrs. Dalloway*(1925), *To the Lighthouse* (1927).
2. Hermione Lee. *Virginia Woolf*. New York: A. A. Knopf, 1997.

Topics for Further Study

1. How is the story different from a traditional one?
2. What does the author say about modern life and modern man in the story?
3. What is the theme of the story?

VIII Contemporary Period

William Golding
(1911~1993)

About the Author

Golding was born in a small village in Cornwall, and educated at Marlborough Grammar School and Oxford. Golding followed his parents' wishes to study natural sciences until his second year at Oxford, when he changed his focus on to English literature. After graduation, he worked briefly as a theatre actor and director, and producer with small theatre companies, and then as a teacher of English. He published his first work as a volume, *Poems* in 1935. During World War II, he served in the Royal Navy in command of a rocket ship and participated in the battle of Normandy.

After the war, Golding resumed teaching and started to write novels. His experience in World War II had a profound influence on his view of life, and he felt doubtful about human innocence, and revealed the dark side of human heart in many of his works. His first novel, *Lord of the Flies*, appeared in 1954 after it had been rejected by 21 publishers. It was an immediate success, the sales of which enabled Golding to retire from teaching and devote himself fully to writing. His other works include *The Inheritors* (1955), *Pincher Martin* (1956), *The Brass Butterfly* (play, 1958), *Free Fall* (1959), *The Pyramid* (1967), *Darkness Visible* (1979) and *Rites of Passage* (1980).

His work is characterized by the exploration of the darkness of human beings and spiritual and ethical questions. A recurrent theme of his works is the conflict between humanity's intrinsic cruelty and the civilized "superego". His novels tend to reveal the dark side of human nature, especially in the face of difficulty and being left alone. Not even children are innocent.

Golding is good at making use of allusions, mythology and Christian symbolism, making his fiction allegorical. The symbolism of his novels is often more important than action. His characters, images, and settings go beyond the merely literal surface to interpret universal truths about human nature.

Golding was awarded the Booker Prize for literature in 1980 for his novel *Rites of Passage*, and the Nobel Prize for literature in 1983. He was also knighted in 1983. He left his last novel *The Double Tongue* in draft (published in 1995) when he died on June 19, 1993. Golding was one of the most acclaimed writers of the second half of the 20th century.

★ Lord of the Flies

About the Novel

During an unnamed time of war, an aeroplane carrying a party of schoolboys, about 6 to 12 years old, crashes on a desert island, but many of the boys survive the crash. Ralph and Piggy obtain a conch and use it to call the other boys from across the island. Ralph is chosen to be their leader by vote. Jack acts as leader of the other castaway members of his choir, and covets the leadership position. Ralph and Piggy lead the boys with attempt to set up a democratic society. Jack leads his choir to hunt for food. The youngest of the boys, generally known as "littluns", spend most of the day searching for fruit to eat. One day, a ship passes by the island, but does not stop because the fire has burned out. Piggy blames Jack for letting the fire die. Jack punches Piggy, and breaks one piece of the lens of his glasses. A little boy named Phil tells how he had a nightmare and when he awoke, he saw something moving among the trees. Simon admits that Phil probably saw him, for he was walking in the jungle that night. They begin to worry about the supposed beast.

A pilot parachutes down the island, and dies. The next morning the twins Sam and Eric see the pilot and assume that the pilot is the Beastie. Jack leaves the group to create a new tribe. Most of the older boys eventually join him. Jack and the hunters kill a pig, and they cut off the head and leave it on a stick as an offering for the beast. Simon finds the pig's head, and he dubs it the Lord of the Flies because of the insects swarming around it. When he sees the dead pilot, he realizes this is what other boys perceived to be the beast. He rushes down the mountain to alert others of his finding. The boys take him as the beast, and kill him. Ralph and Piggy took part in the murder, but try to justify their behaviour as acting out of fear and instinct. Ralph, Piggy, and the twins, Sam and Eric do not join Jack's tribe, but work on keeping the fire going by themselves.

The four boys go to appeal Jack as civilized people. Jack takes Sam and Eric as prisoners and orders them to be tied up. Piggy is killed by a rolling rock tipped by a hunter boy. Jack declares himself chief. Ralph runs away, and hides himself near the castle rock. The next day, his tribe tries to hunt him down, and set a forest fire, which is seen by a passing naval vessel, and one of the ship's officers comes ashore and rescues the boys. For the first time on the island, Ralph cries, weeping for the "end of innocence" "darkness of man's heart", and his dead friend, Piggy.

Chapter 9
A View to a Death

Over the island the build-up of clouds continued. A steady current of heated air rose all day from the mountain and was thrust to ten thousand feet; revolving masses of gas piled up the static until the air was ready to explode. By early evening the sun had gone and a brassy glare had taken the place of clear daylight. Even the air that pushed in from the sea was hot and held no refreshment. Colors drained from water and trees and pink surfaces of rock, and the white and brown clouds brooded. Nothing prospered but the flies who blackened their lord and made the spilt guts look like a heap of glistening coal. Even when the vessel broke in Simon's nose and the blood gushed out they left him alone, preferring the pig's high flavor.

With the running of the blood, Simon's fit passed into the weariness of sleep. He lay in the mat of creepers while the evening advanced and the cannon continued to play. At last he woke and saw dimly the dark earth close by his cheek. Still he did not move but lay there, his face sideways on the earth, his eyes looking dully before him. Then he turned over, drew his feet under him and laid hold of the creepers to pull himself up. When the creepers shook the flies exploded from the guts with a vicious¹ note and clamped back on again. Simon got to his feet. The light was unearthly². The Lord of the Flies hung on his stick like a black ball.

Simon spoke aloud to the clearing.

"What else is there to do?"

Nothing replied. Simon turned away from the open space and crawled through the creepers till he was in the dusk of the forest. He walked drearily between the trunks, his face empty of expression, and the blood was dry round his mouth and chin. Only sometimes as he lifted the ropes of creeper aside and chose his direction from the trend of the land, he mouthed words that did not reach the air.

Presently the creepers festooned the trees less frequently and there was a scatter of pearly light from the sky down through the trees. This was the backbone of the island, the slightly higher land that lay beneath the mountain where the forest was no longer deep jungle. Here there were wide spaces interspersed³ with thickets⁴ and huge trees and the trend of the ground led him up as the forest opened. He pushed on, staggering sometimes with his weariness but never stopping. The usual brightness was gone from his eyes and he walked with a sort of glum⁵ determination like an old man.

A buffet of wind made him stagger and he saw that he was out in the open, on rock, under a brassy sky. He found his legs were weak and his tongue gave him pain all the time. When the wind reached the mountain-top he could see something happen, a flicker of blue stuff against brown clouds. He pushed himself forward and the wind came again, stronger now, cuffing⁶ the forest heads till they ducked and roared. Simon saw a humped thing suddenly sit up on the top and look down at him. He hid his face, and toiled on.

The flies had found the figure too. The life-like movement would scare them off for a moment so that they made a dark cloud round the head. Then as the blue material of the parachute collapsed the corpulent⁷ figure would bow forward, sighing, and the flies settle once more.

Simon felt his knees smack the rock. He crawled forward and soon he understood. The tangle of lines showed him the mechanics of this parody;

he examined the white nasal bones, the teeth, the colors of corruption. He saw how pitilessly the layers of rubber and canvas[8] held together the poor body that should be rotting away. Then the wind blew again and the figure lifted, bowed, and breathed foully at him. Simon knelt on all fours and was sick[9] till his stomach was empty. Then he took the lines in his hands; he freed them from the rocks and the figure from the wind's indignity.

At last he mined away and looked down at the beaches. The fire by the platform appeared to be out, or at least making no smoke. Further along the beach, beyond the little river and near a great slab of rock, a thin trickle of smoke was climbing into the sky. Simon, forgetful of the flies, shaded his eyes with both hands and peered at the smoke. Even at that distance it was possible to see that most of the boys—perhaps all the boys—were there. So they had shifted camp then, away from the beast. As Simon thought this, he turned to the poor broken thing that sat stinking by his side. The beast was harmless and horrible; and the news must reach the others as soon as possible. He started down the mountain and his legs gave beneath him. Even with great care the best he could do was a stagger.

"Bathing," said Ralph, "that's the only thing to do."

Piggy was inspecting the looming sky through his glass.

"I don't like them clouds. Remember how it rained just after we landed!"

"Going to rain again."

Ralph dived into the pool. A couple of littluns were playing at the edge, trying to extract comfort from a wetness warmer than blood. Piggy took off his glasses, stepped primly into the water and then put them on again. Ralph came to the surface and squirted[10] a jet of water at him.

"Mind my specs," said Piggy. "If I get water on the glass I got to get out and clean 'em."

Ralph squirted again and missed. He laughed at Piggy, expecting him to retire meekly as usual and in pained silence. Instead, Piggy beat the water with his hands. "Stop it!" he shouted. "D'you hear?"

Furiously he drove the water into Ralph's face.

"All right, all fight," said Ralph. "Keep your hair on".

Piggy stopped beating the water.

"I got a pain in my head. I wish the air was cooler."

"I wish the rain would come."

"I wish we could go home."

Piggy lay back against the sloping sand side of the pool. His stomach protruded and the water dried on it. Ralph squirted up at the sky. One could guess at the movement of the sun by the progress of a light patch among the clouds. He knelt in the water and looked round.

"Where's everybody?"

Piggy sat up.

"P'raps they're lying in the shelter."

"Where's Samneric?"

"And Bill?"

Piggy pointed beyond the platform.

"That's where they've gone. Jack's party."

"Let them go," said Ralph, uneasily, "I don't care."

"Just for some meat—"

"And for hunting," said Ralph, wisely, "and for pretending to be a tribe, and putting on war-paint."

Piggy stirred the sand under water and did not look at Ralph.

"P'raps we ought to go too."

Ralph looked at him quickly and Piggy blushed.

"I mean—to make sure nothing happens."

Ralph squirted water again.

Long before Ralph and Piggy came up with Jack's lot, they could hear the party. There was a stretch of grass in a place where the palms left a wide band of turf[11] between the forest and the shore. Just one step down from the edge of the turf was the white, blown sand of above high water, warm, dry, trodden. Below that again was a rock that stretched away towards the lagoon. Beyond was a short stretch of sand and then the edge of the water. A fire burned on the rock and fat dripped from the roasting pig-meat into the invisible flames. All the boys of the island, except Piggy, Ralph, Simon, and the two tending the pig, were grouped on the turf. They were laughing, singing, lying, squatting, or standing on the grass, holding food in their hands. But to judge by the greasy faces, the meat-eating was almost done; and some held coco-nut shells in their hands and were drinking from them. Before the party had started a great log had been dragged into the center of the lawn and Jack, painted and garlanded[12], sat there like an idol. There were piles of meat on green leaves near him, and fruit, and coco-nut shells full of drink.

Piggy and Ralph came to the edge of the grassy platform and the boys, as they noticed them, fell silent one by one till only the boy next to Jack was talking. Then the silence intruded even there and Jack turned where he sat. For a time he looked at them and the crackle of the fire was the loudest noise over the bourdon of the reef. Ralph looked away; and Sam, thinking that Ralph had turned to him accusingly, put down his gnawed bone with a nervous giggle. Ralph took an uncertain step, pointed to a palm tree, and whispered something inaudible to Piggy; and they both giggled like Sam. Lifting his feet high out of the sand, Ralph started to stroll past. Piggy tried to whistle.

At this moment the boys who were cooking at the fire suddenly hauled off a great chunk of meat and ran with it towards the grass. They bumped Piggy who was burnt, and yelled and danced. Immediately, Ralph and the crowd of boys were united and relieved by a storm of laughter. Piggy once more was the center of social derision so that everyone felt cheerful and normal.

Jack stood up and waved his spear.

"Take them some meat."

The boys with the spit gave Ralph and Piggy each a succulent[13] chunk. They took the gift, dribbling. So they stood and ate beneath a sky of thunderous brass that rang with the storm-coming.

Jack waved his spear again.

"Has everybody eaten as much as they want?"

There was still food left, sizzling on the wooden spits, heaped on the green platter. Betrayed by his stomach, Piggy threw a picked bone down on the beach and stooped for more.

Jack spoke again, impatiently.

"Has everybody eaten as much as they want?"

His tone conveyed a warning, given out of the pride of ownership, and the boys ate faster while there was still time. Seeing there was no immediate likelihood of a pause, Jack rose from the log that was his throne and sauntered to the edge of the grass. He looked down from behind his paint at Ralph and Piggy. They moved a little further off over the sand and Ralph watched the fire as he ate. He noticed without understanding, how the flames were visible now against the dull light. Evening was come, not with calm beauty, but with the threat of violence.

Jack spoke.

"Give me a drink."

Henry brought him a shell and he drank, watching Piggy and Ralph over the jagged rim. Power lay in the brown swell of his forearms: authority sat on his shoulder and chattered in his ear like an ape.

"All sit down."

The boys ranged themselves in rows on the grass before him but Ralph and Piggy stayed a foot lower, standing on the soft sand. Jack ignored them for the moment, turned his mask down to the seated boys and pointed at them with the spear.

"Who is going to join my tribe?"

Ralph made a sudden movement that became a stumble. Some of the boys turned towards him.

"I gave you food," said Jack, "and my hunters will protect you from the beast. Who will join my tribe?"

"I'm chief," said Ralph, "because you chose me. And we were going to keep the fire going. Now you run after food—"

"You ran yourself!" shouted Jack. "Look at that bone in your hands!"

Ralph went crimson.

"I said you were hunters. That was your job."

Jack ignored him again.

"Who'll join my tribe and have fun?"

"I'm chief," said Ralph tremulously. "And what about the fire? And I've got the conch—"

"You haven't got it with you," said Jack, sneering. "You left it behind. See, clever? And the conch doesn't count at this end of the island—"

All at once the thunder struck. Instead of the dull boom there was a point of impact in the explosion.

"The conch counts here too," said Ralph, "and all over the island."

"What are you going to do about it then?"

Ralph examined the ranks of boys. There was no help in them and he looked away, confused and sweating. Piggy whispered.

"The fire—rescue."

"Who'll join my tribe?"

"I will."

"Me."

"I will."

"I'll blow the conch," said Ralph breathlessly, "and call an assembly."

"We shan't hear it."

Piggy touched Ralph's wrist.

"Come away. There's going to be trouble. And we've had our meat."

There was a blink of bright light beyond the forest and the thunder exploded again so that a littlun started to whine[14]. Big drops of rain fell among them making individual sounds when they struck.

"Going to be a storm," said Ralph, "and you'll have rain like when we dropped here. Who's clever now? Where are your shelters? What are you going to do about that?"

The hunters were looking uneasily at the sky, flinching from the stroke of the drops. A wave of restlessness set the boys swaying and moving aimlessly. The flickering light became brighter and the blows of the thunder were only just bearable. The littluns began to run about, screaming.

Jack leapt on to the sand.

"Do our dance! Come on! Dance!"

He ran stumbling through the thick sand to the open space of rock beyond the fire. Between the flashes of lightning the air was dark and terrible; and the boys followed him, clamorously. Roger became the pig, grunting and charging at Jack, who side-stepped. The hunters took their spears, the cooks took spits, and the rest clubs of fire-wood. A circling movement developed and a chant. While Roger mimed the terror of the pig, the littluns ran and jumped on the outside of the circle. Piggy and Ralph, under the threat of the sky, found themselves eager to take a place in this demented[15] but partly secure society. They were glad to touch the brown backs of the fence that hemmed in the terror and made it governable.

"Kill the beast! Cut his throat! Spill his blood!"

The movement became regular while the chant lost its first superficial excitement and began to beat like a steady pulse. Roger ceased to be a pig and became a hunter, so that the center of the ring yawned emptily. Some of the littluns started a ring on their own; and the complementary circles went round and round as though repetition would achieve safety of itself. There was the throb and stamp of a single organism.

The dark sky was shattered by a blue-white scar. An instant later the noise was on them like the blow of a gigantic whip. The chant rose a tone in agony.

"Kill the beast! Cut his throat! Spill his blood!"

Now out of the terror rose another desire, thick, urgent, blind.

"Kill the beast! Cut his throat! Spill his blood!"

Again the blue-white scar jagged above them and the sulfurous explosion beat down. The littluns screamed and blundered about, fleeing from the edge of the forest, and one of them broke the ring of biguns in his terror.

"Him! Him!"

The circle, became a horseshoe. A thing was crawling out of the forest. It came darkly, uncertainly. The shrill screaming that rose before the beast was like a pain. The beast stumbled into the horseshoe.

"Kill the beast! Cut his throat! Spill his blood!"

The blue-white scar was constant, the noise unendurable. Simon was crying out something about a dead man on a hill.

"Kill the beast! Cut his throat! Spill his blood! Do him in!"

The sticks fell and the mouth of the new circle crunched and screamed. The beast was on its knees in the center, its arms folded over its face. It was crying out against the abominable noise, something about a body on the hill. The beast struggled forward, broke the ring and fell over the steep edge of the rock to the sand by the water. At once the crowd surged after it, poured down the rock, leapt on to the beast, screamed, struck, bit, tore. There were no words and no movements but the tearing of teeth and claws.

Then the clouds opened and let down the rain like a waterfall. The water bounded from the mountain-top, tore leaves and branches from the trees, poured like a cold shower over the struggling heap on the sand. Presently the heap broke up and figures staggered away. Only the beast lay still, a few yards from the sea. Even in the rain they could see how small a beast it was; and already its blood was staining the sand.

Now a great wind blew the rain sideways, cascading the water from the forest trees. On the mountain-top the parachute filled and moved; the figure slid, rose to its feet, spun, swayed down through a vastness of wet air and trod with ungainly[16] feet the tops of the high trees; falling, still falling, it sank towards the beach and the boys rushed screaming into the darkness. The parachute took the figure forward, furrowing the lagoon, and bumped it over the reef and out to sea.

Toward midnight the rain ceased and the clouds drifted away, so that the sky was scattered once more with the incredible lamps of stars. Then the breeze died too and there was no noise save the drip and trickle of water that ran out of clefts[17] and spilled down, leaf by leaf, to the brown earth of the island. The air was cool, moist, and clear; and presently even the sound of the water was still. The beast lay huddled on the pale beach and the stains spread, inch by inch.

The edge of the lagoon became a streak of phosphorescence[18] which advanced minutely, as the great wave of the tide flowed. The clear water mirrored the clear sky and the angular bright constellations. The line of phosphorescence bulged about the sand grains and little pebbles; it held them each in a dimple of tension, then suddenly accepted them with an inaudible syllable and moved on.

Along the shoreward edge of the shallows the advancing clearness was full of strange, moonbeam-bodied creatures with fiery eyes. Here and there a larger pebble clung to its own air and was covered with a coat of pearls. The tide swelled in over the rain-pitted sand and smoothed everything with a layer of silver. Now it touched the first of the stains that seeped from the broken body and the creatures made a moving patch of light as they gathered at the edge. The water rose farther and dressed Simon's coarse hair with brightness. The line of his cheek silvered and the turn of his shoulder became sculptured marble. The strange attendant creatures, with their fiery eyes and trailing vapors, busied themselves round his head. The body lifted a fraction of an inch from the sand and a bubble of air escaped from the mouth with a wet plop. Then it turned gently in the water.

Somewhere over the darkened curve of the world the sun and moon were pulling, and the film of water on the earth planet was held, bulging slightly on one side while the solid core turned. The great wave of the tide moved farther along the island and the water lifted. Softly, surrounded by a fringe of inquisitive bright creatures, itself a silver shape beneath the steadfast constellations, Simon's dead body moved out toward the open sea.

Notes

1. vicious: cruel; having or showing hate and the desire to hurt.
2. unearthly: not natural; as if of a spiritual world; ghostly.
3. interspersed: to set(something) here and there among other things.
4. thickets: a thick growth of bushes and small trees.
5. glum: sad; in low spirits, especially because of disappointment.
6. cuffing: to strike (a person or animal) lightly with the open hand.

7. corpulent: very fat.
8. canvas: strong rough cloth used for tents, sails, bags, etc.
9. sick: upset in the stomach, so as to want to throw up what is in it; nauseated.
10. squirted: to hit or cover with such a stream of liquid.
11. turf: the surface of the soil with the grass and roots growing in it.
12. garlanded: to put one or more circle of flowers, leaves on someone.
13. succulent: thick and fleshy.
14. whine: to complain (too much) in an unnecessarily sad voice.
15. demented: mad; of unbalanced mind.
16. ungainly: not graceful; awkward in movement; clumsy.
17. clefts: a space, crack, opening, or split.
18. phosphorescence: the giving out of light with little or no heat.

Questions for Understanding

1. What does Simon do to the figure on the mountainside?
2. Why does Simon want so badly to talk to the boys?
3. How do Jack's leadership style and personality differ from Ralph's?
4. Who emerges from the jungle with the secret of the beast?
5. Under what circumstances does Simon die?

Aspects of Appreciation

1. Themes and major characters

Lord of the Flies has been interpreted in varying ways over the years since its publication. During the 1950s and 1960s, many readings of the novel claimed that *Lord of the Flies* dramatizes the history of civilization. Some believe that the novel explores some fundamental religious issues. Others approach the novel through the theories of the psychoanalyst Sigmund Freud, who advocates that human mind is the site of a constant battle among different impulses—the id (instinctual needs and desires), the ego (the conscious, rational mind) and the superego (the sense of conscience and morality). Still others maintain that Golding writes the novel as a criticism of the political and social institutions of the West.

First of all, *Lord of the Flies* is an allegorical novel, and the characters and objects in the novel are infused with symbolic significance that conveys the novel's central themes and ideas.

Ralph represents order, leadership, and civilization. Piggy represents the scientific and intellectual aspects of civilization. Jack represents unbridled savagery and the desire for power. Simon represents natural human goodness. Roger represents brutality and blood lust at the most extreme. Sam and Eric are a pair of twins closely allied with Ralph. They fall victim to Jack's manipulation and coercion.

To the extent that the boys' society resembles a political state, the littluns might be seen as the common people, while the older boys represent the ruling classes and political leaders. The relationships that develop between the older boys and the younger ones emphasize the older boys' connection to either the civilized or the savage instinct: civilized boys like Ralph and Simon use their power to protect the younger boys and advance the good of the group; savage boys like Jack and Roger use their power to gratify their own desires, treating the littluns as objects for their own amusement.

2. Golding prefers *Lord of the Flies* to be called "a fable", which it certainly is. A fable is a veiled story about the truth of human existence. It is generally, as is the case with *Aesop's Fables*, timeless and placeless because of the universally applicable nature of the verities revealed. Golding's fable here is one about the nature of man. Instead of recreating and replicating their civilized way of life in a new, bleak environment as Robinson Crusoe does, the boys of *Lord of the Flies* simply return to the primitive, pristine state of human existence and mentality, and repeats the dark, tragic side of human history of tyranny, violence, fanaticism, intolerance, and confrontation. Thirsty for power and blood, and resorting to barbaric rituals and superstitions, they fight and kill each other, thus revealing the naked heart of darkness that exists at the center of their beings. This is probably what the title of the book means.

Suggested Further Reading

Mark Kinkead-Weekes and Ian Gregor. *William Golding: A Critical Study of the Novels* (Third Edition). Faber and Faber, 2002.

Topics for Further Study

1. What is the significance of the figure of the beast in the novel?
2. There are many symbols in this novel. Point out the symbols in the selection and state their significance.

3. In what way is *Lord of the Flies* a novel about power? How about the power of symbols? How about the power of a person to use symbols to control a group?

Doris Lessing
(1919~2013)

About the Author

Doris Lessing, the winner of 2007 Nobel Prize for Literature, is one of the most successful prolific British novelists of the recent decades. She was born in Persia (now Iran) of British parents and lived in Rhodesia (now Zimbabwe) until she settled down in England in 1949. Basically a realist, she took interest in writing in the mythic mode in the 1970s. In the 1980s she reverted back to the realistic mode, though still exhibiting some traces of fantasy at times. Since 1990s, she has been writing a good number of short stories. Doris Lessing's themes are wide and varied: social problems, political concerns, racial questions and feminist views on life and love relationships, but she focuses mostly on black-white relations and on the life of the woman in a male-oriented world. Her commitment to life and society is evident in all her fiction. Her major works include the five novels of her *Children of Violence* series (1952~1969), *The Golden Notebook* (1962), *Briefing for a Descent into Hell* (1971), *Canopus in Argos: Archives* (1979~1983), *The Diaries of Jane Somers* (1983~1984), *The Fifth Child* (1988), and many volumes of short stories such as *A Man and Two Women*.

Given the multinational background of her upbringing, Lessing is always attracted to the spiritual and cultural resources of other nations. Her interesting mystic belief systems, particularly the Islamic Sufism, have inspired some of her later works, among which are a series of science fiction.

She died peacefully at home in London on November 17, 2013.

★ A Road to the Big City

About the Work

The story takes place in Johannesburg and describes two country girls who are willing to be deluded by the false values of the city life.

Jansen, a middle-aged traveler has to stay for several hours in Johannesburg, a modern city in South Africa because of a mistake in his train ticket. As he sits at a station restaurant, two young girls come up to him. Marie has just arrived in the city. She has run away from home with money sent by her sister Lilla, who is obviously a prostitute. They had a poor life back at home, for their father works as a railway worker. Lured by the city life, Lilla left home a year ago for a big city and wrote letters home about her wonderful job and comfortable life. Lilla wants to turn her innocent sister Marie into a prostitute, too. When they meet Jansen, Lilla makes her younger sister, Marie, tempt the young man. But Jansen warns Marie what will happen to her. Marie does not understand his words, being too excited by the luxurious new life she is seeing for the first time in the city. Jansen decides to save Marie, and takes her to the railway station, where he himself must also catch a train. He buys her a ticket, gives her some money and finds her a seat, then goes to find his own train. From the window he sees Marie running back to the city even though she now understands what is in store for her.

The social problems in big cities and the moral decay of the young generation that the author focuses on are fully revealed in the story.

The train left at midnight, not at six. Jansen's flare of temper[1] at the clerk's mistake died before he turned from the counter: he did not really mind. For a week he had been with rich friends, in a vacuum of wealth[2], politely seeing the town through their eyes[3]. Now, for six hours, he was free to let the dry and nervous air of Johannesburg strike him direct[4]. He went into the station buffet. It was a bare place, with shiny brown walls and tables arranged regularly. He sat before a cup of strong orange-coloured tea, and because he was in the arrested, dreamy frame of mind of the uncommitted traveller[5], he was the spectator at a play which could not hold his attention. He was about to leave, in order to move by himself through the streets, among the people, trying to feel what they were in this city, what they had which did not exist, perhaps, in other big cities—for he believed that in every place there dwelt a daemon[6] which expressed itself through the eyes and voices of those who lived there—when he heard someone ask: Is this place free? He turned quickly, for there was a quality in the voice which could not be mistaken. Two girls stood beside him, and the one who had spoken sat down without waiting for his response; there were many empty tables in the room. She wore a tight short black dress, several brass chains, and high shiny black shoes. She was a tall broad girl with colorless hair ridged tightly round her head, but given a bright surface so that it glinted like metal. She immediately lit a cigarette and said to her companion: "Sit down for God's sake." The other girl shyly slid into the chair next to Jansen, averting her face as he gazed at her, which he could not help doing; she was so different from what he expected. Plump, childish, with dull hair bobbing in fat roils on her neck, she wore flowered and flounced dress and flat white sandals on bare and sunburned feet. Her face had the jolly friendliness of a little dog. Both girls showed Dutch ancestry[7] in—the broad blunt planes of cheek and forehead; both had small blue eyes, though one pair was surrounded by sandy lashes and the other by black varnished fringes.

The waitress came for an order. Jansen was too curious about the young girl to move away. "What will you have?" he asked. "Brandy," said the older one at once. "Two brandies," she added, with another impatient look at her sister—there could be no doubt that they were sisters.

"I haven't never drunk brandy," said the younger with a giggle of surprise. "Except when Mon gave me some sherry at Christmas." She blushed as the older said despairingly, half under her breath, "Oh God preserve me from it!"

"I came to Johannesburg this morning," said the little one to Jansen confidingly. "But Lilla has been here earning a living for a year."

"My God!" said Lilla again. "What did I tell you? Didn't you hear what I told you?" Then, making the best of it, she smiled professionally[8] at Jansen and said, "Green[9]! You wouldn't believe it if I told you. I was green when I came, but compared with Marie…" She laughed angrily.

"Have you been to Joburg before this day?" asked Marie in her confiding way.

"You are passing through," stated Lilla, with a glance at Marie. "You can tell easy if you know how to look."

"You're quite right," said Jansen.

"Leaving tomorrow perhaps?" asked Lilla.

"Tonight," said Jansen.

Instantly Lilla's eyes left Jansen, and began to rove about her, resting on one man's face and then the next. "Midnight," said Jansen, in order to see her expression change.

"There's plenty time," she said, smiling.

"Lilla promised I could go to the bioscope[10]," said Marie, her eyes becoming large. She looked around the station buffet, and because of her way of looking, Jansen tried to see it differently. He could. It remained for him a bare, brownish, dirty sort of place, full of badly-dressed and dull people. He felt as one does with a child whose eyes widen with terror or delight at the sight of an old woman muttering down the street, or a flowering tree. What hunched black crone from fairy tale, what celestial tree does the child see? Marie was smiling with charmed amazement.

"Very well," said Jansen, "let's go to the flicks."

For a moment Lilla calculated, her hard blue glance moving from Jansen to Marie. "You take Marie," she suggested, direct to Jansen, ignoring her sister. "She's green, but she's learning." Marie half-rose with a terrified look. "You can't leave me," she said.

"Oh my God!" said Lilla resignedly. "Oh all right, Sit down baby. But I've a friend to see I told you."

"But I only just came."

"All right, all right, sit down." I said. "He won't bite you."

"Where do you come from?" asked Jansen.

Marie said a name he had never heard.

"It's not far from Bloemfontein," explained Lilla.

"I went to Bloemfontein once," said Marie, offering Jansen this experience. "The bioscope there is big. Not like near home."

"What is home like?"

"But does your father do?"

"He works on, the railway," Lilla said quickly.

"He's ganger[11]," said Marie, and Lilla rolled her eyes up and sighed.

Jansen had seen the gangers' cottages, the frail little shacks along the railway lines, miles from any place, where the wasting flapped whitely on the lines over patches of garden, and the children ran out to wave to the train that passed shrieking from one wonderful fabled town to the next.

"Mom is old-fashioned," said Marie. She said the word "old-fashioned" carefully; it was not hers, but Lilla's; she was tasting it in the way she sipped at the brandy, trying it out, determined to like it. But the emotion was all her own; all the frustration of years was in her, ready to explode into joy. "She doesn't want us to be in Joburg. She says it is wrong for girls."

"Did you run away?" asked Jansen.

Wonder filled the child's face. "How did you guess I ran away?" She said, with a warm admiring smile at Lilla; "My sister sent me the money. I didn't have none at all. I was alone with Mom and Dad and my brothers are working on the copper mines."

"I see," Jansen saw the lonely girl in the little house by the railway lines, helping with the chickens and the cooking, staring hopelessly at the fashion papers, watching the trains pass, too old now to run out and wave and shout, but staring at the fortunate people at the windows with grudging envy, and reading Lilla's letters week after week: "I have a job in an office. I have a new dress. My young man said to me." He looked over the table at the two fine young South African women, with their broad and capable look, their strong bodies, their health, and he thought: Well, it happens every day. He glanced at his watch and Marie said at once: "There's time for the bioscope, isn't there?"

"You and your bioscope," said Lilla. "I'll take you tomorrow afternoon." She rose, said to Jansen in an offhand way: "Coming?" and went to the door. Jansen hesitated, then followed Marie's uncertain but friendly smile.

The three went into the street. Not far away shone a large, white building with film stars kissing between thin borders of coloured shining lights. Streams of smart people went up the noble marble steps where splendid men in uniform welcomed them. Jansen, watching Marie's face, was able to see it like that. Lilla laughed and said: "We're going home, Marie. The pictures aren't anything much. There's better things to do than picture." She winked at Jansen.

They went to a two-roomed flat in a suburb. It was over a grocery store called Mac's Golden Emporium. It had tinned peaches, dried fruit, dressed dolls and rolls of cotton stuffs in the window. The flat had new furniture in it. There was a sideboard with bottles and a radio. The radio played: "Or would you like to swing on a star, carry, moonbeams home in a jar, and be better off than you are[12] ..."

"I like the words," said Marie to Jansen, listening to them with soft delight. Lilla said: "Excuse me, but I have to phone my friend," and went out.

Marie said: "Have a drink," She said it carefully. She poured brandy, the tip of her tongue held between her teeth, and she spilled the water. She carried the glass to Jansen, and smiled in unconscious triumph as she set it down by him. Then she said, "Wait," and went into the bedroom. Jansen adjusted himself on the juicy upholstery of a big chair. He was annoyed to find himself here. What for? What was the good of it? He looked at himself in the glass over a sideboard. He saw a middle-aged gentleman, with a worn indulgent face[13], dressed in a grey suit and sitting uncomfortably in a very ugly chair. But what did Marie see when she looked at him? She came back soon, with a pair of black shiny shoes on her broad feet, and a tight red dress, and pretty face painted over her own blunt honest face. She sat herself down opposite him, as she had seen Lilla sit, adjusting the poise of her head and shoulders. But she forgot her legs, which lay loosely in front of her, like a schoolgirl's.

"Lilla said I could wear her dresses," she said, lingering over her sister's generosity. "She said today I could live here until I earned enough to get my own flat. She said I'd soon have enough." She caught her breath. "Mom would be mad."

"I expect she would," said Jansen drily; and saw Marie react away from him. She spread her red skirts and faced him politely, waiting for him to make her evening[14].

Lilla came in, turned her calculating, good humoured eye from her sister to Jansen, smiled, and said: "I'm going out a little. Oh, keep your hair on. I'll be back soon. My friend is taking me for a walk."

The friend came in and took Lilla's arm, a large, handsome sunburned man who smiled with a good-time smile at Marie. She responded with such a passion of admiration in her eyes that Jansen understood at once what she did not see when she looked at himself. "My, my," said this young man with easy warmth to Marie. "You're a fast learner, I can see that."

"We'll be back," said Lilla to Marie, "Remember what I said." Then to Jansen, like a saleswoman: "She's not bad. Anyhow she can't get herself into any trouble here at home." The young man slipped his arm around her, and reached for a glass off the sideboard with his free hand. He poured brandy, humming with the radio: "in a shady nook, by a babbling brook[15] …" He threw back his head, poured the brandy down, smiled broadly at Jansen and Marie, winked and said: "Be seeing you[16]. Don't forget to wind up the clock and put the cat out." Outside on the landing he and Lilla sang: "Carry moonbeams home in a jar, be better off than you are …" They sang their way down to the street. A car door slammed, an engine roared. Marie darted to the window, and said bitterly: "They've gone to the pictures."

"I don't think so," said Jansen. She came back, frowning, preoccupied with responsibility. "Would you like another drink?" she asked, remembering what Lilla had told her. Jansen shook his head, and sat still for a moment, weighted with inertia. Then he said, "Marie, I want you to listen to me." She leaned forward dutifully, ready to listen, but this was not as she had gazed at the other man[17], the warm, generous, laughing singing young man. Jansen found many words ready on his tongue, disliked them, and blurted, "Marie, I wish you'd let me send you back home tonight." Her face dulled. "No, Marie, you really must listen." She listened politely, from behind her dull resistance. He used words carefully, out of the delicacy of his compassion[18], and saw how they faded into meaninglessness in the space between him and Marie[19]. Then he grew brutal and desperate, because he had to reach her. He said "This sort of life isn't as much fun as it looks"; and "Thousands of girls all over the world choose the easy way because they're stupid, and afterwards they're sorry". She dropped her lids, looked at her feet in her new high shoes, and shut herself off from him. He used the words whore and prostitute; but she had never heard them except as swearwords, and did not connect them with herself. She began repeating, over and over again, "My sister's a typist; she's got a job in an office."

He said angrily, "Do you think she can afford to live like this on a typist's pay?"

"Her gentleman friend gives her things, he's generous, she told me so," said Marie doubtfully.

"How old are you, Marie?"

"Eighteen," she said, turning her broad freckled wrist, where Lilla's bracelet caught the light.

"When you're twenty-five you'll be out on the streets picking up any man you see, taking them to hotels…"

At the word "hotel" her eyes widened; he remembered she had never been in a hotel; they were something lovely on the cinema screen.

"When you're thirty you'll be an old woman."

"Lilla said she'd look after me. She promised me faithfully," said Marie, in terror at his coldness. But what he was saying meant nothing to her, nothing at all. He saw that she probably did not know what the word prostitute meant; that the things Lilla had told her meant only lessons in how to enjoy the delights of this city.

He said, "Do you know what I'm here for? Your sister expects you to take off your clothes and get into bed and …" He stopped. Her eyes were wide open, fastened on him, not in fear, but in the anxious preoccupation of a little girl who is worried she is not behaving properly. Her hands had moved to the buckle of her belt, and she was undoing it[20].

Jansen got up, and without speaking he gathered clothes that were obviously hers from off the furniture, from off floor. He went into the bedroom and found a suitcase and put her things into it. "I'm putting you on to the train tonight," he said.

"My sister won't let you," she cried out. "She'll stop you."

"Your sister's a bad girl," said Jansen, and saw, to his surprise, that Marie's face showed fear at last. Those two words, "bad girl" had more effect than all his urgent lecturing.

"You shouldn't say such things," said Marie, beginning to cry. "You shouldn't never say someone's a bad girl." They were her mother's words, obviously, and had hit her hard, where she could be reached. She stood listless in the middle of the floor, weeping, making no resistance. He tucked her arm inside his and led her downstairs. You'll marry a nice man soon, Marie, he promised. "You won't always have to live by the railway lines."

"I don't never meet no man, except Dad." She said, beginning to tug at his arm again.

He held her tight until they were in a taxi. There she sat crouched on the edge of the seat, watching the promised city sweep past. At the station, keeping a firm hold on her, he bought her a ticket and gave her five pounds, and put her into a compartment and said, "I know you hate me. One day you'll know I'm right and you'll be glad." She smiled weakly, and huddled herself into her seat, like a cold little animal, staring sadly out of the window.

He left her, running, to catch his own train which already stood waiting on the next platform.

As it drew out of the station he saw Marie waddling desperately on her tall heels along the platform, casting scared glances over her shoulder. Their eyes met; she gave him an apologetic smile, and ran on. With the pound notes clutched loosely in her hand she was struggling her way through the crowds back to the lights, the love, the joyous streets of the promised city[21].

Notes

1. flare of temper: anger.
2. in a vacuum of wealth: spending all the money.
3. For a week … through their eyes: For a week he had lived in a circle of rich friends, which isolated him from the life of other classes and at the same time made him observe what happened in the town from his rich friends' angle.
4. strike him direct: blow him freely.
5. because he was in the arrested, dreamy frame of mind of the uncommitted traveler: because his mind was caught in a dreamy state as if he was a traveler who stayed outside this world.
6. a daemon: same as demon, which means an evil spirit, referring to something mysterious here.
7. ancestry: blood relationship.
8. smiled professionally: referring to Lilla's flirtatious smile as an experienced prostitute.
9. green: inexperienced.
10. the bioscope: the early movie theatre.
11. ganger: railway switchman whose job is to pull railway switches from one set of tracks to another when necessary.
12. better off than you are: lead a better life than you have right now.
13. with a worn indulgent face: with a tired but kind face.
14. to make her evening: to spend some money for her company in the evening.
15. in a shady nook, by a babbling brook: in a sheltered place by a murmuring stream.
16. Be seeing you: See you soon.
17. the other man: referring to Jansen himself, who looked so different from the one he used to be.
18. out of the delicacy of his compassion: due to the consideration of his sympathy for Marie.
19. saw how they faded into meaninglessness in the space between him and Marie: Jansen tried to weaken the relation between him and Marie.
20. undoing: loosing.
21. promised city: hopeful city.

Questions for Understanding

1. Why does Marie insist on visiting "bioscope"? What does the action indicate?
2. What kind of road is the naive girl Marie taking from her home to the big city?
3. What does the big city symbolize?
4. What is the theme of the story?

Aspects of Appreciation

1. This short story takes place in Johannesburg, the biggest and most modern city in South Africa. Its theme may be the lure of a big city's life to people who live poor, boring lives in the countryside, regardless of the dangers that face a naive person in the city.
2. This story illustrates, on the one hand, the differences between the city and the countryside; and on the other hand, the willingness of people to be deluded by false values, for both Lilla and Marie have deliberately chosen their fate.
3. Doris Lessing is deeply involved in the changing patterns of thought and culture in the western world. There is great continuity between her life and her work. Ever since her first novel, *The Grass Is Singing* (1950), Lessing began her critical exploration of sexual relationship, gender roles, social and racial repression, and the violent potential of resistance and subversion. She is remarkable for her bold experiment in the form of writing, her deep insight into the contemporary social mores, her wide range of subject matters and her profound exploration of the social issues of the time.

Suggested Further Reading

Doris Lessing. *A Man and Two Women* (a short story collection, 1963), *The Grass Is Singing* (1950) and *The Golden Notebook* (1962).

Topics for Further Study

1. What is the basic conflict of the story?
2. What does the author want to express out of the sufferings of Marie?
3. Discuss Lessing's realistic style of writing in "A Road to the Big City".

John Fowles
(1926~2005)

About the Author

John Fowles was born in Essex, England in 1926, educated at Bedford School and served in the Royal Marines for some time. Then he spent four years at Oxford and took his B. A. degree in French in 1950. There he was influenced by the writings of the French existentialists. After his graduation, he worked as a teacher in several universities in France, Greece and London respectively. In 1963, with the publication and success of his novel, *Collector*, he gave up his teaching and became a full-time writer.

Fowles is at once a popular and a serious novelist. He never fails to fascinate his readers. Reading him can always be an enjoyable experience. His stories are basically traditional in nature, or love stories in its various forms, that present little or no obscurity in comprehension. However, the way he wrote his novels merits particular attention. There seems to be some kind of pattern that underpins his stories: the hero undertakes a quest, with the guidance of some wise man, and finds the woman he loves and becomes spiritually whole. Fowles's major novels include *The Collector* (1963), *The Magus* (1965), *The French Lieutenant's Woman* (1969), *The Ebony Tower* (1974), *Daniel Martin* (1977) and *Mantissa* (1982). Fowles also wrote a miscellany of other things such as poetry, short fiction, essays, and philosophy.

★ The French Lieutenant's Woman

About the Novel

This novel is considered to be Fowles's masterpiece. It is set in Victorian England. Charles Smithson, the protagonist, is a true-to-form Victorian gentleman, expecting to inherit a title and wealth from his uncle, and get married to a rich young lady, Ernestina Freeman. Then he meets Sarah Woodruff, a woman of disrepute, who is said to have been a mistress for a French lieutenant. Hence her nickname, the French lieutenant's woman. She is unusually pretty and her gloom adds remarkably well to her attraction. Charles seeks the advice of a doctor, Dr. Grogan, the prototype of a modern psychologist, and learns more about her. He feels so irresistibly drawn to her with time that his passion soon amounts to obsession. He has an affair with her in a hotel and becomes the object of the vicious scandal that his servant spreads about him. The event discredits him thoroughly in the eyes of his leisured class, so that he is ruined and ostracized. When he packs up and goes to the hotel for Sarah, however, he is dismayed to find her already gone. Then he spends a long time and does everything humanly possible to search for her and finds her eventually.

The story ends, as the novel suggests, in more ways than one: one of these, in union, as the two reunite and live happily ever after; and another, in separation, when Sarah rejects him, not even telling him that she has borne him a daughter. Other suggestions for possible endings include Charles' vision of his marrying Ernestina and the author's narrative scheme to have him die in the course of his quest.

Chapter 55

Charles arrived at the station[1] in ridiculously good time the next morning, and having gone through the ungentlemanly business of seeing his things loaded into the baggage van and then selected an empty first-class compartment, he sat impatiently waiting for the train to start. Other passengers looked in from time to time, and were rebuffed by that Gorgon stare[2] (this compartment is reserved for non-lepers) the English have so easily at command. A whistle sounded, and Charles thought he had won the solitude he craved. But then, at the very last moment, a massively bearded face appeared at his window. The cold stare was met by the even colder stare of a man in a hurry to get aboard.

The late comer muttered a "Pardon me, sir" and made his way to the far end to the compartment. He sat, a man of forty or so, his top hat firmly square, his hands on his knees, regaining his breath. There was something rather aggressively secure about him; he was perhaps not quite a gentleman … an ambitious butler[3] (but butlers did not travel first class) or a successful lay preacher-one of the bullying tabernacle[4] kind, a would-be Spurgeon[5], converting souls by scorching them with the cheap rhetoric of eternal damnation. A decidedly unpleasant man, thought Charles, and so typical of the age—and therefore emphatically to be snubbed if he tried to enter into conversation.

As sometimes happens when one stares covertly[6] at people and speculates about them, Charles was caught in the act and reproved[7] for it. There was a very clear suggestion in the sharp look sideways that Charles should keep his eyes to himself. He hastily directed his gaze outside his window and consoled himself that at least the person shunned intimacy as much as he did.

Very soon the even movement lulled Charles into a douce[8] daydream. London was a large city; but she must soon look for work. He had the time, the resources, the will; a week might pass, two, but then she would stand before him; perhaps yet another address would slip through his letter box. The wheels said it: she-could-not-be-so-cruel, she-could-not-be-so-cruel, she-could-not-be-so-cruel, the train passed through the red and green valleys towards Cullompton[9]. Charles saw its church, without knowing where the place was, and soon afterwards closed his eyes. He had slept poorly that previous night.

For a while his traveling companion took no notice of the sleeping Charles. But as the chin sank deeper and deeper-Charles had taken the precaution of removing his hat—the prophet-bearded man began to stare at him, safe in the knowledge that his curiosity would not be surprised.

His look was peculiar: sizing, ruminative[10], more than a shade disapproving, as if he knew very well what sort of man this was(as Charles had believed to see very well what sort of man he was) and did not much like the knowledge of the species. It was true that, unobserved, he looked a little less frigid[11] and authoritarian a person; but there remained about his features an unpleasant aura of self-confidence—or if not quite confidence in self, at least a confidence in his judgment of others, of how much he could get out of them, expect from them, tax[12] them.

A stare of a minute or so's duration, of this kind, might have been explicable. Train journeys are boring; it is amusing to spy on strangers; and so on. But this stare, which became positively cannibalistic[13] in its intensity, lasted far longer than a minute. It lasted beyond Taunton[14], though it was briefly interrupted there when the noise on the platform made Charles wake for a few moments. But when he sank back into his slumbers, the eyes fastened on him again in the same leechlike manner[15].

You may one day come under a similar gaze. And you may—in the less reserved context of our own century—be aware of it. The intent watcher will not wait till you are asleep. It will no doubt suggest something unpleasant, some kind of devious[16] sexual approach… a desire to know you in a way you do not want to be known by a stranger. In my experience there is only one profession that gives that particular look with its bizarre blend of the inquisitive and the magistral[17]; of the ironic and the soliciting[18].

Now could I use you?

Now what could I do with you?

It is precisely, it has always seemed to me, the look an omnipotent[19] god—if there were such an absurd thing—should be shown to have. Not at all what we think of as a divine look; but one of a distinctly mean and dubious[20] (as the theoreticians of the nouveau roman[21] have pointed out) moral quality. I see this with particular clarity on the face, only too familiar to me, of the bearded man who stares at Charles. And I will keep up the pretense no longer.

Now the question I am asking, as I stare at Charles, is not quite the same as the two above. But rather, what the devil am I going to do with you? I have already thought of ending Charles's career here and now; of leaving him for eternity on his way to London. But the conventions of Victorian fiction, allowed no place for the open, the inconclusive ending; and I preached earlier of the freedom characters must be given[22]. My problem is simple—what Charles wants is clear? It is indeed. But what the protagonist[23] wants is not so clear; and I am not at all sure where she is at the moment. Of course if these two were two fragments of real life, instead of two figments[24] of my imagination, the issue of the dilemma is obvious: the one want combats the other want, and fails or succeeds, as the actuality may be. Fiction usually pretends to conform to the reality: the writer puts the conflicting wants in the ring[25] and then describes the fight but in fact fixes the fight, letting that want he himself favors win. And we judge writers of fiction both by the skill they show in fixing the fights (in other words, in persuading us that they were not fixed) and by the kind of fighter they fix in favor of: the good one, the tragic one, the evil one, the funny one, and so on.

But the chief argument for fight-fixing is to show one's readers what one thinks of the world around one-whether one is a pessimist, an optimist, what you will. I have pretended to slip back into 1867, but of course that year is in reality a century past. It is futile to show optimism or pessimism, or anything else about it, because we know what has happened since.

VIII. Contemporary Period

So I continue to stare at Charles and see no reason this time for fixing the fight upon which he is about to engage. That leaves me with two alternatives. I let the fight proceed and take no more than a recording part in it; or I take both sides in it. I stare at that vaguely effete[26] but not completely futile face. And as we near London, I think I see a solution; that is, I see the dilemma is false. The only way I can take no part in the fight is to show two versions of it. That leaves me with only one problem: I cannot give both versions at once, yet whichever is the second will seem, so strong is the tyranny of the last chapter, the final, the "real" version.

I take my purse from the pocket of my frock coat. I extract a florin[27], I rest it on my right thumbnail; I flick it, spinning, two feet into the air and catch it in my left hand.

So be it. And I am suddenly aware that Charles has opened his eyes and is looking at me. There is something more than disapproval in his eyes now; he perceives I am either a gambler or mentally deranged. I return his disapproval and my florin to my purse. He picks up his hat, brushes some invisible speck of dirt(a surrogate for myself) from its nap[28] and places it on his head.

We draw under one of the great cast-iron[29] beams that support the roof of Paddington station[30]. We arrive, he steps down to the platform, beckoning to a porter. In a few moments, having given his instructions, he turns. The bearded man has disappeared in the throng.

※ ※

Notes

1. the station: the station at Lyme, the town where the story is set.
2. Gorgon stare: ferocious stare. Gorgon: (Greek Mythology) each of the three sisters, with snakes for hair, who had the power to turn anyone who looked at them to stone.
3. butler: the chief manservant of a house.
4. tabernacle: (in biblical use) a fixed or movable habitation, typically of light construction.
5. Spurgeon: Charles Spurgeon (1834 ~ 1892), a Puritan preacher in London.
6. covertly: secretly.
7. reproved: criticized or reprimanded.

8. douce: (chiefly Scottish) sober, gentle, and sedate.
9. Cullomption: name of a station on the way to London.
10. ruminative: thoughtful.
11. frigid: showing no friendliness or enthusiasm; stiff or formal in behaviour or style.
12. tax: confront (someone) with a fault or wrongdoing; criticize.
13. cannibalistic: (of the eyes) looking murderous.
14. Taunton: the county town of Somerset, in southwest England.
15. leechlike manner: (of the eyes) persistently or clingingly staring at (Charles).
16. devious: indirect or showing a skillful use of underhand tactics to achieve goals.
17. magistral: authoritative or arrogant.
18. soliciting: asking for or trying to obtain (something) from someone.
19. omnipotent: (of a deity) having unlimited power; able to do anything.
20. dubious: doubting or suspect.
21. nouveau roman: (French) literally "new novel", a style of avant-garde French novel that came to prominence in the 1950s. It rejected the plot, character, and omniscient narrator central to the traditional novel in an attempt to reflect more faithfully the sometimes random nature of experience.
22. I preached earlier of the freedom characters must be given: In chapter 13, the narrator (i.e. the fictitious author of this novel) expressed his idea of writing, saying that if he wished him (Charles) to be a real character, he would respect his freedom and abandon any seemingly holy plan he had made for him.
23. protagonist: the heroine of the novel, Sarah.
24. figment: a thing that someone believes to be real but that exists only in their imagination.
25. ring: a roped enclosure for boxing or wrestling.
26. effete: no longer capable of effective action.
27. florin: a former British coin and monetary unit worth two shillings.
28. He…brushes some invisible speck of dirt (a surrogate for himself) from its nap: This sentence means that Charles brushes his hat on which there is no dirt at all, the gesture just indicating he is tired of me, and eager to get rid of me as he does with the dirt.
29. cast-iron: of or like iron.

30. Paddington station: name of a tube or subway station in London.

Questions for Understanding

1. Who is the bearded man in this selection? Who is the "I" interfering into the narration at the second half of this selection? What does the narrator mean when he says "I will keep up the pretense no longer"?
2. Why does the bearded man look at Charles with "the look an omnipotent god... should be shown to have"? What does it imply?
3. Fowles uses "inquisitive" "magistral" "ironic" and "soliciting" to describe the narrator's "particular look". What is your perception of the narrator?

Aspects of Appreciation

1. Although critics have seen his formal experiments in different ways, Fowles has been, in a very serious sense, regarded as a postmodernist novelist. He enjoys experimenting with a number of important things relating to fiction such as points of view, the notion of time, metafiction, parody, the ways a story ends, and emphasis on his characters' efforts to internalize their harrowing experiences.
2. This novel is metafictional in more than one way. Metafiction, a postmodernist form of writing about fiction in the form of fiction, is a style of fictive narrative that tries to tell the readers that fiction is fiction and is not an illusion of reality as the realists have tried to "deceive" the readers into believing. All through *The French Lieutenant's Woman*, the author keeps telling the readers (and throwing in all sorts of reminders such as Hitler, radar, and TV) that, although the story is about Victorian England, it is a fictional story, not a reality. Furthermore, contrary to traditional realists who try to make their fiction look like reality, metafiction writers feel skeptical about the idea of authentic representation of reality and write novels not so much to tell a story as to shock the readers' expectations. In this connection, they tend to use burlesque and parody as a means of subverting the readers' sense of complacency. Burlesque or parody is a manner of writing in which an effort is made to imitate an original in order to poke fun at it or to reveal the discrepancy between the imitation and the original. The story of *The French Lieutenant's Woman* is an obvious parody of the Victorian, traditional realistic, narrative method; it is a good story telling until the author feels the urge to jog his readers out of their comfortable mode of

reception and their anxious search for the real story. He does this by alerting them to the fact that their search will end in failure as there is nothing like the real story.
3. The ending of the story of *The French Lieutenant's Woman* is interesting though confusing to some readers. Out of the few options that the author has provided, there are two notable endings that we may examine in more detail. The happy conclusion of the story occurs when Charles, after a persistent painstaking search, finally finds Sarah and their daughter Lalage. They unite and live happily together ever after. This should have satisfied the taste of the Victorian readers, who attached importance to wholesome social functioning and family value. But Fowles's are contemporary readers, who are well acquainted with the modern philosophies such as nihilism and existentialism, and have been through the baptism of modern life. The tragic ending may be provided to cater to their relish. It is interesting to note that the story itself has already prepared the readers for a tragic resolution. First, the woman Sarah is not portrayed as a Victorian woman, pure and simple. She is endowed with the qualities of the new, modern age, which is just around the corner in the new century. She does not like the idea of marriage and rejects Charles's offer. Then the man Charles, seasoned as he is with all life's experiences, is no longer a Victorian gentleman, pure and simple, either. He has become an independent individual standing right at the threshold of the modern time. In face of Sarah's rebuttal, he makes his own choice, accepts the situation and leaves graciously, and turns over a new page in his life.

Suggested Further Reading

1. John Fowles. *The Ebony Tower* (a collection of Short Stores, 1974).
2. Katherine Tarbox. *The Art of John Fowles*. Athens, GA: University of Georgia Press, 1998.

Topics for Further Study

1. Charles is living in Victorian England. Do you think the bearded man who he meets on the train is Charles contemporary? Where does the bearded man come from? Please comment on his pretense and function in the novel.
2. What is Fowles going to do with the ending of the novel according to this selection? Why?

3. Please make a comparison between the narrative voice in *David Copperfield*, which is a typical Victorian novel, and that in *The French Lieutenant's Woman*, which is pseudo-Victorian.

Antonia Susan Byatt
(1936~)

About the Author

A. S. Byatt is a well-known contemporary British novelist and critic, and sister to the novelist, Margaret Drabble. She was born on August 24, 1936 in Sheffield, England. After being educated at two independent schools (Sheffield High school and York Mount School), she went on to Newnham College, Cambridge, Bryn Mawr College in the USA, and Somerville College, Oxford. In 1959, she married the economist, Ian Charles Rayner Byatt, with whom she had a daughter, as well as a son who was killed in a car accident at the age of 11. The marriage was dissolved in 1969. She has two daughters with her second husband, Peter John Duffy. Among several academic posts, she has been a senior lecturer at University College, London, the fellow of the Royal Society of Literature, and the judge on many literary award panels including the Hawthornden Prize, the Booker, David Higham Prize for Fiction, and the Betty Trask Award. Byatt has been a professional writer since 1983. So far she has published nearly 30 books, including novels such as *The Shadow of the Sun* (1964), *The Game* (1967), *The Virgin in the Garden* (1978), *Still Life* (1985), *Possession: A Romance* (1990), *Babel Tower* (1997), *A Whistling Woman* (2002), *The Children's Book* (2009), *Ragnarok: The End of the Gods* (2011), and some collections of short stories or novellas, such as *Sugar and Other Stories* (1987), *Angels and Insects* (1992), *The Matisse Stories* (1993), *The Djinn in the Nightingale's Eye* (1994), *Elementals: Stories of Fire and Ice* (1998) and *Little Black Book of Stories* (2003).

Byatt's *Still Life* won The PEN/ Macmillan Silver Pen Award in 1986, and her *Possession: A Romance* won the prestigious Booker Prize in 1990.

On her 8-day China tour in 2012, A. S. Byatt took part in cultural exchanges with famous Chinese contemporary writers as well as Chinese reseachers, creating important links between Chinese and Western literature.

★ Possession: A Romance

About the Novel

Possession is an exhilarating novel of wit and romance, an intellectual mystery and a triumphant love story. It is a tale of a pair of young scholars researching the lives of two Victorian poets. Roland Michell happens to discover two drafts of letters by the renowned Victorian poet, Randolph Henry Ash, to an anonymous woman, who was identified later as the poetess Christabel LaMotte. This excites Roland as he becomes aware that the new discovery may enable him to make a breakthrough in the Ash scholarship. He then manages to get in touch with a LaMotte scholar, Dr. Maud Bailey, and persuades her to cooperate with him to uncover the story behind the correspondence. They search the room where Christabel used to live and find the letters that have remained untouched for over a hundred years. The young scholars' quest inevitably attracts the jealous attention of the competitive academic world, and all too soon the quest becomes a chase. Linking the life experiences of Ash and LaMotte with their works, Maud and Roland gradually redress their previous misinterpretation. They finally recreate in their relationship the romance of the poets.

Byatt deftly plays with literary genres (romantic quest, campus satire, detective story, myth, fairy tale) as Maud and Roland become deeply involved in the unfolding story of a secret relationship between the Victorian poets Randolph Henry Ash and Christabel LaMotte. She has also produced a multitude of voices, and the narration within narration is not only a feature of this novel, but typical of her fiction.

Chapter Two

A man is the history of his breaths and thoughts, acts, atoms and wounds, love, indifference and dislike; also of his race and nation, the soil that fed him and his forebears, tile stones and sands of his familiar places, long-silenced battles and struggles of conscience, of the smiles of girls and the slow utterance of old women, of accidents and the gradual action of inexorable law, of all this and something else too, a single flame which in every way obeys the laws that pertain to Fire itself, and yet is lit and put out from one moment to the next, and can never be relumed in the whole waste of time to come[1].

So Randolph Henry Ash, ca. 1840, when he was writing *Ragnarok*[2], a poem in twelve books, which some saw as a Christianising of the Norse myth and some trounced as atheistic and diabolically despairing. It mattered to Randolph Ash what a man was, though he could, without undue disturbance have written that general pantechnicon of a sentence using other terms, phrases and rhythms and have come in the end to the same satisfactory evasive metaphor. Or so Roland thought, trained in the post-structuralist deconstruction of the subject. If he had been asked what Roland Michell was, he would have had to give a very different answer.

In 1986 he was twenty-nine, a graduate of Prince Albert College, London (1978) and a PhD of the same university (1985). His doctoral dissertation was entitled *History, Historians and Poetry? A Study of the Presentation of Historical "Evidence" in the Poems of Randolph Henry Ash*. He had written it under the supervision of James Blackadder, which had been a discouraging experience. Blackadder was discouraged and liked to discouraged others. (He was also a stringent scholar.) Roland was now employed, part-time, in what was known as Blackadder's "Ash Factory"[3] (why not Ashram? Val had said) which operated from the British Museum, to which Ash's wife, Ellen, had given many of the manuscripts of his poems, when he died. The Ash Factory was funded by a small grant from London University and a much larger one from the Newsome Foundation in Albuquerque, a charitable Trust of which Mortimer Cropper was a Trustee. This might appear to indicate that Blackadder and Cropper worked harmoniously together on behalf of Ash. This would be a misconception. Blackadder believed Cropper to have designs on those manuscripts lodged with, but not owned by, the British Library, and to be worming his way into the confidence and goodwill of the owners by displays of munificence and helpfulness. Blackadder, a Scot, believed British writings should stay in Britain and be studied by the British. It may seem odd to begin a description of Roland Michell with an excursus into the complicated relations of Blackadder, Cropper and Ash, but it was in these terms that Roland most frequently thought of himself when he did not think in terms of Val.

He thought of himself as a latecomer. He had arrived too late for things that were still in the air but vanished, the whole ferment and brightness and journeyings and youth of the 1960s, the blissful dawn of what he and his contemporaries saw as a pretty blank day. Through the psychedelic years he was a schoolboy in a depressed Lancashire cotton town, untouched alike by Liverpool noise and London turmoil. His father was a minor official in the County Council. His mother was a disappointed English graduate. He thought of himself as though he were an application form, for a job, a degree, a life, but when he thought of his mother, the adjective would not be expurgated. She was disappointed. In herself, in his father, in him. The wrath of her disappointment had been the instrument of his education, which had taken place in a perpetual rush from site to site of a hastily amalgamated three-school comprehensive, the Aneurin Bevan school, combining Glasdale Old Grammar School, St. Thomas à Becket's C of E Secondary School and the Clothier's Guild Technical Modern School. His mother had drunk too much stout, "gone up the school", and had him transferred from metal work to Latin, from Civic Studies to French; she had paid a maths coach with the earnings of a paper-round she had sent him out on. And so he had acquired an old-fashioned classical education, with gaps where teachers had been made redundant or classroom chaos had reigned. He had done what was hoped of him, always, had four As at A Level, a First, a PhD. He was now essentially unemployed, scraping a living on part-time tutoring, dogsbodying for Blackadder and some restaurant dishwashing. In the expansive 1960s he would have advanced rapidly and involuntarily, but now he saw himself as a failure and felt vaguely responsible for this.

He was a small man, with very soft, startling black hair and small regular features. Val called him Mole which he disliked. He had never told her so.

He lived with Val, whom he had met at a Freshers' tea party in the Student Union when he was eighteen. He believed now though this belief may have been a mythic smoothing of his memory, that Val was the first person his undergraduate self had spoken to, socially that was, not officially. He had liked the look of her, he remembered, a soft, brown uncertain look. She had been standing on her own, holding a teacup in front of her, not looking about her but rather fixedly out of the window, as though she expected no one to approach and invited no one. She projected a sort of calm, a lack of strife, and so he went over to join her. And since then they had never not been together. They signed up for the same courses and joined the same societies; they sat together in seminars and went together to the National Film Theatre; they had sex together and moved together into a one-roomed flat in their second year. They lived frugally off a diet of porridge and lentils and beans and yogurt; they drank a little beer, making it spin out; they shared book-buying; they were both entirely confined to their grants, which did not go far in London, and could not be supplemented with holiday earnings, for these had vanished with the oil crisis. Val had been, Roland was sure, partly responsible for his First. (Along with his mother and Randolph Henry Ash.) She simply, expected it of him, she made him always say what he thought, she argued points, she worried constantly about whether she was, whether they both were, working hard enough. They quarrelled hardly at all and when they did it was almost always because Roland expressed concern about Val's reserve with the world in general, her refusal to advance opinions in class, and later, even to him. In the early days she had had lots of quiet opinions, he remembered, which she had offered him, shyly slyly, couched as a kind of invitation or bait. There had been poems she had liked. Once she had sat up naked in his dark digs and recited Robert Graves:

> She tells her love while half asleep,
> In the dark hours.
> With trail-words whispered low:
> As Earth stirs in her winter sleep
> And puts out grass and flowers
> Despite the snow,
> Despite the falling snow.

She had a rough voice gentled, between London and Liverpool, as the group voice was. When Roland began to speak, after this, she put a hand over his mouth, which was as well, for he had nothing to say. Later, Roland noticed, as he himself had his successes, Val said less and less, and when she argued, offered him increasingly his own ideas, sometimes the reverse side of the knitting, but essentially his. She even wrote her Required Essay on "Male Ventriloquism[4]: The Women of Randolph Henry Ash". Roland did not want this. When he suggested that she should strike out on her own, make herself noticed, speak up, she accused him of "taunting" her. When he asked, what did she mean, "taunting", she resorted, as she always did when they argued, to silence. Since silence was also Roland's only form of aggression they would continue in this way for days, or, one terrible time when Roland directly criticised "Male Ventriloquism", for weeks. And then the fraught silence would modulate into conciliatory monosyllable, and back to their peaceful co-existence. When Finals came, Roland did steadily and predictably well. Val's papers were bland and minimal, in large confident handwriting, well laid-out. "Male Ventriloquism" was judged to be good work and discounted by the examiners as probably largely by Roland, which was doubly unjust, since he had refused to look at it, and did not agree with its central proposition, which was that Randolph Henry Ash neither liked nor understood women, that his female speakers were constructs of his own fear and aggression, that even the poem-cycle, Ask to Embla[5], was the work, not of love but of narcissism, the poet addressing his Anima. (No biographical critic had ever satisfactorily identified Embla.) Val did very badly. Roland had supposed she had expected this, but it became dreadfully obvious that she had not. There were tears, night-long, choked, whimpering tears, and the first tantrum.

Val left him for the first time since they had set up house, and went briefly "home". Home was Croydon, where she lived with her divorced mother in a council flat, supported by social security, supplemented occasionally by haphazard maintenance payments from her father, who was in the Merchant Navy and had not been seen since Val was five. Val had never, during their time together, proposed to Roland that they visit her mother, though Roland had twice taken her to Glendale, where she had helped his father wash up, and had taken his mother's jeering deflation of their way of life in her stride, telling him, "Don't worry, Mole. I've seen it all before. Only mine drinks. If you lit a match in our kitchen, it'd go up with a roar."

When Val was gone, Roland realized, with a shock like a religious conversion, that he did not want their way of life to go on. He rolled over, and spread his loosened limbs in the bed, he opened windows, he went to the Tate Gallery alone and looked at the dissolving blue and gold air of Turner's Norham Castle. He cooked a pheasant for his rival in the departmental rat-race, Fergus Wolff, which was exciting and civilised, although the pheasant was tough and full of shot. He made plans, which were not plans, but visions of solitary activity and free watchfulness, things he had never had. After a week, Val came back, tearful and shaky, and declared that she meant at least to earn her living, and would take a course in shorthand-typing. "At least you want me", she told Roland, her face damp and glistening. "I don't know why you should want me, I'm no good, but you do." "Of course I do," Roland had said. "Of course."

When his DES grant ran out, Val became the breadwinner, whilst he finished his PhD. She acquired an IBM. golfball typewriter and did academic typing at home in the evenings and various well-paid tempting jobs during the day. She worked in the City and in teaching hospitals, in shipping firms and art galleries. She resisted pressure to specialise. She would not be drawn out to talk about her work to which she almost never referred without the adjective "menial". "I must do just a few more menial things before I go to bed" or, more oddly, "I was nearly run over on my menial way this morning." Her voice acquired a jeering note, not unfamiliar to Roland, who wondered for the first time what his mother had been like before her disappointment, which in her case was his father and to some extent himself. The typewriter clashed and harried him at night, never rhythmical enough to be ignored.

There were now two Vals. One sat silently at home in old jeans and unevenly hanging long creepy shirts, splashed with murky black and purple flowers. This one had lusterless brown hair, very straight, hanging about a pale, underground face. Just sometimes, this one had crimson nails, left over from the other who wore a tight black skirt and a black jacket with padded shoulders over a pink silk shirt and was carefully made up with pink and brown eyeshadow, brushed blusher along the cheekbone and plummy lips. This mournfully bright menial Val wore high heels and a black beret. She had beautiful ankles, invisible under the domestic jeans. Her hair was rolled into a passable pageboy and sometimes tied with a black ribbon. She stopped short of perfume. She was not constructed to be attractive. Roland half wished that she was, that a merchant banker would take her out to dinner, or a shady solicitor to the Playboy Club. He hated himself for these demeaning fantasies, and was reasonably afraid that she might suspect he nourished them.

If he could get a job, it might be easier to initiate some change. He made applications and was regularly turned down. When one came up in his own department there were 600 applications. Roland was interviewed, out of courtesy he decided, but the job went to Fergus Wolff, whose track record was less consistent, who could be brilliant or bathetic, but never dull and right, who was loved by his teachers whom he exasperated and entranced, where Roland excited no emotion more passionate than solid approbation. Fergus was also in the right field, which was literary theory. Val was more indignant than Roland about this event, and her indignation upset him as much as his own failure, for he liked Fergus and wanted to be able to go on liking him. Val found one of her insisting words for Fergus too, one which was askew and inaccurate. "That pretentious blonde bombshell" she said of him. "That pretentious sexpot." She liked to use sexist wolf-whistle words as a kind of boomerang. This embarrassed Roland, since Fergus, transcended any such terminology; he was indeed blond, and he was indeed sexually very successful, and that was an end to it. He came to no more meals, and Roland feared Fergus thought this was a function of his, Roland's, resentment.

When he got home that evening he could smell that Val was in a mood. The basement was full of the sharp warmth of frying onions, which meant she was cooking something complicated. When she was not in a mood, when she was apathetic, she opened tins or boiled eggs, or at most dressed an avocado. When she was either very cheerful or very angry, she cooked. She stood at the sink, chopping courgettes and aubergines, when he came in, and did not look up, so he surmised that the mood was bad. He put down his bag quietly. They had a cavernous basement room which they had painted apricot and white, to cheer it up; it was furnished with a double divan, two very old arm-chairs with curvaceous rolled arms and head-rests, plum and plushy and dusty, a second-hand stained-oak office desk, where Roland worked, and a newer varnished beech desk, where the typewriter sat. These were back to back on the long side-walls each with their Habitat anglepoise, Roland's black, Val's rose-pink. On the back wall were bookcases, made of bricks and planks, sagging under standard texts, most of them jointly owned, some duplicated. They had put up various posters; a British Museum poster from the Koran, intricate and geometric, a Tate advertisement for a Turner exhibition.

Roland possessed three images of Randolph Henry Ash. One, a photograph of the death mask which was one of the central pieces in the Stant Collection of Harmony City, stood on his desk. There was a puzzle about how this bleak, broad-browed carved head had come into existence, since there also existed a photograph of the poet in his last sleep, still patriarchally bearded. Who had shaved him, when? Roland had wondered, and Mortimer Cropper had asked in his biography, *The Great Ventriloquist*, without finding an answer. His other two portraits were photographic copies, made to order, of the two portraits of Ash in the National Portrait Gallery. Val had banished these to the dark of the hall. She said she did not want him staring at her, she wanted a bit of her life to herself, without having to share it with Randolph Ash.

In the dark hall the pictures were difficult to see. One was by Manet and one was by G. F. Watts[6]. The Manet had been painted when the painter was in England in 1867, and had some things in common with his portrait of Zola. He had shown Ash, whom he had met previously in Paris, sitting at his desk, in a three-quarters profile, in a carved mahogany chair. Behind him was a kind of triptych with ferny foliage, to the left and right, enclosing a watery space in which rosy and silver fish shone between pondweeds. The effect was partly to set the poet amongst the roots of a wood or forest, until, as Mortimer Cropper had pointed out, one realised that the background was one of those compartmentalized Wardian cases, in which the Victorians grew plants in controlled environments, or created self-sustaining ponds, in order to study the physiology of plants and fishes. Manet's Ash was dark, powerful, with deepset eyes under a strong brow, a vigorous beard and a look of confident private amusement. He looked, watchful and intelligent, not ready to move in a hurry. In front of him on his desk were disposed, various objects, an elegant and masterly still life to complement the strong head and the ambivalent natural growths. There was a heap of rough geological specimens, including two almost spherical stones, a little like cannon balls, one black and one a sulphurous yellow, some ammonites and trilobites, a large crystal ball, a green glass inkwell, the reticulated skeleton of a cat, a heap of books, two of which could be seen to be the *Divina Commedia* and *Faust*, and an hourglass in a wooden frame. Of these, the inkwell, the crystal ball, the hourglass, the two named books and two of the others, which had been painstakingly identified as *Quixote and Lyell's Geology*, were now in the Stant Collection, where a room had been arranged, Wardian cases and all, to resemble the Manet setting. The chair had also been collected, and the desk itself.

The portrait by Watts was mistier and less authoritative. It had been painted in 1876 and showed an older and more ethereal poet, his head rising, as is common with Watts's portraits, from a vague dark column of a body into a spiritual light. There was a background but it had darkened. In the original portrait it could be vaguely made out as a kind of craggy wild place; in this photographic reproduction it was no more than thickenings and glimmerings in the black. The important features of this image were the eyes, which were large and gleaming, and the beard, a riverful of silvers and creams, whites and blue-greys, channels and forks resembling da Vinci's turbulences, the apparent source of light. Even in the photograph, it shone. These pictures, Roland considered, seemed somehow more real as well as more austere, because they were photographs. Less full of life, the life of the paint, but more realistic, in the modern sense, according to modern expectations. They were a bit the worse for wear; the flat was not clean and was damp. But he had no money to renew them.

At the end of the room the window opened onto a little yard, with steps to the garden, which was visible between railings in the upper third of their window. Their flat was described as a garden flat when they came to see it, which was the only occasion on which they were asked to come into the garden into which they were later told they had no right of entry. They were not even, allowed to attempt to grow things in tubs in their black area, for reasons vague but peremptory, put forward by their landlady, an octogenarian Mrs. Irving, who inhabited the three floors above them in a rank civet rug amongst unnumbered cats, and who kept the garden as bright and wholesome and well-ordered as her living-room was sparse and decomposing. She had enticed them in like an old witch, Val said, by talking volubly to them in the garden about the quietness of the place, giving them each a small, gold, furry apricot from the espaliered trees along the curving brick wall. The garden was long, thin, bowery, with sunny spots of grass, surrounded by little box hedges, its air full of roses, swarthy, damask, thick ivory, floating pink, its borders restraining fantastic striped and spotted lilies, curling bronze and gold, bold and hot and rich. And forbidden. But they did not know that in the beginning, as Mrs. Irving expatiated in her cracked and gracious voice on the high brick wall which dated from the Civil War, and earlier still, which had formed one boundary of General Fairfax's lands when Putney was a separate village, when Cromwell's Trained Bands assembled there, when the Putney Debates on liberty of conscience were held in St Mary's Church on the bridge. Randolph Henry Ash had written a poem purporting to be spoken by a Digger in Putney. He had even come there to look at the river at low tide, it was in Ellen Ash's Journal, they had brought a picnic of chicken and parsley pie. That fact, and the conjunction of Marvell's patron, Fairfax, with the existence of the walled garden of fruit and flowers were enough to tempt

Roland and Val into the garden flat, with its prohibited view.

In spring their window was lit from above by the yellow glow of a thick row of bright daffodils. Tendrils of Virginia creeper crept down as far as the window-frame, and progressed on little circular suckers across the glass, at huge vegetable speed. Swathes of jasmine, loose from a prolifically flowering specimen on the edge of the house, occasionally fell over their bailing, with their sweet scent, before Mrs. Irving, clothed in her gardening gear of Wellingtons and apron, over the seated and threadbare tweed suit in which she had first enticed them in, came and bound these back. Roland had once asked her if he could help in the garden, in exchange for the right to sit there sometimes. He had been told that he didn't know the first thing about it, that the young were all the same, destructive and careless, that Mrs. Irving set a value on her privacy. "You would think," said Val, "that the cats would do the garden no good." That was before they found the patches of damp on their own kitchen and bathroom ceilings, which, when touched with a finger, smelled unmistakably of cat-piss. The cats too, were under prohibition, confined to quarters. Roland thought, they ought to look for somewhere else, but held back from proposing it, because he was not the breadwinner, and because he didn't want to do anything so decisive, in terms of himself and Val.

Val put before him grilled marinated lamb, ratatouille and hot Greek bread. He said, "Shall I get a bottle of wine?" and Val said, disagreeably and truthfully, "You should have thought of that some time back; it'll all go cold." They ate at a card-table, which they unfolded and folded again, after.

"I made an amazing discovery today," he told her,

"Oh?"

"I was in the London Library. They've got R. H. Ash's Vico. His own copy. They keep it in the safe. I had it brought up and it was absolutely bursting at the seams with his own notes, all tucked in, on the backs of bills and things. And I'm ninety per cent sure no one had looked at them, ever, not since he put them there, because all the edges were black and the lines coincided..."

"How interesting," Flatly.

"It might change the face of scholarship. It could. They let me read them, they didn't take it away. I'm sure no one knew it was all there."

"I expect they didn't".

"I'll have to tell Blackadder. He'll want to see how important it is, make sure Cropper hasn't been there…"

"I expect he will, yes."

It was a bad mood.

"I'm sorry, Val, I'm sorry to bore you. It does look exciting."

"That depends what torns you on. We all have our little pleasures of different kinds, I suppose."

"I can write it up. An article. A solid discovery. Make me a better job prospect."

"There aren't any jobs." She added, "And if there are, they go to Fergus Wolff."

He knew his Val: he had watched her honorably try to prevent herself from adding that last remark.

"If you really think what I do is so unimportant…"

"You do what turns you on," said Val. "Everyone does, if they're lucky, if there is anything that turns them on. You have this thing about this dead man. Who had a thing about dead people. That's OK but not everyone is very bothered about all that. I see some things, from my menial vantage point. Last week when I was in that ceramics export place, I found some photographs under a file in my boss's desk. Things being done to little boys. With chains and gags and—dirt—This week, ever so efficiently filing records for this surgeon, I just happened to come across a sixteen-year-old who had his leg off last year—they're fitting him with an artificial one, it takes months, they're incredibly slow—and it's started up for certain now in his other leg, he doesn't know, but I know, I know lots of things. None of them fit together, none of them makes any sense. There was a man who went off to Amsterdam to buy some diamonds, I helped his secretary book his ticket, first class, and his limousine, smooth as clockwork, and as he's walking along a canal admiring the housefronts someone stabs him in the back, destroys a kidney, gangrene sets in, now he's dead. Just like that. Chaps like those use my menial services, here today, gone tomorrow. Randolph Henry Ash wrote long ago. Forgive me if I don't care what he wrote in his Vico."

"Oh, Val, such horrible things, you never say—".

"Oh, it's all very interesting, my menial keyhole observations, make no mistake. Just it doesn't make sense and it leaves me nowhere. I suppose I envy you, piecing together old Ash's world-picture. Only where does that leave you, old Mole? What's your world-picture? And how are you ever going to afford to get us away from dripping cat-piss and being on top of each other?"

Something had upset her, Roland reasonably deduced. Something that had caused her to use the phrase "turn you on" several times, which was uncharacteristic. Perhaps someone had grabbed her. Or had not done so. No, that was unworthy. Anger and petulance did turn her on, he knew. He knew more than was quite good for him about Val. He went across and stroked the nape of her neck, and she sniffed and stiffened and then relaxed. After a bit, they moved over to the bed.

He had not told her, and could not tell her, about his secret theft. Late that night, he looked at the letters again, in the bathroom. "Dear Madam, since our extraordinary conversation, I have thought of nothing else." "Dear Madam, since our pleasant and unexpected conversation I have thought of little else." Urgent, unfinished. Shocking. Roland had never been much interested in Randolph Henry Ash's vanished body; he did not spend time visiting his house in Russell Street, or sitting where he had sat, on stone garden seats; that was Cropper's style. What Roland liked was his knowledge of the movements of Ash's mind, stalked through the twists and turns of his syntax, suddenly sharp and clear in an unexpected epithet. But these dead letters troubled him, physically even, because they were only beginnings. He did not imagine Randolph Henry Ash, his pen moving rapidly across the paper, but he did have the thought of the pads of the long-dead fingers which had held and folded these half-covered sheets, before preserving them in the book, instead of jettisoning them. Who? He must try to find out.

※ ※

Notes

1. This epigraph is from Ash' epic *Ragnarok* which is about the philosophical relationship between an individual and the history. Several of the 28 chapters in *Possession* begin with an epigraph from the poems or writings by the two Victorian poets, Ash or LaMotte, to hint at the important images or ideas in the chapter.
2. Ragnarok: The epic by the fictitious character, Ash, in the novel. In Scandinavian Mythology, Ragnarok means the final battle between the

gods and the powers of evil.
3. Ash Factory: The Research Centre in the charge of the historian, Professor Blackadder. Notice: the word "ash" (similar to dirt) is banteringly used to hint that the research is meaningless.
4. Male Ventriloquism: a performance of male vocal mimicry in which an entertainer who makes one's voice appear to come from a dummy of a man. Here it is to satirize the female characters in Ash's work, who have no say and function as dummies of men do.
5. Ask to Embla: The first man and woman made by the gods in Scandinavian Mythology, similar to Adam and Eve in the Bible. Here Ash regards himself as Ask and writes a poem entitled *Ask to Embla* to hint at his secret love for LaMotte.
6. In *Possession*, A. S. Byatt mentions a lot of real historical figures and events, and here the pictures of Ash are alleged to be painted by the renowned painters Manet and G. F. Watts. Therefore, the fictional world appears incredibly authentic.

Questions for Understanding

1. What is the point of view the narrator adopts here in this chapter? Is it omniscient or limited?
2. Why does Val call Roland "old Mole"? What does the word "mole" suggest to you?
3. Give a description of the young couple Roland and Val presented in this chapter, and comment especially on the condition of their living place next to the "forbidden" garden. What is the symbolic meaning of the garden here if associated with Eden?

Aspects of Appreciation

1. The noticeable feature

The title *Possession*, part historical and part contemporary fiction, refers to issues of ownership and independence between lovers, the practice of collecting historically significant cultural artifacts, and to the possession that a biographer has for his subject. The novel incorporates many different styles and devices: diaries, letters and poetry, in addition to third-person narration. *Possession* is as concerned with the present day as it is with the Victorian era, pointing out the differences between the two periods and satirizing such things as modern academia and mating rituals.

2. The plot feature

The novel concerns the relationship between two fictional Victorian poets, Randolph Henry Ash (Whose life and work are loosely based on those of the English poet Robert Browning or Alfred Tennyson, whose work is more constant with the themes that are portrayed as Ash, as well as his being poet-laureate to Queen Victoria) and Christabel LaMotte (similarly based on Christina Rossetti), as revealed to present day academics as Roland Michell and Maud Bailey. Following a trail of clues from various letters and journals, they attempt to uncover the truth about Ash and LaMotte's past before it is discovered by rival colleagues.

3. The use of the epigraph

In *Possession*, epigraphs are used to head several chapters, particularly those early on in the novel. Byatt uses them as a structural device, primarily for a substantive function, to outline the common themes which formulate in that particular chapter. Each epigraph serves to point the reader to important images or ideas that are going to be expanded upon throughout the chapter. This is manifest in Chapter One, wherein the epigraph is used to introduce the novel. As the first thing the reader will see, it serves to incorporate not only those themes primarily used in that chapter, but also themes frequented throughout the novel as a whole.

Suggested Further Reading

1. A. S. Byatte. *Still Life*, Chatto & Windus, 1985.
2. A. S. Byatt. *Little Black Book of Stories*, Chatto and Windus, 2003.
3. Catherine Burgass. *A. S. Byatt's Possession: A Reader's Guide*, London: Continuum, 2002.

Topics for Further Study

1. What is the significance of the novel's title "Possession"? Do you think it has more than one meaning?
2. What does the concept of "possession" mean to the characters in the novel? In what sense can "possession" be seen as the theme of the book?

Dylan Thomas
(1914~1953)

About the Author

Dylan Marlais Thomas (1914 ~ 1953), the most important modern Welsh poet, sees biology as a magical transformation producing unity out of diversity and in his poetry he seeks a poetic ritual to celebrate this unity. His major themes are natural forces such as life of nature, the forces of birth, sex and death, and the powerful feelings that they create. So he eulogizes the unity of all life, the continuing process of life and death and new life. He also sees men and women as locked in cycles of growth, love, procreation, new growth, death, and new life again.

His poems are passionate, full of life, energy and feeling, with great strength and power. Besides, they are musical and imaginative typical of the Welsh. The closely woven, sometimes self-contradictory images from the Bible, Welsh folklore and Freud are also characteristic of his poetry.

His major works are *18 Poems* (1934), *Twenty-Five Poems* (1936), *Deaths and Entrances* (1946), *In Country Sleep* (1952) and *Collected Poems* (1952). His most notable poems include "Fern Hill" "Ballad of the Long-legged Bait" "Do Not Go Gentle into That Good Night" and "And Death Shall Have No Dominion". In addition to poetry, he wrote short stories and scripts for film and radio, of which his radio play *Under Milk Wood* (1954) is the most famous. His public readings, particularly in America, won him great acclaim; his sonorous voice with a subtle Welsh lilt became almost as famous as his works.

★ Fern Hill[1]

About the Poem

By using seemingly simple but highly expressive language and rich imagery, the poem recollects the memory of the speaker's childhood, depicts a tale of growing up and creates an idyllic world of children. In the end of the poem the reader is reminded of the passage of time and the theme of mortality begins to intrude on the youthful paradise.

Now as I was young and easy under the apple boughs
About the lilting² house and happy as the grass was green,
The night above the dingle³ starry,
Time let me hail and climb
Golden in the heydays of his⁴ eyes,
And honoured among wagons I was prince of the apple towns
And once below a time I lordly had the trees and leaves
Trail with daisies and barley
Down the rivers of the windfall light⁵.

And as I was green and carefree, famous among the barns
About the happy yard and singing as the farm was home,
In the sun that is young once only,
Time let me play and be
Golden in the mercy of his means,
And green and golden I was huntsman and herdsman, the calves
Sang to my horn, the foxes on the hills barked clear and cold,
And the sabbath⁶ rang slowly
In the pebbles of the holy streams.

All the sun long it was running, it was lovely, the hay
Fields high as the house, the tunes from the chimneys, it was air
And playing, lovely and watery
And fire green as grass.
And nightly under the simple stars
As I rode to sleep the owls were bearing the farm away,
All the moon long I heard, blessed among stables, the nightjars⁷
Flying with the ricks⁸, and the horses
Flashing into the dark.

And then to awake, and the farm, like a wanderer white
With the dew, come back, the cock on his shoulder: it was all
Shining, it was Adam and maiden⁹,
The sky gathered again
And the sun grew round that very day.
So it must have been after the birth of the simple light
In the first, spinning place, the spellbound horses walking warm

Out of the whinnying green stable
On to the fields of praise.

And honoured among foxes and pheasants[10] by the gay house
Under the new made clouds and happy as the heart was long,
In the sun born over and over,
I ran my heedless[11] ways,
My wishes raced through the house high hay
And nothing I cared, at my sky blue trades[12], that time allows
In all his tuneful turning so few and such morning songs
Before the children green and golden
Follow him out of grace.

Nothing I cared, in the lamb white days, that time would take me
Up to the swallow thronged loft by the shadow of my hand,
In the moon that is always rising,
Nor that riding to sleep
I should hear him fly with the high fields
And wake to the farm forever fled from the childless land.
Oh as I was young and easy in the mercy of his means,
Time held me green and dying
Though I sang in my chains like the sea.

※ ※

Notes

1. Fern Hill was the name of the small farm where as a boy in the 1920s the poet spent several summers with his aunt Ann Jones.
2. lilting: light, tripping, joyful.
3. dingle: small, wooded valley.
4. his: the third person singular refers to Time personified in the poem.
5. windfall light: possible of quite a few interpretations, "light coming through the gaps of the tree leaves" or "light reflected upon apples brought down by wind" are only a few.
6. sabbath: it can be understood as the ringing of church bell in Sabbath.
7. nightjars: 欧夜鹰。
8. ricks: a large pile of dried grass or straw.

9. Adam and maiden: Adam and Eve, meaning "fresh" or "brand-new".
10. pheasants: a large bird with a long tail.
11. heedless: careless or carefree.
12. trades: games.

Questions for Understanding

1. How do you understand "young and easy"(Line 1, Stanza 1) and "happy as the grass was green" (Line 2, Stanza 1) respectively? Do you think this kind of association of different qualities reasonable?
2. How do you understand "Time let me hail and climb" (Line 4, Stanza 1) and "Time let me play"(Line 4, Stanza 2)? Do you think treating time as the subject logical?
3. How do you understand "once below a time" (Line 7, Stanza 1), "All the sun long"(Line 1, Stanza 3) and "All the moon long"(Line 7, Stanza 3)?
5. What are the original idioms or phrases upon which the above expressions are based?
6. Can you justify the poet's change(transformation) of the original idioms into the present ones in the poem?
7. How effective are these changed(transformed) expressions in conveying the theme(s) of the poem?
8. Can you find more similar phrases in the poem other than what are mentioned in questions 1, 3 and 5?
9. How do you understand such expressions as "forever fled" "childless land" "green and dying" and "sang in my chains"?
10. Which words have religious connotations? How do they contribute to the tone?
12. What might be the theme(s) of the poem?

Aspects of Appreciation

1. The poem is a recollection of the childhood spent upon the poet's aunt's farm that was marked by joy and happiness. In this seemingly innocent and joyous childhood memory recollected from an older age, there is suggestion of passage of time, change and inevitable death. All the images, transformation of idioms and other devices are all centred upon the two major themes: childhood innocence and passage of time and oppositional elements such as "green and golden" and "green and dying" abound in the poem.

2. Different stylistic devices are used in the poem. (1) creative transformation of idioms: "once below a time" "All the sun long" "All the moon long" "young and easy" "green and carefree" "happy as the grass was green" and "happy as the heart was long". (2) transferred epithet and projection of emotions: transferred epithets abound in the poem (See Knowledge of Literature). (3) condensed images and multiplicity of meanings, such as "the rivers of the windfall light", "huntsman and herdsman" and "lamb white days". All these devices are used to strengthen the two major themes above mentioned: childhood memory and dominion of time or mortality.
3. The poem makes use of abundant images, symbols and sound devices, and they interweave into a magical picture of childhood which is full of colors and sounds.

Suggested Further Reading

Other poems by Dylan Thomas: "Do Not Go Gentle into That Good Night" "The Force that Through the Green Fuse Drives the Flower" "A Refusal to Mourn the Death, by Fire, of a Child in London" and "And Death Shall Have No Dominion".

Topics for Further Study

1. The poem seems to move through the cycles of the days as the persona recollects his youth. Why is this cycle particularly significant for this poem?
2. Childhood has often been used to express a state of human innocence. How does the narrator of the poem see childhood?
3. Comment on Dylan Thomas's poetry in view of tradition of Romanticism and against the background of modernism.

Knowledge of Literature

Transferred epithet and its expanded use

Transferred epithet is a poetic device in which an adjective is transferred from the noun it would ordinarily precede to another noun, thus giving a pleasant shock-effect. A typical and classical example of the transferred epithet may be the line from the first stanza of Thomas Gray's famous poem "Elegy Written in a Country Churchyard": "The plowman homeward plods his weary way", in which the word "weary" is transferred from its normal place before the word "plowman" to before the word "way". More recent and more complex examples can be found in Dylan Thomas's "Fern Hill". Instead of "the lilting boy about the house", there is "lilting house"; instead of "whinnying horses" there is "whinnying … stable". More examples from the poem are "happy yard" "gay house" "heedless ways". The profuse use of transferred epithets are very appropriate to the subject and the theme of the poem. In the eye of the child, the world tends to change according to his wishes and he tends to project his own emotions into the inanimate world. The poet also uses the device of transferred epithet to a wider range from within the sentence to beyond the sentence: "In the sun that is young once only" "in the lamb white days". In these two examples though one of the two involved nouns is not present, its presence can be inferred. Actually it is the child that is young once only and it is the child that is as innocent as lamb white. What is more important is that this stylistic feature is appropriate to a child's mentality which tends to project into the inanimate and the non-human human feelings and give them human quality. Other types of epithets are the Homeric epithet and ironic epithet etc.

Philip Larkin
(1922~1985)

About the Author

Born on August 9, 1922, in Coventry, England, Philip Arthur Larkin was commonly regarded as one of the greatest English poets of the latter half of the twentieth century; he was also a novelist and a jazz critic. Larkin had an uneventful life, and worked in a few libraries as a librarian throughout his life.

As a poet, Larkin has a relatively small production. In his lifetime, he only published four collections, titled *The North Ship* (1945), *The Less Deceived* (1955), *The Whitsun Weddings* (1964) and *High Windows* (1974). He was offered but declined the Poet Laureateship in 1984. His poetry is often associated with "The Movement" poets of the 1950s.

Larkin's poetry is characterized by its ordinary and colloquial style with clarity, a quiet and reflective tone, ironic understatement and a direct engagement with commonplace experiences. In his poems, the speakers often adopt a detached view in observing ordinary people doing ordinary things, but the reader is more than often led to further meditations about the deeper philosophical significance of the observation. His subjects vary a lot, but death and fatalism are among the recurring themes in his poetry.

His verse language is flexible but highly structured, often metaphoric and symbolic. Under the placid surface of simplicity, the reader can often detect a profundity and sometimes a transcendent beauty.

★ Toads

About the Poem

What is work to a person? Do we work for pleasure or for money? What is the relation between one's profession and one's interest? These are some of the questions Larkin addresses in this poem. For Larkin, the ugliness of a toad best represents the undesirable work.

In this poem, Larkin gives account of two "toads". One is work that offers no pleasure; the other an internal desire for "the fame and the girl and the money". Even though the speaker is rational enough to denounce the control of both toads, he recognizes in the end that one cannot be totally free from either restraint.

Why should I let the toad *work*
Squat on my life?
Can't I use my wit as a pitchfork[1]
And drive the brute off?

Six days of the week it soils[2]
With its sickening poison—
Just for paying a few bills!
That's out of proportion.

Lots of folk live on their wits:
Lecturers, lispers[3],
Losels[4], loblolly-men[5], louts[6]—
They don't end as paupers[7];

Lots of folk live up lanes
With fires in a bucket,

Eat windfalls and tinned sardines[8]—
they seem to like it.

Their nippers[9] have got bare feet,
Their unspeakable wives
Are skinny as whippets[10]—and yet
No one actually *starves*.

Ah, were I courageous enough
To shout *Stuff your pension*[11]!
But I know, all too well, that's the stuff
That dreams are made on:

For something sufficiently toad-like
Squats in me, too;
Its hunkers are heavy as hard luck,
And cold as snow,

And will never allow me to blarney[12]
My way of getting
The fame and the girl and the money
All at one sitting.

I don't say, one bodies the other
One's spiritual truth;
But I do say it's hard to lose either,
When you have both.

Notes

1. pitchfork: a farm tool with a long handle and two long curved metal points, used especially for lifting hay.
2. soils: to make something dirty, especially with waste from the body.
3. lispers: here they refer those "affecting the air of sophisticated culture", not someone suffering from a speech impediment.
4. losel: a worthless person.

5. loblolly means "thick glue"; "loblolly-men" refers to those who flatter a lot.
6. lout: a rude, violent man.
7. pauper: someone who is very poor.
8. sardines: small fatty fish usually canned.
9. nipper: informal British English, a child.
10. whippet: a small thin racing dog like a greyhound.
11. stuff something: spoken language, used to say angrily or rudely that you do not care about something or do not want something.
12. blarney: influence or urge by gentle urging, caressing, or flattering.

Questions for Understanding

1. How does a toad resemble work?
2. What is "out of proportion"? Why?
3. What kinds of people are "lectures, lispers, losels, loblolly-men, louts"? What do they have in common?
4. Who are the people that "live up lanes / with fires in a bucket, eat windfalls and tinned sardines"?
5. What is "something sufficiently toad-like" that "squats in me"?

Aspects of Appreciation

1. The poetic credo of Larkin

Larkin differs from many of his contemporaries in that he dislikes Modernist poetry's irrationalities and subversions of traditional conventions. For him, "every poem must be its own sole freshly created universe" and therefore relatively independent of the tradition. Modern poetry, mostly made up by myths and allusions, creates a distance between art and the common readership. His poems are in general anti-modernism, accessible, empirical, but thought-provoking. It is no wonder that Larkin enjoys sustained popularity among common English people who like poetry.

2. The colloquial diction

In this poem, Larkin employs colloquial language to give the poem a secular taste. This is an inheritance dating back from William Wordsworth's "language really spoken by men". In the poem, "lispers, losels, loblolly-men, louts" are informal nicknames, while "nipper" is local dialect; "stuff your pension" is swearing language, and "the fame and the girl and the money" is as plain as it can be. Larkin's poems are meant for the reading public, and this type of word-choice makes it closer and more popular with ordinary people.

3. The imagistic imagination

Larkin told an interviewer that it was "pure genius" of him to associate tedious work with the image of a detestable toad. It is true that the image of the toad has become not only the long-standing aftertaste of the poem but also a symbolic image for Larkin's poetry. The more we read into this poem, the more we are impressed with the similarities between work and a toad, and the more we are convinced of Larkin's imaginative genius which contributes to his established reputation as a great poet.

4. Psychological insight

By turning his sight into the inner world, Larkin reveals the role one's desires play in shaping a person's values and attitudes. His frank admission of his weakness before fame, women and money can produce an echo in every reader's bosom.

★ Cut Grass

About the Poem

Cut grass is scarcely noticeable for ordinary people. However, for Larkin, it signifies death of low, unimportant ones. In this poem, the grass that is mown is described as dying, while in other surrounding plants, life is blooming in the early summer. There is no relation, no sympathy and no communication between cut grass and chestnut flowers, hedges, lilac, Queen Anne's lace, and high-builded cloud; there is no connection between life and death. The perspective of the poem is from the ground to the sky, moving slowly and steadily, just like the way life decays. The brevity of the poem may also resemble the shortness of life.

> Cut grass lies frail:
> Brief is the breath
> Mown stalks exhale.
> Long, long the death
>
> It dies in the white hours
> Of young-leafed June

With chestnut flowers,
With hedges snowlike strewn,

White lilac bowed,
Lost lanes of Queen Anne's lace[1],
And that high-builded cloud
Moving at summer's pace.

Notes

1. Queen Anne's lace: a widely naturalized Eurasian herb with finely cut foliage and white compound umbels of small white or yellowish flowers and thin yellowish roots.

Questions for Understanding

1. What image of the cut grass is presented in the first stanza?
2. What is the most conspicuous rhetoric device used to depict the cut grass?
3. What is the "white hours"?
4. Why is June "young-leafed"? What does it have to do with the death of the cut grass?
5. What is the general picture of the other plants? How do they relate to the cut grass?
6. What is the tone of the speaker? Is there any display of personal emotion?

Aspects of Appreciation

1. The plainness and precision of diction

Larkin's poetic language is noted for simple, plain but precise diction. T. S. Eliot once remarked that Larkin "often makes words do what he wants". His acute observations of a floral summer are vividly textualized with just a few words, and none of them is beyond ordinary usage. The reader can feel the transient beauty of a June day with some sentimental associations of death and go on to reflect on the philosophical significance of such a simple poem.

2. Absence of emotions of the poet

In this poem, Larkin does not make his own voice heard or his personal emotions felt. Instead, the depiction of various plants, especially in the last two stanzas, is by means of a list of noun phrases plus a few attributives. This gives the poem an objectivity free of personal emotions. When talking about the poem, Larkin once remarked: "Its trouble is that it's 'music', i. e. pointless crap." The lack of the poet's voice makes the poem a unified, individual existence, with a potential for multiple interpretations.

3. The theme of death

The unremarkable death of the cut grass is given central attention in this poem, with a background of vigorous summer plants. But even in those living plants, a sign of death is creeping in: hedges are strewn, the lilac is bowed, and Queen Anne's lace is lost. Amid a life-buoyant summer, the overt and covert presence of death is almost everywhere, whose control is forthcoming and inevitable. This undertone gives the poem a touch of melancholy and regret: life is transient, and the beauty of life is fragile.

Suggested Further Reading

Philip Larkin: "Next, Please" "Days" "Church Going" "The Whitsun Weddings" "Mr. Bleaney" and "High Windows", etc.

Topics for Further Study

1. A comparative study of the death theme in "Cut Grass" and Robert Frost's "Design".
2. A comparison of Philip Larkin's image of toad with Romantic or Modernist images.
3. Differences between Larkin's poetics and that of T. S. Eliot-led Modernism.
4. Analyse the characteristics of the poetry of Philip Larkin and the Movement.
5. The English tradition of poetry and Philip Larkin's role.

Knowledge of Literature

"The Movement" is a name coined by J. D. Scott in 1954 on the *Spectator* to designate some contemporary English writers, among whom Kingsley Amis, Philip Larkin, Donald Davie, D. J. Enright, John Wain, Elizabeth Jennings, Thom Gunn and Robert Conquest are the most noteworthy. They are "bored by the despair of the Forties, not much interested in suffering and extremely impatient of poetic sensibility". The tone is generally one of "middlebrow skepticism, conformist disrespect, and ironical common sense". They reject Romantic excess and join "the post-war wave of ironical, level headed sobriety". Philip Larkin and his poem "Church Going" are considered epitomes for the Movement literature.

Ted Hughes
(1930~1998)

About the Author

Edward James Hughes (1930 ~ 1998), known as Ted Hughes, is regarded as one of the important English poets in the 20th century. His major works include *The Hawk in the Rain* (1957), *Lupercal* (1960), *Wodwo* (1967), *Crow* (1970), *Gaudete* (1977) and *Remains of Elmet* (1979). In his characteristic poems of animals and plants, he developed his own poetic voice and poetic technique of animal symbolism, with keen observation of the world of creatures, strong feelings and urgent, brilliant images. His poems are often harsh, vigorous and unsentimental, written in rough, sometimes disjointed lines, emphasizing the cunning and savagery of animal life. He was concerned with strong and sometimes violent forces of nature, writing with great power of imagination as if from inside the birds and animals. He had a view of man as being both opposed by the primitive forces of nature and also as containing those same forces within himself.

Ted Hughes was British Poet Laureate from 1984 until his death. He was married from 1956 to 1963 to the famous American poet Sylvia Plath, who committed suicide in 1963 at the age of 30. His part in the relationship became controversial, but his last poetic work, *Birthday Letters* (1998), explored their complex relationship and put him in a significantly better light.

★ Hawk Roosting

About the Poem

One of the most famous Hughes's poems and most anthologized one, "Hawk Roosting" first appeared in his *Lupercal* published in 1960. This is a famous poem of the poet's and a very special one in that the image of the bird was quite new and striking in the history of English literature.

VIII. Contemporary Period

The poem centres on the consciousness of a bird of prey and the whole poem is a monologue of, or psychology about, the hawk. The bird, perched on the top of the trees, inspects the land below him and has some arrogant ideas of himself.

> I sit in the top of the wood, my eyes closed.
> Inaction, no falsifying dream
> Between my hooked head and hooked feet:
> Or in sleep rehearse perfect kills and eat.
>
> The convenience of the high trees!
> The air's buoyancy[1] and the sun's ray
> Are of advantage to me;
> And the earth's face upward for my inspection.
>
> My feet are locked upon the rough bark.
> It took the whole of Creation[2]
> To produce my foot, my each feather:
> Now I hold Creation in my foot
>
> Or fly up, and revolve it all slowly—
> I kill where I please because it is all mine.
> There is no sophistry in my body:
> My manners are tearing off heads—
>
> The allotment of death.
> For the one path of my flight is direct
> Through the bones of the living.
> No arguments assert my right:
>
> The sun is behind me.
> Nothing has changed since I began.
> My eye has permitted no change.
> I am going to keep things like this.

Notes

1. buoyancy: the power to make something float.
2. Creation: the whole universe.

Questions for Understanding

1. What is the bird's personality?
2. Is this poem a matter-of-fact description of the hawk and his psychology or does it have symbolic or allegorical meanings?
3. Explain the title "Hawk Roosting" in terms of the character of the hawk. What may be the difference(s) between "Hawk Roosting" and "Roosting Hawk"?
4. What are characteristics of Hughes's poetry as seen in this poem?

Aspects of Appreciation

1. Image of the hawk

The hawk in this poem is proud, vain, arrogant, self-centred, egotistic, violent, cruel and blood-thirsty. Seen from another perspective, the hawk lives according to the rules of its own morality; and it is sufficient unto itself and at one with its environment.

2. Symbolism of the hawk

The hawk may be a symbol of humanity, like a dictator or a Hitler; or a symbol of violent force of nature (or nature itself). Nature now is no longer the nature in Wordsworth's poetry which was organic, whole, and in harmony with man. Nature now is disjointed and violent because man has done violence to nature and modern society and industry have destroyed the harmony between man and nature.

3. Sound image of the hawk

The title gives the hint for the dominant sounds of the hawk: the leading consonant is [h] in the word "Hawk" and the leading vowel sound is [u] or the similar one [uː] in the word "Roosting". According to Geoffrey Leech certain consonants can be regarded as hard ones and some can be regarded as soft ones. Throughout the poem there are altogether eight words which have [h] sound and there are also eight words which contain the dominant vowel sound [u] or the similar one [uː]. Because the title contains these two sounds and because the words which contain these sounds are key words about the bird's characteristics and its action, these two sounds can be regarded as sound image of the hawk. [h] is associated with the word "hard", thus it suggests hardness of the rock and firmness of the bird's posture and hard-heartedness.

4. Rough poetry of Hughes
  (1) use of long and short irregular lines;
  (2) use of cacophony: words combining consonant sounds that do not permit an easy flow of pronunciation, but rather produce sharpness or harshness;
  (3) pauses within the lines.

5. Irony in the hawk

There is dramatic irony or situational irony. The hawk thinks that he has power to keep the world like this forever, but we know that it is not true.

Suggested Further Reading

Ted Hughes's poems: "Thought Fox" "Thistles" and "Thrushes".

Topics for Further Study

1. Compare similar poems about birds of prey in English and American literature (e. g. "The Eagle" By Alfred Tennyson and "Hurt Hawk" by Robinson Jeffers) to see the change or differences in the image of the bird in literary tradition. What does the change suggest about the change in view of nature, literary ideas and social or moral values?
2. In view of intertexuality, see how meanings can be enriched by reading in a larger cultural context or literary tradition implied by the poems of the eagle or the hawk.

Knowledge of Literature

Intertexuality is a term coined by Julia Kristeva to designate the various relationships that a given text may have with other texts. These intertextual relationships include anagram, allusion, adaptation, translation, parody, pastiche, imitation and other kinds of transformation. The idea of intertextuality emphasizes the relationship between one text and another, the tie of all texts and the importance of the texts themselves rather than the external world.

Seamus Heaney
(1939~2013)

About the Author

Sometimes regarded as the most important British poet after W. B. Yeats, Seamus Heaney is another giant in the Irish literary tradition. As one of the few poets whose works both please the general public reader and attract the academic interests, Heaney was awarded the 1995 Noble prize for "works of lyrical beauty and ethical depth, which exalt everyday miracles and the living past".

Seamus Heaney was born as the first of nine children in a Catholic family in the Protestant north of Ireland. Unlike some of his brothers who committed themselves to the land, Heaney received education in St. Columb's College and then in Queen's University at Belfast, and became a teacher. Nevertheless, in Heaney's poetry, his connections with childhood, the land, nature and traditions of Ireland are omnipresent. His poems mark a respect and a responsibility toward the native and the mythic elements in the Irish culture.

Heaney grew up witnessing the turbulence of the Irish social turmoil and terrorism. His poems, therefore, bear a sometimes intricate relationship with the political currents in its contemporary milieu. Politics is a source of inspiration for his poems, but most of the time, is only subtly detectable.

Heaney is also known for his translation of *Beowulf* into modern English, and his critical essays on Thomas Hardy and Philip Larkin.

★ Digging

About the Poem

As the first poem of his first book, "Digging" is a definitive representation for Heaney's poetry in theme and artistic flavor. Simple as it is, the poem is rich in rural description and compassion for farmers toiling their field generation after generation. "Digging" in his memory, Heaney not only goes deeper in his family history, from father to grandfather, but also discovers a deeper respect for the tradition of the family and a voice of independence and maturity.

Between my finger and my thumb
The squat[1] pen rests; as snug[2] as a gun.

Under my window a clean rasping[3] sound
When the spade sinks into gravelly[4] ground:
My father, digging. I look down

Till his straining rump[5] among the flowerbeds
Bends low, comes up twenty years away
Stooping[6] in rhythm through potato drills
Where he was digging.

The coarse boot nestled[7] on the lug[8], the shaft
Against the inside knee was levered firmly.
He rooted out tall tops, buried the bright edge deep
To scatter new potatoes that we picked
Loving their cool hardness in our hands.

By God, the old man could handle a spade,
Just like his old man.

My grandfather could cut more turf in a day
Than any other man on Toner's bog[9].
Once I carried him milk in a bottle
Corked sloppily with paper. He straightened up
To drink it, then fell to right away
Nicking[10] and slicing neatly, heaving sods
Over his shoulder, digging down and down
For the good turf. Digging.

The cold smell of potato mold[11], the squelch[12] and slap
Of soggy[13] peat[14], the curt[15] cuts of an edge
Through living roots awaken in my head.
But I've no spade to follow men like them.

Between my finger and my thumb
The squat pen rests.
I'll dig with it.

※ ※

Notes

1. squat: short and wide or fat, in a way that is not attractive.
2. snug: warm, comfortable and protected, especially from the cold.
3. rasping: (of sound) harsh and unpleasant.
4. gravelly: full of or containing many small stones.
5. rump: a person's bottom.
6. stooping: bend forward and down.
7. nestled: settle comfortably and warmly in a soft place.
8. lug: a part of something that sticks out, used as a handle or support.
9. bog: an area of low wet muddy ground, sometimes containing bushes or grasses(沼泽地).
10. nicking: make a small cut in.
11. mold: a soft green, grey, or black substance that grows on food which has been kept too long, and on objects that are in warm, wet air.
12. squelch: a sucking sound as when feet are lifted from thick sticky mud.
13. soggy: moist and unpleasantly heavy.
14. peat: a soft black or brown substance formed from decaying plants just under the surface of the ground, especially in cool wet areas.
15. curt: abrupt.

Questions for Understanding

1. Who are the people mentioned in the poem? What do you know about their life?
2. Are those images, sound and smells real or just memories?
3. What kind of feeling does the speaker hold for his father and grandfather?
4. What do you suppose they are "digging" respectively, the grandfather, father and the son?
5. How could the speaker dig with a pen instead of a spade? What might be the symbolic significance of digging?
6. What may contribute to the speaker's determination of "digging with his pen"?

★ The Forge

About the Poem

One of the popular poems by Heaney, "The Forge" takes an episodic look at a forge recollected from childhood memory. In the poem, the speaker presents a view of the forge shop, the forging process and the blacksmith. The blacksmith, ostensibly unhappy about his professional prospect, evokes mythological and religious associations with his "immovable" anvil. Metaphorically, the process of forging can be seen as the creative process for a poet: dark, unpredictable and painstaking. The symbolic undercurrents in this poem extend beyond the sphere of everyday life.

> All I know is a door into the dark.
> Outside, old axles and iron hoops[1] rusting;
> Inside, the hammered anvil[2]'s short-pitched ring,
> The unpredictable fantail[3] of sparks
> Or hiss when a new shoe toughens in water.
> The anvil must be somewhere in the centre,
> Horned as a unicorn[4], at one end square,
> Set there immoveable: an altar
> Where he expends[5] himself in shape and music.
> Sometimes, leather-aproned, hairs in his nose,
> He leans out on the jamb[6], recalls a clatter
> Of hoofs where traffic is flashing in rows;
> Then grunts and goes in, with a slam and a flick
> To beat real iron out, to work the bellows[7].

Notes

1. hoop: a large ring of plastic, wood or iron.
2. anvil: a heavy iron block on which pieces of hot metal are shaped using a hammer(铁砧).
3. fantail: fan-shaped tail or end(扇形).

4. unicorn: an imaginary animal like a white horse with a long straight horn growing on its head(独角兽).
5. expend: to use or spend a lot of energy in order to do something.
6. jamb: a post that forms the side of a door or window.
7. bellows: apparatus for driving air into or through something(风箱).

Questions for Understanding

1. Have you any experience of forging? What kind of work is it?
2. Who is the speaker? What is his viewpoint?
3. What is an anvil? What role does it play in the forging? In what way does it resemble the altar?
4. What is your general impression of the blacksmith? What does his "grunt" suggest?
5. Can you hear the sound of "a slam and a flick"?
6. Do you remember things from childhood that have disappeared now? Is there any particular emotion between you and them?

Aspects of Appreciation

1. Detailed depiction of farming life

The early experience of farming life is an inexhaustible source of inspiration for Heaney. In his poems, we can find the vivid pictures of farming on the hard soil of Northern Ireland. Every detail is taken account of, so that the reader may have a firsthand experience of nature and life in that area.

2. The local flavor

Much of Seamus Heaney's poetry is devoted to the depiction of local surroundings in Northern Ireland where he was born. Always conscious of its geographical features, he asserts an Irish identity despite his English education and inhabitation. The legends and myths of Northern Ireland are explored to the fullest in his poetry.

3. The relationship with tradition

In "Digging" as well as many other poems, Heaney explores the complexity of the relationship with his ancestors, sometimes with respect and awe, and sometimes ambivalence. The relationship to the tradition also defines the development of the poet's psychological self. In the reflection of his ancestors, family or the nation, Heaney discovers his identity and literary genuineness.

Suggested Further Reading

Seamus Heaney's poems: "Follower" "The Brauballe Man" "Punishment" "Casualty" "The Skunk" "Station Island" "The Sharping Stone" and "Exposure".

Topics for Further Study

1. Seamus Heaney and the Irish literary consciousness: the influence of W. B. Yeats and James Joyce.
2. Heaney's poetry and the political issues of Northern Ireland.
3. Seamus Heaney on the English language and translation.

Knowledge of Literature

Irish poetic tradition

Ireland has seen two traditions in poetry: one in the local Irish language, the other in English. Both traditions have influenced each other and formed a variety of poetic works.

Early Irish poetry dated back to the 6th century, mainly short lyrics on such themes as religion and nature. Some poems in tales and sagas contributed another source of its origin. During medieval times, bardic poetry came into fashion, exploring the country's rich history and tradition. After the 1603 conquest, Gaelic tradition of poetry flourished. In the 18th century, poems in English grew and English gradually became the dominant language of poetry. Irish themes and techniques, however, were preserved as heritages and combined with the language. In late 19th century, under the influence of French symbolism, W. B. Yeats, among others, established the Celtic Revival literary movement, focusing on Irish contents for poetic creation. Yeats inspired many younger poets, among whom Seamus Heaney is most eminent. From his first collection of poems, Heaney is devoted to the values of his tribe, searching "for images and symbols adequate to [his] predicament", while keeping distance from political propaganda.

John Osborne
(1929~1994)

About the Author

John James Osborne(1929~1994) was born in Fulham, London, in a family of a commercial artist. He worked as a journalist for a short period of time before he associated himself with the theatre. First he spent a few years as an actor with a provincial theatrical company, during which he began to try his hand at play-writing. His first play was performed in 1950, but it was not until 1956, when *Look Back in Anger* was staged in the Royal Court Theatre, that Osborne finally made his name. The play brought the biggest shock to the English theatre since George Bernard Shaw in the first decade of the twentieth century. *Look Back in Anger* was followed by *Epitaph for George Dillon* (1957), *The Entertainer* (1957), *Luther* (1961), *A Patriot for Me* (1965) and *Watch it Come Down* (1976). The subject matter of Osborne's plays varies considerably, including the life of Martin Luther, the leader of Protestant Reformation in Germany in the early sixteenth century. Although Osborne expresses occasionally an ambivalent nostalgia for the past, the out-burst of anger against contemporary world, which made him known as an "Angry Young Man" in the 1950s, remains the basic tone of his drama.

★ Look Back in Anger

About the Play

On the surface, *Look Back in Anger* is just another adultery story. In the first act the other woman arrives; in the second she persuades the wife to leave, and then she goes to bed with the husband; in the third the wife returns, the other woman leaves, the husband and wife are reconciled. But, Osborne does not write a morality play and the meaning of his play lies deep in his portrayal of the characters. The dominant tone of *Look Back in Anger* is fury, anger for the world that the characters are living in and also for the past of their world. The staging of the play in the mid-fifties was not accidental. A number of writers at that time were either questioning or attacking various aspects of the Establishment. *Look Back in Anger* became not only the focal point but virtually the Bible of the under-thirty generation in England then.

Act I (Excerpt)

[The Porters' one-room flat in a large Midland town. Early evening. April.

The scene is a fairly large attic room, at the top of a large Victorian house. The ceiling slopes down quite sharply from L. to R. Down R. are two small low windows. In front of these is a dark oak dressing table. Most of the furniture is simple, and rather old. Up R. is a double bed, running the length of most of the back wall, the rest of which is taken up with a shelf of books. Down R. below the bed is a heavy chest of drawers, covered with books, neckties, and odds and ends, including a large, tattered toy teddy bear and soft, woolly squirrel. Up L. is a door. Below this a small wardrobe. Most of the wall L. is taken up with a high, oblong window. This looks out on to the landing, but light comes through it from a skylight beyond. Below the wardrobe is a gas stove, and, beside this, a wooden food cupboard, on which is a small, portable radio. Down C. is a sturdy dining table and three chairs, and, below this, L. and R., two deep, shabby leather armchairs.

At rise of curtain, Jimmy and Cliff[1] are seated in the two armchairs R. and L., respectively. All that we can see of either of them is two pairs of legs, sprawled way out beyond the newspapers, which hide the rest of them from sight. They are both reading. Beside them, and between them, is a jungle of newspapers and weeklies. When we do eventually see them, we find that Jimmy is a tall, thin young man about twenty-five, wearing a very worn tweed jacket and flannels. Clouds of smoke fill the room from the pipe he is smoking. He is a disconcerting mixture of sincerity and cheerful malice, of tenderness and free-booting cruelty; restless, importunate, full of pride, a combination which alienates the sensitive and insensitive alike. Blistering honesty, or apparent honesty, like his, makes few friends. To many he may seem sensitive to the point of vulgarity. To others, he is simply a loudmouth. To be as vehement as he is is to be almost noncommittal. Cliff is the same age, short, dark, big-boned, wearing a pullover and grey, new, but very creased trousers. He is easy and relaxed, almost to lethargy, with the rather sad, natural intelligence of the self-taught. If Jimmy alienates love, Cliff seems to exact it—demonstrations of it, at least, even from the cautious. He is a soothing, natural counterpoint to Jimmy. Standing L., below the food cupboard, is Alison. She is leaning over an ironing board. Beside her is a pile of clothes. Hers is the most elusive personality to catch in the uneasy polyphony of these three people. She is tuned in a different key, a key of well-bred malaise that is often drowned in the robust orchestration of the other two. Hanging over the grubby, but expensive, skirt she is wearing is a cheery red shirt of Jimmy's, but she manages somehow to look quite elegant in it. She is roughly the same age as the men. Somehow, their combined physical oddity makes her beauty more striking than it really is. She is tall, slim, dark. The bones of her face are long and delicate. There is a surprising reservation about her eyes, which are so large and deep they should make equivocation impossible. The room is still, smoke-filled. The only sound is the occasional thud of Alison's iron on the board; it is one of those chilly Spring evenings, all cloud and shadows. Presently, Jimmy throws his paper down.]

Jim: Why do I do this every Sunday? Even the book reviews seem to be the same as last week's. Different books—same reviews. Have you finished that one yet?

Cli: Not yet.

Jim: I've just read three whole columns on the English Novel. Half of it's in French. Do the Sunday papers make you feel ignorant?

Cli: Not 'arf.

Jim: Well, you are ignorant. You're just a peasant. [To Alison] What about you? You're not a peasant are you?

Ali: [Absently] What's that?

Jim: I said do the papers make you feel you're not so brilliant after all?

Ali: Oh—I haven't read them yet.

Jim: I didn't ask you that. I said—

Cli: Leave the poor girlie alone. She's busy.

Jim: Well, she can talk, can't she? You can talk, can't you? You can express an opinion. Or does the White Woman's Burden[2] make it impossible to think?

Ali: I'm sorry. I wasn't listening properly.

Jim: You bet you weren't listening. Old Porter talks, and everyone turns over and goes to sleep. And Mrs. Porter gets 'em all going with the first yawn.

Cli: Leave her alone, I said.

Jim: [Shouting] All right, dear. Go back to sleep. It was only me talking. You know? Talking? Remember? I'm sorry.

Cli: Stop yelling. I'm trying to read.

Jim: Why do you bother? You can't understand a word of it.

Cli: Uh huh.

Jim: You're too ignorant.

Cli: Yes, and uneducated. Now shut up, will you?

Jim: Why don't you get my wife to explain it to you? She's educated. [To her] That's right, isn't it?

Cli: [Kicking out at him from behind his paper] Leave her alone, I said.

Jim: Do that again, you Welsh ruffian, and I'll pull your ears off. [He bangs Cliff's paper out of his hands]

Cli: [Leaning forward] Listen—I'm trying to better myself. Let me get on with it, you big, horrible man. Give it me. [Puts his hand out for paper]

Ali: Oh, give it to him, Jimmy, for heaven's sake! I can't think!

Cli: Yes, come on, give me the paper. She can't think.

Jim: Can't think! [Throws the paper back at him] She hasn't had a thought for years! Have you?

Ali: No.

Jim: [Picks up a weekly] I'm getting hungry.

Ali: Oh, no, not already!

Cli: He's a bloody pig.

Jim: I'm not a pig. I just like food—that's all.

Cli: Like it! You're like a sexual maniac—only with you it's food. You'll end up in the *News of the World*, boy, you wait. James Porter, aged twenty-five, was bound over last week after pleading guilty to interfering with a small cabbage and two tins of beans on his way home from "The Builder's Arms." The accused said he hadn't been feeling well for some time, and had been having black-outs. He asked for his good record as an air-raid warden, second class, to be taken into account.

Jim: [Grins] Oh, yes, yes, yes. I like to eat. I'd like to live too. Do you mind?

Cli: Don't see any use in your eating at all. You never get any fatter.

Jim: People like me don't get fat. I've tried to tell you before. We just burn everything up. Now shut up while I read. You can make me some more tea.

Cli: Good God, you've just had a great potful! I only had one cup.

Jim: Like hell! Make some more.

Cli: [To Alison] Isn't that right? Didn't I only have one cup?

Ali: [Without looking up] That's right.

Cli: There you are. And she only had one cup too. I saw her. You guzzled the lot.

Jim: [Reading his weekly] Put the kettle on.

Cli: Put it on yourself. You've creased up my paper.

Jim: I'm the only one who knows how to treat a paper, or anything else, in this house. [Picks up another paper] Girl here wants to know whether her boy friend will lose all respect for her if she gives him what he asks for. Stupid bitch.

Cli: Just let me get at her, that's all.

Jim: Who buys this damned thing? [Throws it down] Haven't you read the other posh paper yet[3]?

Cii: Which?

Jim: Well, there are only two posh papers on a Sunday[4]—the one you're reading, and this one. Come on, let me have that one, and you take this.

Cli: Oh, all right. [They exchange] I was only reading the Bishop of Bromley. [Puts out his hand to Alison] How are you, dullin?

Ali: All right, thank you, dear.

Cli: [Grasping her hand] Why don't you leave all that, and sit down for a bit? You look tired.

Ali: [Smiling] I haven't much more to do.

Cli: [Kisses her hand, and puts her fingers in his mouth] She's a beautiful girl, isn't she?

Jim: That's what they all tell me. [His eyes meet hers]

Cli: It's a lovely, delicious paw you've got. Ummmmm. I'm going to bit it off.

Ali: Don't! I'll burn his shirt.

Jim: Give her her finger back, and don't be so sickening. What's the Bishop of Bromley say?

Cli: [Letting go of Alison] Oh, it says here that he makes a very moving appeal to all Christians to do all they can to assist in the manufacture of the H-Bomb.

Jim: Yes, well, that's quite moving, I suppose. [To Alison] Are you moved, my darling?

Ali: Well, naturally.

Jim: There you are: even my wife is moved. I ought to send the Bishop a subscription. Let's see. What else does he say. Dumdidumdidumdidum. Ah, yes. He's upset because someone has suggested that he supports the rich against the poor. He says he denies the difference of class distinctions. "This idea has been persistently and wickedly fostered by—the working classes!" Well!

[He looks up at both of them for reaction, but Cliff is reading, and Alison is intent on her ironing.]

Jim: [To Cliff] Did you read that bit?

Cli: Um?

[He has lost them, and he knows it, but he won't leave it.]

Jim: [To Alison] You don't suppose your father could have written it, do you?

Ali: Written what?

Jim: What I just read out, of course.

Ali: Why should my father have written it?

Jim: Sounds rather like Daddy, don't you think?

Ali: Does it?

Jim: Is the Bishop of Bromley his nom de plume[5], do you think?

Cli: Don't take any notice of him. He's being offensive. And it's so easy for him.

Jim: [Quickly] Did you read about the woman who went to the mass meeting of a certain American evangelist at Earls Court? She went forward, to declare herself for love or whatever it is, and, in the rush of converts to get to the front, she broke four ribs and got kicked in the head. She was yelling her head off agony, but with 50,000 people putting all they'd got into "Onward Christian Soldiers", nobody even knew she was there. [He looks up sharply for a response; but there isn't any.] Sometimes, I wonder if there isn't something wrong with me. What about that tea?

Cli: [Still behind paper] What tea?

Jim: Put the kettle on. [Alison looks up at him.]

Ali: Do you want some more tea?

Jim: I don't know. No, I don't think so.

Ali: Do you want some, Cliff?

Jim: No, he doesn't. How much longer will you be doing that?

Ali: Won't be long.

Jim: God, how I hate Sundays! It's always so depressing, always the same. We never seem to get any further, do we? Always the same ritual. Reading the papers, drinking tea, ironing. A few more hours, and another week gone. Our youth is slipping away. Do you know that?

Cli: [Throws down paper] What's that?

Jim: [Casually] Oh, nothing, nothing. Damn you, damn both of you, damn them all.

    Cli: Let's go to the pictures. [To Alison] What do you say, lovely?

    Ali: I don't think I'll be able to. Perhaps Jimmy would like to go. [To Jimmy] Would you like to?

    Jim: And have my enjoyment ruined by the Sunday night yobs[6] in the front row? No, thank you. [Pause] Did you read Priestley's[7] piece this week? Why on earth I ask, I don't know. I know damned well you haven't. Why do I spend ninepence on that damned paper every week? Nobody reads it except me. Nobody can be bothered. No one can raise themselves out of their delicious sloth. You two will drive me round the bend soon—I know it, as sure as I'm sitting here. I know you're going to drive me mad. Oh, heavens, how I long for a little ordinary human enthusiasm. Just enthusiasm—that's all. I want to hear a warm, thrilling voice cry out Hallelujah[8]! [He bangs his breast theatrically.] Hallelujah! I'm alive! I've an idea. Why don't we have a little game? Let's pretend that we're human beings, and that we're actually alive. Just for a while. What do you say? Let's pretend we're human. [He looks from one to the other.] Oh, brother, it's such a long time since I was with anyone who got enthusiastic about anything.

    Cli: What did he say?

    Jim: [Resentful of being dragged away from his pursuit of Alison] What did who say?

    Cli: Mr. Priestley.

    Jim: What he always says, I suppose. He's like Daddy—still casting well-set glances back to the Edwardian twilight from his comfortable, disenfranchised wilderness. What the devil have you done to those trousers?

    Cli: Done?

    Jim: Are they the ones you bought last week-end? Look at them. Do you see what he's done to those new trousers?

    Ali: You are naughty, Cliff. They look dreadful.

    Jim: You spend good money on a new pair trousers, and then sprawl about in them like a savage. What do you think you're going to do when I'm not around to look after you? Well, what are you going to do? Tell me?

    Cli: [Grinning] I don't know. [To Alison] What am I going to do, lovely?

    Ali: You'd better take them off.

    Jim: Yes, go on. Take 'em off. And I'll kick your behind for you.

Ali: I'll give them a press while I've got the iron on.

Cli: O. K. [Starts taking them off] I'll just empty the pockets. [Takes out keys, matches, handkerchief]

Jim: Give me those matches, will you?

Cli: Oh, you're not going to start up that old pipe again, are you? It stinks the place out. [To Alison] Doesn't it smell awful?

[Jimmy grabs the matches, and lights up]

Ali: I don't mind it. I've got used to it.

Jim: She's a great one for getting used to things. If she were to die, and wake up in paradise—after the first five minutes, she'd have got used to it.

Cli: [Hands her the trousers] Thank you, lovely. Give me a cigarette, will you?

Jim: Don't give him one.

Cli: I can't stand the stink of that old pipe any longer. I must have a cigarette.

Jim: I thought the doctor said no cigarettes?

Cli: Oh, why doesn't he shut up?

Jim: All right. They're your ulcers. Go ahead, and have a bellyache, if that's what you want. I give up. I give up. I'm sick of doing things for people. And all for what?

[Alison gives Cliff a cigarette. They both light up, and she goes on with her ironing]

Jim: Nobody thinks, nobody cares, no beliefs, no convictions and no enthusiasm. Just another Sunday evening.

[Cliff sits down again, in his pullover and shorts.]

Jim: Perhaps there's a concert on. [Picks up Radio Times] Ah. [Nudges Cliff with his foot] Make some more tea.

[Cliff grunts. He is reading again.]

Jim: Oh, yes. There's Vaughan Williams[9]. Well, that's something, anyway. Something strong, something simple, something English. I suppose people like me aren't supposed to be very patriotic. Somebody[10] said—what was it—we get our cooking from Paris (that's a laugh), our politics from Moscow, and our morals from Port Said. Something like that, anyway. Who was it? [Pause] Well, you wouldn't know anyway. I hate to admit it, but I think I can understand how her Daddy must have felt when he came back from India, after all those years away. The old Edwardian brigade do make their brief little world look pretty tempting. All homemade cakes and croquet, bright ideas, bright uniforms. Always the same picture: high summer, the long days in the sun, slim volumes of verse, crisp linen, the smell of starch. What a romantic picture. Phony, too, of course. It must have rained sometimes. Still, even I regret it somehow, phony or not. If you've no world of your own, it's rather pleasant to regret the passing of someone else's. I must be getting sentimental. But I must say it's pretty dreary living in the American Age—unless you're an American, of course. Perhaps all our children will be Americans. That's a thought, isn't it? [He gives Cliff a kick, and shouts at him.] I said that's a thought!

Cli: You did?

Jim: You sit there like a lump of dough, I thought you were going to make me some tea. [Cliff groans. Jimmy turns to Alison.] Is your friend Webster coming tonight?

Ali: He might drop in. You know what he is.

Jim: Well, I hope he doesn't. I don't think I could take Webster tonight.

Ali: I thought you said he was the only person who spoke your language.

Jim: So he is. Different dialect but same language, I like him. He's got bite, edge, drive—

Ali: Enthusiasm.

Jim: You've got it. When he comes here, I begin to feel exhilarated. He doesn't like me, but he gives me something, which is more than I get from most people. Not since—

Ali: Yes, we know. Not since you were living with Madeline. [She folds some of the clothes she has already ironed, and crosses to the bed with them.]

Cli: [Behind paper again] Who's Madeline?

Ali: Oh, wake up, dear. You've heard about Madeline enough times. She was his mistress. Remember? When he was fourteen. Or was it thirteen?

Jim: Eighteen.

Ali: He owes just about everything to Madeline.

Cli: I get mixed up with all your women. Was she the one all those years older than you?

Jim: Ten years.

Ch: Proper little Marchbanks[11], you are!

Jim: What time's that concert on? [Checks paper]

Cli: [Yawns] Oh, I feel so sleepy. Don't feel like standing behind that blinking sweet-stall[12] again tomorrow. Why don't you do it on your own, and let me sleep in?

Jim: I've got to be at the factory first thing, to get some more stock, so you'll have to put it up on your own. Another five minutes.

[Alison has returned to her ironing board. She stands with her arms folded, smoking, staring thoughtfully.]

Jim: She had more animation in her little finger than you two put together.

Cli: Who did?

Ali: Madeline.

Jim: Her curiosity about things, and about people was staggering. It wasn't just a naive nosiness. With her, it was simply the delight of being awake, and watching.

[Alison starts to press Cliff's trousers.]

Cli: [Behind paper] Perhaps I will make some tea, after all.

Jim: [Quietly] Just to be with her was an adventure. Even to sit on the top of a bus with her was like setting out with Ulysses.

Cli: Wouldn't have said Webster was much like Ulysses. He's an ugly little devil.

Jim: I'm not talking about Webster, stupid. He's all right though, in his way. A sort of female Emily Bronte. He's the only one of your friends [To Alison] who's worth tuppence, anyway. I'm surprised you get on with him.

Ali: So is he, I think.

Jim: [Rising to window R., and looking out] He's not only got guts, but sensitivity as well. That's about the rarest combination I can think of. None of your other friends have got either.

Ali: [Very quietly and earnestly] Jimmy, please don't go on.

[He turns and looks at her. The tired appeal in her voice has pulled him up suddenly. But soon gathers himself for a new assault. He walks C., behind Cliff, and stands, looking down at his head]

Jim: Your friends—there's shower for you.

Cli: [Mumbling] Dry up. Let her get on with my trousers.

Jim: [Musingly] Don't think I could provoke her. Nothing I could do would provoke her. Not even if I were to drop dead.

Cli: Then drop dead.

Jim: They're either militant like her Mummy and Daddy. Militant, arrogant, and full of malice. Or vague. She's somewhere between the two.

Cli: Why don't you listen to that concert of yours? And don't stand behind me. That blooming droning on behind me gives me a funny feeling down the spine.

[Jimmy gives his ears a twist and Cliff roars with pain. Jimmy grins back at him]

Cli: That hurt, you rotten sadist! [To Alison] I wish you'd kick his head in for him.

Jim: [Moving in between them] Have you ever seen her brother? Brother Nigel? The straight-backed, chinless wonder from Sandhurst[13]? I only met him once myself. He asked me to step outside when I told his mother she was evil-minded.

Cli: And did you?

Jim: Certainly not. He's a big chap. Well, you've never heard so many well-bred commonplaces come from beneath the same bowler hat. The Platitude from Outer Space—that's Brother Nigel. He'll end up in the Cabinet one day, make no mistake. But somewhere at the back of that mind is the vague knowledge that he and his pals have been plundering and fooling everybody for generations. [Going upstage, and turning] Now Nigel is just about as vague as you can get without being actually invisible. And invisible politicians aren't much use to anyone—not even to his supporters! And nothing is more vague about Nigel than his knowledge. His knowledge of life and ordinary human beings is so hazy, he really deserves some sort of decoration for it—a medal inscribed "For Vaguery in the Field." But it wouldn't do for him to be troubled by any stabs of conscience, however vague. [Moving down again] Besides, he's a patriot and an Englishman, and he doesn't like the idea that he may have been selling out his countrymen all these years, so what does he do? The only thing he can do—seek sanctuary in his own stupidity. The only way to keep things as much like they always have been as possible, is to make any alternative too much for your poor, tiny brain to grasp, it takes some doing nowadays. It really does. But they knew all about character building at Nigel's school, and he'll make it all right. Don't you worry, he'll make it. And, what's more, he'll do it better than anybody else!

[There is no sound, only the plod of Alison's iron. Her eyes are fixed on what she is doing. Cliff stares at the floor. His cheerfulness has deserted him for the moment. Jimmy is rather shakily triumphant. He cannot allow himself to look at either of them to catch their response to his rhetoric, so he moves across to the window, to recover himself, and look out]

Jim: It's started to rain. That's all it needs. This room and the rain. [He's been cheated out of his response, but he's got to draw blood somehow. Conversationally] Yes, that's the little woman's family. You know Mummy and Daddy, of course. And don't let the Marquess of Queensberry manner[14] fool you. They'll kick you in the groin while you're handing your hat to the maid. As for Nigel and Alison—[In a reverent, Stuart Hibberd[15] voice.] Nigel and Alison. They're what they sound like: sycophantic, phlegmatic, and pusillanimous.

Cli: I'll bet that concert's started by now. Shall I put it on?

Jim: I looked up that word the other day. It's one of those words I've never been quite sure of, but always thought I knew.

Cli: What was that?

Jim: I told you—pusillanimous. Do you know what it means?

[Cliff shakes his head]

Jim: Neither did I really. All this time, I have been married to this woman, this monument to non-attachment, and suddenly I discover that there is actually a word that sums her up. Not just an adjective in the English language to describe her with—it's her name! Pusillanimous! It sounds like some fleshy Roman matron, doesn't it? The Lady Pusillanimous seen here with her husband Sextus, on their way to the Games. [Cliff looks troubled, and glances uneasily at Alison]

Poor old Sextus! If he were put into a Hollywood film, he's so unimpressive, they'd make some poor British actor play the part. He doesn't know it, but those beefcake Christians will make off with his wife in the wonder of stereophonic sound before the picture's over. [Alison leans against the board, and closes her eyes.] The Lady Pusillanimous has been promised a brighter easier world than old Sextus can ever offer her. Hi, Pusey! What say we get the hell down to the Arena, and maybe feed ourselves to a couple of lions, huh?

Ali: God help me, if he doesn't stop, I'll go out of my mind in a minute.

Jim: Why don't you? That would be something, anyway. [Crosses to chest of drawers R.] But I haven't told you what it means yet, have I?

[Picks up dictionary] I don't have to tell her—she knows. In fact, if my pronunciation is at fault, she'll probably wait for a suitably public moment to correct it. Here it is. I quote: Pusillanimous. Adjective. Wanting of firmness of mind, of small courage, having a little mind, mean-spirited, cowardly, timid of mind. From the Latin *pusillus*, very little, and *animus*, the mind. [Slams the book shut] That's my wife! That's her, isn't it? Behold the Lady Pusillanimous. [Shouting hoarsely] Hi, Pusey! When's your next picture?

[Jimmy watches her, waiting for her to break. For no more than a flash, Alison's face seems to contort, and it looks as though she might throw her head back, and scream. But it passes in a moment. She is used to these carefully rehearsed attacks, and it doesn't look as though he will get his triumph tonight. She carries on with her ironing. Jimmy crosses, and switches on the radio. The Vaughan Williams concert has started. He goes back to his chair, leans back in it, and closes his eyes]

Ali: [Handing Cliff his trousers] There you are, dear. They're not very good, but they'll do for now.

[Cliff gets up and puts them on.]

Cli: Oh, that's lovely.

Ali: Now try and look after them. I'll give them a real press later on.

Cli: Thank you, you beautiful, darling girl. [He puts his arms round her waist, and kisses her. She smiles, and gives his nose a tug. Jimmy watches from his chair.]

Ali: [To Cliff] Let's have a cigarette, shall we?

Cli: That's a good idea. Where are they?

Ali: On the stove. Do you want one, Jimmy?

Jim: No, thank you, I'm trying to listen. Do you mind?

Cli: Sorry, your lordship.

[He puts a cigarette in Alison's mouth, and one in his own, and lights up. Cliff sits down, and picks up his paper. Alison goes back to her board. Cliff throws down paper, picks up another, and thumbs through that]

Jim: Do you have to make all that racket?

Cli: Oh, sorry.

Jim: It's quite a simple thing, you know—turning over a page. Anyway, that's my paper. [Snatches it away]

Cli: Oh, don't be so mean!

Jim: Price ninepence, obtainable from any news-agent's. Now let me hear the music, for God's sake. [Pause. To Alison] Are you going to be much longer doing that?

Ali: Why?

Jim: Perhaps you haven't noticed it, but it's interfering with the radio.

Ali: I'm sorry. I shan't be much longer.

[A pause. The iron mingles with the music. Cliff shifts restlessly in his chair. Jimmy watches Alison, his foot beginning to twitch dangerously. Presently, he gets up quickly, crossing below Alison to be the radio, and turns it off.]

Ali: What did you do that for?

Jim: I wanted to listen to the concert, that's all.

Ali: Well, what's stopping you?

Jim: Everyone's making such a din—that's what's stopping me.

Ali: Well, I'm very sorry, but I can't stop everything because you want to listen to music.

Jim: Why not?

Ali: Really, Jimmy, you're like a child.

Jim: Don't try and patronize me. [Turning to Cliff] She's so clumsy. I watch for her to do the same things every night. The way she jumps on the bed, as she were stamping on someone's face, and draws the curtains back with a great clatter, in that casually destructive way of hers. It's like someone launching a battleship. Have you ever noticed how noisy women are? [Crosses below chairs to L. C.] Have you? The way they kick the floor about, simply walking over it? Or have you watched them sitting at their dressing tables, dropping their weapons and banging down their bits of boxes and brushes and lipsticks? [He faces her dressing table.] I've watched her doing it night after night. When you see a woman in front of her bedroom mirror, you realize what a refined sort of a butcher she is. [Turns in] Did you ever see some dirty old Arab, sticking his fingers into some mess of lamb fat and gristle? Well, she's just like that. Thank God they don't have many women surgeons! Those primitive hands would have your guts out in no time. Flip! Out it comes, like the powder out of its box. Flop! Back it goes, like the powder puff on the table.

Cli: [Grimacing cheerfully] Ugh! Stop it!

Jim: [Moving upstage] She'd drop your guts like hair clips and fluff all over the floor. You've got to be fundamentally insensitive to be as noisy and as clumsy as that. [He moves C., and leans against the table.] I had a flat underneath a couple of girls once. You heard every damned thing those bastards did, all day and night. The most simple, everyday actions were a sort of assault course on your sensibilities. I used to plead with them. I even got to screaming the most ingenious obscenities I could think of, up the stairs at them. But nothing, nothing, would move them. With those two, even a simple visit to the lavatory sounded like a medieval siege. Oh, they beat me in the end—I had to go. I expect they've still at it. Or they're probably married by now, and driving some other poor devils out of their minds. Slamming their doors, stamping their high heels, banging their irons and saucepans—the eternal flaming racket of the female.

[Church bells start ringing outside]

Jim: Oh, hell! Now the bloody bells have started! [He rushes to the window.] Wrap it up, will you? Stop ringing those bells! There's somebody going crazy in here! I don't want to hear them!

Ali: Stop shouting! [Recovering immediately] You'll have Miss Drury up here.

Jim: I don't give a damn about Miss Drury—that mild old gentlewoman doesn't fool me, even if she takes in you two. She's an old robber. She gets more than enough out of us for this place every week. Anyway, she's probably in church, [Points to the window] swinging on those bloody bells! [Cliff goes to the window, and closes it]

Cli: Come on, now, be a good boy. I'll take us all out, and we'll have a drink.

Jim: They're not open yet. It's Sunday. Remember? Anyway, it's raining.

Cli: Well, shall we dance? [He pushes Jimmy round the floor, who is past the mood for this kind of fooling] Do you come here often?

Jim: Only in the mating season. All right, all right, very funny. [He tries to escape, but Cliff holds him like a vise.] Let me go.

Cli: Not until you've apologized for being nasty to everyone. Do you think bosoms will be in or out, this year?

Jim: Your teeth will be out in a minute, if you don't let go!

[He makes a great effort to wrench himself free, but Cliff hangs on. They collapse to the floor C., below the table, struggling. Alison carries on with her ironing. This is routine, but she is getting close to breaking point, all the same. Cliff manages to break away, and finds himself in front of the ironing board. Jimmy springs up. They grapple.]

Ali: Look out, for heaven's sake! Oh, it's more like a zoo every day!

[Jimmy makes a frantic, deliberate effort, and manages to push Cliff on to the ironing board, and into Alison. The board collapses. Cliff falls against her, and they end up in a heap on the floor. Alison cries out in pain. Jimmy looks down at them, dazed and breathless.]

Cli: [Picking himself up] She's hurt. Are you all right?

Ali: Well, does it look like it!

Cli: She's burnt her arm on the iron.

Jim: Darling, I'm sorry.

Ali: Get out!

Jim: I'm sorry, believe me. You think I did it on pur—

Ali: [Her head shaking helplessly] Clear out of my sight!

[He stares at her uncertainly. Cliff nods to him, and he turns and goes out of the door.]

※※※※※※※※※※※※※※※※※※※※※※※※※※※※※※

Notes

1. Cliff: Cliff Lewis, who shares the flat with the Porters.
2. The term "White Man's Burden" was coined in 1899 by Rudyard Kipling, an English author, to refer to the white people's obligation to manage the affairs of the supposedly backward non-white people in English colonies. Here Jimmy coins a similar term.
3. posh: smart, elegant.
4. two posh papers: *The Times* and *The Observer*.
5. nom de plume: pen name.
6. yobs: slow-thinking foolish fellows.
7. Priestley: John Boynton Priestley, English author.
8. Hallelujah: (Hebrew) Praise the Lord.
9. Vaughan Williams: an English composer.
10. somebody: George Orwell, an English author. Port Said: a port in Egypt.
11. Marchbanks: a character in G. B. Shaw's *Candida*, who, at the age of eighteen, falls in love with the thirty-three-year-old Candida.
12. sweet-stall: candy stand.
13. Sandhurst: the site of the Royal Military College.
14. the Marquess of Queensberry manner: rules for boxing drawn by the

Marquess of Queensberry in 1867.
15. Stuart Hibberd: a BBC news commentator.

Questions for Understanding

1. Work out a list of the things that Jimmy Porter complains about in Act One. What kind of attitude does Jimmy have toward the past, the present, and the future?
2. Explain in a few sentences the state of mind of Jimmy Porter. Does this have something to do with the time when the play was staged?

Aspects of Appreciation

1. The setting of the play

The play takes place in the Porters' one-room flat, a fairly large attic room. The furniture is simple and rather old: a double bed, dressing table, book shelves, chest of drawers, dining table, and three chairs, two shabby leather arm chairs. The drab setting of the play emphasizes the contrast between the idealistic Jimmy and the dull reality of the world surrounding him.

2. Critical reception

Critical reception was strongly mixed: some detested the play and the central character, but most recognized Osborne as an important new talent and the play as emotionally powerful. They also recognized the play as one that fervently spoke of the concerns of the young in post-war England. Although the first production of *Look Back in Anger* was not initially financially successful, after an excerpt was shown on BBC the box office was overwhelming. Osborne was publicized as the "Angry Young Man" and the success of *Look Back in Anger* opened the door to other young writers who dealt with contemporary problems.

Suggested Further Reading

John Osborne's *The Entertainer*, *A Patriot for Me* and *Watch it Come Down*.

Topics for Further Study

The image of "Angry Young Man" in *Look Back in Anger*.

Harold Pinter
(1930~2008)

About the Author

Harold Pinter(1930~2008), a Nobel Prize winner in 2005, was born in East London into a Jewish family. The subject matter of Pinter's plays is the contemporary life of the English people, very often the life of those at the bottom of the social ladder. Compared with other contemporary English dramatists, Pinter has been studied by quite a few scholars and critics. Naturally, critics tend to attach labels to Pinter's dramatic work, but he denies all these labels, insisting that his plays are original, coming out of himself, as a natural response to his environment. *The Room* (1957) was followed by *The Birthday Party* (1958), *The Caretaker* (1960), *The Dumb Waiter* (1960), *The Lover* (1963), *The Homecoming* (1965), *Old Times* (1971), *No Man's Land* (1975) and *Betrayal* (1978). Pinter is far from a realistic writer and in his plays it is almost impossible to locate specific information concerning the characters' background, identity and motive. To Pinter, these three issues do not only exist in his plays; they are the very issues to which contemporary philosophy and literature have been searching for an answer.

★ The Dumb Waiter

About the Play

Like Pinter's first play, *The Room*, the one-act play *The Dumb Waiter* is also set in a room enclosed by a dark, mysterious world outside. The plot is simple. Two professional assassins, Ben and Gus, are waiting for their order in the basement of a totally uninhabited derelict building. This room that they are in must have been the kitchen of a restaurant because there is a dumb waiter and speaking tube to be used for communication with the restaurant upstairs. A tension is being built up since the two men do not trust each other. Suddenly the dumb waiter begins to work and slips of paper with food orders come down. At first, the orders are for ordinary English food, but gradually the order becomes more and more exotic. When the order for tea comes, Gus becomes indignant because they have tried in vain to make themselves a cup of tea. When he leaves to drink a glass of water in the kitchen, instructions come from above. It seems that the victim has arrived. Then the door opens and Gus is pushed in without his jacket or his revolver. The two partners face each other when the curtain falls.

[Scene: A basement room. Two beds, flat against the back wall. A serving hatch, closed, between the beds. A door to the kitchen and lavatory, left. A door to a passage, right.

Ben is lying on a bed, left, reading a paper. Gus is sitting on a bed, right, tying his shoelaces, with difficulty. Both are dressed in shirts, trousers and braces.

Silence.

Gus ties his laces, rises, yawns and begins to walk slowly to the door, left. He stops, looks down, and shakes his foot.

Ben lowers his paper and watches him. Gus kneels and unties his shoe-lace and slowly takes off the shoe. He looks inside it and brings out a flattened matchbox. He shakes it and examines it. Their eyes meet. Ben rattles his paper and reads. Gus puts the matchbox in his pocket and bends down to put on his shoe. He ties his lace, with difficulty. Ben lowers his paper and watches him. Gus walks to the door, left, stops, and shakes the other foot. He kneels, unties his shoe-lace, and slowly takes off the shoe. He looks inside it and brings out a flattened cigarette packet. He shakes it and examines it. Their eyes meet. Ben rattles his paper and reads. Gus puts the packet in his pocket, bends down, puts on his shoe and ties the lace.

He wanders off, left.

Ben slams the paper down on the bed and glares after him. He picks up the paper and lies on his back, reading.

Silence.

A lavatory chain is pulled twice off, left, but the lavatory does not flush.

Silence.

Gus re-enters, left, and halts at the door, scratching his head.

Ben slams down the paper.]

Ben: Kaw! [He picks up the paper] What about this? Listen to this! [He refers to the paper]

A man of eighty-seven wanted to cross the road. But there was a lot of traffic, see? He couldn't see how he was going to squeeze through. So he crawled under a lorry.

Gus: He what?

Ben: He crawled under a lorry. A stationary lorry.

Gus: No?

Ben: The lorry started and ran over him.

Gus: Go on!

Ben: That's what it says here.

Gus: Get away.

Ben: It's enough to make you want to puke, isn't it?

Gus: Who advised him to do a thing like that?

Ben: A man of eighty-seven crawling under a lorry!

Gus: It's unbelievable.

Ben: It's down here in black and white.

Gus: Incredible.

[Silence. Gus shakes his head and exits. Ben lies back and reads.

The lavatory chain is pulled once off left, but the lavatory does not flush.

Ben whistles at an item in the paper.

Gus re-enters]

Gus: I want to ask you something.

Ben: What are you doing out there?

Gus: Well, I was just—

Ben: What about the tea?

Gus: I'm just going to make it.

Ben: Well, go on, make it.

Gus: Yes, I will. [He sits in a chair. Ruminatively] He's laid on some very nice crockery this time, I'll say that. It's sort of striped. There's a white stripe.

[Ben reads]

Gus: It's very nice. I'll say that.

[Ben turns the page]

Gus: You know, sort of round the cup. Round the rim. All the rest of it's black, you see. Then the saucer's black, except for right in the middle, where the cup goes, where it's white.

[Ben reads]

Gus: Then the plates are the same, you see. Only they've got a black stripe—the plates—right across tbe middle. Yes, I'm quite taken with the crockery.

Ben: [still reading] What do you want plates for? You're not going to eat.

Gus: I've brought a few biscuits.

Ben: Well, you'd better eat them quick.

Gus: I always bring a few biscuits. Or a pie. You know I can't drink tea without anything to eat.

Ben: Well, make the tea then, will you? Time's getting on.

[Gus brings out the flattened cigarette packet and examines it]

Gus: You got any cigarettes? I think I've run out.

[He throws the packet high up and leans forward to catch it]

Gus: I hope it won't be a long job, this one.

[Aiming carefully, he flips tile packet under his bed]

Gus: Oh, I wanted to ask you something.

Ben: [slamming his paper down] Kaw!

Gus: What's that?

Ben: A child of eight killed a cat!

Gus: Get away.

Ben: It's a fact. What about that, eh? A Child of eight killing a cat!

Gus: How did he do it?

Ben: It was a girl.

Gus: How did she do it?

Ben: She—[He picks up the paper and studies it] It doesn't say.

Gus: Why not?

Ben: Wait a minute. It just says—Her brother, aged eleven, viewed the incident from the toolshed.

Gus: Go on!

Ben: That's blood ridiculous.

[Pause]

Gus: I bet he did it.

Ben: Who?

Gus: The brother.

Ben: I think you're right.

[Pause]

Ben: [slamming down the paper] What about that, eh? A kid of eleven killing a cat and blaming it on his little sister of eight! It's enough to—[He breaks off in disgust and seizes the paper. Gus rises.]

Gus: What time is he getting in touch? [Ben reads] What time is he getting in touch?

Ben: What's the matter with you? It could be any time. Any time.

Gus: [moves to the foot of Ben's bed] Well, I was going to ask you something.

Ben: What?

Gus: Have you noticed the time that tank takes to fill?

Ben: What tank?

Gus: In the lavatory.

Ben: No. Does it?

Gus: Terrible.

Ben: Well, what about it?

Gus: What do you think's the matter with it?

Ben: Nothing.

Gus: Nothing?

Ben: It's got a deficient ballcock, that's all.

Gus: A deficient what?

Ben: Ballcock.

Gus: No? Really?

Ben: That's what I should say.

Gus: Go on! That didn't occur to me. [Gus wanders to his bed and presses the mattress.] I didn't have a very restful sleep today, did you? It's not much of a bed. I could have done with another blanket too. [He catches sight of a picture on the wall.] Hello, what's this? [Peering at it] "The First Eleven[1]". Cricketers. You seen this, Ben?

Ben: [reading] What?

Gus: The first eleven.

Ben: What?

Gus: There's a photo here of the first eleven.

Ben: What first eleven?

Gus: [studying the photo] It doesn't say.

Ben: What about that tea?

Gus: They all look a bit old to me. [Gus wanders downstage, looks out front, then all about the room.] I wouldn't like to live in this dump. I wouldn't mind if you had a window, you could see what it looked like outside.

 Ben: What do you want a window for?

 Gus: Well, I like to have a bit of a view, Ben. It whiles away the time. [He walks about the room.] I mean, you come into a place when it's still dark, you come into a room you've never seen before, you sleep all day, you do your job, and then you go away in the night again.

 [Pause]

 Gus: I like to get a look at the scenery. You never get the chance in this job.

 Ben: You get your holidays, don't you?

 Gus: Only a fortnight.

 Ben: [lowering the paper] You kill me. Anyone would think you're working every day. How often do we do a job? Once a week? What are you complaining about?

 Gus: Yes, but we've got to be on tap though, haven't we? You can't move out of the house in case a call comes.

 Ben: You know what your trouble is?

 Gus: What?

 Ben: You haven't got any interests.

 Gus: I've got interests.

 Ben: What? Tell me one of your interests.

 [Pause]

 Gus: I've got interests.

 Ben: Look at me. What have I got?

 Gus: I don't know. What?

 Ben: I've got my woodwork. I've got my model boats. Have you ever seen me idle? I'm never idle. I know how to occupy my time, to its best advantage. Then when a call comes, I'm ready.

 Gus: Don't you ever get a bit fed up?

 Ben: Fed up? What with?

 [Silence]

 [Ben reads. Gus feels in the pocket of his jacket, which hangs on the bed]

 Gus: You got any cigarettes? I've run out. [The lavatory flushes off left.] There she goes. [Gus sits on his bed.] No, I mean, I say the crockery's good. It is. It's very nice. But that's about all I can say for this place. It's worse than the last one. Remember that last place we were in?

Last time, where was it? At least there was a wireless there. No, honest. He doesn't seem to bother much about our comfort these days.

Ben: When are you going to stop jabbering?

Gus: You'd get rheumatism in a place like this, if you stay long.

Ben: We're not staying long. Make the tea, will you? We'll be on the job in a minute.

[Gus picks up a small bag by his bed and brings out a packet of tea. He examines it and looks up]

Gus: Eh, I've been meaning to ask you.

Ben: What the hell is it now?

Gus: Why did you stop the car this morning, in the middle of that road?

Ben: [lowering the paper] I thought you were asleep.

Gus: I was, but I woke up when you stepped. You did stop, didn't you?

[Pause]

Gus: In the middle of that road. It was still dark, don't you remember? I looked out. It was all misty. I thought perhaps you wanted to kip², but you were sitting up dead straight, like you were waiting for something.

Ben: I wasn't waiting for anything.

Gus: I must have fallen asleep again. What was all that about then? Why did you stop?

Ben: [picking up the paper] We were too early.

Gus: Early? [He rises] What do you mean? We got the call, didn't we, saying we were to start right away. We did. We shoved out on the dot. So how could we be too early?

Ben: [quietly] Who took the call, me or you?

Gus: You.

Ben: We were too early.

Gus: Too early for what?

[Pause]

Gus: You mean someone had to get out before we got in? [He examines the bedclothes] I thought these sheets didn't look too bright. I thought they ponged³ a bit. I was too tired to notice when I got in this morning. Eh, that's taking a bit of a liberty, isn't it? I don't want to share my bed-sheets. I told you things were going down the drain. I mean, we've always had clean sheets laid on up till now. I've noticed it.

Ben: How do you know those sheets weren't clean?

Gus: What do you mean?

Ben: How do you know they weren't clean? You've spent the whole day in them, haven't yon?

Gus: What, you mean it might be my pong? [He sniffs sheets.] Yes. [He sits slowly on bed] It could be my pong, I suppose. It's difficult to tell. I don't really know what I pong like, that's the trouble.

Ben: [referring to the paper] Kaw!

Gus: Eh, Ben.

Ben: Kaw!

Gus: Ben.

Ben: What?

Gus: What town are we in? I've forgotten.

Ben: I've told you. Birmingham.

Gus: Go on!

[He looks with interest about the room.]

Gus: That's in the Midlands. The second biggest city in Great Britain. I'd never have guessed. [He snaps his fingers] Eh, it's Friday today, isn't it? It'll be Saturday tomorrow.

Ben: What about it?

Gus: [excited] We could go and watch the Villa[4].

Ben: They're playing away.

Gus: No, are they? Caarr! What a pity.

Ben: Anyway, there's no time. We've got to get straight back.

Gus: Well, we have done in the past, haven't we? Stayed over and watched a game, haven't we? For a bit of relaxation.

Ben: Things have tightened up, mate. They've tightened up.

[Gus chuckles to himself.]

Gus: I saw the Villa get beat in a cup tie once. Who was it against now? White shirts. It was one-all at half-time. I'll never forget it. Their opponents won by a penalty. Talk about drama. Yes, it was a disputed penalty. Disputed. They got beat two-one, anyway, because of it. You were there yourself.

Ben: Not me.

Gus: Yes, you were there. Don't you remember that disputed penalty?

Ben: No.

Gus: He went down just inside the area. Then they said he was just acting. I didn't think the other bloke touched him myself. But the referee had the ball on the spot.

Ben: Didn't touch him! What are you talking about? He laid him out flat!

Gus: Not the Villa. The Villa don't play that sort of game.

Ben: Get out of it.

[Pause]

Gus: Eh, that must have been here, in Birmingham.

Ben: What must?

Gus: The Villa. That must have been here.

Ben: They were playing away.

Gus: Because you know who the other team was? It was the Spurs. It was Tottenham Hotspur[5].

Ben: Well, what about it?

Gus: We've never done a job in Tottenham.

Ben: How do you know?

Gus: I'd remember Tottenham.

[Ben turns on his bed to look at him.]

Ben: Don't make me laugh, will you?

[Ben turns back and reads. Gus yawns and speaks through his yawn.]

Gus: When's he going to get in touch?

[Pause]

Gus: Yes, I'd like to see another football match. I've always been an ardent football fan. Here, what about coming to see the Spurs tomorrow?

Ben: [tonelessly] They're playing away.

Gus: Who are?

Ben: The Spurs.

Gus: Then they might be playing here.

Ben: Don't be silly.

Gus: If they're playing away they might be playing here. They might be playing the Villa.

Ben: [tonelessly] But the Villa are playing away.

[Pause. An envelope slides under the door, right. Gus sees it. He stands, looking at it.]

Gus: Ben.

Ben: Away. They're all playing away.

Gus: Ben, look here.

Ben: What?

Gus: Look.

[Ben turns his head and sees the envelope. He stands.]

Ben: What's that?

Gus: I don't know.

Ben: Where did it come from?

Gus: Under the door.

Ben: Well, what is it?

Gus: I don't know.

[They stare at it.]

Ben: Pick it up.

Gus: What do you mean?

Ben: Pick it up!

[Gus slowly moves towards it, bends and picks it up.]

Ben: What is it?

Gus: An envelope.

Ben: Is there anything on it?

Gus: No.

Ben: Is it sealed?

Gus: Yes.

Ben: Open it.

Gus: What?

Ben: Open it!

[Gus opens it and looks inside.]

Ben: What's in it?

[Gus empties twelve matches into his hand.]

Gus: Matches.

Ben: Matches?

Gus: Yes.

Ben: Show it to me.

[Gus passes the envelope. Ben examines it.]

Ben: Nothing on it. Not a word.

Gus: That's funny, isn't it?

Ben: It came under the door?

Gus: Must have done.

Ben: Well, go on.

Gus: Go on where?

Ben: Open the door and see if you can catch anyone outside.

Gus: Who, me?

Ben: Go on!

[Gus stares at him, puts the matches in his pocket, goes to his bed and brings a revolver from under the pillow. He goes to the door, opens it, looks out and shuts it.]

Gus: No one.

[He replaces the revolver.]

Ben: What did you see?

Gus: Nothing.

Ben: They must have been pretty quick.

[Gus takes the matches from pocket and looks at them.]

Gus: Well, they'll come in handy.

Ben: Yes.

Gus: Won't they?

Ben: Yes, you're always running out, aren't you?

Gus: All the time.

Ben: Well, they'll come in handy then.

Gus: Yes.

Ben: Won't they?

Gus: Yes, I could do with them. I could do with them too.

Ben: You could, eh?

Gus: Yes.

Ben: Why?

Gus: We haven't got any.

Ben: Well, you've got some now, haven't you?

Gus: I can light the kettle now.

Ben: Yes, you're always cadging matches. How many have you got there?

Gus: About a dozen.

Ben: Well, don't lose them. Red too. You don't even need a box.

[Gus probes his ear with a match.]

Ben: [slapping his hand] Don't waste them! Go on, go and light it.

Gus: Eh?

Ben: Go and light it.

Gus: Light what?

Ben: The kettle.

Gus: You mean the gas.

Ben: Who does?

Gus: You do.

Ben: [his eyes narrowing] What do you mean, I mean the gas?

Gus: Well, that's what you mean, don't you? The gas.

Ben: [powerfully] If I say go and light the kettle I mean go and light the kettle.

Gus: How can you light a kettle?

Ben: It's a figure of speech! Light the kettle. It's a figure of speech!

Gus: I've never heard it.

Ben: Light the kettle! It's common usage!

Gus: I think you've got it wrong.

Ben: [menacing] What do you mean?

Gus: They say put on the kettle.

Ben: [taut] Who says?

[They stare at each other, breathing hard.]

Ben: [deliberately] I have never in all my life heard anyone say put on the kettle.

Gus: I bet my mother used to say it.

Ben: Your mother? When did you last see your mother?

Gus: I don't know, about—

Ben: Well, what are you talking about your mother for?

[They stare]

Ben: Gus, I'm not trying to be unreasonable, I'm just trying to point out something to you.

Gus: Yes, but—

Ben: Who's the senior partner here, me or you?

Gus: You.

Ben: I'm only looking after your interests, Gus. You've got to learn, mate.

Gus: Yes, but I've never heard.

Ben: [vehemently] Nobody says light the gas! What does the gas light?

Gus: What does the gas?

Ben: [grabbing him with two hands by the throat, at arm's length] THE KETTEL, YOU FOOL!

[Gus takes the hands from his throat.]

Gus: All right, all right.

[Pause]

Ben: Well, what are you waiting for?
Gus: I want to see if they light.
Ben: What?
Gus: The matches.
[He takes out the flattened box and tries to strike.]
Gus: No.
[He throws the box under the bed. Ben stares at him. Gus raises his foot.]
Gus: Shall I try it on here?
[Ben stares. Gus strikes a match on his shoe. It lights.]
Gui: Here we are.
Ben: [wearily] Put on the bloody kettle, for Christ's sake.
[Ben goes to his bed, but, realising what he has said, stops and half turns. They look at each other. Gus slowly exits, left. Ben slams his paper down on the bed and sits on it, head in hands.]
Gus: [entering] It's going.
Ben: What?
Gus: The stove.
[Gus goes to his bed and sits.]
Gus: I wonder who it'll be tonight.
[Silence]
Gus: Eh, I've been wanting to ask you something.
Ben: [putting his legs on the bed] Oh, for Christ's sake.
Gus: No. I was going to ask you something.
[He rises and sits on Ben's bed]
Ben: What are you sitting on my bed for?
[Gus sits]
Ben: What's the matter with you? You're always asking me questions. What's the matter with you?
Gus: Nothing.
Ben: You never used to ask me so many damn questions. What's come over you?
Gus: No, I was just wondering.
Ben: Stop wondering. You've got a job to do. Why don't you just do it and shut up?
Gus: That's what I was wondering about.
Ben: What?

Gus: The job.
Ben: What job?
Gus: [tentatively] I thought perhaps you might know something.
[Ben looks at him]
Gus: I thought perhaps you—I mean—have you got any idea—who it's going to be tonight?
Ben: Who what's going to be?
[They look at each other]
Gus: [at length] Who it's going to be.
[Silence]
Ben: Are you feeling all right?
Gus: Sure.
Ben: Go and make the tea.
Gus: Yes, sure.
[Gus exits, Ben looks after him. He then takes his revolver from under the pillow and checks it for ammunition. Gus re-enters]
Gus: The gas has gone out.
Ben: Well, what about it?
Gus: There's a meter[6].
Ben: I haven't got any money.
Gus: Nor have I.
Ben: You'll have to wait.
Gus: What for?
Ben: For Wilson.
Gus: He might not come. He might just send a message. He doesn't always come.
Ben: Well, you'll have to do without it, won't you?
Gus: Blimey.
Ben: You'll have a cup of tea afterwards. What's the matter with you?
Gus: I like to have one before.
[Ben holds the revolver up to the light and polishes it.]
Ben: You'd better get ready anyway.
Gus: Well, I don't know, that's a bit much, you know, for my money.
[He picks up a packet of tea from the bed and throws it into the bag.]
Gus: I hope he's got a shilling, anyway, if he comes. He's entitled to have. After all, it's his place, he could have seen there was enough gas for a cup of tea.

Ben: What do you mean, it's his place?

Gus: Well, isn't it?

Ben: He's probably only rented it. It doesn't have to be his place.

Gus: I know it's his place. I bet the whole house is. He's not even laying on any gas now either. [Gus sits on his bed.] It's his place all right. Look at all the other places. You go to this address, there's a key there, there's a teapot, there's never a soul in sight—[He pauses.] Eh, nobody ever hears a thing, have you ever thought of that? We never get any complaints, do we, too much noise or anything like that? You never see a soul, do you? —except the block who comes. You ever noticed that? I wonder if the walls are sound-proof. [He touches the wall above his bed.] Can't tell. All you do is wait, eh? Half the time he doesn't even bother to put in an appearance, Wilson.

Ben: Why should he? He's a busy man.

Gus: [thoughtfully] I find him hard to talk to, Wilson. Do you know that, Ben?

Ben: Scrub round it, will you?

[Pause]

Gus: There are a number of things I want to ask him. But I can never get round to it, when I see him.

[Pause]

Gus: I've been thinking about the last one.

Ben: What last one?

Gus: That girl.

[Ben grabs the paper, which he reads]

Gus: [Rising, looking down at Ben] How many times have you read that paper?

[Ben slams the paper down and rises.]

Ben: [angrily] What do you mean?

Gus: I was just wondering how many times you'd—

Ben: What are you doing, criticizing me?

Gus: No, I was just—

Ben: You'll get a swipe round your earhole if you don't watch your step.

Gus: Now look here, Ben—

Ben: I'm not looking anywhere! [He addresses the room] How many times have I—! A bloody liberty!

Gus: I didn't mean that.

Ben: You just get on with it, mate. Get on with it, that's all.

[Ben gets back on the bed]

Gus: I was just thinking about that girl, that's all.

[Gus sits on his bed.]

Gus: She wasn't much to look at, I know, but still. It was a mess though, wasn't it? What a mess. Honest, I can't remember a mess like that one. They don't seem to hold together like men, women. A looser texture, like. Didn't she spread, eh? She didn't half spread. Kaw! But I've been meaning to ask you. [Ben sits up and clenches his eyes.] Who clears up after we've gone? I'm curious about that. Who does the clearing up? Maybe they don't clear up. Maybe they just leave them there, eh? What do you think? How many jobs have we done? Blimey, I can't count them. What if they never clear anything up after we've gone.

Ben: [pityingly] You mutt. Do you think we're the only branch of this organisation? Have a bit of common. They got departments for everything.

Gus: What cleaners and all?

Ben: You birk!

Gus: No, it was that girl made me start to think—

[There is a loud clatter and racket in the bulge of wall between the beds, of something descending. They grab their revolvers, jump up and face the wall. The noise comes to a stop. Silence. They look at each other. Ben gestures sharply towards the wall. Gus approaches the wall slowly. He bangs it with his revolver. It is hollow. Ben moves to the head of his bed, his revolver cocked. Gus puts his revolver on his bed and pats along the bottom of the centre panel. He finds a rim. He lifts the panel. Disclosed is a serving-hatch, a "dumb waiter." A wide box is held by pulleys. Gus peers into the box. He brings out a piece of paper.]

Ben: What is it?

Gus: You have a look at it.

Ben: Read it.

Gus: [Reading] Two braised steak and chips. Two sago puddings. Two teas without sugar.

Ben: Let me see that. [He takes the paper.]

Gus: [To himself] Two teas without sugar.

Ben: Mmnn.

Gus: What do you think of that?

Ben: Well—

[The box goes up. Ben levels his revolver.]

Gus: Give us a chance! They're in a hurry, aren't they?

[Ben re-reads the note. Gus looks over his shoulder.]

Gus: That's a bit—that's a bit funny, isn't it?

Ben: [Quickly] No. It's not funny. It probably used to be a cafe here, that's all. Upstairs. These places change hands very quickly.

Gus: A cafe?

Ben: Yes.

Gus: What, you mean this was the kitchen, down here?

Ben: Yes, they change hands overnight, these places. Go into liquidation. The people who run it, you know, they don't find it a going concern[7], they move out.

Gus: You mean the people who ran this place didn't find it a going concern and moved out?

Ben: Sure.

Gus: Well, who's got it now?

[Silence]

Ben: What do you mean, who's got it now?

Gus: Who's got it now? If they moved out, who moved in?

Ben: Well, that all depends—

[The box descends with a clatter and bang. Ben levels his revolver. Gus goes to the box and brings out a piece of paper.]

Gus: [Reading] Soup of the day. Liver and onions. Jam tart.

[A pause. Gus looks at Ben. Ben takes the note and reads it. He walks slowly to the hatch. Gus follows. Ben looks into the hatch but not up it. Gus puts his hand on Ben's shoulder. Ben throws it off. Gus puts his finger to his mouth. He leans on the hatch and swiftly looks up it. Ben flings him away in alarm. Ben looks at the note. He throws his revolver on the bed and speaks with decision.]

Ben: We'd better send something up.

Gus: Eh?

Ben: We'd better send something up.

Gus: Oh! Yes. Yes. Maybe you're right.

[They are both relieved at the decision.]

Ben: [Purposefully] Quick! What have you got in that bag?

Gus: Not much.

[Gus goes to the hatch and shouts up it.]

Gus: Wait a minute!

Ben: Don't do that!

[Gus examines the contents of the bag and brings them out, one by one.]

Gus: Biscuits. A bar of chocolate. Half a pint of milk.

Ben: That's all?

Gus: Packet of tea.

Ben: Good.

Gus: We can't send the tea. That's all the tea we've got.

Ben: Well, there's no gas. You can't do anything with it, can you?

Gus: Maybe they can send us down a bob[8].

Ben: What else is there?

Gus: [Reaching into bag] One Eccles cake.

Ben: One Eccles cake?

Gus: Yes.

Ben: You never told me you had an Eccles cake.

Gus: Didn't I?

Ben: Why only one? Didn't you bring one for me?

Gus: I didn't think yuu'd be keen.

Bell: Well, you can't send up one Eccles cake, anyway.

Gus: Why not?

Ben: Fetch one of those plates.

Gus: All right.

[Gus goes towards the door, left, and stops.]

Gus: Do you mean I can keep the Eccles cake then?

Ben: Keep it?

Gus: Well, they don't know we've got it, do they?

Ben: That's not the point.

Gus: Can't I keep it?

Ben: No, you can't. Get the plate.

[Gus exits, left. Ben looks in the bag. He brings out a packet of crisps. Enter Gus with a plate.]

Ben: [Accusingly, holding up the crisps.] Where did these come from?

Gus: What?

Ben: Where did these crisps come from?

Gus: Where did you find them?

Ben: [Hitting him on the shoulder] You're playing a dirty game, my lad!

Gus: I only eat those with beer!

Ben: Well, where were you going to get the beer?

Gus: I was saving them till I did.

Ben: I'll remember this. Put everything on the plate.

[They pile everything on to the plate. The box goes up without the plate.]

Ben: Wait a minute!

[They stand.]

Gus: It's gone up.

Ben: It's all your stupid fault, playing about!

Gus: What do we do now?

Ben: We'll have to wait till it comes down.

[Ben puts the plate on the bed, puts on his shoulder holster, and starts to put on his tie.]

Ben: You'd better get ready.

[Gus goes to his bed, puts on his tie, and starts to fix his holster.]

Gus: Hey, Ben.

Ben: What?

Gus: What's going on here?

[Pause]

Ben: What do you mean?

Gus: How can this be a cafe?

Ben: It used to be a cafe.

Gus: Have you seen tile gas stove?

Ben: What about it?

Gus: It's only got three rings.

Ben: So what?

Gus: Well, you couldn't cook much on three rings, not for a busy place like this.

Ben: [Irritably] That's why the service is slow!

[Ben puts on his waistcoat.]

Gus: Yes, but what happens when we're not here? What do they do then? All these menus coming down and nothing going up. It might have been going on like this for years.

[Ben brushes his jacket.]

Gus: What happens when we go?

[Ben puts on his jacket.]

Gus: They can't do much business.

[The box descends. They turn about. Gus goes to the hatch and brings out a note.]

Gus: [Reading] Macaroni Pastitsio. Ormitha Macaromrada.

Ben: What was that?

Gus: Macaroni Pastitsio. Ormitha Macarounada.

Ben: Greek dishes.

Gus: No.

Ben: That's right.

Gus: That's pretty high class.

Ben: Quick before it goes up.

[Gas puts the plate in the box.]

Gus: [Calling up the hatch] Three McVitie and Price! One Lyons Red Label! One Smith's Crisps! One Eccles cake! One Fruit and Nut!

Ben: Cadbury's.

Gus: [Up the hatch] Cadbury's!

Ben: [Handling the milk] One bottle of milk.

Gus: [Up the hatch] One bottle of milk! Half a pint! [He looks at the label.] Express Dairy! [He puts the bottle in the box.]

[The box goes up.]

Gus: Just did it.

Ben: You shouldn't shout like that.

Gus: Why not?

Ben: It isn't done.

[Ben goes to his bed.]

Ben: Well, that should be all right, anyway, for the time being.

Gus: You think so, eh?

Ben: Get dressed, will you? It'll be any minute now.

[Gus puts on his waistcoat. Ben lies down and looks up at the ceiling.]

Gus: This is some place. No tea and no biscuits.

Ben: Eating makes you lazy, mate. You're getting lazy, you know that? You don't want to get slack on your job.

Gus: Who me?

Ben: Slack, mate, slack.

Gus: Who me? Slack?

Ben: Have you checked your gun? You haven't even checked your gun. It looks disgraceful, anyway. Why don't you ever polish it?

[Gus rubs his revolver on the sheet. Ben takes out a pocket mirror and straightens his tie.]

Gus: I wonder where the cook is. They must have had a few, to cope with that. Maybe they had a few more gas stoves. Eh! Maybe there's another kitchen along the passage.

Ben: Of course there is! Do you know what it takes to make an Ormitha Macarounada?

Gus: No, what?

Ben: An Ormitha—! Buck your ideas up[9], will you?

Gus: Takes a few cooks, eh?

[Gus puts his revolver in its holster.]

Gus: The sooner we're out of this place the better.

[He puts on his jacket.]

Gus: Why doesn't he get in touch? I feel like I've been here years.

[He takes his revolver out of its holster to check the ammunition.] We've never let him down though, have we? We've never let him down. I was thinking only the other day, Ben. We're reliable, aren't we?

[He puts his revolver back in its holster.]

Gus: Still, I'll be glad when it's over tonight. [He brushes his jacket.] I hope the bloke's not going to get excited tonight, or anything. I'm feeling a bit off. I've got a splitting headache.

[Silence. The box descends. Ben jumps up. Gus collects the note.]

Gus: [Reading] One Bamboo Shoots, Water Chestnuts and Chicken. One Char Siu and Beansprouts.

Ben: Beansprouts?

Gus: Yes.

Ben: Blimey.

Gus: I wouldn't know where to begin.

[He looks back at the box. The packet of tea is inside it. He picks it up.]

Gus: They've sent back the tea.

Ben: [Anxious] What'd they do that for?

Gus: Maybe it isn't tea-time.

[The box goes up. Silence]

Ben: [Throwing the tea on the bed, and speaking urgently.] Look here. We'd better tell them.

Gus: Tell them what?

Ben: That we can't do it, we haven't got it.

Gus: All right then.

Ben: Lend us your pencil. We'll write a note.

[Gus, turning for a pencil, suddenly discovers the speaking-tube, which hangs on the right wall of the hatch facing his bed.]

Gus: What's this?

Ben: What?

Gus: This.

Ben: [Examining it.] This? It's a speaking-tube.

Gus: How long has that been there?

Ben: Just the job. We should have used it before, instead of shouting up there.

Gus: Funny I never noticed it before.

Ben: Well, come on.

Gus: What do you do?

Ben: See that? That's a whistle.

Gus: What, this?

Ben: Yes, take it out. Pull it out. [Gus does so.] That's it.

Gus: What do we do now?

Ben: Blow into it.

Gus: Blow?

Ben: It whistles up there if you blow. Then they know you want to speak. Blow. [Gus blows. Silence]

Gus: [Tube at mouth] I can't hear a thing.

Ben: Now you speak! Speak into it!

[Gus looks at Ben, then speaks into the tube.]

Gus: The larder's bare!

Ben: Give me that!

[He grabs the tube and puts it to his mouth.]

Ben: [Speaking with great deference] Good evening. I'm sorry to—bother you, but we just thought we'd better let you know that we haven't got anything left. We sent up all we had. There's no more food down here.

[He brings the tube slowly to his ear.]

Ben: What? [To mouth] What? [To ear. He listens. To mouth] No, all we had we sent up. [To ear. He listens. To mouth] Oh, I'm very sorry to hear that. [To ear. He listens. To Gus]The Eccles cake was stale. [He listens. To Gus] The chocolate was melted. [He listens. To Gus] The milk was sour.

Gus: What about the crisps?

Ben: [Listening] The biscuits were mouldy. [He glares at Gus. Tube to mouth] Well, we're very sorry about that. [Tube to ear] What? [To mouth] What? [To ear] Yes. Yes. [To mouth] Yes certainly. Certainly. Right away. [To ear. The voice has ceased. He hangs up the tube.]

Ben: [Excitedly] Did you hear that?

Gus: What?

Ben: You know what he said? Light the kettle! Not put on the kettle! Not light the gas! But light the kettle!

Gus: How can we light the kettle?

Ben: What do you mean?

Gus: There's no gas.

Ben: [Clapping hand to head] Now what do we do?

Gus: What did he want us to light the kettle for?

Ben: For tea. He wanted a cup of tea.

Gus: He wanted a cup of tea! What about me? I've been wanting a cup of tea all night!

Ben: [Despairingly] What do we do now?

Gus: What are we supposed to drink?

[Ben sits on his bed, staring.]

Gus: What about us? [Ben sits.] I'm thirsty too. I'm starving. And he wants a cup of tea. That beats the band[10], that does.

[Ben lets his head sink on to his chest.]

Gus: I could do with a bit of sustenance myself. What about you? You look as if you could do with something too.

[Gus sits on his bed.]

Gus: We send him up all we've got and he's not satisfied. No, honest, it's enough to make the cat laugh. Why did you send him up all that stuff? [Thoughtfully] Why did I send it up?

[Pause]

Gus: Who knows what he's got upstairs? He's probably got a salad bowl. They must have something up there. They won't get much from down here. You notice they didn't ask for any salads? They've probably got a salad bowl up there. Cold meat, radishes, cucumbers. Watercress. Roll mops.

[Pause]

Gus: Hardboiled eggs.

[Pause]

Gus: The lot. They've probably got a crate of beer too. Probably eating my crisps with a pint of beer now. Didn't have anything to say about those crisps, did he? They do all right, don't worry about that. You don't think they're just going to sit there and wait for stuff to come up from down here, do you? That'll get them nowhere.

[Pause]

Gus: They do all right.

[Pause]

Gus: And he wants a cup of tea.

[Pause]

Gus: That's past a joke, in my opinion.

[He looks over at Ben, rises, and goes to him.]

Gus: What's the matter with you? You don't look too bright. I feel like an Alka-Seltzer myself.

[Ben sits up]

Ben: [In a low voice] Time's getting on.

Gus: I know. I don't like doing a job on an empty stomach.

Ben: [Wearily] Be quiet a minute. Let me give you your instructions.

Gus: What for? We always do it the same way, don't we?

Ben: Let me give you your instructions.

[Gus sighs and sits next to Ben on the bed. The instructions are stated and repeated automatically]

Ben: When we get the call, you go over and stand behind the door.

Gus: Stand behind the door.

Ben: If there's a knock on the door you don't answer it.

Gus: If there's a knock on the door I don't answer it.

Ben: But there won't be a knock on the door.

Gus: So I won't answer it.

Ben: When the bloke comes in—

Gus: When the bloke comes in—

Ben: Shut the door behind him.

Gus: Shut the door behind him.

Ben: Without divulging your presence.

Gus: Without divulging my presence.
Ben: He'll see me and come towards me.
Gus: He'll see you and come towards you.
Ben: He won't see you.
Gus: [Absently] Eh?
Ben: He won't see you.
Gus: He won't see me.
Ben: But he'll see me.
Gus: He'll see you.
Ben: He won't know you're there.
Gus: He won't know you're there.
Ben: He won't know you're there.
Gus: He won't know I'm there.
Ben: I take out my gun.
Gus: You take out your gun.
Ben: He stops in his tracks.
Gus: He stops in his tracks.
Ben: If he turns round—
Gus: If he turns round—
Ben: You're there.
Gus: I'm there.
[Ben frowns and presses his forehead]
Gus: You've missed something out—
Ben: I know. What?
Gus: I haven't taken my gun out, according to you.
Ben: You take your gun out—
Gus: After you've closed the door.
Ben: After you've closed the door.
Gus: You've never missed that out before, you know that?
Ben: When he sees you behind him—
Gus: Me behind him—
Ben: And me in front of him—
Gus: And you in front of him—
Ben: He'll feel uncertain—
Gus: Uneasy.
Ben: He won't know what to do.
Gus: So what will he do?

Ben: He'll look at me and he'll look at you.
Gus: We won't say a word.
Ben: We'll look at him.
Gus: He won't say a word.
Ben: He'll look at us.
Gus: And we'll look at him.
Ben: Nobody says a word.
[Pause]
Gus: What do we do if it's a girl?
Ben: We do the same.
Gus: Exactly the same?
Ben: Exactly.
[Pause]
Gus: We don't do anything different?
Ben: We do exactly the same.
Gus: Oh.
[Gus rises, and shivers.]
Gus: Excuse me.
[He exits through the door on the left. Ben remains sitting on the bed, still. The lavatory chain is pulled once off left, but the lavatory does not flush. Silence. Gus re-enters and stops inside the door, deep in thought. He looks at Ben, then walks slowly across to his own bed. He is troubled. He stands, thinking. He turns and looks at Ben. He moves a few paces towards him.]

Gus: [Slowly in a low, tense voice.] Why did he send us matches if he knew there was no gas?

[Silence. Ben stares in front of him. Gus crosses to the left side of Ben, to the foot of his bed, to get to his other ear.]

Gus: Ben. Why did he send us matches if he knew there was no gas?
[Ben looks up.]
Gus: Why did he do that?
Ben: Who?
Gus: Who sent us those matches?
Ben: What are you talking about?
[Gus stares down at him.]
Gus: [Thickly] Who is it upstairs?
Ben: [Nervously] What's one thing to do with another?

Gus: Who is it, though?

Ben: What's one thing to do with another?

[Ben fumbles for his paper on the bed.]

Gus: I asked you a question.

Ben: Enough!

Gus: [With growing agitation] I asked you before. Who moved in? I asked you. You said the people who had it before move out. Well, who moved in?

Ben: [Hunched] Shut up.

Gus: I told you, didn't I?

Ben: [Standing] Shut up!

Gus: [Feverishly] I told you before who owned this place, didn't I? I told you.

[Ben hits him viciously on the shoulder.]

Gus: I told you who ran this place, didn't I?

[Ben hits him viciously on the shoulder.]

Gus: [Violently] Well, what's he playing all these games for? That's what I want to know. What's he doing it for?

Ben: What games?

Gus: [Passionately, advancing] What's he doing it for? We've been through our tests, haven't we? We got right through our tests, years ago, didn't we? We took them together, don't you remember, didn't we? We've always done our job. What's he doing all this for? What's the idea? What's he playing these games for?

[The box in the shaft comes down behind them. The noise is this time accompanied by a shrill whistle, as if falls. Gus rushes to the hatch and seizes the note.]

Gus: [Reading] Scampi!

[He crumples the note, picks up the tube, takes out the whistle, blows and speaks.]

Gus: WE'VE GOT NOTHING LEFT! NOTHING! DO YOU UNDERSTAND?

[Ben seizes the tube and flings Gus away. He follows Gus and slaps him hard, back-handed, across the chest.]

Ben: Stop it! You maniac!

Gus: But you heard!

Ben: [Savagely] That's enough! I'm warning you!

[Silence. Ben hangs the tube. He goes to his bed and lies down. He picks up his paper and reads. Silence. The box goes up. They turn quickly, their eyes meet. Ben turns to his paper. Slowly Gus goes back to his bed, and sits. Silence. The hatch falls back into place. They turn quickly, their eyes meet. Ben turns back to his paper. Silence. Ben throws his paper down.]

Ben: Kaw!

[He picks up the paper and looks at it.]

Ben: Listen to this!

[Pause]

Ben: What about that, eh?

[Pause]

Ben: Kaw!

[Pause]

Ben: Have you ever heard such a thing?

Gus: [Dully] Go on!

Ben: It's true.

Gus: Get away.

Ben: It's down here in black and white.

Gus: [Very low] Is that a fact?

Ben: Can you imagine it.

Gus: It's unbelievable.

Ben: It's enough to make you want to puke, isn't it?

Gus: [Almost inaudible] Incredible.

[Ben shakes his head. He puts the paper down and rises. He fixes the revolver in his holster. Gus stands up. He goes towards the door on the left.]

Ben: Where are you going?

Gus: I'm going to have a glass of water.

[He exits. Ben brushes dust off his clothes and shoes. The whistle in the speaking-tube blows. He goes to it, takes the whistle out and puts the tube to his ear. He listens. He puts it to his mouth.]

Ben: Yes. [To ear. He listens. To mouth] Straight away. Right. [To ear. He listens. To mouth] Sure we're ready.

[To ear. He listens. To mouth] Understand. Repeat. He has arrived and will be coming in straight away. The normal method to be employed. Understood. [To ear. He listens. To mouth] Sure we're ready.

[To ear. He listens. To mouth] Right. [He hangs the tube up.] Gus!

[He takes out a comb and combs his hair, adjusts his jacket to diminish the bulge of the revolver. The lavatory flushes off left. Ben goes quickly to the door, left.

Ben: Gus!

[The door right opens sharply. Ben turns, his revolver levelled at the door.

Gus stumbles in.

He is stripped of his jacket, waistcoat, tie, holster and revolver.

He stops, body stooping, his arms at his sides.

He raises his head and looks at Ben.

A long silence.

They stare at each other.]

Notes

1. "The First Eleven": a school's top team of cricketers.
2. kip: nap.
3. ponged: smelled.
4. Villa: Aston Villa, popularly known as "the Villa", Birmingham's football team.
5. the Spurs: a football team. Tottenham: in north London.
6. a meter: one that controls the supply of gas and must be fed with shilling coins.
7. a going concern: an active profitable business.
8. bob: shilling.
9. buck your ideas up: Try to improve yourself.
10. beats the band: is too much.

Questions for Understanding

1. When the first order for food comes down from upstairs, Ben discovers that Gus has kept something hidden from him. How does this discovery affect the relationship between the two hired gunmen?
2. Who, between the two, is in command? And who is smarter?
3. Is Ben aware that Gus is the next victim before Gus is pushed into the room? How do you know?

Aspects of Appreciation

1. Aspects of Pinters's dramatic art

The Dumb Waiter exhibits two important aspects of Pinter's dramatic art. In his plays, communication between characters is conducted at a variety of levels. Speech is only part of the means of communication, and speech itself consists of words, gestures, pauses, and word plays. To Pinter, silence and hesitation in speech convey a layer of meaning one wants to express. At the same time, Pinter is a master of ambiguity. When we come to the end of play, we still have a number of questions in our minds: How does this mysterious organization work? Why is Gus the next victim? Does Ben kill his partner? We do not seem to be able to find any definite answer from the play. However, this is exactly what Pinter has expected—leaving his audience arguing with each other when they leave the theatre.

2. Gus's frequent trips to the bathroom

Gus bemoans the dull routine of life, and nothing is more mundane and repetitive than the act of going to the bathroom; one fills up, then empties out. Moreover, the waste itself returns in some form, so even that is recycled. He cannot escape the routines of life and is thus highly aware of them, especially in the way they relate to his poverty. Ben, on the other hand, does not go to the bathroom throughout *The Dumb Waiter* and seems less concerned with his own repetitive station, and feels they are "fortunate" to have their jobs. Finally, the toilet flushes on a delay, so that after each trip to the bathroom there is a silence from the toilet—one that complements the many silences in conversation—and then it often interrupts the men later—one of the frequent interruptions by objects (the dumb waiter, speaking tube, and envelope are the others).

Suggested Further Reading

Pinter's *The Room* (1957) and *The Homecoming* (1965).

Topics for Further Study

1. The effect of having the play set in one place without time stoppage.
2. The use of props in the play (guns, matches, sheets, the photo of cricket players, etc.).
3. Gus's and Ben's attitudes toward money and class.

VIII. Contemporary Period

Knowledge of Literature

A one-act play is a play that has only one act, as distinct from plays that occur over several acts. One-act plays may consist of one or more scenes. In recent years the 10-minute play known as "flash drama" has emerged as a popular sub-genre of the one-act play, especially in writing competitions. The origin of the one-act play may be traced to the very beginning of drama: in ancient Greece, *Cyclops*, a satyr play by Euripides, is an early example.

References

1. Abrams, Mike Howard. *A Glossary of Literary Terms* (7th edition). Beijing: Foreign Language Teaching and Research Press & Thomson Learning, 2004.
2. Baldick, Chris. *Oxford Concise Dictionary of Literary Terms*. Shanghai: Shanghai Foreign Language Education Press, 2000.
3. Booz, Elizabeth B. *A Brief Introduction to Modern English Literature*. Shanghai: Shanghai Foreign Language Education Press, 1984.
4. Bradbury, Malcolm. *The Modern British Novel* 1878～2001 (Revised Edition). London: Penguin Books, 2001.
5. Brooks, Cleanth & Robert Penn Warren. *Understanding Poetry* (4th ed.). Beijing: Foreign Language Teaching and Research Press and Thomson Learning, 2004.
6. Brooks, Cleanth & Robert Penn Warren. *Understanding Fiction* (3rd ed.). Beijing: Foreign Language Teaching and Research Press and Pearson Education, 2004.
7. Chaucer, Geoffrey. *The Canterbury Tales*. Trans. Nevill Coghil. Baltimore, MD: Penguin Books, 1969.
8. Conrad, Peter. *The History of English Literature*. Philadelphia: U of Pennsylvania P, 1987.
9. Daily, Melody Richardson, et al. *Instructor's Guide to The Riverside Anthology of Literature*. Boston: Houghton Mifflin, 1988.
10. Drabble, Margaret. Ed. *The Oxford Companion to English Literature* (6th ed.). Beijing: Foreign Language Teaching and Research Press and Oxford University Press, 2005.
11. Ford, Boris. Ed. *The Pelican Guid to English Literature* (7): *The Modern Age*. Baltimore, U.S.A. & Mitcham, Australia: Penguin

Books, 1961.
12. Kennedy, X. J.. *An Introduction to Poetry* (7th ed.). Glenview, Illinois: Scott, Foresman and Company, 1990.
13. Kirkland, James W. *Poetry: Sight and Insight*. New York: Random House, 1982.
14. Lazarus, Arnold. & H. Wendell Smith. *A Glossary of Literature and Composition*. Urbana, Illinois: Grosset and Dunlap, 1983.
15. McEwan, Neil. *The Survival of the Novel: British Fiction in the Later Twentieth Century*. London: The Macmillan Press Ltd, 1985.
16. Muller, Gilbert H. & John A. Williams. *The McGraw-Hill Introduction to Literature*. New York: McGraw-Hill, 1985.
17. *Oxford Companion to 20th Century Poetry*. Shanghai: Shanghai Foreign Language Education Press, 2000.
18. Peck, John and Martin Coyle. New York: *A Brief History of English Literature*. Palgrave, 2002.
19. Richetti, John. Ed. *The Columbia History of the British Novel*. Beijing: Foreign Language Teaching and Research Press and Columbia University Press, 2005.
20. Roberts, Edgar V. & Henry E. Jacobs. *Literature: An Introduction to Reading and Writing*. Englewood Cliffs, New Jersey: Prentice-Hall, 1986.
21. 常耀信著:《英国文学简史》。天津:南开大学出版社,2006。
22. 陈红、段汉武主编:《英国文学选读新编:20世纪卷》。武汉:华中师范大学出版社,2010。
23. 陈嘉编:《英国文学作品选读》(1－3册)。北京:商务印书馆,1984。
24. 戴桂玉编著:《新编英美文学欣赏教程》。北京:中国社会科学出版社,2001。
25. 丁廷森主编:《英国文学选读》。重庆:重庆大学出版社,2005。
26. 刁克利编著:《英国文学经典选读》(上、下)。北京:外语教学与研究出版社,2008。
27. 刁克利主编:《英美文学欣赏》。北京:中国人民大学出版社,2003。
28. 杜瑞清等编:《20世纪英国小说选读》(增订版)。西安:西安交通大学出版社,2006。
29. 范存忠:《英国文学史纲》。成都:四川人民出版社,1983。
30. 郭群英主编:《英国文学新编》(上、下)。北京:外语教学与研究出版社,2003。
31. 何功杰:《英诗选读》。合肥:安徽教育出版社,1998。

32. 李公昭主编:《新编英国文学选读》(修订版)。西安:西安交通大学出版社,2005。
33. 李公昭主编:《新编英国文学教程》(上、下)。北京:世界图书出版公司,1998。
34. 刘丹编:《英美文学选读》。北京:知识产权出版社,2004。
35. 刘洊波主编:《英美文学名著赏析》(上)。广州:华南理工大学出版社,2005。
36. 刘意青等著:《简明英国文学史》。北京:外语教学与研究出版,2008。
37. 罗经国编注:《新编英国文学选读》(上、下)。北京:北京大学出版社,1996。
38. 宁一中等主编:《英美小说选读》。长沙:湖南师范大学出版社,2004。
39. 彭家海主编:《新编英国文学教程》。武汉:华中科技大学出版社,2006。
40. 瞿世镜、任一鸣著:《当代英国小说》。上海:上海译文出版社,2008。
41. 申富英等主编:《新编英国文学教程》。济南:山东大学出版社,2004。
42. 孙汉云编著:《英国文学教程》。南京:河海大学出版社,1999。
43. 王虹编:《英国文学阅读与欣赏》。广州:华南理工大学出版社,2000。
44. 王军主编:《英国短篇小说赏析》。北京:新华出版社,2007。
45. 王丽丽编著:《二十世纪英国文学史》。济南:山东大学出版社,2001。
46. 王佩兰等主编:《英国文学史及作品选读》。长春:东北师范大学出版社,2006。
47. 王守仁主编:《英国文学选读》(第三版)。北京:高等教育出版社,2011。
48. 王新春编著:《英国文学选读》。哈尔滨:东北林业大学出版社,2006。
49. 王佐良等主编:《英国文学名篇选注》。北京:商务印书馆,1991。
50. 吴伟仁编:《英国文学史及选读》(1—2册)。北京:外语教学与研究出版社,1995。
51. 吴翔林编注:《英美文学选读》(第三版)。北京:北京大学出版社,2007。
52. 杨岂深等主编:《英国文学选读》(1—3册)。上海:上海译文出版社,1981~1984。
53. 袁宪军等编:《英语小说导读》。北京:北京大学出版社,2004。
54. 张伯香主编:《英国文学教程》(修订版)(上、下)。武汉:武汉大学出版社,2005。
55. 张伯香主编:《英国文学教程学习指南》。武汉:武汉大学出版社,2006。
56. 张伯香主编:《英美经典小说赏析》。武汉:武汉大学出版社,2005。
57. 赵太和编:《现代英国文学教程》。北京:北京师范大学出版社,1990。